In Sheep's Clothing

To: Alana —

Thank you for your incredible work!

With lots of affection,

[signature] 2/24

In Sheep's Clothing

The Idolatry of White Christian Nationalism

Edited by George Yancy and Bill Bywater
Foreword by J. Kameron Carter

ROWMAN & LITTLEFIELD
Lanham • Boulder • New York • London

Published by Rowman & Littlefield
An imprint of The Rowman & Littlefield Publishing Group, Inc.
4501 Forbes Boulevard, Suite 200, Lanham, Maryland 20706
www.rowman.com

86-90 Paul Street, London EC2A 4NE

Copyright © 2024 by The Rowman & Littlefield Publishing Group, Inc.

All rights reserved. No part of this book may be reproduced in any form or by any electronic or mechanical means, including information storage and retrieval systems, without written permission from the publisher, except by a reviewer who may quote passages in a review.

British Library Cataloguing in Publication Information Available

Library of Congress Cataloging-in-Publication Data Available

978-1-5381-8328-1 (cloth: alk. paper)
978-1-5381-8329-8 (pbk: alk. paper)
978-1-5381-8330-4 (ebook)

∞™ The paper used in this publication meets the minimum requirements of American National Standard for Information Sciences—Permanence of Paper for Printed Library Materials, ANSI/NISO Z39.48-1992.

Bill dedicates this book to Duncan, who must live with all of this. George dedicates this book to Easter, his great-great-great-grandmother, free in Africa and enslaved in America.

Contents

Acknowledgments — xi

The Religion of Whiteness: A Foreword — xiii
J. Kameron Carter

Introduction — 1
George Yancy

Introduction — 11
Bill Bywater

Opening Poem: Mary Magdalene Sings — 15
Becky Thompson

Chapter 1: White Christians and the US Corporate-Warrior State — 17
Mark Lewis Taylor

Chapter 2: White Mob Logic — 39
Karen Teel

Chapter 3: The "Promised Land" in Christian Nationalist Rhetoric: The Persistent Vision of Christianity as a Religion of Conquest — 51
Brock Bahler

Chapter 4: Discipleship or Duplicity?: A Christian "No" to White Christian Nationalism — 71
Anna Floerke Scheid

Chapter 5: White Christians Warring against Democracy: A Long History — 85
Joe Feagin

Chapter 6: The Pedagogy of Hegemony: A History of Christian
   Nationalism, Narrative Wars, and School Dominance   103
   Todd M. Mealy

Chapter 7: "Who Do You Say That I Am?"   127
   Laurie Cassidy

Chapter 8: The Theological Irony of White Christian Nationalism:
   A View from the South   145
   Leah Kalmanson

Chapter 9: Christian Churches in North America and the
   Imperatives of the Dialogue of Action toward Restitution and
   Restorative Justice for Blacks, Latinos/Latinx, and Native
   Americans   157
   Marinus Chijioke Iwuchukwu

Chapter 10: "Legitimate Political Discourse": January 6 and the
   Brutality of White Theodicy   167
   Biko Mandela Gray

Chapter 11: Philosophical Ends and Theological Beginnings: The
   Logos, the Nigger, and Whiteness in American Christianity   179
   Timothy J. Golden

Chapter 12: Misogyny and the Stench of White Supremacist
   Christianity   205
   Traci C. West

Chapter 13: "Where Is the Love?": Christian Nationalism and the
   Politics of Exclusion   221
   Kathy Glass

Chapter 14: The Life and Death of Queen Elizabeth II: Defender
   of the Faith, Supreme Governor of the Church of England, and
   Manifestation of the White Colonial Gaze   235
   Kimberley Ducey

Chapter 15: "The Order" of the Day: Lessons, Philosophical and
   Otherwise, from Childhood at the Heart of American Christian
   Nationalism   255
   James Garrison

Chapter 16: Victims of the Cross: Violence and Apocalyptic
   Discourse in Christian Nationalism   269
   Sheldon George

Chapter 17: White Solidarity on Campus and the Sin of Neutrality 279
Elisabeth Vasko

Chapter 18: Can White Christian Nationalists and Donald Trump Be Overcome? 289
Josiah Ulysses Young III

Chapter 19: Revolution and the Soul of White Christianity 299
Dean J. Johnson

Chapter 20: The Hidden White Flesh of White Christian Nationalism: Anthropological Docetism and the Forging of Idols 313
José Francisco Morales Torres

Chapter 21: On White Christian Violence 329
Anthony Paul Smith

Closing Poem: Original Sin 343
Michael Simms

Index 351

About the Contributors 371

Acknowledgments

The editors, George Yancy and Bill Bywater, would like to thank Natalie Mandziuk, our editor at Rowman & Littlefield, for her initial enthusiasm for this book. We would also like to thank Yu Ozaki, assistant acquisitions editor, and Anna Keyser, assistant production editor, for their patience and professional care with the manuscript. We would like to thank all the brilliant contributors for their deep insights, critical engagements, and passionate drive and for their collective commitment to fighting against authoritarianism in terms of how it expresses itself within the context of white Christian nationalism. The world that we collectively envision is not one that is simply free of variegated forms of violence but one where we actively install justice, especially for those embodied voices, precarious groups, that are constantly under political attack and attempted erasure. We would also like to thank the brilliant scholar J. Kameron Carter for writing such a powerful foreword. We especially thank him for agreeing to write the foreword with such alacrity given the time constraints.

 I (George) would like to take a moment to express deep regret regarding the sudden death of Marinus Chijioke Iwuchukwu. Marinus was a colleague of mine who taught in the theology department at Duquesne University. Not too long after I received a submission from Marinus, I received information about his passing. Although I could not get any feedback regarding any edits, I felt that it was my obligation and honor to publish his chapter within this important text. I wish our dear brother great peace. I would also like to thank my children and Susan. There is so much in this world that isn't right; indeed, tragically, the truth of the matter is that so much about what is going on in our world is dreadful, alarming, and, I would imagine, unspeakable if we knew the whole truth. And yet, we must speak and speak up. Because of your presence, living my life is far more enjoyable and durable. I would especially like to thank my son Gabriel for his love of family and his desire to discover our family history and extended family connections. As I write, he is busy tracking down our ancestors. I know that they are honored by his efforts. I would also like to thank my colleague Bill Bywater. The two of us have taught together, had multiple and generative philosophical exchanges, and broken bread together on numerous occasions (I'm pretty sure that our fondest gastronomic memories have to do with eating pancakes and bacon). This is the first book we have worked on together. It was both an honor and a pleasure to produce this book with Bill. We worked on this book like hand and glove. Thanks, Bill.

Thank you, George, for including me in this project, it is, as always, a pleasure and an inspiration to work with you! A very big thank-you, also, to our authors who took time to contribute to this collection. As I tried to make clear in my introduction, they have done fine work on revealing the historical depth and contemporary danger of the ideology called *white Christian nationalism*. It really is not Christian, but *surely* it is white. Congratulations to you all for creating an important document that will help others understand the danger this ideology presents.

The Religion of Whiteness: A Foreword

J. Kameron Carter

A growing list of journalists, scholars, and public intellectuals have been giving important attention to the new white supremacy that is currently afoot. At the heart of this "white reconstruction," as one writer has put it, is a virulent authoritarianism in the heart of democracy itself that has led to the buckling of democratic institutions.[1] Hence, much of the attention given to the new white supremacy has focused on the rise of white nationalism in the United States under the presidency of Donald J. Trump and its ongoing persistence after his presidency. As we know, the twin crises of democracy and white nationalism culminated in the January 6th (2021) mob attack on the U.S. Capitol. Inspired and egged on by then-outgoing President Trump, the mob attack sought to affect a coup against the government by killing then-Vice President Mike Pence to prevent him from overseeing the electoral college vote count, which in the U.S. system of government is the final formal step in certifying the election and moving forward with the transfer of power from one presidency to the next.

This collection of essays and poems joins the growing list of writings increasingly concerned with the problem of the new iteration, genre, or version of white supremacy. However, what makes this book so important to the conversations and public debates on this urgent issue is the attention it gives the religiosity of white nationalism. That is, though its main or most explicit task is examining the specifically Christian logics that animate white Christian nationalism today and trying to think Christianity otherwise or outside of a white Christian nationalistic framework, something larger is at stake in this book. The writings of the poets and scholars that George Yancy and Bill Bywater bring together here calls attention to the very whiteness, indeed, to *the religion of whiteness* (more on what I mean by this phrase momentarily), on which white Christian nationalism in both its U.S. form and in its various global iterations today rests. Put differently, and to resort to a metaphor, if white Christian nationalism is the tip of the iceberg, there is a larger, though submerged part of the iceberg.

But what is that larger, more expansive though unseen part of the iceberg? It is whiteness itself, which is at once sociologically and historically related to the group of people called "white people" and yet something not just equal to individual white people. More still, that submerged part of the iceberg concerns whiteness as *religion*. But we must slow down when we come to this word, religion, and resist our default, taken-for-granted, common sense around this term. To answer the question, *what is Whiteness?*, we must also ask, *what is religion?*

Derived from the Latin verb *relegere* ("to bind together" and even "to write law") and Latin noun *religio* ("binding" and "writings") and bequeathed to us through the writings of the ancient Roman statesman and philosopher Marcus Tullius Cicero and then repurposed by European Christianity and Enlightenment philosophers in the context of colonial conquest, contact, and exchange in trans-Atlantic commerce, religion concerns the many practices of binding together a socius, a community, or even the State around an exclusionary "We."[2] This we can only be a we by producing an other, a them, as an undemocratic enemy or threat or invader or the like. In short, religion as such is a term of politics, and the political is as such a term of religion. This is evident in the phrase that heads the preamble to the U.S. Constitution:

> We the People of the United States, in Order to form a more perfect Union, establish Justice, insure domestic Tranquility, provide for the common defence, promote the general Welfare, and secure the Blessings of Liberty to ourselves and our Posterity, do ordain and establish this Constitution for the United States of America.

This is a statement of religion, specifically of what we might call "American Religion." It aims to bind together a "We," and yet as a document of the State it does so through an excluded "them" (even if not explicitly articulated). What this means is that as a document of constituting a we and thus as a document of "we-ing" over against a "them-ing," the U.S. Constitution is fundamentally a document of religion. To turn the word religion back into a verb, the U.S. Constitution is a document of "religion-ing." It religions us. What I am proposing here—and what the book you are holding proposes—is intended to shake us from our too easy, inherently Protestant ways of thinking about religion as a private thing of the heart and what have you. What we see here is religion as not confined to formal, religious institutions like churches, or synagogues, or mosques, and the like. What we see instead is religion as a political phenomenon of statecraft and/as racecraft. This is the larger iceberg that I am calling attention to: whiteness as religion.

Indeed, this is what the writer and cultural critique W. E. B. Du Bois was getting at just about a century ago in his essay, "The Souls of White Folk." A chapter in his book *Darkwater: Voices from Within the Veil* (1920), "The Souls of White Folk" (the companion document to his more well-known book, *The Souls of Black Folk* of 1903) gifts to us the phrase *the religion of whiteness* as a conceptual device through which Du Bois sought to understand how whiteness was reconstructing itself in the historical moment of the aftermath of World War I in 1919. This is when European and U.S. colonialism was taking on new forms, when antiblack violence in the form of lynching was surging, when a global pandemic was afoot (what was then called "the Spanish Flu"), when the conditions were emerging for a global economic crisis (what would become the Great Depression), and finally when European fascism was starting to emerge. In *Darkwater*, a collection of historical and creative writings comprised of essays, poems, and short stories, Du Bois proposed a counternarrative of the origins of the Great War and of the travails of the West itself, including the United States, at the time. Key to Du Bois's proposed counternarrative was to situate the origins of the United States within a broader framework of Western Man's will to rule the planet, and how that project was imploding upon itself. In other words, Du Bois sought to position the United States within a global ideological system. This broader ideological system of power, what he called *"whiteness,"* he insisted be understood in the opening pages of his reflection on "the souls of white folk" as a political-theological system, indeed, as *"religion"* in terms apposite to what I outlined above, and further still as a type of apocalyptic cosmology. Du Bois himself put it this way:

> I do not laugh. I am quite straight-faced as I ask soberly:
>
> "But what on earth is whiteness that one should so desire it?" Then always, somehow, some way, silently but clearly, I am given to understand that whiteness is the ownership of the earth forever and ever, Amen!
>
> Now what is the effect on a man or a nation when it comes passionately to believe such an extraordinary dictum as this? That nations are coming to believe it is manifest daily. Wave on wave, each with increasing virulence, is dashing *this new religion of whiteness* on the shores of our time.[3]

Here, Du Bois aligns whiteness not first and foremost with white skin, but rather as a practice of belief in and devotion to a certain civilizational ethos. That civilizational ethos concerns the material-capitalist logics of property ownership that extract or thieve value from the earth itself and from the dark poor of the earth. That is, whiteness is a program premised on stolen land and stolen life. This is the practice of ownership. Indeed, this will to ownership is not just terrestrial (to extract from the earth and its darkened poor), but celestial, for in the very next paragraph following the above quotation, Du Bois further says, "Everything considered, the title to *the universe* claimed by White Folk is faulty."[4] Whiteness is the practice of title, of cosmic entitlement. (Which, as an aside, is interesting, given then President Trump's public opining at one time that the U.S. should colonize the moon and given recent exercises by the billionaire class to travel to outer space. But I [do not] digress . . .). Put differently, Whiteness is premised upon a settler cosmology that grounds (in the very taking of ground) the imaginary institution of property in the constitution of the modern state.

Fortunately, the story of whiteness as religion, whiteness as political theology, and whiteness as theft of the earth and the cosmos is not a closed one in which we are cynically, if not pessimistically, trapped. There are other practices of belonging to and intimacy with each other, ways of artistic living, that are not exclusionary. There are ways of be-ing without antagonistically them-ing or other-ing. Arguably, our greatest intellectual, cultural, and political challenge today is to produce languages for this non-exclusionary, species-entangled, and incomplete Us-ness. But that's a story for another day and another book.[5] The gift of this book, *In Sheep's Clothing: The Idolatry of White Christian Nationalism*, is that it begins to bring overdue attention to the specific religiosity of whiteness through its attention to white Christian nationalism. I commend and recommend it without reservation.

NOTES

1. Rodríguez, Dylan. *White Reconstruction: Domestic Warfare and the Logics of Genocide* (New York: Fordham University Press, 2020).

2. I am necessarily condensing a lot of things here regarding the etymology of religion and its history. I point the interested reader to the following texts for more information: Carlin A. Barton and Daniel Boyarin, *Imagine No Religion: How Modern Abstractions Hide Ancient Realities* (New York: Fordham University Press, 2016); J. Kameron Carter, *The Anarchy of Black Religion: A Mystic Song* (Durham, N.C.: Duke University Press, 2023); David Chidester, *Empire of Religion: Imperialism and Comparative Religion* (Chicago, IL: University of Chicago Press, 2014); Charles H. Long, *Significations: Signs, Symbols, and Images in the Interpretation of Religion* (Aurora, CO: The Davies Group Publishers, 1995); Tomoko Masuzawa, *The Invention of World Religions: Or, How European Universalism Was Preserved in the Language of Pluralism* (Chicago: University of Chicago Press, 2005).

3. Du Bois, W. E. B. "The Souls of White Folk" in *Darkwater: Voices From Within the Veil* (Amherst, NY: Humanity Books, 2002), 56 (emphasis mine).

4. Ibid. 57 (emphasis added).
5. See J. Kameron Carter, *The Anarchy of Black Religion* and *The Religion of Whiteness: An Apocalyptic Lyric* (New Haven, CT: Yale University Press, forthcoming).

Introduction

George Yancy

As I thought and rethought about how to begin this brief introduction, I couldn't find the words. There was part of me that felt that whatever I had to say about the pernicious historical and contemporary hydraulics of *white* Christian nationalism—its "Doctrine of Discovery" perpetuated (in the name of "God") by imperialistic European monarchs to justify the genocide of Indigenous Peoples; its enslavement and brutalization of Black bodies; its lynching and rape of Black bodies; its signifying evil/terrorism in the form of white robes and hoods; its maintenance of "law and order" as racist machinations and tactics of surveillance and control of Black mobility and agency; its ecocide through neoliberal, capitalist logics; its anti-intellectualism and glorification of ignorance that is passed off as "knowledge"; its violent and dehumanizing practices of Othering and hatred of human beings who defy the discursive strictures of normative whiteness; its sycophantic and antidemocratic displays (along with the urine and feces) on January 6, 2021; its deeply troubling and idolatrous claims that Donald Trump is somehow religiously "anointed" and something of a "savior" figure; its fascistic efforts to repress and control our critical imaginations through book banning and the demonization of critical race theory (CRT); and its attempts at erasing the critical discourse (systemic racism, for example) that is necessary to name the ugly reality of the US—would not be enough.

The delineation of historical and contemporary facts about various forms of white Christian nationalism is *necessary*, crucial, if we are to collectively name this shameless updated Constantinian manifestation where *hesed* (i.e., loving kindness) has been supplanted by, or inextricably entangled with, "the instruments of death, war, and conquest."[1] Yet, and this brings me back to my failure to find the words to begin this brief introduction, so much more is needed.

There are times when I would like to think that I am being "radical," that I am one of those "heroic" figures who refuses to accept the status quo. Surely I must be doing something radical given that as a professor I was placed on what is called "The Professor Watchlist," which is a conservative website created by a conservative youth group known as Turning Point USA. The job of this watchlist is to monitor professors who teach so-called leftist propaganda. It is reminiscent of George Orwell's *1984*.[2] There were some scholars who wrote to me to give me a virtual high five for having made the infamous list. As much as I know that white Christian nationalism is a site of poisonous "us-versus-them" ideology, despicable idolatry, violence, lockstep conformism, anti-Black racism, homophobia, and white nation-building, I am also keen to keep track of my own deep failures. Being attentive to my own failures is not designed to move away from the fundamental and urgent need to bring truth to bear upon the ethically catastrophic problems intrinsic to white Christian nationalism. I want to make it clear that when I rage against white Christian nationalism, I also rage against my own pretensions and failures, which is by no means to conflate these with white Christian nationalism.

I see myself as a hopeful Christian theist. My hope is not simply some abstract gesture or emotional filler, as it were, in the *absence* of indubitable proof for the existence of God. That feels too noncommittal. Rather, my hope functions as a form of striving, a commitment and steadfastness, that hangs onto a promise. You see, my hope is not defined by a convenient instance of deus ex machina. My hope is embodied in the desired unfolding of a promise, a promise that is predicated on *hesed*, agape, justice, kindness, and the eradication of social evil. It is also predicated upon an anticipated world where we dwell together in absolute peace. Those who may have read my critical work on whiteness and anti-Blackness, where my philosophical sensibilities are impacted by the powerful insights of Afro-pessimism, will perhaps find these disclosures odd. But you see, I don't desire the end of *the* world, I desire the end of *this* world, *a* world. It is *this* world of *white* Christian nationalism, and of other forms of social evil, that *must go*.

Even as a hopeful Christian theist, even as a so-called dangerous professor, I am ensconced in a world where I am not innocent. There are times when I tremble as I think about calling myself a hopeful *Christian* theist. I tremble because I think about what this really looks like in action, what it really looks like in practice. I think about the weight of the commitment, and I know that I have failed. I can't recall the last time that I stopped to care for a stranger who was ill, hungry, or beaten or for the refugee seeking a place called home because of their war-torn country. This doesn't mean that I've never given money to a person whose hand is reached out in my direction, but shit, they will be back tomorrow and the day after tomorrow. So, what have I done? I can tell you what I have not done. I have not eradicated *systemic poverty*.

That is weighty; that is a burden; that feels like a call to which I have not responded.

And, sure, I teach courses that challenge whiteness. I write about these issues and give lectures, both nationally and internationally, about the conscious and insidious ways in which whiteness is violent. After such talks, I am left with a nagging sense of defeatism: Nothing will change! Yet, I will give another talk, white people will be moved, some might even cry, I will receive an honorarium and be taken out to dinner, but the systemic hegemony and privilege of whiteness will continue, which means that anti-Black violence will perdure. As Joy James states, "I'm petty bourgeois. The way I suffer is not how impoverished others suffer, or the incarcerated suffer at Rikers or in maximum security."[3] This doesn't mean that I have ceased to be Black within an anti-Black US, but I trust you get the point. I'm neither suggesting that it is futile to identify as a Christian, nor am I saying that academics who do the work of fighting against social injustice should stop. My point is that we need to *tarry* with our contradictions, our pretensions, the ways in which we are held captive by the very structures that we critique. Indeed, perhaps we need to face the reality of how such structures paradoxically enable our critiques. After all, neoliberal structures are consumptive.

Just when we think or feel as though we are holier than thou, the thoroughly converted, those possessed by a form of epistemic certainty, perhaps it is then that we have lost our way. Just when we become inebriated by our own internalized exaggerated sense of "revolutionary" vigilance, radical rebellion, when we become academic/intellectual "stars" who, unlike others, believe that we have the most critical insights on what ails the world, I would ask that we step back and ask: Who pays the bills? Where do I sleep at night? How do I find time to write, to think such lofty thoughts? Who the hell do I think I am when the Doomsday Clock is now ninety seconds to midnight? These questions, and so many more, when faced with brute honesty, remind me of the words of Rabbi Abraham Joshua Heschel, "If all agony were kept alive in memory, if all turmoil were told, who could endure tranquility?"[4] Heschel also observes that "an honest estimation of the moral state of society will disclose: *some are guilty, but all are responsible.*"[5]

Now that I have said what *I needed* to say, let me be clear. White Christian nationalism is dangerous. I don't say this as a political abstraction; I say this as a warning. Perhaps this is also why I had so much trouble finding an entry into this introduction. Part of white Christian nationalism is what we observed at the Capitol on January 6, 2021. There were some who chanted, "Hang Mike Pence!" It has been said that Trump supported the hanging of Pence.[6] From testimony, the implication is that Trump and his minions were prepared to commit murder. When white people are prepared to kill other white people (indeed, the vice president of the US) based on a lie (the Big

Lie that Trump won the election), what the hell do you think Trump and his white Christian nationalist followers would do to a Black embodied person like me or like you? After all, we are deemed the abject. Learn about the history of the lynching of Black bodies by white Christian folk (who brought their white children along to watch) and the answer to that question is terrifying. What was it that Trump wanted Pence to do? According to one Trump tweet, "Mike Pence didn't have the courage to do what should have been done to protect our Country and our Constitution."[7] And what was that? Pence should have attempted to overturn an official and valid certification of electoral votes. In short, Trump wanted Pence to act against, at least in this case, a functioning aspect of democracy, to undo the majority vote, to render nugatory the expressed desire of the demos. That is the stench of fascism, a form of fascism led by someone who referred to himself as "the chosen one." He is, according to his white theological hyperbole and repugnant grandiosity, "the elect." Then again, the entire white Christian nationalist/supremacist mise-en-scène at the Capitol functioned to buttress such a lie.

There were signs that read, "Jesus Saves," "In God We Trust," "Jesus is my Savior, Trump is my President," "Trump is President, Christ is King," and flags that read, "Make America Godly Again." There were large crosses paraded and prayers performed in and outside the Capitol. Support for the Big Lie was apparently underwritten by those whites who believed that something (dare I say) "transcendent" was at stake, where the rule of a certain white theological absolutism had been placed under threat by those ("never Trumpers") who wanted to call into question the "divinity" and manifest destiny of Trump—the white "deliverer." My sense is that protesters were not only fighting with a sense of white nationalist "duty" but also fighting with a religious zeal to do "God's work." In short, what we witnessed was an example of unhinged fanaticism. Carrying signs of a white Jesus (the one with blue eyes) at the attempted coup reinforced the semiotic whiteness and theologically exclusionary/violent logics at play.

As we know, the stench of fascism, the audacity of the Republican Thought Police or "Thinkpol" (the *1984* dystopian reference is intended) deepened. Republicans referred to the attack on the Capitol as "legitimate political discourse."[8] It is this level of attempted mystification and obscurantism that forces me as a Black philosopher to rethink my relationship to Auguste Rodin's *The Thinker*. I want to scream. Yet, it isn't just Advard Munch's *The Scream* that will suffice. It is a scream that is unleashed after staring long and hard into the ethical abyss of the US, its ignominy and history of prevarication, bloodlust, and death-dealing fantasies and realities. It is a form of repugnance expressed by Frederick Douglass where he powerfully critiqued the condemnable duplicity of white Christianity: "I am filled with unutterable loathing when I contemplate the religious pomp and show, together with the horrible inconsistencies, which [everywhere] surround me."⁹ It is the lament felt by Black people who were forcefully brought to this country by white people to satisfy their materialist, malicious greed, desire, pleasure, and gratuitous violence. And it was in the name of their "white God" that they justified their actions. Rabbi Heschel writes, "What is an idol? *Any god who is mine but not yours*, any god concerned with me but not with you, *is an idol*."¹⁰ How can the God/gods of a white Christian fascist be concerned with me? Then again, I imagine that there is always room for a "Nigger" in such a white supremacist theology. The truth of that claim is beyond philosophical *aporia*; rather, it is one that is laden with existential *agony*. To know that Black bodies—"Niggers"—are necessary for the libidinal and psychic coherence¹¹ of white life (dare I say even white theology) is to shudder in the face of such a monstrous theological metaphysics.

In its white imperial neediness, the US (I could have written Rome) needs the death of Black bodies in both spectacular and mundane forms. It is necessary to watch the "Niggers." Hiding beneath their facade is the hidden "superpredator" waiting to strike.¹² "Niggers" are always already deemed "immoral," "unclean," "wretched," and "pollutants." Indeed, with their audacity to reclaim their humanity, to reclaim their being, they are "enemies" of the State. Imagine that! This is a case where Black ontology is a site of troublemaking, a site to be subjected to imperial, carceral logics. It is here that white Christian nationalists need to be reminded that it was the hegemonic power of the empire (etymologically, to command) of Rome that put the historical Jesus to death. It makes sense that white Christian nationalists would refuse to focus on the supremacist machinations that put Jesus to death. It is best not to think of the messiness of embodied subjugation at the hands of brute hegemonic power. I would argue that white Christian nationalists "mask the insurrectionist and mundane political meanings of his [Jesus's] imperial torture-death."¹³ This is what white supremacy does; it masks, and it conceals. In doing so, white Christian nationalism is a form of betrayal of "the core meanings of Jesus's life and teachings."¹⁴ As Cornel West notes, "Most American Constantinian Christians are unaware of their imperialistic identity because they do not see the parallel between the Roman empire that put Jesus to death and the American empire that they celebrate."¹⁵

Having now found my words in this text, I want to reiterate: White Christian nationalism is dangerous. It is as dangerous as the fanaticism of Nazism. If successful, all who oppose it (indeed, all whose "differences" it attempts to define within its fixed logics) will be trampled to death. It is a fanaticism born of domination, political repression, and xenophobia. In this case, white Christian nationalists refuse to remove the mask that allows them to "proudly profess their allegiance to the flag and the cross not realizing that just as the cross was a bloody indictment of the Roman empire, it is a powerful critique of the American empire."[16] The mask enables white Christian nationalists/ Constantinian Christians to "sell their precious souls for a mess of imperial pottage based on the false belief that they are simply being true to the flag and the cross."[17] James Baldwin was critical of a conceptualization of God that didn't "make us larger, freer and more loving."[18] Baldwin would have no patience for a white Christian nationalist conception of God because it would make us smaller, render us captive, and hateful. Regarding that concept of God, I agree with Baldwin that it is time we abandoned it. White Christian nationalism is predicated on conquest. The subjugation and dispossession of others is what conquest looks like. Deep suffering and murderous catastrophe are what it leaves in its wake. Think here of Gaza.

White Christian nationalism is parasitic, hegemonic, binaristic, and ontologically hierarchical. James Cone argues, "Love is a refusal to accept whiteness. To love is to make a decision against white racism."[19] In stream with Cone, I would argue that white Christian nationalism is a refusal to accept love; it is a decision against love. Love un-sutures in the face of those who have been and are being dehumanized by racism, sexism, classism, genderism, heterosexism, ableism, nativism, State oppression, and colonial occupation. Love refuses the arbitrary power of empires that are invested in forms of governmentality that produce cowards and bystanders who remain silent as precious human beings are valued on the cheap. Love resists the eradication of critical thinking and the love of wisdom. The eradication of critical thinking is consistent with the banning of books. Both are motivated to repress dissent. As West writes, "To be a Christian—a follower of Jesus Christ—is to love wisdom, love justice, and love freedom."[20] West concludes, "This is the radical love in Christian freedom and the radical freedom in Christian love that embraces Socratic questioning [and] prophetic witness."[21] As Paulo Freire also reminds us, "To glorify democracy [though not something to be made into another idol] and to silence the people is a farce."[22] Indeed, it is a travesty for white Christian nationalists to worship an authoritarian figure like Trump, one who habitually lies, who abuses and disparages historical memory,[23] and who is an admirer of authoritarian figures around the globe—Vladimir Putin, Kim Jong Un, and Tayyip Erdogan, to name a few.

The love of wisdom, radical freedom, and Socratic questioning are anathema to authoritarian strongmen and imperial domination. There is no space for mutual kenosis, a form of emptying where reciprocal learning flourishes. Yet, kenosis is necessary for white Christian nationalists. They need to rid themselves of fear, hatred, xenophobia, idolatry, conceptions of racial "purity," myths that seduce them into believing that they are *the* "white saviors of the world," the "*white* chosen ones." What is needed are apostates who are prepared to reject the idolatry of white Christian nationalism. We need those who are prepared to imperil the lie of "safety." What we need is an apocalypse vis-à-vis whiteness. I want the reader to understand the double meaning captured by the term. On the one hand, *apocalypse* means destruction. As an unethical structure, whiteness must come to an end. That much is clear. On the other hand, *apocalypse* means, etymologically, to uncover. And to uncover is to face the truth about whiteness, which means to face its emptiness, and then to relinquish a lie that covers itself as the truth. That will require both a scream and a profound lament—*a necessary loss*.

In Sheep's Clothing: The Idolatry of White Christian Nationalism is an urgent text. As the title suggests, we are faced with a disguise that passes (for many) for "innocence," indeed, religious "purity." It is a cloak of deception that involves an active maintenance and encouragement of ignorance. Within the context of the US, white Christian nationalism is the enemy of the demos; it is predicated on the authoritarianism and militarism[24] of the State and seeks to maintain fascistic control over everything within its reach. This isn't new. As West writes, "With Constantine's conversion, a terrible co-joining of church and state was institutionalized."[25] He continues, "Constantine himself seems to have converted to Christianity partly out of political strategy and imperial exigency, and then proceeded to use the cloak of Christianity for his own purposes of maintaining power."[26] It is the use of this cloak that is important here. I would argue that foundational to the US is an imperial theo-political confluence of colonial violence, Manichaean racism, nativism, and a problematic philosophical anthropology that has deep soteriological and hamartiological implications that run deep and that differentially and hierarchically mark racialized bodies. From Megyn Kelly's claim that Jesus is white, to former President Trump's hubristic and megalomaniacal claim that he is the "chosen one" or the "King of Israel," we are in serious trouble. Contemporary manifestations of white Christian nationalism are deeply entangled in issues from women's political rights over their own bodies to the rejection of critical thought itself.

We are living in a deep crisis in the US, one that is fueled by tyrannical figures who are more than prepared to deploy as much paramilitary violence as is needed to suppress forms of resistance to injustice. White Christian nationalism seems to be propelled by a self-fulfilling eschatology that it may tragically create. West asks, "Are not our nihilistic imperial rulers [think here of just two, Trump and Ron DeSantis] and their Constantinian followers leading us on a similar path—the suffocating of prophetic voices and viewpoints that challenge the status quo?"[27] It is not difficult for me to imagine the dismantlement of US democracy as we know it. To get a sense of some of the necessary forces, just think here of the intensification of book banning; holding libraries and curricular materials captive; the violent suppression of critical thought; the proliferation of fake news; paramilitary expansion and escalation in US streets; the continuing cultivation and deepening of a politics of resentment;

the divisive use of zero-sum logics; greater corporate (oligarchic) elite power; the development of more sophisticated forms of a politics of distraction; regressive policies that attack and restrict the agency that women have over their bodies; the further increase in policing and mass incarceration; the refusal of the (non-white) stranger based on the nativist policy to "Make America Great Again"; and the emergence of more skillfully deceitful and tyrannical "demagogues to promote nationalistic policies."[28] Combine all of this with white Christian nationalism, where God and Jesus are believed to be white (and Santa, too) and on the side of those who have State power, well, how can one lose?

The book that you have before you consists of a cadre of twenty-three scholars engaged in critical, insightful, and profound analyses of white Christian nationalism. Some critically engage and trace deep and insightful historical dynamics that uncover white Christian nationalism as the theo-ideological racist mythos and brutal/violent regime that it is, revealing that what is occurring in the US at this moment isn't an inaugural event. Others provide searing autobiographical explorations that situate white privilege and power at the locus of white Christian nationalism, revealing the mundanity of whiteness without severing it from white Christian nationalist sensibilities. Still others analytically tease out the dynamics involved in the white psyche vis-à-vis white Christian nationalism, revealing deep theological implications (e.g., misogyny, white loss, the fear of incoherence, or where whiteness is explored as a theodicy). Poetry is also deployed as a revelatory discourse to uncover the hidden. All the scholars in this text provide important sites of intervention where the question, "How can they lose?" is profoundly called into question. This is a text that rejects white nationalist theological arrogance, authoritarianism, and the equation of racial whiteness with "divinity." It is a text that opposes white Christian nationalism's xenophobic violence and its conceptualization of God as wedded to the American flag. Indeed, this text is undergirded by a form of praxis that resists and takes a stand against white Christian nationalism's enthrallment with its own graven image—*whiteness*.

NOTES

1. Miguel A. De La Torre, "Constantinian Christianity," *Good Faith Media*, January 30, 2008, https://goodfaithmedia.org/constantinian-christianity-cms-12212/.

2. Indeed, after I discovered that I was placed on "The Professor Watchlist," I decided to write an article for the *New York Times* titled "I Am a Dangerous Professor," November 30, 2016, https://www.nytimes.com/2016/11/30/opinion/i-am-a-dangerous-professor.html?_r=0.

3. Joy James, *In Pursuit of Revolutionary Love: Precarity, Power, Communities* (Brussels: Divided Publishing, 2022), 175.

4. Abraham Joshua Heschel, *Abraham Joshua Heschel: Essential Writings*, ed. Susannah Heschel (Maryknoll, NY: Orbis Books, 2011), 178.

5. Heschel, *Abraham Joshua Heschel*, 69.

6. Betsy Woodruff Swan and Kyle Cheney, "Trump Expressed Support for Hanging Pence during Capitol Riot, January 6 Panel Told," *Politico*, May 25, 2022, https://www.politico.com/news/2022/05/25/trump-expressed-support-hanging-pence-capitol-riot-jan-6-00035117.

7. Swan and Cheney, "Trump Expressed Support for Hanging Pence during Capitol Riot, January 6 Panel Told."

8. Jonathan Weisman and Reid J. Epstein, "G.O.P. Declares January 6 Attack 'Legitimate Political Discourse,'" *New York Times*, February 4, 2022, https://www.nytimes.com/2022/02/04/us/politics/republicans-jan-6-cheney-censure.html.

9. Frederick Douglass, *Narrative of the Life of Frederick Douglass, an American Slave, Written by Himself*, ed. David W. Blight (New York: Bedford/St. Marin's Press, 1993), 105.

10. Heschel, *Abraham Joshua Heschel*, 66.

11. On theorizing the various ways in which civil society, and the Human, acquire psychic and narrative coherence vis-à-vis the Black body (or anti-Black racism), see Frank B. Wilderson III, *Afropessimism* (New York: Liverlight Publishing, 2020).

12. Carroll Bogert, "Analysis: How the Media Created a 'Superpredator' Myth That Harmed a Generation of Black Youth," *NBC News*, November 20, 2020, https://www.nbcnews.com/news/us-news/analysis-how-media-created-superpredator-myth-harmed-generation-black-youth-n1248101.

13. George Yancy and Mark L. Taylor, "Christianity Is Empty If It Doesn't Address the Racist Carceral State," *Truthout*, September 26, 2021, https://truthout.org/articles/christianity-is-empty-if-it-doesnt-address-the-racist-carceral-state/.

14. Yancy and Taylor, "Christianity Is Empty If It Doesn't Address the Racist Carceral State."

15. Cornel West, *Democracy Matters: Winning the Fight Against Imperialism* (New York: Penguin Books, 2004), 150.

16. West, *Democracy Matters*, 150.

17. West, *Democracy Matters*, 151.

18. James Baldwin, *The Fire Next Time* (New York: Modern Library, 1962/1995), 46.

19. James H. Cone, *A Black Theology of Liberation* (Maryknoll, NY: Orbis Books, 2010), 78.

20. West, *Democracy Matters*, 172.

21. West, *Democracy Matters*, 172.

22. Paulo Freire, *Pedagogy of the Oppressed*, 30th Anniversary Edition (New York: Continuum International Publishing Group, 2000), 72.

23. Henry Giroux, *American Nightmare: Facing the Challenge of Racism* (San Francisco, CA: City Lights Books, 2018), 119.

24. West, *Democracy Matters*, 148.

25. West, *Democracy Matters*, 148.

26. West, *Democracy Matters*, 148.
27. West, *Democracy Matters*, 159.
28. Giroux, *American Nightmare*, 258. Giroux powerfully theorizes a politics of resentment and regressive politics within the context of Donald Trump's fascistic aims and efforts.

Introduction

Bill Bywater

The chapters collected here make it abundantly clear that Europeans, followed by colonists in North America and then citizens of the United States, committed terrible atrocities under the guise of Christianity, as Brock Bahler and Laurie Cassidy demonstrate. These atrocities began with the Catholic Church but were also undertaken by Protestant leaders. Even the late Queen Elizabeth II, as Kimberley Ducey points out, ignored the racist violence within her realm. In the US today, in addition to many so-called evangelistic Christians, we find politicians and assorted cultural commentators also proposing to limit the rights and freedoms of individuals under the cover of Christianity. As Leah Kalmanson argues, these Christians, politicians, and pundits—their names are legion, from Pope Nicholas V to Megyn Kelly, as our authors demonstrate—are making the universal God of Christianity into a local deity that supports a specific race and place while it is deliberately blind to the oppression caused by this local deity, as José Francisco Morales Torres observes, and insistent on the "innocence" and "goodness" of the individuals who worship it, as Biko Mandela Gray points out. The authors within this text accurately refer to such processes as white Christian nationalism to fully illustrate its locality of race and nation. Laurie Cassidy suggests that this is deicide. The *imago Dei* is ruined when Jesus is identified as white. She suggests that this process of whitening equates the innocence and goodness of Jesus with that of whites so that whites can ignore, or repress without hesitation, Jesus's real identity as a person of color. And, as Kathy Glass argues, this involves the repression of Jesus's values of loving our neighbors and supporting those who have the least to privilege white racial identity. This identity includes a disembodiment that neglects not only the flesh of Jesus but also the suffering flesh of those who are oppressed by white supremacy, Torres argues.

Timothy J. Golden describes this deicide as a reduction of God's transcendence to an immanence in which the *imago Dei* becomes an *imago hominis*—God created in the image of white men whose idea of the US as a Christian nation includes racist violence and oppression, as Golden and Joe Feagin argue, but that also supports a hypermasculinity, as Dean J. Johnson notes, which Mark Lewis Taylor sees as a devotion to the US as a corporate-warrior state. Taylor's engaging point is quite consistent with Karen Teel's observations about the role of the violent white mob in the history of the US, from lynching, to the invasion of the Capitol on January 6, 2021, and the violence of colonization, as Anthony Paul Smith describes it. Elisabeth Vasko points out that the norms of whiteness are reenacted in a manner that allows whites to avoid any responsibility for the terror that results from their violent actions. This includes, too, the violence of misogyny, which, for Traci C. West, is at the heart of Christian white supremacy. Nonwhite girls and women—Native American and Black—are at the center of this mistreatment. White women and white girls are also subject to control under the aegis of "family values" that will save them from "impurity."

Sheldon George's analysis that whites' sense of victimhood and the accompanying feeling that they are losing or have lost some important dimension of their identity as people of color (and I would add of alternative sexualities) claims that more social recognition for themselves is at the root of all this violence, which brings to mind James Garrison's discussion of eliminationism and Todd M. Mealy's examination of replacement theory. From the age of six to the present day, James Garrison powerfully explores his experiences as a target for elimination by white bullies who see him as a threat, especially when their desires for fulfillment are thwarted. Mealy traces white people's concerns about being replaced by people of color, especially Black people, from the Lost Cause movement right after the Civil War through the Ku Klux Klan to present "memory laws," which attempt, through education, to control our national story by eliminating the importance of people of color and people of alternative sexualities to tell stories in which whites who conform to traditional gender roles are always the heroes.

This overview combining eighteen of our chapters leaves me with the impression that any Christian church or individual worthy of the name should be condemning white Christian nationalism as not really Christian at all but, rather, as a heresy that is a manifestation of deicide. Those who wrap themselves in this idolatry are not professing a mutually respectful religious faith but pursuing a divisive and violent ideology that seeks for its proponents the power to control the lives of US citizens as well as the nature of citizenship itself. Josiah Ulysses Young III argues that progressive theologians must challenge this debauched Christianity. He also points out that all believers must adopt a humane ethics to push white Christian nationalism back into the shadows. Ann Floerke Scheid, Marinus Chijioke Iwuchukwu, and Torres argue that there is a Christian tradition that embodies a humane ethics and is not a heresy of deicide—Christianity as developed and practiced by people of color who were subject to slavery and oppression in the Americas. Torres introduces us to Father Ernesto Cardenal of Nicaragua, who re-sings the Psalms in a way that makes clear how the Christian message applies to the lives of the poor and oppressed. Iwuchukwu seeks restorative justice for Black and brown people in the US via the recognition by white churches of their historic and current role in supporting racism. Scheid introduces the work of Black theologians who describe Black Christianity as embracing God as a savior who will lead Black people out of slavery, as God led the Israelites out of Egypt and who raised Jesus in defiance of the powers who crucified him.

These authors' findings lead me to advocate that white Christians and their churches who are not already embracing deicide should apprentice themselves to Black Christianity. Because the idea of apprenticeship is so tightly linked to the idea of mastering a trade or a body of knowledge, let me make clear that the apprenticeship I propose does not advocate that whites become "masters" of Black Christianity! The apprenticeship I propose is one of growth, not mastery. It is what takes place when persons and institutions nondefensively open themselves to learning from those who have traditionally been excluded, regarded as the Other. That is, it is a process of learning about the lives, the experiences, the values, and the joys and sorrows of those who have been disregarded by learning about the hymns they sing, the biblical passages they treasure, and the holidays they celebrate and how they celebrate them in Black churches that are concerned with social justice and take seriously those who are oppressed by hegemonic systems. Beyond what happens on Sundays, growth by white people must include an understanding of how white lives are intertwined with Black lives; how the successes whites may experience as self-generated through a problematic system of "meritocracy" are actually grounded in the lives of those whom whites tend to ignore; and how white people experience themselves—their bodies, feelings, and thoughts—as they move from place to place, which is very different from the ways in which Black people experience themselves as they move within or through those same places. As many of our authors suggest, white people have a great deal to learn about the lives of Native Americans, Latino/Latinas, and Black people if these traditionally marginalized people are to be fully embraced, with the dignity and love to which they are entitled, as the sisters and brothers of white people.

These concerns lead us into the wider world of our democracy in the US. John Dewey, our greatest philosopher of democracy, described it, in part, as follows:

> [D]emocracy is a *personal* way of individual life; that it signifies the possession and continual use of certain attitudes, forming personal character and determining desire and purpose in all the relations of life. . . . Belief in the Common Man is a familiar article in the democratic creed. That belief is without basis and significance save as it means faith in the potentialities of human nature as that nature is exhibited in every human being irrespective of race, color, sex, birth and family, of material or cultural wealth. . . . [I]f, in our daily walk and conversation, we are moved by racial, color or other class prejudice; indeed, by anything save a generous belief in their possibilities as human beings, *a belief which brings with it the need for providing conditions which will enable these capacities to reach fulfillment.* . . . Intolerance, abuse, calling of names because of differences of opinion about religion or politics or business, as well as because of differences of race, color, wealth or degree of culture are treason to the democratic way of life.[1]

White Christian nationalism is a threat to Christianity when it commits deicide under its banner. It also commits democracide by violating every one of the conditions that Dewey posits as central to our democracy. This ugly nationalism does not place faith in the potentiality of our fellow citizens "irrespective of race, color, sex." If you are not white and not cisgender, you are in danger of special State scrutiny and will be viciously marked by degrading names. It is also likely that the State will be unwilling to provide the conditions that will enable you to be fulfilled and flourish. If you are not white and not cisgender, it is unlikely that any generous belief in your possibilities will be extended to you.

If you are white and cisgender, you had better not extend a generous belief in the possibilities of those who are not, nor should you advocate for providing conditions that will enable the capacities of such people, that is, if you want to stay clear of scrutiny. If you are a cisgender white woman (or man), do not mention birth control or abortion in any other than negative terms. Oh, and do not strive for justice. In this book, *In Sheep's Clothing: The Idolatry of White Christian Nationalism*, the authors strive for justice, and they critique white Christian nationalism as a form of empire, as a political regime of exclusion, and as a form of fanaticism that longs for racial "purity."

NOTE

1. John Dewey, "Creative Democracy—The Task Before Us," in *The Later Works, Volume 14: 1939–1941*, edited by Jo Ann Boydston (Carbondale: Southern Illinois University Press, 1991), 226–27. Second set of italics added.

Opening Poem
Mary Magdalene Sings

Becky Thompson

If your god is the color of a white sheet who shoots up
a baby's bris, if your god stalks abortion clinics,

scaring cardinals in neighboring trees, or rampages
the Capitol as if it were his destiny, if your god builds

fortresses on stolen land, ambushes families traveling
peacefully by caravan, then my name is Deborah,

judge and prophet with military chops. My name
is Delilah, who snipped off my lover's locks.

My name is Jezebel who dressed in red,
refused to limit who shared my bed.

My names are the women erased
by the Latter-Day Saints.

My name is Mary Magdalene ignored by Gnostic
restraints. My god is not hate that refuses

to wear a humble hat. My god is not lay down
like a tattered place mat. My god outsmarts

an ornery band, calls on Fannie Lou Hamer to help us
understand, reminds us of faith that refuses to shun,

disarms the gun that leaves no space to run. My god
meets your god and plays Sweet Honey in the Rock.

My god is a marigold, neither bought nor sold, sees
your god and kneels to our collective woes. My god

reaches out to your god, is not frightened or subdued.
My god knows we're all born precious, that we all exit too.

ABOUT THIS POEM

I was raised by a teen mother who ran from the Mormon Church after being baptized 142 times to save the souls of the unsaved. She now refers to the church as a cult. As I watched coverage of the January 6 attack at the Capitol and heard twisted Christian justifications for racist hate crimes, I wondered what the forgotten women of the Bible might say. The early multiracial feminist classic *God's Fierce Whimsy* by the Mud Flower Collective and Anne Swinfen's writing have been helpful in imagining such conversations, as has the work of liberation theologians (Howard Thurman, Dr. Reverend Katie Cannon, and Oscar Romero) who never ceded the Bible to fantasies of a racist state.

Chapter 1

White Christians and the US Corporate-Warrior State

Mark Lewis Taylor

AFFECTIVE PROVOCATIONS AND THEORETICAL POSTURES

There are white Christians with fascist aspirations who provoke in me—the white Christian theologian that I am—outrage and even disgust and some shame that I ever could have been associated with Christianity. Also problematic to me, however, are the white Christians who, while distancing themselves from fascist aspirants, offer up routine accommodations to a US imperial apparatus, one also heavily laden with white supremacist force. By this apparatus, I mean the many institutional and social mechanisms of control (local, national, global) that reinforce the powerful dynamics of corporate capitalists' rule as these dynamics interplay continuously with the equally powerful dynamics of military-carceral rule. As shorthand, I refer to this apparatus as the US corporate-warrior state.

Both Christian fascist aspirants and Christian adherents to US empire are racialized and racist formations. Both are enabled by, and expressions of, white supremacy and anti-Blackness.

Steeped in raciality as they both are, however, each deploys a distinctive apparatus of domination. It is hard to draw a sharp line of demarcation, but fascists display their totalitarian and brutal apparatus more out in the open. The adherents to empire tend to fold the brutal and totalitarian features of fascism into a larger world mission with a commandeering political influence of global reach, which normalizes, justifies, and often masks the fascist features to which they often resort. In this chapter, I will argue that the continuing white adherence to the US corporate-warrior state's imperial apparatus is the more serious white supremacist formation with which we must wrestle. It is more serious because it is a more expansive matrix of power, one that functions regularly as the very condition for the possibility of the growing white Christian fascist aspirants in the US today. If I could put it in a nutshell: White imperial wars abroad reinforce white rule at home in its many forms.[1] The US military power and surveillance apparatus, which especially targets Black, Indigenous, and other people of color in poorer countries abroad, is often also a practice that inflicts the technologies of control and repression on poor racialized communities at home. In one concentrated example, we can see this in the imprisonment of Black American employee of the CIA Jeffrey Sterling, who for his exposure of racial discrimination in the CIA and the inadequacies in US attempts to subvert Iran's nuclear program, was sent to prison on trumped-up charges under the Espionage Act. He paid dearly, both for his critique of empire and his Blackness.[2]

So, as dangerous as white fascist tendencies are, I often find white liberal Christian adherents to the US empire's corporate-warrior state to provoke in me deeper consternation, a slower burning but more pervading outrage, disgust, and, again, some shame that I ever could be associated with it. As a white professor of theology in neoliberal academe, I am of course embedded in the very matrix of the US corporate-warrior apparatus I decry. Maybe what is especially disturbing about this white devotion to the corporate-warrior state is its announced "liberalism" and the cults of respectability in which it can clothe itself. This is no new tendency. Harvard historian Caroline Elkins writes in her recent book, *Legacy of Violence: A History of the British Empire*, of that empire's long legacy of advocating "reform" and "liberal" values while colonizing with imperial means. Precisely this "liberal imperialism" and the often astounding brutal "legalized lawlessness" that it dared to call a "civilizing" process do much to provoke fascist reaction as well as revolution.[3] The US empire, too, uses its politicians' "liberal" claims of guarding democracy and progress to justify its incursions and imposed chaos and subjugation.[4] Recall the US invasion of Iraq, about which former Vice President Dick Cheney intoned in advance, "We will be greeted as liberators."[5] To the contrary, the war quickly put Iraq into debilitating chaos,[6] leaving it in many ways worse off. "An estimated 300,000 people have died from direct war violence in Iraq, while the reverberating effects of war continue to kill and sicken hundreds of thousands more."[7]

The fascism that liberals decry is often a consequence of the imperial wars they support. White soldiers returning from Vietnam, Iraq, and Central America have been key catalysts of militant white supremacism and fascism at home.[8] The role of US war-making today is rarely critiqued by so-called "liberals." Consider how the architects of US imperial policies in 2023, whether they be Republican or Democrat, routinely came together to renounce Trump daily and his white nationalist fascism, while rarely if ever questioning the US imperial wars abroad, the corporate concentration of wealth, or the surveillance capitalism so entrenched today. I grant that sometimes we need to support, at least temporarily, the "liberal" apparatus to counter rising white fascism's threat. Recall Fred Hampton's famous words, "Nothing is more important than stopping fascism because fascism is gonna stop us all."[9] But in the same speech in which these words were delivered Hampton also linked US fascism to international "neocolonialism" as practiced, for example, in Africa and in Haiti. White fascists were a problem, but they were a piece with what he termed in that speech "megalomaniac warmongers." To put it another way, those thinking themselves "liberal" opponents to fascism are often by their support of US wars the very conditions that make fascism a possibility.

My negative judgments here about the two forms of racist Christianity—white Christian fascism and white Christian liberalism—which are both embedded in white supremacism, and my deeper consternation about the white liberal Christian adherents to US empire should not be misunderstood. Three possible misunderstandings need to be addressed.

First, the dissenting positions I take about the US imperial project do not prohibit my critical loyalty to a nation still experimenting with the possibility of a people's democracy. I especially maintain a strong sense of belonging to the land across which "America" has colonized. I maintain that sense despite the expansion of the nation's founding violence of Indigenous dispossession and Black subjugation, which are now maintained by means of its corporate organization of wealth and military/carceral powers—in short, by its corporate-warrior elite. In the US, the ongoing struggle to free and nurture the land and its peoples—the complexity of all this—is something I take to be
• beautiful. I value belonging to that complexity. So, despite my critique of the US imperial project, I still value the struggle to define, refine, and radically transform what it means to be a US citizen.

Second, the criticisms that this chapter offers of white Christianity, and the discomfort I have with it, should not be taken as meaning my complete relinquishment of elements of Christian tradition. In fact, I write as one who takes with both personal and professional seriousness the gift of key intelligent claims that can be made for a faith in movements and institutions that remember the life and witness of Jesus of Nazareth. I will end this chapter pointing in the direction of that faith. This enables me to affirm those white folk inside various churches, at their margins, or perhaps pushed outside of church spaces, who are resisters to white Christianity as I will define it here. They wield elements of Christian traditions against white Christianity, in both its fascist and liberal, imperial forms.

Third, although this chapter places my criticism of white Christian fascist aspirations *within* the larger and more forceful criticism of white Christian adherence to US empire, the fascist aspirations do require a specific and forceful criticism. It is important to do so. The oft-referenced assault by a white mob on the US Capitol on January 6, 2021, is just one example of what must be resisted. I watched the event, as did many others, as members of the mob turned US flag poles into spears or batons to batter those in their way. The colors they carried included a flag of the Confederacy, just one sign of the refuse collected from America's white supremacist past and present.[10]

Standing out from this detritus on January 6 were emblems and slogans of Christian culture made into props for assault. "Jesus in 2024" read one Trumpster's banner at the Capitol. "Holy Bible" was printed on another rioter's T-shirt. Christian crosses appeared among those who flashed white supremacist hand signs. The simple wood frame set out to "hang Mike Pence" featured a horizontal crossbeam and a vertically hanging noose, together figuring another kind of crucifix, that crucible of US history's racist lynchings, primarily of African Americans, but also of Mexicans and Chinese. White Christians have long been present among lynching crowds. On January 6, they cavorted with the emerging forces of coalescing white power movements in the US, as Neo-Nazi, Aryan Nation, and Proud Boys all jockeyed under the cross, hungry for a power to make their white America great again. Once inside the US Senate chamber, the so-called "QAnon Shaman" and his friends mounted the dais up front and chanted a number of stock phrases of Christian nationalism against the "socialist and globalist traitors" ("We invoke the name of Jesus Christ!" "Our dear Heavenly Father, we pray . . . ," and so on).[11] All this is the stuff of a dangerous past and a threatening present. It augurs a predominantly white Christian fascist future. But again, we dare not carve out "white Christian fascists" from other forms of white Christianity and its politics, especially knowing that there are critics of the white fascists who yet support the US corporate-warrior state uncritically. We thus must undertake some critical thinking about what we mean when we speak or write of "white Christianity."

WHITE CHRISTIANITY

"White Christianity" is an expression that fuses the name of one of the so-called religions, here "Christianity," with a racializing term, here "white." But in this fusion of terms—one about religion, another about race—there often remain hidden two other complex dynamics, that is, the making of Christianity as "religion" and the making of whiteness as a "race." These dynamics of "making" operate not only in our usage of the expression often today, but also in the long histories of Christianity and whiteness. Again, my position in this chapter is that even as we rage against and resist white

Christianity, in both its fascist and imperial forms, we do best to point our focused resistance toward something bigger than what "white Christianity" usually names, toward the larger complex of power relations in which it is embedded and which it supports. Looking at these two dynamics of making exposes the embeddedness of white Christianity in its larger complex of power relations.

WHITE CHRISTIANITY AS RELIGION-MAKING

When I claim that white Christianity is religion-making I refer, first, to a long history of Christian thinkers, particularly theologians, who played crucial roles in generating the notion of "religion" as a category for social discourse and academic study. Second, the making of the general notion of "religion" was bound up with the plural "religions," the latter often set in a comparative relation one to another, usually arranged hierarchically. A most obvious example of this is found in early European agents in commercial exchange with African peoples who began to name something called "fetish religion" in Africa or "the religion of the Blacks,"[12] both often discussed within a panoply of other "religions" such as Islam, Judaism, Buddhism, Hinduism, and so on. Here, I do not emphasize so much how European Christians set various religions into hierarchical relation one to another, though that was often done. In the above list of religions, for example, fetish religion and religion of the Blacks were clearly hierarchically subordinate to other "major" ones, especially Christianity, but also often to Islam, Buddhism, and so on.

The major distinction that I want to stress here is that which set Christianity as the "true religion" (*vera religio*) over other "lesser" spiritualities and visions, other religions.[13] The making of the very notion of "religion" and of "the religions" emerges as predominantly Christian and European discoveries and colonizing agents encountered other peoples. Historian of religions Brent Nongbri reminds readers in his *Before Religion: A History of a Modern Concept* that the notion of religion/religions is a "relic of Christian polemic,"[14] which is a product of Christian self-understanding achieved through contestation with other encountered cultures and peoples. The notion of religion/religions that emerged with European modernity did so precisely in this time of colonializing powers in Africa, the Americas, and elsewhere.[15] Even though some converts from colonized populations themselves touted modes of Christian supremacy,[16] the primary formulation and impetus for religion-making that forged Christian supremacy was done by white Christian thinkers embedded in processes of the European coloniality of power.

Similarly, religious studies scholar Richard King, in *Orientalism and Religion: Postcolonial Theory, India and "The Mystic East,"* demonstrates how the very notions of "religion" and "mysticism" came into current parlance and scholarly use as a result of complex power shaped by "Western (Judeo-Christian/secular) paradigms." Scholars still find it difficult, King reminds us, to get free from this era in which European, predominantly white Christian culture, shaped definitions of religion. Additional historical and theoretical analyses would foreground many nuances in this development, but the basic point is this: It was largely white theology's cultural and intellectual communities that "made religion." Further, when the plural form, "the religions," is used today, there persists a pervasive Christian-inflected hierarchical attitude to the "other" religions. Judith Butler noticed this with respect to US society, wherein Christianity functions still as the "legitimate religion." Even amid the poly-religiosity and secularity of US society, Butler discerns Christianity's taking on a "legitimacy" in the ways it provides certain "cultural preconditions of the public." Unlike Buddhism, Hinduism, Islam, and other spiritual or religious traditions, the communities named "Christian" long have offered to US public life "symbols circulating freely within the public." It remains difficult, for example, to imagine candidates for US president who think it beneficial to their political interests to wear a crescent or other religious symbols on their suit lapel or on display on a necklace. Christianity and its symbols are allowed greater acceptance, while public limits are placed on "other" symbols and traditions "that are considered to threaten the foundation of secular life" or that often are "considered ostentatious or threatening to democracy itself."[17] All this is part of the way Christianity is continually "made" as a religion and then made to be preferred, set forth as supreme.

In US history, there are many sites at which we can view this religion-making. The very founding of the US nation is integrally bound up with Christians' views of their religion's supremacy. One doesn't need to access only today's Christian conservative press to find antagonism toward and a continual Othering of Islam over and against Christianity. From before the founding of the US government, from 1789 to its early decades, this Othering, the making of an antagonism between Christian and Muslim religions, was continually being manufactured by Christian-dominated culture. Christians shared with early political leaders in the North American colonies an opposition between Christianity and Islam manufactured as an antagonism between the "civilized" and the "barbaric." As historian Richard Allison writes in *The Crescent Observed: The United States and the Muslim World, 1776–1815*, "The Americans inherited this understanding of the Muslim world and pursued this enemy more relentlessly than the Europeans had done."[18] Early American preachers and theologians like Cotton Mather celebrated American victories over Muslim cultures. Mather, a staunch Calvinist, not only stoked religious devotion by emphasizing the religious inferiority of Islam, but he also fueled intellectual hubris when he highlighted the limits of Muslim philosophy and intellectual life. Thus, Muslim intellectual knowledge on even natural matters was allegedly corrupted. Mather intoned, "May our Devotion exceed the Mahometan as much as our Philosophy!" The white Christian "making" of Islam as Other in Europe, as in America, became ever more intense during the first wars of the US on the international stage against the depicted Muslims of Tripoli, the "Barbary Pirates" who were disrupting British and US sea commerce. The Othered Muslim, as in early depictions of "the Moor" often were imaged in art and literary description in ways to remind also of additionally Othered peoples, enslaved Blacks and Native Americans whose lives and spiritual sensibilities also occupied subjugated positions vis-à-vis the US national project. White Christians were full participants in, and key fomenters of, the "specter of Islam" and of all "Moorish" peoples, as foils against which Christians made themselves and against which US national identity made itself.[19]

In sum, white Christianity as a religion-making force was from US beginnings embedded in the larger apparatus of power that enabled it and which it still reinforces. That is to say, White Christianity not only "makes" and remakes other religions as Other to its own superiority as Christian, but also, in making this religious superiority—and this is crucial for the argument I am making in this chapter—it does so as a religious legitimizer of the US nation-state or, better, of the "U.S. empire-state."[20] In this sense, the imperialist and nationalist reflexes of the US are at least partially indebted to white Christianity's religion-making dynamic. From the formation of the US Constitution and through its many court rulings in the earliest periods of the nation, it is clear that an expansionist reflex, the taking in of more lands and peoples, was the aim.[21] Of course, this was touted as an enlightened "liberal imperialism," to recall again historian Elkins's term whereby an expanding governance by the US over "lesser" peoples" (Muslim, Indigenous, Black, Mexican/Latin American, Asian)—all within what Thomas Jefferson termed an "empire of liberty"[22]—would ensure a world order of freedom.

WHITE CHRISTIANITY AS RACE-MAKING

In white Christianity's making of religion, of its superiority as *vera religio* vis-à-vis those religions made Other and subordinate to it, there is still more going on. I refer to white Christianity's making of race. As white Christianity forged its *Christian* supremacy in the making of religion, it also made *white* supremacy. As such, religion-making and race-making are closely intertwined in white European white Christianity. In fact, there are many indications that white Christian theology prompted and sustained white supremacism, even if now white supremacism is itself a matrix broader than Christian forms of supremacy and racism.

Two recent theologians are exemplary in laying bare Christian traditions' entailment in the making of race as a hierarchical construct. J. Kameron Carter highlights European white Christianity's race-making force in its abstraction from and stigmatization and repression of Jewish peoples that took place from early medieval to mainstream Enlightenment periods. Jeanine Hill Fletcher underscores many of Carter's points but exposes in more detail white Christians' race-making in the US founding. The contributions of both theologians, however—as both Carter and Fletcher ably indicate—need also to be seen within the context of European and Western relations of colonialism and imperialism.

Carter views "modern racial discourse" and race-making as developing within "Christian theological discourse and missiological practice."[23] Pervading all this is a mode of Othering, not only of the needy Other, but also of the heathen Other. In Carter's view, the primary mode of this Othering as it generated European modernity's white supremacy is the Othering of the Jew.[24] The problem of the Jew as Othered is compounded by the fact that Christian theologians and philosophers "severed" themselves from their faith's own Jewish roots. The very early "antisemitic" trope of Jews as "Christ-killers," a stark case of religious Othering, developed further in the making of the Jews as a "racial" group, raced as persons of "the East" and inferior, with a closer relation to the material world, in contrast to the purity of more Aryan-cast figurations of Jesus.[25] In so doing, Christians racialized their religion and made race and racism. In so doing, they also created whiteness and white supremacy. In Carter's words, "Christian theology provided the inner architecture of modern racial reasoning."[26]

This theo-racial project is prominent for Carter in the mainstream Enlightenment figure Immanuel Kant. He provided a "political cultural nationalism of whiteness" as the pervasive ethos of his cosmopolitanism.[27] In Kant's religious musings, Jesus is "de-Judaized" in favor of a Europeanized cosmopolitan Christ. Kant's anthropology, for the sake of this European provincial and supremacist vision, also yields a skewed ethnocentric and racist view of the "four-fold races." These are built upon "a binary opposition between white and nonwhite flesh qua white and Jewish flesh, between occidental whiteness and oriental (Palestinian) Jewishness."[28] Jews, then, are seen in Carter's critique as the primary "aliens within" (within white Christian Europe) and so paradigmatic for the viewing and treating of "aliens without" (encountered in European colonization of those on other continents).[29]

Carter may limit too much the scope of Christianity's race-making by viewing its horizon of Otherness as set primarily by the Jew. I suggest that Christianity's severance from its Jewish roots, and its many de-Judaizing impulses, constitute but one necessary but not sufficient pillar in the theological racism of colonial modernity. Indeed, Judaeophobia and antisemitism and its racialist tendencies go back to the start of Christian movements. But antisemitism's vicious animating of modern white supremacy occurred in a reciprocal relation with the Othering that Christian colonizers forged amid and against their many colonized. Carter seems to emphasize this also, as in his more recent writings on "Black Malpractice (A Poetics of the Sacred)."[30] It was not only a matter of projecting the alien Jew within upon the "non-Jewish alien without." Historian Patrick Wolfe, a theorist of settler colonialism and race, writes:

> Reciprocally, colonialism subsequently came to furnish a racialized mythology that could be displaced back onto stigmatized minorities within Europe itself.
> In other words, Jews came relatively late to race—or, rather, race came late to Jews. *Through colonial practice*, a doctrine devised to rank subjugated peoples from outside Europe became discursively available to be redirected inwards, onto emancipated European Jews, refurbishing their theoretically outmoded exteriority. At that point Judaeophobia, an age-old European practice, took on the distinctive features of racial antisemitism, a post-Enlightenment discourse which, as Hannah Arendt pointed out, had been significantly *prefigured in the colonial world*.[31]

Moreover, in addition to this racializing move from without, there were also, in both medieval and especially early modern periods, a host of different "aliens within" alongside Jews to fuel a race-making Christianity. This was especially true in emergent large cities of Europe. Many "aliens" of the darker nations were ready-to-hand to enliven the racist white imaginary of white theology.[32] But even when Jews were lifted up as the primary, most villainous of all Others, their villainy in the white imaginary was due not only to their Jewishness but also to their alleged and projected sensuousness, their materiality, their being more "of the flesh" and, thus, a challenge posed to the alleged purity of whiteness and its imagined call to rule over the dark and the opaque projected onto so many colonized peoples. I am suggesting that as white theology made itself counter to Jews, it did so also in countering itself to material flesh generally. Such a countering of material flesh was also for whites to be apprehensive and ambivalent about, to be repressive of their "excessively black pit" (or "black hollow," as another translator has it), which Frantz Fanon named whites' own oft repressed and fleshly, finite being.

In this dimension of whites' sensibility, wrote Fanon, "the most immoral instincts and unmentionable desires slumber."[33]

Christian theology's stripping its savior and message of "Jewish flesh," as Carter puts it, is part of a veritable war against the flesh, highlighted by numerous histories of Western Christianity's contemptus mundi ("contempt for the world"). Historian David Stannard mines this tradition to explain aspects of colonizers' rationalization of genocide in the Americas. Racialized flesh—Indigenous, African, "Moorish"—were seen as of "the wild" and often portrayed in what whites saw as their "sensuous worst." As such, they "symbolized everything the Christian's ascetic contemptus mundi tradition was determined to eradicate, even as that tradition also acknowledges that the wild one's very *same* carnal and uncivilized sinfulness gnawed at the soul of the holiest saint."[34] Thus, to follow Fanon's logic here again, white supremacy's imagined views of colonized subjects entailed a projection of European whites' own fragile and dreaded embodiment. In the white imaginary, the white self, fearing its own opaque "hollow" or "pit," projected its self-loathing and dread onto those whose opaqueness made them seemingly appropriate targets onto whom whites could displace their discomfort with and hatred of their own repressed embodiment.[35] Moreover, it is part of what might be called a dialectics of psycho-political oppression that this white discomfort with whites' own selves became the means of whites' securing against Black life their comfort in economic, political, and racial life. Philosopher George Yancy has often theorized this point, most recently stating directly to white readers in his book *Backlash*: "And it is as you reap comfort from being white that we suffer for being black and people of color. This is how we are tied to each other."[36] These psycho-political dialectics of embodiment, which tie white and black, whites and people of color, are also at work in the broader matrix within which Christian theology mobilized against the Jewish Others, and from which Christian contemptus mundi traditions helped "make race."

In turning back to the US nation-state, we will also find white Christianity's dynamic of race-making and religion-making coming together. Historian Ron Takaki interprets the US founding as infused with an understanding of the young nation's republican virtue, which drew heavily from Christian-infused moral asceticism.[37] Building the US empire-state then could be felt as a moral virtue of purification. But it is especially Christian theologian Jeanine Hill Fletcher who has clarified how in North America and the US "in the development of the university knowledge of White supremacy, the theology of Christian supremacy played a pivotal role as bedrock to the White racial frame."[38] In the founding and governance of early North American colleges, usually run by Christian ministers who also were its teachers, Fletcher finds the Christian supremacist teachings that in systems of university production made white supremacist ideas "appear reasonable."[39] When in his first presidential term George Washington was beginning what would be a large period of Indigenous wars in the northwest territories, based on his own and America's slavery-based plantocracy, the universities' Christian supremacy and race-making white supremacy were already putting in place the basic pillars of Christian and white supremacy, in what Fletcher terms the "religio-racial project" of white Christianity. In 1783, she quoted a sermon by Yale President Ezra Stiles from historian Craig Steven Wilder's study *Ebony and Ivy*:

> Stiles lauded the rise of the "whites" whose numerical growth alone proved divine favoritism toward the children of Europe. God intended the Americas of "a new enlargement of Japhet," the minister began, invoking the curse of Ham, and Europe's children were quickly filling the continents. It was "God's good providence," the president continued, that the vanishing of nonwhite people would also erase the moral problem of dispossession and enslavement.[40]

Here Stiles links the children of Europe to the good son of Noah, Japheth, these names coming from the Genesis story about the curse of the "bad son," Ham. Stiles was tapping into a long-standing European Christian colonizers' religio-racial-geopolitical vision. Ham was linked to Africa. Shem, the other son, to Asia. Noah's sons' names were actually written onto the regions shown on European maps dating from at least the tenth century. Europe was "Japheth," and through another ideological step the Americas were seen as "Japheth's inheritance," a bestowal due him as Noah's good son, who did not look on his father's nakedness. This gave theological license to the later white "Japheths" to colonize and enslave others.[41] Fletcher discusses the "curse of Ham myth" as it coursed through various US theologians and white communities, and compiles numerous examples of Christian educators and ministers crafting white supremacy from this and other religious sources.[42] Needless to say, this does not constitute an indictment of all or any Christians. After all, whites do not make up the majority of Christians in the US, much less of Christians the world over.[43] What is at fault is white Christianity's mobilization and enabling of thinkers in university and church environments who provided the "symbolic capital" for a white supremacy built upon Christian supremacy. That symbolic capital was necessary, as Fletcher shows, to the economic and social capital of the US white supremacist national project. Those of us who have benefited from this white supremacist project are obliged to work to dethrone these forms of capital by refiguring faith and spiritual practice in symbolic terms and by working in the fight for economic and political reparations, and more. What is crucial to note here, however, about Carter's and Fletcher's historical sketches of white Christianity is that they both display how this race-making Christianity was embedded in a matrix of colonial and imperial aspiration, formative in both Europe and the US.

Nowhere does this dynamic of race-making intertwined with religion-making show itself more dramatically than in Fletcher's reach back into Christian history for her critique of the fourth-century Nicene Creed that is still used throughout many Christian churches. The creed exemplifies—provides a kind of rhetorical discipline for—the "theo-logic" of the religio-racial project of white supremacy. True enough, the well-known first part of the creed does not show the problematic *racial* theo-logic, opening as it does with the following lines:

> I believe in one God,
> The Father almighty,
> Maker of heaven and earth,
> Of all things visible and invisible.

One can infer from this, Fletcher observes, that "there is a basic equality . . . in the singular unity of the created world."[44] But it is in the creed's second part, where the divinity of Christ is asserted and, in a marked particular way, as "the *only* begotten son," that the founder of Christianity becomes the singular and sole savior of the world. "Jesus as both human and divine bridges the opposition of divinity and humanity in his very being and creates the conditions for others to bridge that opposition as well."[45] In this way, those humans who belong to this "only begotten" filial son, and who become affiliated with this Jesus, become valuable as "the saved." The distinctive marking of the "saved" from the "unsaved" is not simply an observable variance among a panoply of different forms of humanity. No, here instead, Fletcher emphasizes, is difference marked as deficiency. Religious Otherization creates a particular stance toward thinking about difference, one that imposes a hierarchy of value. The divinized particular Jesus, and the valued saved believers affiliated with him, are marked off from non-Christian, unsaved Others. "Difference is not only deficient; it is gravely deficient in matters of salvific proportion." In this religion-making, Otherness is the poisoning of difference, forging distinctions and ranks of worth essential to hierarchical structuring.

Note where we have now arrived. We do not have white Christianity simply as a racist Christianity. Instead, through and beyond that racism, we have white Christianity as a phenomenon that remains continually generative of the repressive regime of European and US colonial modernity. White Christianity's long history of race-making, strengthened also by its religion-making dynamic, has expanded its field of force. This field of force is neither just "white," nor is it just "Christian." White Christianity is operative as a force in its thriving, in animating and legitimizing economic power and military enforcement. Today that field is made of transnational corporate power with global war-making capacity. Such a field of force made up of economic and military power is the hallmark of imperialism. Geopolitically, today, this imperialism is wielded primarily by global North European powers together with the US. However, although much US power has been challenged and perhaps is waning, it is arguably still the most determinative economic power and one with a still-unrivaled military supremacy to back its geopolitical and economic interests. To maintain its imperial policies, the US—as from its beginnings—deploys an apparatus of power that is not just economic and military (allied with nations across the global North and the elite sectors of the colonized world, too); it also continually shores up its cultural and ideological power through many national ceremonies, education and university systems, and multiple forms of media venues—its so-called "soft power."

There is an important lesson here, and it is the burden of this chapter. If we want to resist the destructive force of white Christianity, especially in the neofascist forms of white Christianity that we see today, we must resist it as the extended field of force that it is, as the imposing and commandeering imperial world power that it has become. This means calling out, exposing, and resisting the US corporate-warrior state, the US's corporate-dominated economy and its imperial war machinery, whether operative covertly or overtly. This kind of resistance and the imaginative transformation needed cannot be undertaken by the church alone. Nor will it be sufficient to see this resistance as interfaith or interreligious. All peoples as humans who share Earth and its climate, its planetary being, must unite in this counter-imperial resistance to the US. I hasten to say here, to those poised to pounce on this as some "un-American" position, that this is in fact the only way to break out the peoples of the US and elsewhere into a generative space of real freedom from systemic coercion, within which a people's democracy can be forged. Being counter to US imperialism is to safeguard and finally begin to build democratic dynamics for all. Antiracist training sessions against white supremacy alone are not sufficient, especially if they are silent about racial capitalism and imperialism (and they usually are). Nor will interfaith sharing beyond Christian supremacy be sufficient. Certainly, it is not enough to cast Christians' lot with any party—Republican, Democrat, Libertarian—in our two-party oligarchy.[46] Both parties fund and rarely question the imperial site of white racism today, the US corporate-warrior state, even if they, especially the Democrats, wax eloquent on matters of diversity, multiculturalism, and other identity issues, important as they may be. Both parties, for example, vote for budgets that fatten the resources of US corporate power and the war economy. White supremacy in the oligarchy operating in the corporate-warrior state of the US puts decision-making above the heads of most citizens, especially those who are Black, Asian-American, Latinx, Indigenous, and poor. This nurtures economic and political dispossession and disenfranchisement in the US, the breeding grounds for fascism and racist resentment.[47] Again, you cannot fight either white supremacism or the white fascism rising with it (Christian or otherwise) without resisting the oligarchic empire-state that makes it strong.[48]

In sum, white supremacy (and its foundational anti-Blackness) and Christian supremacy are inscribed and forcefully holding good over our nation and the world's peoples as a transnational corporate-warrior state that keeps in special travail the "darker nations." And here the real conversation begins, which I have addressed in numerous other works. We face the question: Where and how, in what social movements, do we work to challenge such a corporate-warrior state? I will here just note two organizations/movements that are key today. One is *Black Alliance for Peace* and the other is the Tricontinental Institute for Social Research. The Black Alliance is exemplary in that its wide-angle analysis and critique of white supremacy includes US police abuses in contemporary Atlanta, US wars in Afghanistan and Ukraine, and also US covert wars under the US African Command (AFRICOM) in contemporary Africa.[49] The Tricontinental Institute marshals its critique of white Christianity and white supremacy through an international analytic of the imperial power of global corporate interest and global war-making interests of the US and its allies.[50] My point is primarily not to lobby for participation in only these groups, but more to put them forward as examples of the kind of groups and movements needed among those that challenge the US corporate-warrior state in which destructive white Christianity needs to be resisted.

CONCLUSION—THE CRUCIFIED JESUS IN THE WAKE OF EMPIRE

In closing, we do well to engage critical conversations about which Christian beliefs better aid in resisting and bringing transformative vision and practice amid the current dominance of the US/transnational corporate-warrior state. I will here propose just one key aspect that has been routinely distorted by dominant and expansive white Christianity: namely, the fact that Jesus of Nazareth—and this is one of the very few claims that can be made with historical reliability—suffered an imperial execution, a politically imposed death and torture by a corrupt imperial state.[51] This figure, the one depicted perhaps most powerfully in Brazilian sculptor Guido Rocha's *The Tortured Christ*,[52] reminds us that crucifixion was not just any death. Nor was it a routine capital punishment of a wrongdoer. Its primary purpose was, as crucifixions were generally, to remove the politically dissident or inconvenient from imperial society.[53] This gives special significance to the death of Jesus and, by extension, to any claims that can be made for the transformative impact of his death. Dying *as* he did is what, potentially, puts Christianity's reputed founder at one with all the world's peoples who suffer on the underside of the imperial pontiffs, consuls, and Caesar-like figures and structures of our time.[54]

However, instead of lifting up clearly this potential solidarity of Jesus with the world's poor on the underside of corporate-warrior state systems, all too much of white Christianity has loaded onto the death of Jesus many alternative divine scenarios, as I've called them (i.e., dramas and narratives that distract from the hard historical and political fact of Jesus's torture, death, and its meanings), thus glossing what was constitutive and primary about a crucifixion, namely, its reinforcement of imperial political order by torturous death. Instead, divine scenarios foreground various religious narratives: of God "coming" to Earth in Jesus, perhaps to work a sacrifice on the cross for the forgiveness of human sins, to exemplify love in practice, and so on. All these narratives, which may have some place in the panoply of Christian meanings, often neglect and distract from the fact that Jesus's death was what imperial states do to their dissidents—in Jesus's case, to a dissident storied as one who lived out the radical love borne by long traditions of prophetic protests in Palestine by many, especially the well-known Jewish prophets. Jesus occasioned a release of counterimperial vision and energy for living amid empire.[55] Gospel writers presented him as embracing radical visions of the day; some visions were quite apocalyptic and expectant of the end of the world, but many other visions stressed a new way, made up of many small acts, for living in the shadow of empire. In these ways, he dreamed and acted toward new kin(g)dom of life in the wake of empire, "after" empire. At the heart of Rome's zenith of powerful Augustan rule, Jesus was remembered, after his death especially, as provoking religio-political awareness of empire's comprehensive and brutal, totalizing repression. Crucifixions were not easy to forget. They were empire's way of doing what Franz Kafka's story "In the Penal Colony" depicts colonialism as routinely performing. In that story, Kafka depicts a most macabre machine, one that etches its bloody message, slowly carving it, onto a tortured, strapped down, live body.[56] The message of a European colony's torture machine, or of Roman crucifixions was, "Act up and this may well be your end." These torture-deaths often turned the ruled, even those not actually crucified, into "crucified people," that is, a whole people consigned to be kept alive but in a "social death" subject to torturous repression and imperial dominance and fear targeting especially its racialized and often "feminized" poor.[57]

If we dodge this concrete politicality of Jesus's death, we Christians also then avoid the hard question: How might anything like justice and energy for living emerge from a crucified figure's life and work in the wake of an imperial crucifixion that anchors social death? To answer this question is not easy. Conversations about the potential ways forward amid empire must be critical and continuous, particularly if our calls to such ways forward are to be persuasive and cogent to the world's peoples without invoking magical thinking modes of "resurrection" belief or idealistic conversion scenarios. I will not here repeat my own critical project, which I detail in *Religion, Politics and the Christian Right* and, especially, in *The Executed God: The Way of the Cross in Lockdown America*. Both works trace how life might persist or can reemerge in the shadow of imperial crucifixion and the social deaths of repression, dread, and fear spawned by them. Suffice it to say here, in brief, that the emergence of life comes, as it did when women on the third day after Jesus's death and later at third-day or third-week intervals thereafter, regularly gathered in funerary rituals—as peoples of the Mediterranean then would have done—to stand, sing, and teach around their "special dead," Jesus. There they also narrated their own stories of need and survival, forging communities for love and justice, suffering the stigmas of being a community of the crucified. In that process, there arose a re-membering of the imperially crucified figure, Jesus, a gathering of his body's "members," as it were, together with those others who also were dismembered in various ways, and so in need of being re-membered in the face of brutalizing coloniality and imperiality. All this is a most complex and real "resurrection," a resurgence of re-membering life among the imperially repressed and socially "dead."[58] It is generative of movements. It rivals the power of empire through its organizing in ever greater circles of resistance.

Re-membering *this* Jesus cuts against the grain of white Christianity's *longue durée*, its long-term historical structure. Re-membering this Jesus is not white Christianity's "religion-making" discourse and practice. It is a spirit of faithful resistance that does not confine itself to naming itself a "religion," certainly not one above others; instead, it builds new social bonds and community with crucified peoples in need of re-membering from any and all religions and with those of no religion. This is not an amorphous anti-institutional claim; it means establishing new institutions of remembrance and resistance to rival the white Christian supremacist ones embedded in US imperial ideology and policy.

Similarly, re-membering *this* Jesus cuts against the grain of white Christianity's race-making discourse and practice. Certainly, re-membering this Jesus is not a de-Judaizing or anti-Jewish move, which was so essential to the *longue durée* of white Christianity. Re-membering this Jesus is to ponder and recall a Jewish body whose historical concrete politicality, like that of other bodies in Palestine, was broken, speared, and tortured by crucifying powers—perhaps left to the dogs and birds of prey as were most of the crucified on the way, often, to a mass burial pit.[59] Re-membering a Jesus who suffered from the crosses and burial pits of Rome cuts against the grain of the US *longue durée* that built its government, its mercantilist and industrial economy, as well as its militarized war economy on a founding violence of Black enslavement made possible by dispossession of Indigenous land, of all its ground-down poor.

And, finally, this must be said. If reemergent life is to be known in a community that re-members this Jesus, then we best look for it today among those whose lives have been thrown into the direct path of white Christianity's imperial state power. Such as these are not to be found in the corrupted Christianity that thrives among white Christian fascist aspirants. Nor will it be found among the white Christians feigning respectability while complicit with, silent about, and funding the militarized rule of US empire and imperial culture today. It is to the crucified peoples that we must look. It is with them that we seek to make common cause—if "we" are not in fact ourselves those "crucified peoples." Wherever they may be, they are the ones whose leaders and ancestors have often been among the first to discern not just suffering but also some reemergent life, its re-membering action around the crucified body of Jesus. Working with crucified peoples, as we may be called to do, will require taking stands against the imperial power of today's US corporate-warrior elite. While crucified peoples may have their own proactive powers, taking such stands against that elite will be the means by which any of the rest of us—those of "us" with our positions more proximate to the status and privileges of imperial US power—might taste the reemergent life that persists for all despite the powers of empire.

NOTES

1. Crucial for securing this point is the research by Kathleen Belew, *Bring the War Home: The White Power Movement and Paramilitary America* (Cambridge, MA: Harvard University Press, 2018). See also the crisp and impassioned essay by former US military veteran and Black radical journalist Glen Ford, "The Lies of Empire: Don't Believe a Word They Say," *Black Agenda Report*, July 27, 2022, https://www.blackagendareport.com/lies-empire-dont-believe-word-they-say.

2. "How Jeffrey Sterling Took on the CIA—and Lost Everything," *The Intercept*, June 18, 2015, https://theintercept.com/2015/06/18/jeffrey-sterling-took-on-the-cia-and-lost-everything/. Sterling tells his own story in Jeffrey Sterling, *Unwanted Spy: The Persecution of an American Whistleblower* (New York: Bold Type Books, 2019).

3. Caroline Elkins, *Legacy of Violence: A History of the British Empire* (New York: Alfred A. Knopf, 2022), 140, 203, 452. See, for just one example, the mixes of torture, confinement, and village destruction by the British in twentieth-century Kenya in Elkins, 543–79, particularly pages 556–57.

4. See US historian Richard H. Immerman, *Empire for Liberty: A History of U.S. Imperialism from Ben Franklin to Paul Wolfowitz* (Princeton, NJ: Princeton University Press, 2010), 1–19.

5. Dick Cheney, "Transcript for Sept. 14," *NBC News*, September 14, 2003, https://www.nbcnews.com/id/wbna3080244.

6. Charles Ferguson, *No End in Sight: Iraq's Descent into Chaos* (New York: Public Affairs Group, 2008).

7. "The Costs of the US-Led War in Iraq Since 2003," The Watson Institute, Brown University, March 21, 2023, https://watson.brown.edu/costsofwar/2022/IraqWarCosts.

8. See Belew, *Bring the War Home*, especially the chapter "Mercenaries and Paramilitary Praxis," 77–100.

9. See https://www.youtube.com/watch?v=iR5MoD-X5uM.

10. "Confederate Flag-Waving Man Found Guilty in Capitol Riot Case," *Reuters*, June 15, 2022, https://www.reuters.com/world/us/confederate-flag-waving-man-found-guilty-capitol-riot-case-2022-06-15/.

11. Luke Mogelson, "A Reporter's Footage of the Capitol Siege," *The New Yorker*, January 17, 2021, https://www.youtube.com/watch?v=270F8s5TEKY&ab_channel=TheNewYorker.

12. Sylvester A. Johnson, *African American Religions, 1500–2000: Colonialism, Democracy and Freedom* (New York: Cambridge University Press, 2015), 89.

13. On the notion of "the heathen" in this religion-making process, see Kathryn Gin Lum, *Heathen: Religion and Race in American History* (Cambridge, MA: Harvard University Press, 2022).

14. Brent Nongbri, *Before Religion: A History of a Modern Concept* (New Haven, CT: Yale University Press, 2013), 12.

15. Nongbri, *Before Religion*, 6.

16. Johnson, *African American Religions, 1500–2000*, 49, 67–69.

17. Judith Butler, *Parting Ways: Jewishness as a Critique of Zionism* (New York: Columbia University Press, 2013), 114–15.

18. Robert J. Allison, *The Crescent Observed: The United States and the Muslim World, 1776–1815* (New York: Oxford University Press, 1995), xv.

19. Allison, *The Crescent Observed*, 59.

20. Moon-Kie Jung, "The Racial Constitution of the U.S. Empire-State," in Jung, *Beneath the Surface of White Supremacy: Denaturalizing U.S. Racisms Past and Present* (Stanford, CA: Stanford University Press, 2015), 55–82.

21. Jung, "The Racial Constitution of the U.S. Empire-State," 64–66.

22. Immerman, *Empire for Liberty*, 57–58.

23. J. Kameron Carter, *Race: A Theological Account* (New York: Oxford University Press, 2010), 3.

24. Carter, *Race*, 4.

25. Shawn Kelley, *Racializing Jesus: Race, Ideology and the Formation of Modern Biblical Scholarship* (New York: Routledge, 2005). See discussions especially of "aesthetic fascism," 89–128

26. Carter, *Race*, 4.

27. Carter, *Race*, 81.

28. Carter, *Race*, 104.

29. Carter, *Race*, 81–82.

30. For example, in this later work Carter discusses fascism, following Georges Bataille, as "the right-hand sacred," a politically rightist deployment of the sacred's "wild energies," which renders as impure all that "came to be figured in the Jews *and in other undesirables*" (italics added). Carter's addition "and in other undesirables" here better foregrounds a larger teeming matrix of Others out of which whiteness, racism, and its anti-Blackness were forged. See J. Kameron Carter, "Black Malpractice (A Poetics of the Sacred)," *Social Text* 37, no. 2 (June 2019): 67–107, especially p. 72.

31. Patrick Wolfe, *Traces of History: Elementary Structures of Race* (New York: Verso Books, 2016), 12, emphasis added. Wolfe is citing Hannah Arendt, *The Origins of Totalitarianism* (San Diego, CA: Harvest/Harcourt, 1966), 158–84.

32. Jeffrey Jerome Cohn, *The Postcolonial Middle Ages* (New York: Palgrave Macmillan, 2000), 229–42; David Theo Goldberg, *The Racial State* (Malden, MA: Blackwell Publishing, 2002), 16–34.

33. Frantz Fanon, *Black Skin, White Masks*, translated by Richard Philcox (New York: Grove Press, 2008/1952), 166–67.

34. David E. Stannard, *American Holocaust: The Conquest of the New World* (New York: Oxford University Press, 1992), 149–259, especially p. 171.

35. Fanon, *Black Skin, White Masks*, 166–67.

36. George Yancy, *Backlash: What Happens When We Talk Honestly about Racism in America* (Lanham, MD: Rowman & Littlefield, 2018), 12.

37. Ronald Takaki, *Iron Cages: Race and Culture in 19th-Century America*. Revised edition (New York: Oxford University Press, 2000), 3–15.

38. Jeanine Hill Fletcher, *The Sin of White Supremacy: Christianity, Racism and Religious Diversity in America* (Maryknoll, NY: Orbis Books, 2017), 14.

39. Fletcher, *The Sin of White Supremacy*, 19.

40. Fletcher, *The Sin of White Supremacy*, 17, quoting Craig S. Wilder, *Ebony and Ivy: Race, Slavery and the Troubled History of America's Universities* (New York: Bloomsbury, 2013), 33.

41. Christoph Mauntel, "The T-O Diagram and Its Religious Connotations: A Circumstantial Case," in *Geology and Religious Knowledge in the Medieval World*, edited by Christoph Mauntel (Berlin: De Gruyter, 2021), 57–82.

42. Fletcher, *The Sin of White Supremacy*, 9–29.

43. On the percentage of white Christians in the US, see PRRI, "The American Religious Landscape in 2020," *The 2020 Census of American Religion*, https://www.prri.org/research/2020-census-of-american-religion/. On white Christians globally, see Tish Harrison Warren, "The Global Transformation of Christianity Is Here," *New York Times*, March 26, 2023, https://www.nytimes.com/2023/03/26/opinion/christianity-global-demographics.html.

44. Fletcher, *The Sin of White Supremacy*, 42.

45. Fletcher, *The Sin of White Supremacy*, 43.

46. For one of the best arguments made for the US as oligarchy, see Martin Gilens and Benjamin I. Page, "Testing Theories of U.S. Politics: Elites, Interest Groups and Average Citizens," *Perspectives on Politics* 12, no. 3 (September 2014): 564–81.

47. Du Bois knew this in his own day and documented these conditions as setting for the rise of the Klan and the end of Reconstruction. See W. E. B. Du Bois, *Black Reconstruction, 1860–1880* (New York: The Free Press, 1998/1935), 678.

48. Managing one's voting choices in this context is complex. As one resists white power, whether in fascist or liberal forms in the US, one often must pit them one against another and consider the possibility of voting for one or the other while resisting both. In the case of the 2020 presidential election between Democratic candidate Joe Biden and the Republican Donald Trump, see Mark Lewis Taylor, "Trumpism and Césaire's 'Terrible Boomerang Effect,'" *Counterpunch*, October 30, 2020, https://www.counterpunch.org/2020/10/30/trumpism-and-cesaires-terrible-boomerang-effect/.

49. For a display of the concerns of Black Alliance for Peace, see their website at https://blackallianceforpeace.com/#home-above-fold.

50. Both research and practice—and the arts that nurture both—can be found at the website for the Tricontinental Institute for Research at https://thetricontinental.org/. For a treatment of white neoliberal Christianity see "Religious Fundamentalism and Imperialism in Latin America: Action and Resistance," *Dossier* no. 59, December 19, 2022.

51. See scholar of biblical and early Christian literature John Dominic Crossan, *The Birth of Christianity* (London: Bloomsbury Academic, 1999), 14.

52. Brian Bantum, "Guido Rocha's 'The Tortured Christ,'" *Roots of Justice*, March 20, 2015, https://lent2015.wordpress.com/2015/03/20/guido-rochas-tortured-christ/.

53. Martin Hengel, *Crucifixion* (Philadelphia: Fortress Press, 1977). More recent and thorough is John Granger Cook, *Crucifixion in the Mediterranean World. Wissenschaftliche Untersuchungen zum Neuen Testament* 327 (Tübingen: Mohr Siebeck, 2014).

54. On analogies between Roman and US imperial powers, see Chalmers Johnson, *Nemesis: The Last Days of the American Republic* (New York: Metropolitan Books, 2006), 54–89.

55. On the connection between Jesus's crucifixion and "released energy" that powered early Jesus movements, see scholar Richard A. Horsley, *Jesus and the Powers: Conflict, Covenant and the Hope of the Poor* (Minneapolis, MN: Fortress Press, 2011), 1990–2044.

56. Franz Kafka, "In the Penal Colony," in Kafka, *The Penal Colony: Stories and Short Pieces*, translated by Willa and Edward Muir (New York: Schocken Books, 1948), 191–227

57. On ethnicity, racialization, and targeting of "feminized" nations in Rome, see Davina Lopez, *Apostle to the Conquered: Reimagining Paul's Mission* (Minneapolis, MN: Fortress Press, 2010).

58. For the history and conceptualization of funerary rituals in Jesus's time and a resource for communal thriving, see Kathleen E. Corley, *Maranatha: Women's Funerary Rituals and Christian Origins* (Minneapolis, MN: Fortress Press, 2010), 111–37.

59. For just one of several historians who explore this possibility, see Bart D. Ehrman, *How Jesus Became God: The Exaltation of a Jewish Preacher from Galilee* (New York: HarperOne, 2014), 157–59.

Chapter 2

White Mob Logic

Karen Teel

I

How could they do that? Is anyone else getting tired of this question? As a response to the events of January 6, 2021—indeed, to any display of white power or white solidarity—this reflexive expression of disbelief is beginning to feel disingenuous. Even as it spontaneously arises within my own well-meaning white mind, I sense that something is off, that I'm missing something obvious. Maybe I'm ignoring it on purpose.

I've learned enough history to know that white identity in the US, including my own, has been shaped by a particularly violent form of Christianity. Many contemporary US Americans, especially white US Americans such as myself, think of Christianity as a religion of peace. And for us it is—or at least we believe that it should be.

But this understanding of Christianity and its adherents as inherently peaceful is far from universal. According to the gospels, Jesus himself said, "Do not think that I have come to bring peace on the earth. I have come to bring not peace but the sword."[1] He seems to have been warning his disciples that not all would believe, that their families would be divided, that they would be persecuted. Nowhere is it recorded that he instructed them to take up arms to spread the faith. Nevertheless, as time went by and Christians began to gain social and political power, many came to believe that their use of force was justified, even commanded by God. Christians transmuted the Great Commission into the Great Conquest.[2]

No one did this more effectively than my own ancestors, the Europeans. After the Crusades; after colonialism and slavery; after the Holocaust; after the physical and cultural genocide of Indigenous Peoples; after the murders of Breonna Taylor, Ahmaud Arbery, and George Floyd; after a US president who defended white nationalists while identifying as Christian, why would I find January 6 hard to believe? Of course the mostly white crowd brandished Christian symbols—the Bible, pictures of Jesus. When the *that* in *How could they do that?* refers to racist, colonialist, imperialist, or white supremacist behavior, it is nothing new. It is normal for white Christians. It is how we relate to the world.

I have been working for years to reckon with this. I have not quite come to terms with it, but I have tried to become knowledgeable enough not to be constantly surprised by it. Moreover, as a teacher, I invest considerable energy into urging students to face this history honestly. I attempt to model for them how to engage it matter-of-factly, without indulging in the histrionics that to cynics and realists alike appear calculated to distract us from actively collaborating within and across racial lines to come up with solutions. That is, I aim to model taking responsibility rather than wallowing in guilt or evading the problem altogether. Yet still I feel it in my gut, that fundamentally disbelieving response: *How could they do that?*

Contemplating my own reaction, I see how tenaciously I cling to the third-person pronoun *they*, even though I also am white. I want to distance myself from the marchers, their beliefs and behavior. Yet, as a white person, I have been socialized similarly. If they are people like me, and not mysterious alien creatures, then I can investigate their behavior and their motivations. I just have to summon the willpower.

Indeed, if I am serious about wanting things like "that" to happen less, then as a self-identified "theologian of the white experience," I have to grow up a little.[3] I must own my impact, and the impact of people like me, rather than ceaselessly protesting our supposedly innocent personal intentions. I have to ask *How could they do that?* as a real question rather than a rhetorical one. Then I need to take an honest look at why I am so surprised.

II

The tone in which we ask *How could they do that?* often seems to imply that what happened on January 6 was totally illogical. Why would US citizens try to prevent certified election results from being implemented peacefully? *That makes no sense!*

On reflection, however, it makes perfect sense. First, it made sense to the people who marched on the Capitol that day. They believed that they were fighting for a righteous cause. They believed that the election had been stolen and that they must right that wrong. They probably believed that they were honoring the example of our nation's founders, insofar as they took up arms to fight for liberty against injustice. Indeed, the formal congressional investigation of the events of January 6 concluded that the marchers were following the exhortations, if not the direct orders, of the sitting president, who openly shared and encouraged their belief. Second, those who do not believe that the marchers' cause was righteous nevertheless can easily formulate a reasonable explanation. Perhaps the marchers were misinformed. Perhaps they got carried away. What is clear is that, justifiably or not, the marchers were aggrieved, and they chose a violent way of showing it. One may judge the behavior excessive, but taking context and human psychology into account, one can see how things got to this point.

Thoughtful observers, sympathetic or unsympathetic, might want to dig further. What kind of action was this, exactly? How should history remember this day? As it turns out, some experts aren't sure. More than a year after the Capitol attack, historian Joshua Zeitz facilitated a roundtable in *Politico* in which five historians and "coupologists" debated how to describe what happened on January 6.[4] Was it a demonstration? A riot? An insurrection? An attempted coup? While the panelists discuss analogous events from all over the world, they do not settle on a single term. Significantly, however, they do locate the event within the US's robust, if little-known, tradition of antidemocratic violence. US history contains many incidents in which white people have overreacted to perceived threats to white power. As examples, the experts mention the 1837 killing of Elijah Lovejoy, a white abolitionist minister and journalist; the slaughter of Mexican Americans in response to the Plan of San Diego in 1915; the daily horrors of the Jim Crow South.[5] The Capitol attack appears to fit this pattern.[6]

Despite this insight, the *why* eludes the panelists—perhaps by design. In introducing the roundtable, Zeitz critiques the long-standing myth of national innocence, connecting it to our general inability to recognize the "deep tradition of antidemocratic violence that courses through the veins of American history."[7] In doing so, he questions the claim that *this is not who we are* (another way of saying *How could they do that?*). Yet, stunningly (and perhaps rhetorically), Zeitz then concedes the notion that antidemocratic violence is a thing of the past: "This may not be who we are," he says, "but it's most definitely who we've been."[8] Zeitz implies that previously our belief in our national innocence was false, a way to escape facing up to our own violence; but now US society has become a nonviolent functional democracy, such that antidemocratic violence no longer fits the clear pattern it did before. This move redeploys the myth of national innocence to defer the question of why January 6 happened, even though that question frames the discussion. Zeitz's rhetoric implies that until we find a word that precisely captures the events of January 6, the question of why it happened is unanswerable.

It's tempting to stop where the experts stop. The mystification is sticky, alluring. Why would I want to understand what the Capitol mob was up to?

As a white person myself, if I can understand how they could do that, might that not mean that I am capable of thinking the same way, doing the same thing? I don't want that to be true. By the same token, however, if I want to do all I can to avoid going down the same road, my best bet probably is to figure it out.

III

As the *Politico* panelists discuss, US history contains many precursors to the Capitol attack. But not all violent uprisings are antidemocratic. A complete list would not include colonists fighting Revolutionary War battles, for example, or enslaved people rebelling against their enslavers. Though some might quibble with their methods, we now judge the colonists and the abolitionists to have been on the right side of history. Assuming the 2020 presidential election results were accurate, the Capitol marchers were not. Although their actions may be analyzed productively from numerous angles, one especially illuminating historical category into which they fit is the white mob: a group of people mobilizing to defend white supremacy.

The category of the white mob begs explanation because as an ongoing cultural phenomenon, it is invisible to many. Following the Capitol attack, journalist Victor Luckerson observed, "The white mob exists outside of American mythology, but it has long shaped the nation's reality."[9] That is, while the white mob is not explicitly part of the dominant narrative of the meaning of US culture, it is nevertheless a fundamental component of how society operates. White mob behavior emerges episodically from white supremacist culture, white supremacy being a consistent commitment to white dominance that is individual and collective, conscious and unconscious, stable and fluid.

Building a partial timeline of white mob violence over the last hundred years, Luckerson mentions the Tulsa race riots of 1921 and similar preceding events; the rise of the Ku Klux Klan among well-to-do whites in the 1920s; white resistance to legalized integration throughout the mid- to late twentieth century; Oklahoma's failure to investigate the Tulsa race riots fully in the 1990s; and January 6, 2021. Luckerson clarifies, "The white mob is now turning against the state, threatening the lives of elected officials, desecrating their sacred chambers, and attacking police officers, because the state has failed to uphold its end of the power-hungry mob's bargain."[10] To spell it out, the bargain is white supremacy, white dominance, which philosopher Charles Mills decades ago named *the racial contract*.[11]

The fact that white people usually are not socialized into conscious, explicit awareness of the white mob as such does not mean that it has not existed, sometimes latent but ready to be constituted in an instant. White mob violence is sometimes physical, sometimes not. White mob participants need not be consciously aware that they are defending white supremacy to have that effect. Moreover, an individual need not be white to exhibit white mob behavior. Although white mobs typically are made up mostly or entirely of white people, white dominance is ideological, not necessarily tied to racial identity. This means that white people do not always exhibit white mob behavior, and white mobs can include people of color, as evidently happened on January 6.[12]

Do the Capitol marchers fit in the category of white mob? Compare an example that may strike us as equally extreme: the lynch mob. If ever there was a white mob, a group of citizens acting to defend white dominance, then surely the lynch mob qualifies. And the similarities are many. First, both the lynch mob and the Capitol mob were violent, armed uprisings by ordinary citizens who took extrajudicial measures to bring about their vision of justice. Second, both the lynch mob and the Capitol mob acted with a blatant disregard for facts, defending themselves against a mostly if not wholly imaginary threat. The fantasy of lynchers was the Black rapist; the fantasy of the Capitol marchers was the stolen election. Third, both the lynch mob and the Capitol mob targeted people who are just living their lives (Black people) or doing their jobs (staff and legislators). Fourth, both the lynch mob and the Capitol mob had elements of spontaneity and appeared loosely organized; some people came along for the ride, yet the events had masterminds who planned them out beforehand. Fifth, both the lynch mob and the Capitol mob were led by white people asserting dominance. Sixth, both the lynch mob and the Capitol mob were condoned or sanctioned by some elected officials—lynch mobs by police, sheriffs, and local governments; the Capitol mob by the president himself, among others. Seventh, lynch mobs were condoned by a broad swath of privileged citizens within American society, namely those (mostly white) in control. Likewise, the Capitol mob was condoned by large numbers of citizens, largely those (many white) ideologically aligned with the president just completing his term. Eighth, both lynchers and Capitol marchers claimed their Christian faith as legitimizing their actions. They fought not only for human justice but also for the justice of God.

Other examples of white mob behavior betray the same ideology of white dominance: white protests against racial integration in schools, buses, and lunch counters; white police fending off would-be Black voters with dogs, clubs, and fire hoses; white attacks on Black-owned homes and businesses; white failure to recruit diverse employees or coaches; white complacency in the face of ongoing and pervasive racial inequities; white whining and lawsuits when institutions seek to create space for people of color. The Capitol attack made for dramatic television, but as white mob behavior, it was a quintessentially ordinary event.

White mobs appear motivated by fear that white dominance is diminishing in the US. This fear is perennial. It can be traced to the colonial period, when the English defined themselves as white precisely to claim and maintain power over everyone they defined as nonwhite. White mob violence first occurred as the colonists massacred Indigenous people and enslaved people from Africa. For centuries, as the parameters of whiteness gradually expanded to include all those appearing to be solely of European origin, the fear was stated explicitly. Until the legislative changes of the 1960s, dominant US culture was overtly and proudly white. Once discrimination laws were overturned, whiteness began to be less explicitly celebrated, and some white mob behavior became more subtle. But it never disappeared.

All this time, white people in the United States, including white mob participants, overwhelmingly have been Christian. The colonists, seeking prosperity and freedom of Christian worship, structured colonial law as a system of advantages and privileges for themselves. After independence, when they said *American*, they meant, more or less, *white Christian*. Today, the language has been secularized, but *American* still implicitly means *white Christian*. Anyone who is not white, Christian, and US American, all three, may be regarded with suspicion. While formal adherence to Christianity is declining among white US Americans, most white people who have moved away from organized churches have done so in their own lifetimes. They come from Christian backgrounds, and they act like they believe Christians are supposed to act. In fact, many of them reject institutional Christianity precisely because they judge that too few traditionally affiliated Christians live up to the essence of their faith. They think of themselves as truer to Christian values than those who attend church. Like the US, most white people remain culturally if not confessionally Christian.

Today, as in the past, when it comes to white mob behavior, the *they* in the question *How could they do that?* essentially denotes white Christian US Americans. The white mob is an essential element of the tradition of racism and white supremacy that Christians sowed into the nation's roots and cultivated as it grew. Considering this history, displays of Christian adherence by the Capitol marchers just make sense. The white mob simultaneously claims and is constituted by the power that has always dominated this nation.

IV

The history notwithstanding, one still wonders how it is that our supposedly enlightened, culturally Christian nation has not yet moved definitively beyond white mob violence. After all, what happened on January 6, citizens of a democracy attempting to overturn certified election results, seems to defy the normal rules of logic. For further insight into *how they could do that*, we must analyze the Capitol marchers' thinking. I suggest that, collectively, they were using a particular mode of reasoning that throughout US history has been deployed routinely to rationalize white mob behavior. Specifically, the Capitol mob exhibits what sociologist Steve Martinot calls *racist thinking*, and I will call *white mob logic*.

In racist thinking, Martinot explains, an individual's or group's reasoning exhibits three distinct steps: (1) one grants a widely held assumption about what should be the case; (2) one withholds acknowledgment of pertinent evidence, information, or data; and (3) one maintains unilateral power to determine the facts and the appropriate outcome.[13] For example, lynch mobs seizing on spurious accusations of rape as excuses to murder Black men (1) granted the common belief that rape is unacceptable; (2) conveniently ignored the fact that evidence in the case was missing, circumstantial, or invented; and (3) maintained that it was appropriate for them to administer their version of "justice" by murdering the accused.

Let's break this down in the case of the Capitol marchers. First, they granted the basic assumption, foundational to US democracy, that elections should be fair. No US American could disagree with that. Second, they withheld acknowledgment that, by all formally agreed-on measures, the 2020 presidential election was fair. They dismissed the evidence that the process had worked as it should. Third, they maintained that they had the right to decide that the election was unfair and to take corrective action. They concluded that they were justified in using violence to try to force legislators to change the election's outcome.

Thus, the Capitol marchers used white mob logic to define their attempt to subvert the election's outcome as an endeavor to protect it. White mob logic has been deployed so long and so routinely in the US as to have become an unconscious habit. In white mob logic, lies and distortions are claimed as truth, and attempts to make society conform to it are seen as noble, glorious, and divinely ordained. White mob logic convinced the Capitol marchers that they were on the right side of history—that if Jesus were there, he would fight with them. That is *how they could do that*.

V

Of course, many contemporary US Christians did not identify with the Capitol marchers. Since the 1960s, white people who have adopted a liberal or progressive stance have become deeply invested in seeing ourselves as champions of justice and tolerance, especially when it comes to race relations. It has become de rigueur to repudiate overtly racist or white supremacist behavior and sometimes to critique its organic connection with the imperialist and colonialist history of western Christianity. Moreover, antidemocratic violence seems to repudiate everything our nation stands for. Faced with the events of January 6, which appeared to violate all these conventions at once, shocked progressives exclaimed, *How could they do that?*

The confusion goes beyond not knowing the history of antidemocratic violence. Progressive white Christians tend to believe that Christianity and white supremacy are incompatible. Many of us have never come to terms with the fact that white people confidently relied on biblical arguments to justify slavery, nor with the fact that segregationists believed that separation of the races was the will of the Christian God. For us, seeing Christianity and white supremacy together generates cognitive dissonance. Though we could not name it as such, we were sincerely horrified when, on January 6, we saw Christians engaging in white mob violence. We articulated our distress as disbelief.

Beyond our genuine astonishment, however, we ask *How could they do that?* as if the question is too shocking to answer, not because it is, but because we do not really want to know. Our top priority is to distance ourselves from and not be confused with "them." At least part of our consternation comes from an unspoken awareness that, as white people, we have a lot in common with the Capitol marchers. We want to believe that they do not represent us: *That's not who we are.* Seeing ourselves as peace-loving, tolerant people (who just happen to be white), we insist that we, not they, are the true US Americans, the true Christians. Even those of us who know that our own ancestors helped to create and perpetuate white supremacy instinctively separate this history from our contemporary identities. Surely our beliefs represent the real meaning of Christianity, not the white supremacist beliefs of past eras or those whose actions still, inexplicably, align with them.

Notice how our claims of incredulity endeavor to demonstrate not just that we are different, but that we are better. We are the *good* white people, the *good* white Christians.[14] We need to examine this conviction carefully. After all, in the US, the idea that Christians are or should be "better" is inextricably intertwined with white supremacy. Since Jesus's original followers first preached the Gospel, Christians have believed that their religion is the truth and that their adherence to it makes them more virtuous and more reasonable than other people. It is only very recently that some Christians have begun to question this assumption. Again, the idea that Christians are better than other people is rooted in the idea that Christianity is superior to other religions. And both these ideas have been used to justify racism. Indeed, it was in codifying into law their alleged cultural and religious superiority that colonial European

Christians invented modern racism and white supremacy, including modern white identity itself.[15]

Our belief in progressive superiority is linked to the same tradition. Progressiveness is fundamentally about being better. Having made some progress, we think we are better than less progressive people, including our former, less enlightened selves. Even as we profess to believe in equality, our conviction that we are or should be better remains. We think that believing in equality, justice, and tolerance makes us superior to people who don't. The irony escapes us.

This is the real reason progressives were so shocked on January 6. Deep down, we still think that Christians are, or should be, exceptional. Nothing has touched that yet. And given how US society has developed, thinking that Christians should be better is functionally equivalent to thinking that white people should be better. This is the assumption behind *How could they do that?* We are really asking, *Aren't white people better than that? Aren't we, at least, exceptional?* Whether we sympathize with the marchers or shake our heads, our sense of superiority keeps flexing the power that western Christians have always exerted, from Constantine through Charlemagne and Columbus all the way to the Capitol. January 6 can illuminate our entire history, if we let it.

•

VI

We also can see white progressives' inability to understand January 6 as another manifestation of white mob logic. When we ask *How could they do that?* as though merely uttering the question exonerates us, we (1) grant that antidemocratic behavior is unacceptable; (2) refuse to understand how we are socialized into the same white supremacist culture that brought the marchers to the Capitol; and (3) maintain that it is up to us to decide whether and how our whiteness, and whiteness in general, really matters.

And we decide that it doesn't—or that if it does, there is nothing we can do about it. Rather than resorting to physical violence, like the Capitol marchers, progressive Christians engaging in white mob logic vigorously perform what to the critical observer looks suspiciously like feigned helplessness, like the histrionics mentioned previously. Our disapproval disdains responsibility. We choose not to understand the depth of our racialization as white. We choose not to see that our white racialization exceeds our attempts to be good people, that much of its meaning is not under our control. We choose to believe that our innocence lies in our ignorance.

Yet, whether or not we are aware of it, white people are socialized from birth into a strong mentality of white solidarity. As white people, we feel (though we may not consciously think) that because we have our whiteness in common, we are supposed to stick together. This is why we stop at disbelief. It is not only that we cannot bring ourselves to believe that whiteness (still) confers dominance. We cannot bring ourselves to call out white people for acting white. We cannot bring ourselves to believe that as white people, they have done anything truly bad.

So, we throw up our hands. This is how progressive white Christians honor the compact of white solidarity: by refusing to put serious effort into trying to understand *how they could do that*. This all but guarantees that we won't do anything about it. We are using white mob logic to disregard white mob violence.

VII

Still, it is tempting to protest that Christianity is incompatible with violence; that Jesus taught love, justice, and tolerance; and that the behavior of the Capitol marchers grossly misrepresents his message. And perhaps there is indeed a God who intends Christians to be exceptionally loving, just, and tolerant. Who can say?

That is the point: We can believe, we can hope, but we can't say for sure. The last two thousand years have shown that Christianity does not automatically make its followers more loving or just than non-Christians. For most of its history, Western Christianity has been one of the world's most intolerant institutions. To many it still is. Moreover, Christians disagree about the best way to follow Jesus, and each group believes that their interpretation of the Gospel is the right one. In practice, Christianity does not *really* have whatever meaning any single person or group resolves it to have. Christianity has all the meanings Christians give it; it has the impact of whatever actions Christians actually undertake. Christianity has meant wildly different things throughout its history, and it will mean more in the future.

Insofar as their Christian beliefs helped to motivate them, I can only assume that the Capitol marchers acted in accordance with their faith as they understood it. I may not share their interpretation, but I have to give them credit for having the courage of their convictions. If I want Christianity to have a different impact on the world than theirs, then it is up to me to live my Christianity differently. I can stop insisting that I am better than they are, that my beliefs are more adequate than theirs, and I can focus on living out my own Christian conviction that every human being is equally dignified and precious. If I want my version of Christianity to change the way this nation has always operated, then I must fight for equity and equality with more energy than the Capitol marchers fought to overturn the election.

Confronted with white mob violence, we ask *How could they do that?* as if there is no answer because the answer requires us to do something. Stopping at shocked indignation elegantly continues the venerable tradition of dodging responsibility for white supremacy. That is white mob logic justifying white mob behavior. I don't want to do that anymore.

NOTES

1. Mt 10:34 (*New American Bible*). See also Lk 12:31.
2. For the Great Commission, when the risen Jesus commanded his disciples to preach the Gospel to the world, see Mt 28:18–20.
3. For the phrase "theologian of the white experience," see Karen Teel, "Salving the Wound of Race: Racialized Bodies as Sacrament in the Theology of M. Shawn Copeland," in *T&T Clark Handbook of Theological Anthropology*, edited by Mary Ann Hinsdale and Stephen Okey (London: Bloomsbury Academic, 2021), 294. For white racial accountability as growing up, see Karen Teel, "The Racial Crucible: The Movement for Black Lives as Spiritual Invitation," *Critical Theology* 3, no. 1 (Fall 2020).
4. Joshua Zeitz with Scott Althaus, Ruth Ben-Ghiat, Matt Cleary, and Ryan McMaken, "Ask the 'Coupologists': Just What Was Jan. 6 Anyway?" *Politico*, August 19, 2022, https://www.politico.com/news/magazine/2022/08/19/jan-6-coup-authoritarianism-expert-roundtable-00052281.
5. Zeitz et al., "Ask the 'Coupologists.'"
6. This is my conclusion in response to the panelists' leading question, "Does our reluctance to look at the underside of American history feed our inability to understand January 6 for what it was?" (Zeitz et al., "Ask the 'Coupologists'").
7. Zeitz et al., "Ask the 'Coupologists,'" introductory remarks.
8. Zeitz et al., "Ask the 'Coupologists,'" introductory remarks.
9. Victor Luckerson, "Living in the Age of the White Mob," *The New Yorker*, January 15, 2021, https://www.newyorker.com/news/dispatch/living-in-the-age-of-the-white-mob. A related concept that recently is gaining broader understanding and acceptance is white privilege. White privilege too has been largely invisible to white people yet always powerfully present. For the classic articulation, see Peggy McIntosh, "White Privilege: Unpacking the Invisible Knapsack," *Peace and Freedom* (July/August 1989): 10–12.
10. Luckerson, "Living in the Age of the White Mob."
11. Charles Mills, *The Racial Contract*, 25th anniversary edition with a foreword by Tommie Shelby (Ithaca, NY: Cornell University Press, 2022).
12. As I define the term here, a white mob made up entirely of people of color is possible.
13. Steve Martinot, *The Rule of Racialization: Class, Identity, Governance* (Philadelphia: Temple University Press, 2002), chapter 1. For a detailed theological application of Martinot's concept of racist thinking, see Karen Teel, "Whiteness in

Catholic Theological Method," *Journal of the American Academy of Religion* 87, no. 2 (2019): 401–33.

14. For a concise discussion of "good white Christians," see Jeannine Hill Fletcher, *The Sin of White Supremacy: Christianity, Racism, and Religious Diversity in America* (Maryknoll, NY: Orbis Books, 2017), ix–xiii.

15. Christian theologians argue that supersessionism, the ancient belief that Christianity rendered Judaism obsolete (some Christian churches now formally repudiate this belief), is the origin of white Christian supremacy. For example, see J. Kameron Carter, *Race: A Theological Account* (New York: Oxford University Press, 2008); Willie James Jennings, *The Christian Imagination: Theology and the Origins of Race* (New Haven, CT: Yale University Press, 2010); Fletcher, *The Sin of White Supremacy*.

Chapter 3

The "Promised Land" in Christian Nationalist Rhetoric

The Persistent Vision of Christianity as a Religion of Conquest

Brock Bahler

Christian nationalism has *always* been a component of the American imperialist project and is essential to America's collective *mythos* and memory—or more accurately, its intentional, collective forgetting.[1] At the heart of white Christian nationalism lies the conviction that Christianity is a *religion of conquest*. The rhetoric of politicians who have taken up the banner of Christian nationalism often imitates the language of Christian colonization. One of the most salient metaphors for demonstrating this link between colonization and present-day white Christian nationalism is the religious symbolism of America as an alleged "Promised Land," imagery appropriated from the Hebrew Bible when Joshua leads the conquest of Canaan and annihilates the people who live in the land (Exod. 23:23; Num. 34; Josh. 1; Josh. 8). As Philip Gorski and Samuel Perry note, the "deep story" of American Christian nationalism largely hinges on a mythos about Christian colonizers who read themselves back into the text and reenacted the events—a religious cosplay.[2] Christian nationalists today envision themselves as an extension of this colonialist endeavor while repackaging Promised Land rhetoric for their own political purposes. This interpretive framework is central for understanding the logic that undergirds Christian nationalism's propensity to justify violence, promote antidemocratic policies, and align with white supremacist ideologies such as antisemitism and anti-Black racism.

DIVINE APPOINTMENT, PROPHECY, AND APOCALYPTICISM

Of the New Heaven and Earth which Our Lord has made, and as St. John writes in the Apocalypse.... He made me the messenger for it and showed me where to find it.
—Christopher Columbus[3]

God, I ask you that you help us roll in these dark times . . . that we will seize our Esther and Gideon moments. . . . I pray that . . . we'll seize the power that we had given to us by the Constitution, and as well by you. . . . I pray . . . on the 6th of January that they will rise up . . . and stand firm.
—Doug Mastriano prior to the January 6 Insurrection[4]

Just days before Columbus departed Spain in August 1492, Ferdinand and Isabella expelled or forcibly converted every Jew in Spain.[5] Columbus interpreted his voyage as a continuation of this act, believing global domination of Christianity was the conclusion of Crusade logic.[6] Spain's demonization of Jews and Muslims paved the way for him to develop a proto-racial account of the Taíno people as a "people without religion," a claim that within medieval theology implied they had no souls and were not really people at all.[7] In Columbus's diary, he listed hundreds of Bible verses he believed predicted his role in bringing about Christ's second coming, which would occur shortly after he established a new Garden of Eden.[8] In 1503, he claimed to have had a vision where God was providentially guiding him just as much as God had guided Moses, David, and "the people of Israel when He led them out of Egypt."[9] Columbus was convinced he was uniquely chosen to be at the center of God's historical and apocalyptic plan. He not only believed his actions to be a continuation of the conquests of the Hebrew Bible but also viewed himself as a canonical figure and thus an extension of the inerrancy of Scripture.[10]

Christian nationalists take a page out of this discourse. For example, Lauren Boebert has claimed that the Founding Fathers were divinely inspired when they wrote the Second Amendment.[11] Doug Mastriano believed himself—and the election deniers of 2020—to be modern-day Esthers or Gideons, providentially appointed for "such a time as this" (Esther 4:14), to protest a "godless" government. Members of the New Apostolic Reformation who advocate a form of theocracy believe Mastriano to be a modern-day prophet, and he regularly depicted his campaign in apocalyptic terms as a battle of spiritual warfare in a time of national crisis.

Likewise, leading up to his Florida gubernatorial victory, Ron DeSantis released a campaign ad depicting himself as divinely chosen. Alongside images of DeSantis, the voiceover says: "And on the eighth day, God looked down on his planned paradise and said, 'I need a protector.' So God made a fighter. God said, 'I need somebody who will take the arrows, stand firm in the wake of unrelenting attacks.'"[12] Like Columbus's belief he had unearthed Eden, DeSantis's Florida is a "planned paradise." Like Columbus's violence toward the Taíno people as an extension of the Crusades, DeSantis and Mastriano believed themselves to be engaged in a holy war—"help us roll" being an allusion to Todd Beamer's "let's roll" comment on Flight 93 to combat Muslim terrorists on 9/11. They depict themselves "standing firm" (1 Cor. 16:13) while wearing the "armor of God," which can "extinguish all the flaming arrows of the evil one" (Eph. 6:16).[13] Like colonizers' repeated attempts to demonize Native people, DeSantis and Mastriano suggest Democrats are ultimately guided by the devil.

Resorting to biblical allusions surely speaks to a Christian audience of potential voters, but the symbolism is far more substantive. The language grants divine credence to their endeavors, suggesting that to vote against them is not only un-American but also an *act against God*. Conversely, to vote for them is an act of faith. Additionally, such biblical allusions position voting in a political election as a life-or-death, the-end-is-near proposition. Fear of an unknown future becomes a compelling factor to vote, especially fear of the unknown Other, who is dehumanized to the point of demonization.

AMERICA AS A SITE OF CANAANITE CONQUEST

This is the Land of Promise, possessed by idolators, the Amorite, Amulekite, Moabite, Canaanite. . . . Since we are commanded by God in the Holy Scriptures to take it from them, being idolators, and, by reason of their idolatry and sin, to put them all to the knife.
—Pedro de Santander regarding the colonization of Florida, 1552[14]

When the Israelites came into their Promised Land, they didn't just march in and take it. . . . God had to move in mighty ways to remove their enemies. . . . Our Promised Land is Pennsylvania and we're taking it back.
—Rebbie Mastriano, April 30, 2022[15]

Citing Columbus's voyage, Pope Alexander VI issued *Inter Caetera* (1493), often known as the Doctrine of Discovery. As "the vicarship of Jesus Christ," he claimed he could "give, grant, and assign" *any land* "discovered" by Spanish and Portuguese colonizers not already "in the actual possession of any Christian king."[16] All land was up for the taking to be possessed as private property, and *only Christians* are the rightful owners. Not to be outdone,

England issued its own Doctrine of Discovery under the conquests of John Cabot's voyages (1496–1498).[17]

Christian colonizers quickly framed the Doctrine of Discovery as a reenactment of Israelite entry into the Promised Land as Chosen People, like a New Israel with Native Americans as the "Canaanites." This theological narrative provided metaphysical justification for genocide and profiting from chattel slavery. Like de Santander, in 1513 at a gathering of Spanish theologians, Martin Fernandez de Encisco reasoned: "The Spanish king might very justly send me to require those idolatrous Indians to hand over their land to him for it was given to him by the pope. . . . He might justly wage war against them, kill and enslave those captured in war, precisely as Joshua treated the inhabitants of the land of Canaan."[18] *Inter Caetera*, with its myth that Christians have special title to the land, is essential to American legal history. In *Johnson v. McIntosh* (1823), the Supreme Court cited the papal decree as *legal precedent* for all land title matters between the US and Native Americans. Chief Justice John Marshall claimed "discovery" of America by Christian nations gave them the "sole right of acquiring the soil." In contrast, Native people are depicted as "heathen, and barbarous" and as trespassers on the land.[19] In *Cornet v. Winton* (1826), the Tennessee Supreme Court defended *Johnson v. McIntosh*'s upholding of Christian colonialization on the grounds that the US was simply following the model of "the Israelites under the guidance of Moses and Joshua," who "extirpated the inhabitants of the countries they invaded."[20] This continues to serve as legal precedent for US attitudes about Native rights.[21]

In 1583, Sir George Peckham developed a legal theory of British land rights in Turtle Island that justified the seizure of Indian lands by appeal to the Canaanite conquest.[22] When Anglican colonizers settled Jamestown in 1607, they claimed that "the English" now fulfilled "the role of God's new Chosen."[23] While some settlers initially sought to evangelize Native people, by 1609, Anglican Rev. Robert Gray argued they should "cast out the Canaanites," likening the Virginia settler colonialism to Israel's extermination of the Amalekites.[24]

Both Spanish Catholics and Anglican colonizers depicted the Americas as Canaan and used apocalyptic, prophetic imagery as justification for colonialism long before the Puritans did,[25] yet the Puritans hold a particularly influential place in American religious mythology. Through a Calvinist covenantal framework, the Puritans believed themselves to be establishing a Christian Utopia where white European Christians replaced Israel at the center of God's plan for the world.[26] In 1630, Puritan minister John Cotton preached, "God's people take the Land by Promise . . . the Land of Canaan is called a Land of Promise."[27] Likewise, John Winthrop proclaimed: "The God of Israel is among us . . . men shall say of succeeding plantations, 'may the Lord make it like that of New England.' For we . . . shall be as a city upon a hill."[28] Winthrop maintains that the Puritans are guided by the "God of Israel," implying God's covenant to the ancient Israelites has been shifted over to European Christians. Winthrop is drawing a parallel between England and Jerusalem, the assumed spiritual center of the world. By naming the colony "New England," Winthrop is alluding to passages of the Bible suggesting that God will establish a *New Jerusalem* and claiming that its location is identifiably in the American colonies.[29] Furthermore, in Cotton Mather's seven-volume *Magnalia Christi Americana* (1702), he depicts William Bradford as "the leader of a people in a Wilderness . . . a Moses."[30] John Winthrop is also depicted as Moses, leading the "Chosen People into an American Wilderness" and preparing them for a "heavenly Canaan."[31] Regularly mentioning Joshua's Canaanite conquest, Mather describes Native Americans as "Ammonites" and "Indian Amalekites" who "Worship of the Devil," whereas the Puritans are "New-English Israel."[32]

Today, Christian nationalists invoke similar Promised Land imagery. Doug Mastriano, who has claimed that separation of church and state is a "myth," bypasses the Constitution as a founding text and believes America was intended to be a theocracy in the tradition of William Penn's Quaker settlement of Pennsylvania. Florida governor Ron DeSantis, on the night of his 2022 reelection, described his state as the "promised land."[33] Again, this is politically expedient, because in an August 2021 poll, 30 percent of *all Americans* and more than 50 percent of both white Evangelicals and Republicans agreed that "God intended America to be a new promised land where European Christians could create a society that could be an example to the rest of the world."[34]

Like Cotton Mather, far-right Christian nationalists have repeatedly enacted the Jericho story as a kind of spiritual performance, ritualized incantation, or cosplay. In mid-December of 2020, a "Jericho March" rally was held in Washington, DC, including speeches by Mike Lindell, Eric Metaxas, Michael Flynn, and Doug Mastriano. Participants marched around the US Capitol building while blowing shofars (a Jewish instrument typically now used in Jewish high holy holidays), as if their noise would overturn the election.[35] Other marches were scheduled for January 2–6, and shofars were blown the day of the insurrection. Mastriano then announced his campaign to run for governor of Pennsylvania by having a man donning a Jewish prayer shawl blow a shofar.[36] More recently, after election-denier Kari Lake lost the 2022 Arizona gubernatorial race, supporters performed a Jericho March around the Maricopa County election office in hopes of overturning the democratic election results.[37]

The symbolic meaning of such biblical allusions is not merely to compel Christians to vote for a particular candidate. The Jericho Marches reflect how white Christian nationalists believe they are in a holy war, but now the alleged "pagans" in the so-called Promised Land include socialists, democrats, atheists, LGBTQIA people, Muslims, Jews, Black people, and immigrants.[38] When far-right politicians use terms like *The People* or *patriots* (often contrasted to the antisemitic-laden term *globalists*), they really mean that the mostly white and Christian conservatives who vote for them are the *real* American citizens.[39] Such imagery calls to mind the sustained conspiratorial efforts by Republicans in 2008 claiming Barack Obama was secretly a Muslim (and thus unqualified to be president), or the common ploy in the 1960s to identify Rev. Martin Luther King Jr. as a Communist (and thus an atheist and not truly American). Most disturbingly, by cosplaying a story in which nearly the entire population of Jericho was annihilated, Christian nationalists imply that their metaphors might turn into actual violence (and have) against fellow US citizens they have deemed enemies of God. The violent metaphors are particularly dangerous in how they normalize the dehumanization of political opponents and further encourage verbal and physical attacks upon marginalized communities.

CHRISTIAN NATIONALISM AND THE CONVERGENCE OF ANTI-BLACK RACISM AND ANTISEMITISM

As the Race of Ham or his son Canaan (Parents and Children) are cursed, so Shem (parent and children) is blessed and continued in the place of Blessing, the Church. . . . It is possible that some of the [Native] Americans may be the Posterity of those Canaanites, who after the Wars of Canaan, set up their Pillars in Africa. . . . Jesus the Saviour has follow'd them, and conquer'd them with his Glorious Grace! . . . The Ammonites [Pequot Indians] perceived that they had made themselves to sink before the New-English Israel.
—Cotton Mather (1702)[40]

As a family, we so much love Israel. In fact, I'm going to say we probably love Israel more than a lot of Jews do.
—Rebbie Mastriano, October 29, 2022[41]

The woke agenda has caused millions of Americans to leave these jurisdictions for greener pastures. Now this great exodus of Americans, for those folks, Florida, for so many of them, has served as a promised land.
—Ron DeSantis after winning reelection as governor of Florida, November 8, 2022[42]

In 1624, the shareholders of the Virginia Company gathered, and Alderman Richard Johnson concluded, "As for convertinge of the Infidells itt was an attempt impossible they being descended of ye cursed race of Cham."[43] Cham, or Ham, was one of the three sons of Noah. In Genesis 9, Ham's son Canaan is allegedly cursed to a life of perpetual slavery. Anglicans Robert Johnson and William Strachey claim Native Americans were "direct descendants" of those under God's "heavie curse and punishment" due to "the sin of Ham."[44] Cotton Mather advances this same theory to develop a theologically based taxonomy of race. In the late Middle Ages, European Christians believed all humans came from Noah's three sons, which were then mapped onto landmasses. Shem was typically associated with Asia, Japheth with Europe, and Ham with Africa, and in the European medieval theological anthropology, the "evidence" of this curse was often purported to be black skin.[45] Prior to the "scientific" taxonomy of four races (i.e., Linnaeus's in 1758) or five (i.e., Blumenbach's in 1798), the idea of three races developed from a literalist reading of the Bible.[46] Christians then forced Native Americans into this taxonomy to maintain their belief in the inerrancy of Scripture: *Both* Native Americans and Africans were perceived to be under the "curse" of inferiority and perpetual servitude.

Noticeably, Mather changes the categories: European Christians are now associated with *Shem*. To align with his Calvinist theology and advance supersessionism, he claims the Church replaces ethnic and religious Jews, that Christians are the *real Jews*. During the colonial era, some Christians theorized that Native Americans were members of the so-called Lost Tribes of Israel, and thus were convinced the mass conversion of Native people would result in the end of history.[47] As Native people actively resisted, colonizers abandoned this view and began to envision *themselves* as the descendants of the Lost Tribes of Israel. The British Israelism movement had millions of adherents who claimed Anglo-Saxons were the true Israelites and thus were the "biological heirs" of the promises in the Hebrew Bible, and there was a concerted effort among German theologians to claim major biblical figures were white (a view Kant held).[48] Anti-Native and anti-Black racism is interwoven within and inseparable from this antisemitic logic where Christians are the "real" children of Shem.[49]

Through this theological-genealogical view of race, colonizers promoted "hereditary heathenism," believing being a white European was a guarantee of salvation, whereas being a child of Ham—whether African or Native—signified permanent damnation.[50] Race, first and foremost, symbolized a hierarchical theological binary of God's blessing and cursing, light and darkness, salvation and damnation, but one passed on through blood and revealed in culture.[51] White supremacy as a form of biological essentialism and cultural superiority was allegedly *providentially ordained*, which would come to frame scientific racist efforts for centuries.[52]

Mather believes Black and Native people can be converted to Christianity, yet there remains a divinely sanctioned "separate but equal" where enslavement is their destiny.[53] He depicts their experience of receiving God's grace as an act of colonialist violence,[54] which maps onto both Promised Land imagery and Mather's racial theology. Mather believes those who survived Israel's Canaanite conquest first fled to Africa and then to Turtle Island. For the Canaanite conquest to be completed, now being continued by Euro-Christians, African and Native people must be destroyed or forcibly assimilated. They can obtain eternal salvation but only so long as they embrace whiteness: "Though your *Skins* are of the colour of the *Night*, yet your *Souls* will be washed *White* in the *Blood of the Lamb*."[55]

Interpreted through the history of Christian supersessionism, the logic of Christian nationalists' cultural appropriation of symbolism from the Hebrew Bible (e.g., blowing a shofar, Jericho Marches) implies belief in the superiority of Euro-Christianity in which they can understand Jewish religious texts, symbols, and practices better than Jews understand them themselves. As the so-called "real" Jews, Christian nationalists view themselves as rightfully entitled to Judaism, a spiritualized application of a Cartesian epistemology of becoming "masters and possessors of nature."[56]

Christian supersessionism was a feature of Mastriano's campaign. Mastriano depicted his political opponent, Josh Shapiro—who is a practicing conservative Jew—as a socialist (i.e., un-American) and claimed his children went to an "elitist" school (another common antisemitic slur). Mastriano's legal adviser Jenna Ellis even tweeted: "Josh Shapiro is at best a secular Jew in the same way Joe Biden is a secular Catholic—both are extremists for gender transition surgeries on minors and no limits on abortion."[57] *Secular* here is functioning as a pejorative that not only erases Shapiro's conservative Jewish practices but also delegitimizes the more than 30 percent of American Jews that identify as nonobservant, as well as the majority of American Jews who are registered as Democrats. According to Ellis, the only *real* Jews (and Christians) are those that fully align with far-right conservative political policies[58]—a belief that Donald Trump also advanced in stating that Evangelicals are more faithful Jews than actual Jews due to their agreement with his policies toward Israel.[59] Further, in response to an Israeli journalist asking about Mastriano's ties with Andrew Torba, the well-known openly antisemitic Christian and founder of the social media site GAB, Rebbie Mastriano stated that her Christian proselytizing attempts toward Jews are proof that she loves Israel more than actual Jews—that she is the *real* Jew and progressive Jews are frauds. Not surprisingly, Torba, who publicly endorsed Mastriano's campaign (and whom Mastriano briefly paid as a consultant), advocates supersessionism and depicts Jews as the "Synagogue of Satan" and a "den of vipers."[60]

DeSantis's reference to the "woke agenda," then, reveals how antisemitism is tethered to anti-Black racism within Christian nationalism.

Historically, the term *woke* was coined in African American Vernacular English to refer to Black people staying alert to threats of racial discrimination. Conservatives have subversively coopted the term into a pejorative to refer to social justice movements that seek to openly discuss the long-lasting effects of white supremacy, honestly tell the history of racism in America, or call for reparations. Broadly (and mistakenly) labeled as "Critical Race Theory," conservatives have consistently claimed that such a movement to redress past and present wrongs amounts to a form of reverse racism against white people.[61] This has led to massive state-led efforts to ban books about racism and the Holocaust (and about gay and trans experiences) throughout the country. In Florida, DeSantis passed the "Stop W.O.K.E. Act" to make it illegal to teach about the legacy of white supremacy in public schools, suggesting that the real racists are those who desire to speak out against it.[62] As both Ellis's tweet and DeSantis's political platform reveal, white supremacy is committed to demonizing and policing the lives of LGBTQIA people. DeSantis's "Don't Say Gay" bill banned teaching about gender and trans identity in public schools, claiming that the LGBTQIA community promotes a "woke gender ideology."[63] Christian nationalists and other far-right politicians have sought to erase the existence of trans people from society, often depicting them as "groomers," playing into a common trope suggesting gay men are more prone to commit pedophilia. This should come as no surprise, as white supremacists have a long history of policing sexuality and gender. Indeed, the Nazis deported thousands of gay men to concentration camps, and the first books they banned and burned were on trans research.[64] DeSantis's election night speech, then, is an explicit proclamation that Black and LGBTQIA people are not welcome in the "Promised Land" of Florida, that it is effectively for white Christians. The antisemitic coopting of Promised Land rhetoric becomes divine cover for functionally denying human rights to Black and trans folk and for protecting the power and fragile feelings of white people.

VIOLENCE IN THE NAME OF GOD

> Those that scaped the fire were slaine with the sword; some hewed to peeces. . . . It was a fearful sight to see them thus frying in the fyer, and the streams of blood . . . and horrible was the stincke and sent thereof, but the victory seemed a sweet sacrifice . . . to God who had wrought so wonderfully for them . . . a victory over so proud and insulting an enimie.
> —Puritan William Bradford in *History of Plymouth Plantation* (1651)[65]

> The First Amendment right, which is our right to worship Jesus freely, that's why we have a country. That's why we have Georgia. . . . Our Founding Fathers [came] over here [to] destroy American Indians' homes and their land. They took it. Look at what they went through, the Native Americans, for sacrifice for us to have the freedom we have today.
> —Georgia Republican politician Kandiss Taylor, May 2022[66]

On May 26, 1637, the Puritans surrounded Mystic Fort and burned it to the ground. Up to seven hundred Pequot Indians were killed in the genocidal act, including women, children, and the elderly. The Puritans unanimously justified this event as a providential act of God. Captain John Underhill, in his firsthand account, wrote, "Sometimes the Scripture declareth women and children must perish with their parents. . . . We had sufficient light from the Word of God for our proceedings."[67] Cotton Mather concludes that the people who were burned alive were "Savages" who "were dismissed from a World that was *Burdened* with them," and the victory was evidence of "the Glory of the Englishman's God"—material proof of white Christian supremacy.[68] For Mather, Native people were an inconvenience, expendable for the sake of the greater good—the same logic that undergirds racial capitalism, Enlightenment "progress," America's eugenics program, and conservative rejections of COVID mitigation efforts. But for the Puritans, the easy disposability of Native life was further spiritualized as an act pleasing to God. William Bradford concludes the sheer existence of Native people is an "insult," and yet their flayed, burning flesh functioned as a "sweet sacrifice," like prayers lifted up to God. In the Calvinistic account of Jesus's death, the son of God is foreordained to serve as an atoning sacrifice to appease the angry wrath of the Father-God, who *requires* the death penalty for sin. Within this understanding of the cosmic order, Bradford condones human sacrifice with ease.

Kandiss Taylor was a Republican candidate in the Georgia gubernatorial campaign who lost in the 2022 spring primaries. With "Jesus Guns Babies" emblazoned on the side of her campaign bus as her three-point political platform, Taylor's expansion of Bradford's same theo-logic continues the vision of Christianity as a religion of conquest. Taylor falsely claims that (1) the First Amendment was really intended to only secure the rights of *Christian* worship, (2) the very *purpose* of America as a nation and Georgia as a state is to protect *Christian* worship, (3) the Founding Fathers (which, here, includes all European colonizers) intended to wage acts of ethnic cleansing [OK, that part is true!], and (4) such genocidal acts were a justifiable *sacrifice* to God to guarantee Christian "freedom" today. Taylor reveals that when Christian nationalists talk about freedom, rights, and liberty, they really mean the preservation of the privileges of white Christians at the expense of the rights of others. When she speaks about upholding the Second Amendment, she means the justification of violent Christian acts of conquest for the protection of white property.[69] When she speaks about being pro-life, she really means that some lives are expendable, and really, only white Christian lives matter.

Taylor's conviction that some people can justifiably be determined as expendable—without their consent, input, or agency—aligns with Georgia's brutal history of systemic violence toward Black and Native peoples. In the 1700s, George Whitefield, one of the most famous Christian evangelists of the Great Awakening, founded an orphanage for white boys near Savannah as part of his hope that the state would become a Christian Utopia. But to make the orphanage financially solvent, he enslaved Africans to harvest a 640-acre plantation and profited from their free labor.[70] Then in the nineteenth century, as is well known, Georgia was the site of the "Trail of Tears," where the intentional removal and death of Cherokee Native people under the Indian Removal Act was defended by Presbyterian president Andrew Jackson.

CONCLUSION

Violence has been a constant theme throughout this chapter because at its core Promised Land rhetoric in Christian nationalist ideology is a religious justification for violence, conquest, and imperialist might. Not surprisingly, in the wake of January 6, white Evangelical Protestants are the religious group *most* likely to agree that "true American patriots might have to resort to violence in order to save our country."[71] This should rightly raise alarms about the significant potential that white Christian nationalists might resort to extensive measures of terrorism to achieve their aims. But more sobering, it demands our attention to how Christian nationalism is a threat to American democracy because it has *always* been a threat to democracy by justifying exclusion and violence against Black, Brown, Native, LGBTQIA, and immigrant lives for the sake of economic gain, political power, and religious devotion. For under the dark underbelly of American imperialism and its slavocracy, beneath every iteration of American exceptionalism and its concomitant domestic and foreign policies—from Promised Land to Manifest Destiny, to "the last best hope of man on earth," to "Make America Great Again"—lie the bodies of those who have been deemed disposable in the name of an Almighty God.

NOTES

1. Critical race theorist Kendall Thomas maintains that how legal history is depicted as one of continual progress requires "an ideological strategy of 'organized forgetting'" of the ways legal history often also includes setbacks, unjust rulings,

and subversive resistance to change unjust laws (Thomas, "*Rouge Et Noir* Reread," 483). Here Thomas is referencing Roger Bromley's *Lost Narratives*, which suggests that writing history is as much a matter of "amnesia" as it is an act of remembering, and thus, "What is 'forgotten' . . . [has] been carefully and consciously, not casually and unconsciously, omitted from the narrative economy of remembering" (quoted in Thomas, "*Rouge Et Noir* Reread," 493n115).

2. Gorski and Perry, *The Flag and the Cross*, chap. 2.

3. West and Kling, *The Libro de las profecias*, 60.

4. Dickinson, "Caught on Tape."

5. Ferdinand II and Isabella I, "Edict of Expulsion of the Jews."

6. Parfitt, *The Lost Tribes of Israel*, 27; Columbus, "Letter to the Sovereigns," 195; West and Kling, *The Libro de las profecias*, 62.

7. Maldonaldo-Torres, "Religion, Conquest and Race"; Maldonaldo-Torres, "Race, Religion and Ethics"; Grosfoguel, "The Structure of Knowledge in Westernized Universities," 78; Shohat, "Taboo Memories, Diasporic Visions," 210, 230n12.

8. West and Kling, *The Libro de las profecias*, 60, 109; Parfitt, *The Lost Tribes of Israel*, 140.

9. West and Kling, *The Libro de las profecias*, 54.

10. Columbus claimed his understanding of biblical prophecy was led by "the Holy Spirit who encouraged me with a radiance of marvelous illumination from his sacred Holy Scriptures" (West and Kling, *The Libro de las profecias*, 105).

11. On Twitter, Lauren Boebert said regarding the Second Amendment: "This isn't something that the American forefathers gave us. . . . They [the Founding Fathers] were divinely inspired when they wrote the Constitution and they're just reiterating the revelation they received from God." https://twitter.com/patriottakes/status/1532480786762448896. In a November 2020 poll, sociologists Samuel Perry and Philip Gorski found that up to an astonishing 70 percent of white Evangelicals hold to the view that the Constitution is divinely inspired (Gorski and Perry, *The Flag and the Cross*, 83).

12. Eskin, "Ron DeSantis' Campaign Ad."

13. See also Ceballos, "What Message Is DeSantis Sending with Religious 'Full Armor of God' Rhetoric?"

14. Cited in Newcomb, *Pagans in the Promised Land*, 50. It would be impossible to catalog *every* instance of Promised Land rhetoric during the colonial era, but Newcomb provides dozens of them.

15. This was during a speech at a campaign stop at the Shield of Truth rally in Pennsburg, Pennsylvania. A recording of the speech is available on Twitter at https://twitter.com/KiraResistance/status/1584711662682054656.

16. Alexander VI, *Inter Caetera*. For extensive accounts of the Doctrine of Discovery from a Native perspective, see Charles (Navajo) and Rah, *Unsettling Truths*; Newcomb (Shawnee-Lenape), *Pagans in the Promised Land*; Tinker (Osage), *Missionary Conquest*; Miller (Shawnee) et al., *Discovering Indigenous Lands*; Dunbar-Ortiz, *An Indigenous Peoples' History of the United States*, ch. 11.

17. Miller et al., *Discovering Indigenous Lands*, 17; Newcomb, *Pagans in the Promised Land*, 84.

18. Quoted in Hanke, *The Spanish Struggle*, 32. This statement was made in Valldolid, which would later be the site, in 1550, where Juan Ginés de Sepúlveda and Bartolomé de las Casas would debate whether Native Americans had souls (and were thus worthy of human rights). Sepúlveda claimed they had no souls; de las Casas claimed they did but needed to be converted to Christianity to become civilized. *Both* religio-racial frameworks dominated the colonial era. See also Garcia-Treto, "The Lesson of the Gibeonites," 74.

19. Marshall, *Johnson v. McIntosh*. That same year, with the issuance of the Monroe Doctrine, the US declared that the Doctrine of Discovery had been transferred from European countries to America.

20. Cited in Newcomb, *Pagans in the Promised Land*, 77–78.

21. It undergirds the Supreme Court rulings *Tee-Hit-Ton Indians v. US* (1955), *Oliphant v. Suquamish Indian* (1978), and *Nevada v. Hicks* (2001) and has been cited as precedent as recently as *City of Sherrill v. Oneida Indian Nation of NY* (2005), in a majority opinion written by Ruth Bader Ginsburg. In 2001, US representatives to the United Nations confirmed that treaties with Native American tribes were still interpreted through *Johnson v. McIntosh* (Newcomb, *Pagans in the Promised Land*, xxii, 117, 121, 126).

22. Cave, "Canaanites in a Promised Land," 281.

23. Cave, "Canaanites in a Promised Land," 277.

24. Cave, "Canaanites in a Promised Land," 283; see also 286.

25. Despite his otherwise exceptional research, John Fea wrongly claims, "New England was the place where the notion of America as God's new Israel began" (Fea, *Was America Founded as a Christian Nation?* 63). And Gorski and Perry, despite their extremely important sociological work on white Christian nationalism, inaccurately claim, "[Cotton] Mather was not the first to view the Puritans' wars with the native tribes through a providential lens. But he was arguably the first to view it through an apocalyptic lens as well" (Gorski and Perry, *The Flag and the Cross*, 51). While the Puritans are no doubt important, this complete erasure of Spanish Catholic influence further *compounds* the centering of English-speaking Anglo-Saxon Protestantism so central to the American mythos. Further, by focusing on the Puritans, the result is a complete erasure of over a century of the development of the concept of race and racism.

26. Dunbar-Ortiz, *An Indigenous Peoples' History of the United States*, 308.

27. Cotton, "God's Promise to His Plantation."

28. Winthrop, "A Model of Christian Charity."

29. See Isa. 60:11; 65:17–19; Heb. 12:22; Rev. 21. In 1670, the Puritan Rev. Samuel Danforth compared the Massachusetts Bay Colony to Israel's wandering toward their "promised Inheritance" and likened Puritan leaders to Moses (Danforth, "A Brief Recognition of New England's Errand into the Wilderness," 9, 11, 20). Danforth concludes that the reason the Puritans entered "into the Wilderness" was to establish heaven on Earth, a "pure and faithful dispensation of the Gospel and the Kingdome of God" (19).

30. Mather, *Magnalia Christi Americana*, II.5.

31. Mather, *Magnalia Christi Americana*, II.8. See also V.90.

32. Mather, *Magnalia Christi Americana*, III.64, III.196, VII.42.
33. Rodríguez Ortiz, "'I Have Only Begun to Fight.'"
34. Jones, "Columbus Day or Indigenous Peoples' Day?"; Jenkins, "Survey: 'Great Replacement' Belief Correlates with Christian Nationalist Views."
35. One organizer of the march, Jill Noble, compared their attempt to prevent the democratic election of Joe Biden to the Maccabees, who violently fought against Roman oppression, which is the basis of the Jewish celebration of Hanukkah (Cheney, "Trump-Supporting 'Jericho March' Ends in Protest").
36. Hanau, "Pennsylvania Republican Doug Mastriano Enters Race for Governor with a Shofar Blast."
37. Lemon, "Kari Lake Supporters Reenact Biblical Battle of Jericho in Maricopa Protest."
38. Indeed, according to recent surveys, 63 percent of Republicans believe "being Christian is somewhat or very important to being truly American," and conversely, 74 percent of Republicans claim that Islam is "at odds with American values," while 71 percent of Republicans believe "immigrants threaten American values" (PRRI Staff, "Competing Visions of America").
39. Johnson, *I The People*. Johnson notes how this has been a common rhetorical ploy by Reagan, the Tea Party, and Trump, but noticeably it also appears in Doug Mastriano's concession letter, wherein he describes his campaign as "The People's movement" (Caruso et al., "Republican Doug Mastriano Concedes Pa. Governor's Race").
40. Mather, *Magnalia Christi Americana*, V.68, V.90, VI.62, VII.42.
41. Vigna, "'We Love Israel More Than Most Jews.'"
42. Rodríguez Ortiz, "'I Have Only Begun to Fight.'"
43. Goetz, *The Baptism of Early Virginia*, 60.
44. Cave, "Canaanites in a Promised Land," 284, 285.
45. Keel, "Religion, Polygenism, and the Early Science of Human Origins," 14–15; Goldenberg, "Review: The Development of the Idea of Race"; Harris, *Is Christianity a White Man's Religion?*, 103. Some biblical literalists who promote "Aryan" forms of white supremacy claim Japheth is the father of the Aryan race. Shem is considered the father of the Semites or Jews, and in Aryan-privileged formations of race, Shem is often associated with Asia (and the Middle East) and used to perpetuate Orientalist conceptions of racism. But sometimes (as with the Puritans), Calvinist Christians claimed Europeans were the descendants of Shem, and thus were the "real" Jews.
46. Jennings, *The Christian Imagination*, chapter 2.
47. Parfitt, *The Lost Tribes of Israel*, 58, 62, 66; Benite, *The Ten Lost Tribes*, 3, 141; Gorski and Perry, *The Flag and the Cross*, 52. This view is still held in Mormon theology.
48. Throughout the eighteenth and nineteenth centuries, there was an extensive push by theologians and anthropologists to claim all the main figures of the Bible—including Jesus, Noah, Abraham, and Adam—were white, that the "original design" of the human was whiteness and all others were deviations. In fact, the term *Caucasian* as a designation for being white is well known to derive from the assumption that white people originated from the Caucasus mountains, but what is far less known is

that scholars believed this to be the original home of white people *because that was the location where Noah's Ark landed after the flood* (Kidd, *The Forging of Races*, 24, 44, 204–8; see also Carter, *Race: A Theological Account*, ch. 2.).

49. See Charles and Rah, *Unsettling Truths*, 72–73; Goldenberg, *The Curse of Ham*; Goldenberg, "Review: The Development of the Idea of Race"; Kidd, *The Forging of Races*. Vice President of the Confederacy Alexander Stephens appealed to the Curse of Ham in his vision of the Confederacy: "With us, all of the white race . . . are equal in the eye of the law. Not so with the negro. Subordination is his place. He, by nature, or by the curse against Canaan, is fitted for that condition which he occupies in our system" (Stephens, "Cornerstone Speech"). The curse of Ham was one of several theological racial theories invoked by southern Christians to maintain segregation during the twentieth century (Hawkins, *The Bible Told Them So*).

50. Goetz, *The Baptism of Early Virginia*, 59–63.

51. Mather, *Magnalia Christi Americana*, V.69. Mather's father, Rev. Increase Mather, also promoted hereditary heathenism (Goetz, *The Baptism of Early Virginia*, 63).

52. Notably, in the fifteenth century, Spanish Catholics expressed deep suspicion regarding the (counterfeit) conversions of Jews and Muslims and whether their blood was pure (Maldonaldo-Torres, "Religion, Conquest and Race," 646; Grosfoguel, "The Structure of Knowledge in Westernized Universities," 78). This is another instance in which theological demarcations were the predecessor of the idea of race. In the 1800s some British thinkers claimed that the "blood of our race" of Anglo-Saxons made them uniquely suited for Protestantism (Kidd, *The Forging of Races*, 196). In his 1867 treatise defending slavery, Robert Louis Dabney wrote, "Depraved parents will naturally rear depraved children, unless God interfere by a grace to which they have no claim; so that not only punishment, but the sinfulness, becomes hereditary" (Dabney, *Defence of Virginia*, 102).

53. "The State of your Negroes in this World, must be low, and mean, and abject; a State of Servitude. No great Things in this World, can be done for them. Something then, let there be done, towards their welfare in the World to Come" (Mather, *The Negro Christianized*, 9).

54. Mather, *Magnalia Christi Americana*, VI.62.

55. Mather, *A Good Master Well Served*, 52–53, 54. John Eliot, one of the earliest Puritan missionaries, also promoted this idea that conversion to Christianity implied assimilation into European culture (Gorski and Perry, *The Flag and the Cross*, 52).

56. Descartes, *Discourse on Method*, 35. Latin American Liberation philosopher Enrique Dussel observes that the "ego cogito" is undergirded and preceded by the "ego conquiro" (cited in Grosfoguel, "The Structure of Knowledge," 77).

57. The tweet was made on October 21, 2022. I have saved a screenshot at https://twitter.com/brockbahler/status/1583810264792563712.

58. Given Judaism has long allowed for abortion for centuries (at least dating back to Maimonides), and the Talmud mentions five nonbinary gender categories, Ellis's claim is based on complete ignorance of Jewish thought and practice, which are not "extremist" views.

59. Trump has repeatedly claimed that Jews who vote Democrat are "disloyal" (and thus not real Americans). On October 16, 2022, he posted to his media site Truth Social: "No President has done more for Israel than I have. . . . Our wonderful Evangelicals are far more appreciative of this than the people of the Jewish faith."

60. Torba and Isker, *Christian Nationalism*, 5, 22, 24, 47. Indeed, Torba explicitly names the Pilgrim's Mayflower Compact as the true founding document of America (62, 106).

61. Notably, the "reverse racism" accusation has a long history dating as far back as President Andrew Johnson's opposition to Reconstruction after the end of slavery. In fall 2022, before the Supreme Court conservative lawyers argued that the Indian Child Welfare Act (ICWA), which exists as a reparative measure to decades of ethnic cleansing through the Indian Boarding School system, is a form of reverse racism against potential white (and Christian) adoptive parents.

62. Staff, "Governor DeSantis Announces Legislative Proposal to Stop W.O.K.E. Activism."

63. Diaz, "Florida's Governor Signs Controversial Law." Doug Mastriano also made part of his political platform to end "CRT" and the participation of trans women in sports had he been elected as governor of Pennsylvania.

64. Holocaust Memorial Day Trust, "6 May 1933."

65. Cited in Dunbar-Ortiz, *An Indigenous Peoples' History of the United States*, 63.

66. Stanton, "Native Americans Made 'Sacrifice' for 'Our Right to Worship Jesus.'"

67. Underhill, "Newes from America," 36, University of Nebraska, Lincoln, Digital Commons, https://digitalcommons.unl.edu/cgi/viewcontent.cgi?article=1037&context=etas

68. Mather, *Magnalia Christi Americana*, VII.43.

69. Relatedly, at a campaign event at a local Christian church, Lauren Boebert suggested Jesus wouldn't have died on the cross by the Roman government if he had owned some AR-15s (Loh, "Rep. Lauren Boebert Joked That Jesus Didn't Have Enough AR-15s").

70. Tisby, *The Color of Compromise*, 48.

71. PRRI Staff, "Competing Visions of America." See also Du Mez, *Jesus and John Wayne*, which traces the history of this penchant for violence among American Evangelicals.

BIBLIOGRAPHY

Alexander VI. *Inter Caetera*. Papal Encyclicals. https://www.papalencyclicals.net/Alex06/alex06inter.htm.

Benite, Zvi Ben-Dor. *The Ten Lost Tribes: A World History*. New York: Oxford University Press, 2009.

Carter, J. Kameron. *Race: A Theological Account*. New York: Oxford University Press, 2008.

Caruso, Stephen, Angela Couloumbis, Kate Huangpu, and Katie Meyer. "Republican Doug Mastriano Concedes Pa. Governor's Race 4 Days after Democrat Josh Shapiro Declared Winner." *SpotlightPA*. November 10, 2022. https://www.spotlightpa.org/news/2022/11/pa-governor-election-2022-results-doug-mastriano-no-concession-josh-shapiro/

Cave, Alfred E. "Canaanites in a Promised Land: The American Indian and the Providential Theory of Empire." *American Indian Quarterly* 12, no. 4 (Fall 1988): 277–97.

Ceballos, Ana. "What Message Is DeSantis Sending with Religious 'Full Armor of God' Rhetoric?" *Tampa Bay Times*, September 14, 2022. https://www.tampabay.com/news/florida-politics/2022/09/12/what-message-is-desantis-sending-with-religious-full-armor-of-god-rhetoric/.

Charles, Mark, and Soong-Chan Rah. *Unsettling Truths: The Ongoing, Dehumanizing Legacy of the Doctrine of Discovery.* Downers Grove: IVP, 2019.

Cheney, Jillian. "Trump-Supporting 'Jericho March' Ends in Protest, Burning of BLM Banners." *Religion Unplugged*. December 14, 2020. https://religionunplugged.com/news/2020/12/13/trump-supporting-jericho-march-ends-in-protest.

Columbus, Christopher. "Letter to the Sovereigns 4 March 1493." In *Reading Columbus*. Edited by Margarita Zamora, 190–97. Berkeley: University of California Press, 1993.

Cotton, John. "God's Promise to His Plantation" (1630). https://amlit1.hcommons.org/cottonpromise/.

Dabney, Robert Lewis. *A Defence of Virginia and Through Her, of the South, in Recent and Pending Contests Against the Sectional Party.* New York: E.J. Hale & Son, 1876. https://www.gutenberg.org/files/47422/47422-h/47422-h.htm.

Danforth, Samuel. "A Brief Recognition of New England's Errand into the Wilderness." Cambridge: S.G. and M.J, 1671. https://digitalcommons.unl.edu/cgi/viewcontent.cgi?article=1038&context=libraryscience.

Descartes, Rene. *Discourse on Method.* Translated by Donald Cress. Indianapolis: Hackett, 1993.

Diaz, Jaclyn. "Florida's Governor Signs Controversial Law Opponents Dubbed 'Don't Say Gay.'" *NPR*. March 28, 2022. https://www.npr.org/2022/03/28/1089221657/dont-say-gay-florida-desantis.

Dickinson, Tom. "Caught on Tape: Doug Mastriano Prayed for MAGA to 'Seize the Power' Ahead of Jan. 6." *Rolling Stone*. September 9, 2022. https://www.rollingstone.com/politics/politics-features/doug-mastriano-donald-trump-christian-right-1234589455/.

Du Mez, Kristin Kobes. *Jesus and John Wayne: How White Evangelicals Corrupted a Faith and Fractured a Nation.* New York: Liveright, 2020.

Dunbar-Ortiz, Roxanne. *An Indigenous Peoples' History of the United States.* Boston: Beacon Press, 2014.

Eskin, Amy. "Ron DeSantis' Campaign Ad Says He Was Sent by God to 'Take the Arrows.'" *People*. November 7, 2022. https://people.com/politics/ron-desantis-god-made-fighter-ad/.

Fea, John D. *Was America Founded as a Christian Nation? A Historical Introduction.* Louisville: Westminster John Knox Press, 2016.

Ferdinand II and Isabella I. "Edict of the Expulsion of the Jews (1492)." Foundation for the Advancement of Sephardic Studies and Culture. http://www.sephardicstudies.org/decree.html.

Garcia-Treto, Francisco O. "The Lesson of the Gibeonites: A Proposal for Dialogic Attention as a Strategy for Reading the Bible." In *Hispanic/Latino theology: Challenge and Promise.* Edited by Ada Maria Isasi-Diaz and Fernando F. Segovia, 73–85. Minneapolis: Fortress Press, 1996.

Goetz. *The Baptism of Early Virginia: How Christianity Created Race.* Baltimore: Johns Hopkins University Press, 2012.

Goldenberg, David M. *The Curse of Ham: Race and Slavery in Early Judaism, Christianity, and Islam.* Princeton, NJ: Princeton University Press, 2003.

———. "Review: The Development of the Idea of Race: Classical Paradigms and Medieval Elaborations." *International Journal of the Classical Tradition* 5, no. 4 (Spring 1999): 561–70.

Gorski, Philip S., and Samuel L. Perry. *The Flag and the Cross: White Christian Nationalism and the Threat to American Democracy.* New York: Oxford University Press, 2022.

Grosfoguel, Ramón. "The Structure of Knowledge in Westernized Universities: Epistemic Racism/Sexism and the Four Genocides/Epistemicides of the Long 16th Century." *Human Architecture: Journal of the Sociology of Self-Knowledge* 11, no. 1 (Fall 2013): 73–90.

Hanau, Shira. "Pennsylvania Republican Doug Mastriano Enters Race for Governor with a Shofar Blast." *Jewish Telegraph Agency.* January 9, 2022. https://www.jta.org/2022/01/09/politics/pennsylvania-republican-doug-mastriano-enters-race-for-governor-with-a-shofar-blast.

Hanke, Lewis. *The Spanish Struggle: Justice in the Conquest of America.* Philadelphia: University of Pennsylvania Press, 1949.

Harris, Antipas L. *Is Christianity a White Man's Religion? How the Bible Is Good News for People of Color.* Downers Grove, IL: IVP, 2020.

Hawkins, J. Russell. *The Bible Told Them So: How Southern Evangelicals Fought to Preserve White Supremacy.* New York: Oxford University Press, 2021.

Holocaust Memorial Day Trust. "6 May 1933: Looting of the Institute of Sexology." https://www.hmd.org.uk/resource/6-may-1933-looting-of-the-institute-of-sexology/.

Jenkins, Jack. "Survey: 'Great Replacement' Belief Correlates with Christian Nationalist Views." *Religion News Service.* October 12, 2021. https://religionnews.com/2021/10/12/survey-christian-nationalist-view-of-history-correlates-with-support-for-racist-conspiracy-theory/.

Jennings, Willie James. *The Christian Imagination: Theology and the Origins of Race.* New Haven, CT: Yale University Press, 2010.

Johnson, Paul Elliott. *I The People: The Rhetoric of Conservative Populism in the United States* Birmingham: University of Alabama Press, 2022.

Jones, Robert P. "Columbus Day or Indigenous Peoples Day? The Damaging Christian 'Doctrine of Discovery' at the Heart of the American Identity Crisis." October 8, 2021. https://robertpjones.substack.com/p/columbus-day-or-indigenous-peoples.

Keel, Terence. *Divine Variations: How Christian Thought Became Racial Science*. Stanford, CA: Stanford University Press, 2018.

———. "Religion, Polygenism, and the Early Science of Human Origins." *History of the Human Sciences* 26, no. 2 (2013): 3–32.

Kidd, Colin. *The Forging of Races: Race and Scripture in the Protestant Atlantic World, 1600–2000*. Cambridge: Cambridge University Press, 2006.

Lemon, Jason. "Kari Lake Supporters Reenact Biblical Battle of Jericho in Maricopa Protest." *Newsweek*. November 13, 2022. https://www.newsweek.com/kari-lake-supporters-reenact-biblical-battle-jericho-maricopa-protest-1759158.

Loh, Matthew. "Rep. Lauren Boebert Joked That Jesus Didn't Have Enough AR-15s to Save His Life as She Defended Gun Rights." *Business Insider*. June 15, 2022. https://www.businessinsider.com/lauren-boebert-jesus-didnt-have-ar-15s-save-his-life-2022-6.

Maldonaldo-Torres, Nelson. "AAR Centennial Roundtable: Religion, Conquest, and Race in the Foundations of the Modern/Colonial World." *Journal of the American Academy of Religion* 82, no. 3 (September 2014): 636–65.

———. "Race, Religion and Ethics in the Modern/Colonial World." *Journal of Religious Ethics* 42, no. 4 (2014): 691–711.

Marshall, John. *Johnson v. McIntosh*, 21 U.S. 543 (1823). Accessed at https://supreme.justia.com/cases/federal/us/21/543/#tab-opinion-1922743.

Mather, Cotton. *A Good Master Well Served: A Brief Discourse on the Necessary Properties and Practices of a Good Servant*. Boston: B. Green and J. Allen, 1696.

———. *Magnalia Christi Americana: Or, the Ecclesiastical History of New-England*. London: Thomas Parkhurst, 1702. https://archive.org/details/magnaliachristia00math.

———. *The Negro Christianized. An Essay to Excite and Assist That Good Work, the Instruction of Negro-Servants in Christianity*. Boston: B. Green, 1706.

Miller, Robert J., Jacinta Ruru, Larissa Behrendt, and Tracey Lindberg. *Discovering Indigenous Lands: The Doctrine of Discovery in the English Colonies*. New York: Oxford University Press, 2010.

Newcomb, Steven T. *Pagans in the Promised Land: Decoding the Doctrine of Christian Discovery*. Golden, CO: Fulcrum Publishing, 2008.

Parfitt, Tudor. *The Lost Tribes of Israel: The History of a Myth*. London: Weidenfeld & Nicolson, 2002.

PRRI Staff. "Competing Visions of America: An Evolving Identity or a Culture Under Attack? Findings from the 2021 American Values Survey." *PRRI*. November 1, 2021. https://www.prri.org/research/competing-visions-of-america-an-evolving-identity-or-a-culture-under-attack/#_ftn3.

Rodríguez Ortiz, Omar. "'I Have Only Begun to Fight': Here Are 4 Takeways from DeSantis' Victory Speech." *Miami Herald*. November 9, 2022. https://www.miamiherald.com/news/politics-government/election/article268489932.html.

Shohat, Ella. "Taboo Memories, Diasporic Visions: Columbus, Palestine, and Arab-Jews." In Ella Shohat, *Taboo Memories: Diasporic Voices*, 201–32. Durham, NC: Duke University Press, 2006.

Staff. "Governor DeSantis Announces Legislative Proposal to Stop W.O.K.E. Activism and Critical Race Theory in Schools and Corporations." *FlGov*. Dec. 15, 2021. https://www.flgov.com/2021/12/15/governor-desantis-announces-legislative-proposal-to-stop-w-o-k-e-activism-and-critical-race-theory-in-schools-and-corporations/.

Stanton, Andrew. "Native Americans Made 'Sacrifice' for 'Our Right to Worship Jesus': Taylor." *Newsweek*. May 21, 2022. https://www.newsweek.com/native-americans-made-sacrifice-our-right-worship-jesus-taylor-1708855.

Stephens, Alexander. "Cornerstone Speech." American Battlefield Trust. March 21, 1861. https://www.battlefields.org/learn/primary-sources/cornerstone-speech.

Thomas, Kendall. "*Rouge Et Noir* Reread: A Popular Constitutional History of the Angelo Herndon Case." In *Critical Race Theory: The Key Writings That Formed the Movement*. Edited by Kimberlé Crenshaw, Neil Gotanda, Gary Peller, and Kendall Thomas, 465–94. New York: New Press, 1995.

Tinker, Tink. *Missionary Conquest: The Gospel and Native American Cultural Genocide*. Minneapolis, Fortress, 1993.

Tisby, Jemar. *The Color of Compromise: The Truth about the American Church's Complicity in Racism*. Grand Rapids, MI: Zondervan, 2019.

Torba, Andrew, and Andrew Isker. *Christian Nationalism: A Biblical Guide for Taking Dominion and Discipling Nations*. Gab (self-published), 2022.

Underhill, John. "Newes from America; Or, a New and Experimentall Discoverie of New England" (1638). University of Nebraska, Lincoln, Digital Commons. https://digitalcommons.unl.edu/cgi/viewcontent.cgi?article=1037&context=etas.

Vigna, Paul. "'We Love Israel More Than Most Jews': Doug Mastriano Wife's Response Draws Scrutiny." *PennLive*. October 30, 2022. https://www.pennlive.com/elections/2022/10/we-love-israel-more-than-most-jews-doug-mastriano-wifes-response-draws-scrutiny.html.

West, Delno C., and August Kling, eds. *The Libro de las profecias of Christopher Columbus*. Gainesville: University Press of Florida, 1991.

Winthrop, John. "A Model of Christian Charity" (1630). The American Yawp Reader. https://www.americanyawp.com/reader/colliding-cultures/john-winthrop-dreams-of-a-city-on-a-hill-1630/.

Chapter 4

Discipleship or Duplicity?
A Christian "No" to White Christian Nationalism

Anna Floerke Scheid

My motivation for the work of this chapter is admittedly not merely disinterested scholarship. As an academic specializing in ethics, theology, and religious studies, as a Catholic scholar frequently engaged in what we call "public theology" (theological and religious critical analysis of current social, cultural, and political issues), and as a professor who teaches classes on the intersections of religion with civic and political life, I have grown increasingly alarmed and repulsed by the renewed power, influence, and violence of white Christian nationalism in the US. This chapter is, first and foremost, a firm "No" to white Christian nationalism, to its racism, nativism, xenophobia, anti-Blackness, and antisemitism, from a Catholic scholar who refuses to cede the inclusive and potentially life-giving narrative of Christianity, which the Christian tradition calls the Gospel, or the "good news." Indeed, Christianity should be *good news*.

In *Taking America Back for God: Christian Nationalism in the United States*, sociologists Andrew Whitehead and Samuel Perry define Christian nationalism as "a cultural framework—a collection of myths, traditions, symbols, narratives, and value systems—that idealizes and advocates a fusion of Christianity with American civic life."[1] They also affirm that Christian nationalism does not represent the overall Christian tradition. Instead "the 'Christianity' of Christian nationalism is of a particular sort"; representing "something more than religion . . . it includes nativism, white supremacy, patriarchy, and heteronormativity, along with divine sanction for authoritarian control and militarism. It is as ethnic and political as it is religious."[2] In their research, Whitehead and Perry have found that Christian nationalists are overwhelmingly white, politically conservative, and Evangelical Christians,[3] though many in my own Catholic religious tradition also embrace or accommodate it.[4] Christianity is good news. White Christian nationalism? That is bad news.

One question I begin to address in this chapter is: How does a religious tradition that, at its core, expresses faith in a loving God who creates human beings in the Divine image[5] and invests all human beings with inherent value, worth, and dignity come not only to overlap with but also be responsible for creating and promoting a virulently and violently racist and antisemitic society in which white Christian nationalism captures so many people's imaginations? A related question is: How has the Christian tradition managed in the US to survive authentically as a religious belief system that promotes this God-given dignity and opposes racism, antisemitism, and white Christian nationalism?

Key to answering each of these questions is to insist that Christianity in the US is no monolith, nor has it been at least since the first Africans brought here against their will nevertheless freely chose to embrace the Trinitarian God of Christian doctrine: Father, Son, and Holy Spirit. Therefore, this chapter will trace two trajectories of Christian thought and practice. The two trajectories are similar to what Catholic womanist theologian M. Shawn Copeland on the one hand calls "discipleship," which I think of as an authentic Christianity that embraces Jesus's praxis of the Reign of God for the poor and oppressed, and "duplicity,"[6] or a Christianity that has been distorted to promote the economic, cultural, and political interests of the powerful, on the other hand. The former is the Christianity of the enslaved and their decedents and allies today. The latter is the Christianity of colonizers, enslavers, and white nationalists in the past and present. These two trajectories stand in cacophonous tension in the US today, just as they have throughout US history. To explore them, I will discuss the distortions of Christian theology that enabled colonialism and the slave trade, the embrace of the good news of Christian faith by enslaved Africans in the Americas, and how these two oppositional Christianities function in the US today.

WHITENESS, SALVATION BY CONQUEST, AND THE NEW "CHOSEN PEOPLE"

I was once asked a provocative question: If you could go back in time and change one moment in history, what would it be? The question asks how we would transform our present world through changing the past. Although it was difficult for me to pinpoint a precise moment I would change or a decision I would alter, the clear answer was that I would choose to stop Europeans from colonizing the rest of the world. The commitment of European leaders to establish and carry out colonial projects (including but not limited to the transatlantic slave trade) set Europe on the path to invent race and a racial hierarchy to promote their cultural, economic, and political interests. It was among the most consequential choices for mass dehumanization in written history.

Colonial conquest and the Christian religion became intimately intertwined in the so-called New World. Whether in English Puritan settlements in North America or among Spanish Catholic conquistadors in the Southern Hemisphere, Christian theology became a justifying force for colonialization. In this way, Yale Divinity School scholar of theology and Africana studies Willie James Jennings argues that Christianity quickly and dramatically lost its way. Turning away from Christian discipleship rooted in communion with and fundamental equality among fellow believers, Christianity as colonizing ideology developed a "diseased social imagination."[7] Jennings's argument is a tour de force, critically important, stunningly beautifully written, and far too complex for me to summarize in full here. Nevertheless, it is critical to understand how whiteness and Christianity played significant overlapping roles in justifying the theft (of land and resources), exploitation, and enslavement indicative of colonialism.

Initially, Jennings demonstrates that colonialism required both physical and mental dislocation, as human identity was divorced from the land that particular peoples occupied and transferred to skin color. This dislocation amounts to a "profound and devastating alteration."[8] Tying identity to skin color meant that identity could travel with a person to new lands where identity-as-skin-color would remain fixed, even as the relationship with the land was radically transformed. Whether white-skinned European explorer or dark-skinned kidnaped African slave, identity remained static from place to place, as did the hierarchy in which lighter skin color was presumed to indicate divine preference or election, as well as intellectual and cultural superiority over darker skin color. Significantly, this meant that lighter-skinned (i.e., white) *migrants* could claim superiority to and authority over lands historically inhabited by darker-skinned (i.e., brown and black) native and Indigenous people. White skin dominated all other skin colors over the whole world, regardless of who might have an original claim to the particular land being inhabited, settled, or colonized.[9] It is difficult to overemphasize how strongly this alteration from land-based identity to skin-color-based identity supports white nationalism. It allows white people in North America, a landmass to which they are not indigenous, to uphold the delusion that their claim to belonging in the US is stronger than that of other racial or ethnic groups.

Colonial elites relied not only on the notion that white skin indicated intellectual superiority but also that Christianity indicated religio-cultural superiority. Christian scholars played a significant role in developing a twofold theological rationale that would justify the dehumanization inherent in slavery and colonial exploitation. First, with the help of theologians, and even the Pope,[10] colonizers imagined themselves as agents of God's providential plan to spread the Gospel. They could salve any guilty conscience by resting assured that their conquest was propelled not merely by a lust for gain but by a "soteriological motive"[11]: By bringing Christianity to new lands and people, they were saving the souls of the damned heathens. After describing having "taken [West Africans] by force, and some by barter," one chronicler of colonialism and the slave trade boasts, "A large number of these have been converted to the Catholic faith, and it is hoped by the help of divine mercy that if such progress be continued with them, either those peoples will be converted to the faith or at least the souls of many of them will be gained for Christ."[12] In other words, some of those enslaved had converted to Christianity, and enslavers were hopeful they would be able to enslave and convert even more.

The second aspect of the theological rationale for colonialism remains particularly salient as we consider the present problem of white Christian nationalism and its connection to not only anti-Black racism but also antisemitism. While Europeans invented race to justify slavery and colonialism, imagining a racial hierarchy with themselves at the top was not the first instance of European Christians Othering and hierarchically ordering people for cultural, economic, and political purposes. European Jews had been excluded or marginalized for centuries on specious claims that they were "Christ-killers." Christian hatred of Jews manifest in ghettoizing, pogroms, and other forms of dehumanization and violence, which culminated in the Holocaust. The antisemitic tropes, myths, and stereotypes generated continue to function as fodder for harassing, intimidating, and justifying violence against Jews in the US today.

Antisemitism throughout Christian history has also taken the form of theology, especially the idea sometimes known as replacement theology or, more formally, supersessionism. Supersessionism holds that that Christians replaced Jews as God's chosen people, that is, that the particular place that the Jewish people occupy in the metaphorical heart of God is now the place of Christians. Jews have been exiled once again. Jennings calls supersessionism "the most decisive and central theological distortion that exists in the church."[13] When European Christians already saturated with centuries of antisemitic replacement theology found themselves upon the shores of the Americas, the temptation to see themselves as God's new chosen people entering a new Promised Land proved too great for them to resist.

While today, supersessionism is largely viewed as heretical within both Catholic and Protestant Christian theology, it lingers in the lived practice and imagination of US Christians. White Christian nationalism is one of its descendants. Rev. Dr. Kelly Brown Douglas of Union Theological Seminary explains the development of Manifest Destiny as a theological perspective among early American white theologians. She demonstrates that Manifest Destiny, or "America's divine calling,"[14] was supersessionist. It involved an amalgam of ideas from the Hebrew scriptures, in which God leads the Israelites into the Promised Land, superimposed onto white Protestant colonizers in New England. Early American theologians imagined that white Christian Americans were the new Israel, God's chosen elect, and that the US was the new Promised Land flowing with milk and honey, in other words, promising prosperity for the chosen people. The Puritans and their descendants did not see themselves as stealing land from native peoples but as claiming a homeland that God intended specifically for them.

Whiteness and Christianity were both viewed as necessary indicators of chosenness or Divine election to occupy and rule the Promised Land. As Jennings notes, with the new racial hierarchy emergent in the age of conquest and the old sense of Christian religious superiority over Jews, "the [white] body of the [Christian] European would be the compass marking divine election."[15] To be chosen, and thus to have a claim to the promises of Manifest Destiny, one needed to be white and Christian.

In the wake of colonialism and conquest, through the US revolutionary and civil wars, and well into the mid-twentieth century, American Christians continued to voice perspectives consistent with these two theological developments (salvation-motivated conquest and supersessionism) to justify a host of practices, from slavery, to Western expansion, to Jim Crow laws, and even to "Stand Your Ground Laws" today. Thus, early American Christian theologians like Josiah Strong easily promoted the idea that "North America [would] be the great home of the Anglo-Saxon, the principal seat of his power, the center of his life and influence."[16] Here I discuss three representative theological perspectives of the duplicitous and distorted trajectory of American Christian history that continue to animate white Christian nationalism: that of Cotton Mather, that of Jonathan Edwards, and that of a representative group of mid-twentieth-century pro-segregation preachers.

Seventeenth-century Puritan minister and enslaver Cotton Mather was explicit in employing the soteriological justification for slavery.[17] He believed slavery to be a condition established by God as part of the natural law. He also suggested that converting the enslaved to Christianity might have the presumably happy effect of "dulcifying and mollifying" the enslaved, who, "if they are faithful and honest servants, and if they do cheerfully what they do, because the Lord Jesus Christ has bid them to do it," can be assured that "it can't be long before they die, and then they shall rest from all their labors, and all their troubles, and they shall be companions of angels in the glories of a paradise."[18] Such remarks prompted the influential founder of Black liberation theology, James Cone, roughly two centuries later, to categorize Mather as among those white Christian theologians who "interpreted the gospel according to the cultural and political interests of white people."[19] Christian theology, for Mather, proved a powerful resource for shoring up his own privilege and position at the expense of those for whom he claimed to desire salvation.

Theologian and minister Jonathan Edwards is considered the most influential Christian thinker in early New England. He is known to have enslaved people and to have justified slavery on biblical grounds. Yet Edwards "preached and wrote little on the subject of slavery."[20] For James Cone, it is this absence that shocks an authentic Christian conscience. Cone marvels at the capacity of early American theologians to "do theology as if slavery did not exist." Edwards "could preach and write theological treatises on total depravity, unconditional election, limited atonement, irresistible grace, and the perseverance of the saints without the slightest hint of how these issues related to human bondage."[21] Yet, even as the condition of the enslaved made evidently little impression on Edwards, he was convinced of America's exceptional status in the eyes of God. Edwards's experience of "The Great Awakening" of Christian faith in New England led him to conclude that America was the inevitable site of the Second Coming of Christ.[22] Edwards thus affirms the notion of America as the Promised Land and white Christians as those destined to inhabit it. That American citizenship would be for white people was a given; however, the enslaved, even though they interacted with Edwards every day, were largely invisible in his imagined coming Kingdom of God in the Promised Land of the US.

Finally, I turn to a flurry of Christian theology written in the mid-twentieth century in the form of speeches and sermons that argued that segregation is divinely willed. These sermons are the theological inheritance of those who justified colonialism and slavery, of thinkers like Mather and Edwards, among others. In claiming their inheritance, these mid-century ministers embraced the ideology of white Christian nationalism. While this is certainly not a comprehensive analysis of such pro-segregation sermons, even a cursory reading reveals three common themes. First, pro-segregation Christians viewed the very presence of Black people in North America as a sin. For example, Carey Daniel claims that "God is the original segregationist" because he "put the black race on a huge continent to themselves segregated from other races by oceans of water."[23] That Black people do not all currently live on that continent is a violation of God's will because that is where God put them. Daniel's theological argument makes no reference, nor acknowledges in the slightest, the fact that the ancestors of most African Americans had been brought to North America against their will by force of arms. Similarly, in a sermon titled "God's Plan for the Races," Harold Smith claims that "God gave Africa to our negro friends."[24] Smith admits that the forcible removal of Africans from their homes, the slave trade, and the centuries of slaving in the US were sinful acts perpetrated by the ancestors of white Americans. He argues that white people should never have engaged in the trade of human beings. However, his reasoning suggests that the sinfulness of the slave trade lies in its defiance against "God's plan for segregation," rather than the monumental affront it represents to Black freedom, humanity, and dignity. Smith suggests that the fight to desegregate was a kind of punishment that God inflicted on white people: "We are paying for the sins of our forefathers" who brought Africans out of their proper divinely ordained place, namely Africa.[25] Note that Smith here is suggesting that those suffering under the historical sins of chattel slavery are not so much the descendants of the enslaved but the descendants of slave owners. What is plainly Black suffering and the imposed indignity of segregation is really, for Smith, white suffering in having to bear the supposed indignity of *de*segregation. For Smith, desegregation is not only against the will of God, but it is also allowable by God only as a punishment for white people.

Second, the pro-segregation sermons see no contradiction between the claim that God had ordained Black people to live on the continent of Africa and white people's claim to belong on the continent of North America. If God divinely ordained certain races to stay on certain masses of land, then surely members of the white race ought to live on the continent of Europe. But this suggestion is not even hinted at in the pro-segregation sermons. Why the dissonant leap in logic? The way that the sermons employ the Hebrew scriptures points to an answer: The white ministers have inherited the supersessionism of their colonial ancestors. They see themselves as having replaced the Israelites as God's chosen people, and they see America as white Christians' Promised Land. G. T. Gillespie provides the analogy, arguing that as God instructed Abraham to segregate Hebrews from Gentiles, whites (now in the role of the chosen Hebrews) are to remain separated from all other races (cast in the analogous role of separated Gentiles).[26] America is the land set apart for white Christians; God intended the US to be a white Christian nation.

Third, the sermons all preach that interracial marriage is a grave sin. It is painfully clear in reading the sermons that the white ministers' real fears are less about divine wrath and more about sexual relationships between whites and Blacks and the racially mixed offspring that would result from such unions. The sermons drip with a terror of losing or diluting the imagined purity of whiteness through interracial marriage and what that might mean for the Promised Land for white Christians. Carey Daniel accuses those who oppose segregation of wanting only "one race" that would "mongrelize" his "children and grandchildren."[27] Harold Smith echoes these fears, arguing that desegregation and interracial marriage will make America a "negroid nation of people,"[28] rather than a nation of the racially "pure" people intended by "God's plan for the races."

The theological justifications for colonialism and slavery, Cotton Mather's instructions for catechizing the enslaved, Jonathan Edwards's tendency to ignore human bondage, and mid-twentieth-century pro-segregation preachers all follow the same trajectory of building a duplicitous and distorted Christianity that protects the interests of the powerful and aims to keep America white.

ANOTHER WAY OF BEING AN AMERICAN CHRISTIAN

To voice the unequivocal "No" to white Christian nationalism today and to embrace authentic Christian discipleship in the midst of theological distortion, is necessary. It is nourishing to remember there has always been another Christian history being lived out in the United States. There has always been a story of faith in an inclusive and loving God, growing against all odds, bearing witness to Jesus's preaching of a Kingdom of God for the poor, the vulnerable, and the oppressed, in opposition to an empire for manifesting white power. Black Christians in the so-called New World developed faith in Jesus, whom they believed to be the Son of the same God who had delivered Israelite slaves from bondage in Egypt. In Jesus, they saw their liberator and the inspiration for their survival and resistance. M. Shawn Copeland calls this faith the "dark wisdom" of the enslaved.[29]

Through meticulous research, Copeland traces the faith development of enslaved Christians. As we saw in the example of Cotton Mather, ministers preached to the enslaved a hopeless message that "distort[ed] the love command of Jesus for the sake of profit and racial privilege."[30] They were told that their "bondage [was] part of a natural and divinely ordained social order in which masters were 'God's overseers' and slaves were to obey these masters as if they were obeying God."[31] The enslaved were assured that their condition was willed by God, as they were the inheritors of the biblical curse of Ham, whose lot was "abject bondage."[32]

Why would the enslaved accept such a debasing theological message? How could any of this be "good news" for them, such that they would wish to embrace Christianity as salvific? To argue that they hoped for rewards in a heavenly afterlife, as described by Mather, is too facile a conclusion and, indeed, contrary to the evidence. Black American theologians demonstrate that the enslaved found in Christianity, and perhaps especially in Jesus's crucifixion (with which they could readily relate given the scope and depth of their own suffering) and resurrection, a source of comfort and hope. Perhaps more importantly, though, they also found a source of inspiration to survive and resist the message of, as James Baldwin put it, "a society which spelled out with brutal clarity and in as many ways as possible that you were a worthless human being."[33]

Plumbing the depths of the early African American spirituals, Copeland finds evidence for a faith that confirmed the dignity and humanity of the enslaved. The earliest Black American Christians found that Jesus "understood them and their suffering like no one else. They believed that he was one with them in their otherness and affliction, that he would help them to negotiate this world with righteous anger and dignity."[34] Copeland demonstrates how, despite often being deprived of literacy, the enslaved were nevertheless able to learn and understand that the duplicitous theology of the slavers was a distortion of the Gospel and that the Gospel was indeed good news for the poor, the afflicted, and the vulnerable. Jesus had come to set captives free.[35] The good news is that "God is a heart-fixer and a mind-regulator" who has the power "to grant identity and liberation to an oppressed and humiliated people."[36] In other words, the enslaved discovered affirmation in the Christian Gospel that they were not who white people told them they were; rather, they were valuable and beloved.

Describing his own Christian faith experience in similar terms, Cone notes that the white Christians of his youth in Arkansas "did everything within their power to define black reality, to tell us who we were—and their definition, of course, extended no further than their social, political, and economic interests. They tried to make us believe that God created black people to be white people's servants."[37] Cone shows that the enslaved embraced Christianity because in it they found proof of their humanity and dignity, power for survival, and hope for freedom in the midst of demeaning and deadly white power. "Black slaves," argues Cone, "believed that just as God had delivered Moses and the Israelites from Egyptian bondage, God also will deliver black people from American slavery."[38] Faith in the God of Moses was a form of "self-affirmation"[39] that contrasted jarringly with white ideas about Black personhood. Although the faith of both Black and white people bore a single name—Christianity—they professed and practiced starkly different religions. They shared sacred texts, narratives, and even forms of religious practice. Yet Cone remarks, "When the master and the slave spoke of God, they could not possibly be referring to the same reality."[40]

Even as Jonathan Edwards was largely ignoring human bondage in America and enjoying its privileges in his own home, even as he preached a revival of faith to white Christians, and later even as white ministers declared that God was a segregationist who found the presence of Black people in

North America to be a sin, even in the midst of these theological distortions, Black American Christians embraced Jesus of Nazareth, the Jewish Son of the God of Exodus. They believed that God raised Jesus from the dead as vindication of Jesus's proclamation of the good news of liberation and as God's own judgment upon the sinful exercise of state-sanctioned violence carried out by affixing the body of Jesus to a tree. The enduring faith of the enslaved and segregated, the raped, and the lynched should give us serious pause as we seek to understand Christianity in the US today. The inheritance of Black Christian theology is one of discipleship that rejects racism, xenophobia, and nativism. The inheritance of white Christian nationalism either implicitly or explicitly not only embraces these but also depends on a duplicitous, distorted, and ultimately dehumanizing theology that is not good news.

CONCLUSION: TWO CHRISTIANITIES TODAY

In a longer project, one could continue to trace the contours of these two theological trajectories within American Christian history right into the present day. The distorted path would include secessionist Christians in the era of the Civil War, fighting to maintain the slavocracy they believed to be ordained by God. It would flow through the period of segregationist preaching described herein, and it would find resonance in the 1980s with the Moral Majority. In recent years, we have rediscovered these distortions and begun to call them white Christian nationalism. We saw the symbols of this distorted theology on January 6, 2021, as hundreds of people stormed the US Capitol—the American flag alongside the flag of the Confederacy, banners claiming, "Jesus is my Savior, Trump is my President" (as though these are intrinsically connected), a large wooden cross and a large wooden gallows, and perhaps the perfect symbolic image of white Christian nationalism: a massive picture of a white, blue-eyed, blond-haired Jesus wearing a red MAGA hat. For the rioters of January 6, Jesus is white, Jesus is American, and Jesus votes for Donald Trump.

The other trajectory of American Christian history is less sensationalist. In a longer project we could find traces of it in the post–Civil War Protestant social Gospel movement of Walter Rauschenbusch and the early twentieth-century Catholic Worker Movement of Dorothy Day and Peter Maurin. We would find it flourishing in the theological writings of Dr. Martin Luther King Jr. and in the practices of the Civil Rights Movement. Today it is struggling for theological airtime wherever Christianity enters the public sphere. It can be found among "Christians against Christian Nationalism."[41] It is thriving in academic theology and religious ethics where despite the best efforts of cultural warriors to destroy critical race theory, a multiracial community of scholars in religion and theology embrace its tools to understand and analyze white privilege and the long-lasting effects of unequal power dynamics. Their scholarship takes anti-Black racism and inequality by the horns as part and parcel of serious structural problems in the political and economic systems of the US, which demand serious structural solutions. Outside of academia, Rev. Dr. William Barber's Poor People's Campaign[42] and the Moral Mondays Movement are the inheritors of the trajectory of Christianity that is good news for the poor and vulnerable, for people of color, for LGBTQIA people, and for all allies who see in Jesus Christ the liberator of humankind from all forms of humiliation, dehumanization, and captivity.

For Christians who voice a "No" to white Christian nationalism, who view it as a heretical perversion of the good news of the Gospel, it is critical that we move from the pews to the public sphere. To live our faith in public in this era will be to oppose explicitly the distorted Christianity of white Christian nationalism that seeks to exclude, marginalize, and disempower millions of American citizens in their own nation and on their own land. This will mean combating new efforts at voter suppression and gerrymandering that seek to disenfranchise people of color so that the white vote can have an outsize influence in elections. It will mean working toward immigration reform that welcomes the stranger, especially those fleeing violence and criminal justice reform that "sets captives free" in the spirit of the Gospel. It will mean efforts to protect the vulnerable from gun violence, food insecurity and hunger, environmental disaster, and all forms of exploitation. It will involve interfaith and multiracial relationship-building and solidarity across difference, based in the Christian belief that all people bear the imprint of God.

NOTES

1. Andrew L. Whitehead and Samuel L. Perry, *Taking America Back for God: Christian Nationalism in the United States* (New York: Oxford University Press, 2020), 10.

2. Whitehead and Perry, *Taking America Back for God*, 10.

3. About 80 percent of Christian nationalists identify as Evangelicals (Whitehead and Perry, *Taking America Back for God*, 42). At the same time, across both *Taking America Back for God* and *The Flag and the Cross*, Gorski, Perry, and Whitehead take pains to point out that although Christian nationalists are overwhelmingly politically conservative, white, and Evangelical, it does not follow that to be a white Evangelical is to be a Christian nationalist. In other words, Christian nationalism is not synonymous with political conservatism or Evangelicalism. Moreover, there is a significant minority of white Evangelicals resisting the growing trend of Christian nationalism taking hold in their communities. See Whitehead and Perry, *Taking America Back for God*, 32, and Gorski and Perry, *The Flag and the Cross: White Christian*

Nationalism and the Threat to American Democracy (New York: Oxford University Press, 2022), 10.

4. Whitehead and Perry demonstrate that about 30 percent of those who "accommodate" Christian nationalism (which they describe as "leaning toward accepting it") are Catholics (Whitehead and Perry, *Taking America Back for God*, 33–34).

5. Gen. 1:27.

6. M. Shawn Copeland, *Knowing Christ Crucified: The Witness of African American Religious Experience* (Maryknoll, NY: Orbis Books, 2018).

7. Willie James Jennings, *The Christian Imagination: Theology and the Origins of Race* (New Haven, CT: Yale University Press, 2010), 9.

8. Jennings, *The Christian Imagination*, 40.

9. Jennings, *The Christian Imagination*, 30–31.

10. See, for example, "Bull Romanus Pontifex, January 8, 1455," issued by Pope Nicholas V.

11. Jennings, *The Christian Imagination*, 31. See also 27 on fifteenth-century Portuguese Prince Henry's "holy" motives for conquest.

12. Papal Bull of Pope Nicholas V, quoted in Jennings, *The Christian Imagination*, 27.

13. Jennings, *The Christian Imagination*, 33

14. Kelly Brown Douglas, *Stand Your Ground: Black Bodies and the Justice of God* (Maryknoll, NY: Orbis Books, 2015), 93.

15. Jennings, *The Christian Imagination*, 33.

16. Josiah Strong, *Our Country: Its Possible Future and Its Present Crisis* (New York: Baker & Taylor Co., 1885), 159–60, quoted in Douglas, *Stand Your Ground*, 94.

17. Cotton Mather, "The Negro Christianized: An Essay to Excite and Assist That Good Work, the Instruction of Negro-Servants in Christianity" (1706), Zea E-Books in American Studies, University of Nebraska, Lincoln, Digital Commons.

18. Mather, "The Negro Christianized," 20–21. Exclamation point in the original.

19. James H. Cone, *God of the Oppressed*, rev. ed. (Maryknoll, NY: Orbis Books, 1997), 43.

20. Richard Anderson, "Jonathan Edwards, Sr.," *Princeton and Slavery Project*, https://slavery.princeton.edu/stories/jonathan-edwards.

21. Cone, *God of the Oppressed*, 44.

22. Douglas, *Stand Your Ground*, 14.

23. Carey Daniel, "God the Original Segregationist" (1954), Digital Collections at the University of Southern Mississippi.

24. Harold Smith, "God's Plan for the Races," (1950), 4, Digital Collections at the University of Arkansas.

25. Smith, "God's Plan for the Races," 5.

26. G. T. Gillespie, "A Christian View on Segregation" (1954), 6, University of Mississippi eGrove, Pamphlets and Broadsides.

27. Daniel, "God the Original Segregationist," 6–7.

28. Smith, "God's Plan for the Races," 15.

29. Copeland, *Knowing Christ Crucified*, 3.

30. Copeland, *Knowing Christ Crucified*, 8.

31. Copeland, *Knowing Christ Crucified*, 11.
32. Copeland, *Knowing Christ Crucified*, 11.
33. James Baldwin, "A Letter to My Nephew," *The Progressive Magazine*, December 1, 1962, https://progressive.org/magazine/letter-nephew/.
34. Copeland, *Knowing Christ Crucified*, 26.
35. See Lk 4:16–18.
36. Cone, *God of the Oppressed*, 21.
37. Cone, *God of the Oppressed*, 2.
38. Cone, *God of the Oppressed*, 10.
39. Cone, *God of the Oppressed*, 11.
40. Cone, *God of the Oppressed*, 10.
41. For more information on this important organization, see their website at https://www.christiansagainstchristiannationalism.org/statement.
42. For more information on this important organization, see their website at https://www.poorpeoplescampaign.org.

Chapter 5

White Christians Warring against Democracy

A Long History

Joe Feagin

In a famous address to the 1992 Republican National Convention, the white right-wing politician, public commentator, and future presidential candidate Patrick Buchanan insisted that "there is a religious war going on in this country. It is a cultural war, as critical to the kind of nation we shall be as was the Cold War itself, for this war is for the soul of America."[1] His address was well received, with boisterous cheering from a mostly white Christian crowd of Republicans. In a 1991 commentary, Buchanan had previously insisted that "our Judeo-Christian values" had to be "preserved and our Western heritage is going to be handed down to future generations and not dumped on some landfill called multiculturalism."[2] For him, the relevant US heritage here is white, Christian, and European, as he had made clear elsewhere: "If we had to take a million immigrants in, say, Zulus next year, or Englishmen, and put them in Virginia, what group would be easier to assimilate and would cause less problems for the people of Virginia? There is nothing wrong with us sitting down and arguing that issue that we are a European country, English-speaking country."[3]

In these 1990s commentaries, Buchanan aggressively articulates what has gradually become the central vision of the contemporary Republican party—white Christian nationalism as a bulwark against the current and coming racial demographic and voter change often termed the "browning of America." This political shift in the contemporary Republican Party has been so great that influential political commentator Kevin Phillips argued it is now the "first religious party in U.S. history," one that is a theocratic Christian threat to the US.[4]

This country was built, and continues to be built, on white Christian nationalism, though its face and structure have mutated somewhat over time. Over the course of my eight-plus decades, the white evangelical Christianity—a key component of this white Christian nationalist reality and threat—that I have experienced has changed significantly. In my first couple of decades, the white evangelical Christianity I experienced in East Texas was, for the most part, quietly and routinely linked to white nationalism. Whites around me were generally accepting of their unchallenged white racial status and privilege in the extensive Jim Crow segregation where I grew up. When I left the Deep South part of Texas in 1960, however, this untroubled white privilege was being increasingly, sometimes successfully, challenged.

As organized Black civil rights protests against this institutionally racist system in the South grew, much of that buttressed by Black evangelical morality, the white evangelical Christianity I had experienced in those early decades transmogrified into something quite different. Although important aspects remained similar over subsequent decades, there have been dramatic shifts in the way in which that white evangelical Christianity has become more explicitly supportive of the country's increasingly overt white nationalist framing and politics. While white fears of major racial change were once disproportionately concentrated in the South, as the desegregating 1960s gave way to later decades and to a substantial increase in antiracist protests by African Americans and other Americans of color, extensive and intense white fears of major racial change spread nationwide.

WHITE AMERICAN EXCEPTIONALISM: THE COLONIAL ERA

Most contemporary analyses of white Christian nationalism accent the role of ordinary whites, yet this misses the most important creators and maintainers of this antidemocratic reality, *elite white men*. Conspicuous in the history of white Christian nationalism is the central if not exclusive role of elite European-descended men. They have defined and maintained white Christian nationalism. These men had the most power to create and maintain a country that eventually became the internationally dominant US, one with an overarching and extensive system of elite-white-male dominance. Indeed, a major key to understanding the long history of white Christian nationalism is to understand its three foundational features, which have been interlocked and webbed together now over more than four centuries, European (white),

Christian, and nationalist. This substantively intertwined reality can be seen in every historical era, from the early 1600s to recent decades.

Early on, English Puritans colonized New England, and other white Protestant groups established other North American colonies. These early Christian groups were mostly similar in dogmatic religious beliefs, strict morality, and patriarchal institutions. All were led by elite white men. The colonial leaders of what eventually became the US constantly framed their views of Europeans (whites) and enslaved African Americans and oppressed Native Americans in biblical, principally Christian, terms.

In 1630, ten ships with hundreds of English Puritans greatly expanded the new Massachusetts Bay colony. An early Christian Founding Father, John Winthrop, was a Puritan lawyer aboard the ship *Arbella* in this fleet.[5] Revealing the early and close connection between European Christianity and emerging American nationalism, Winthrop is famous for articulating an early version of American "exceptionalism," another term for early nationalism. This exceptionalism included the idea that the newly emerging country was *qualitatively* different from others because of its values of liberty, Christian morality, and "democratic" institutions. In a famous part of a sermon that he made either onboard *Arbella* or before it departed, Winthrop made the first recorded statement about this exceptionalism. He concluded that sermon with a metaphorical assertion anticipating well the contemporary concept of the US as the dominant societal model for the world: "The Lord will . . . make us a praise and glory that men shall say of succeeding plantations, 'the Lord make it like that of New England.' For we must consider that we shall be as a *city upon a hill. The eyes of all people are upon us.*"[6] Winthrop and fellow Puritans saw themselves as setting a Christian religious and Eurocentric (English) societal example for "all people." These and other English colonists were building a new societal exceptionalism with its distinctive European American identity. Like many of their white Christian descendants today, they arrogantly viewed themselves as "God's chosen people."[7] From the beginning, this view of European America as exceptional in comparison with other countries has been ethnocentric and white Christian nationalist.

Another societal inheritance from these Christian Puritan groups is a socially schizophrenic practice of political "democracy" that is still with us today. Actually, these Puritans did not support substantial democracy and other values of full-fledged political freedom. They did have some representative institutions in their colonial towns, for white male voters only, and their churches often had elected male ministers.[8] Political officials, again elite white men, were often elected but nonetheless typically viewed themselves as responsible mainly to God, not ordinary colonists. Indeed, in a political statement prepared in the 1640s, Winthrop also insisted that "if we should change from a mixed aristocracy to mere democracy, first we should have no warrant in scripture for it: . . . A democracy is, amongst civil nations, accounted the meanest and worst of all forms of government."[9] It seems clear that US "democracy" today, as in the Puritan era, still blends a commitment to a substantially oligarchical political-economic structure but with a veneer of democratic ideals still far from implemented. For a great many white Americans, now as then, Christian religious justification ("warrant") is more important than fully authentic democracy.

Another important inheritance from this early Christian era is the strong white commitment to societal hierarchy and inequality. Most early Protestant colonists accepted and enforced a strong class, gender, and, quite soon, racial hierarchy. In his *Arbella* sermon, Winthrop had made clear this hierarchical commitment: "God Almighty in his most holy and wise providence, hath so disposed of the condition of mankind, as in all times some must be rich, some poor, some high and eminent in power and dignity; others mean and in submission." Winthrop accented these reasons for his hierarchical fatalism: "First to hold conformity with the rest of his world, being delighted to show forth the glory of [God's] wisdom in the variety and difference of the creatures, and the glory of his power in ordering all these differences for the preservation and good of the whole."[10] That is, the (male) Christian God had ordained the inegalitarian societal hierarchy. Given this Eurocentric hierarchical framework, it is not surprising that by the mid-seventeenth century these early Protestant colonists had imported enslaved African workers and also enslaved local Native Americans. Early on, English colonists used terms like *Christians* for themselves and *heathens* or *negroes* for Africans, African Americans, and Native Americans. They soon were emphasizing skin color and purity of ancestry ("blood").[11]

Again, notice that the colonies that eventually became the US were founded on, from the beginning, a white Christianity emphasizing distinctive white exceptionalism (nationalism). Initially that could be seen well in the Puritans' colonization of Native American territories, including in New England, to create their version of a new Christian nation. Each later European American generation has developed its own version of this white Christian nationalism, but that distinctive Christian exceptionalist framing has always been there.

LATER FOUNDERS: THE JEFFERSONIAN ERA AND A NEW US

Interestingly, many prominent founders of the actual US officially created in the late 1700s, again elite white men, did *not* seek the close ties between evangelical or other Christian religious groups and the new US government that had been sought by Puritan-era leaders or that are sought by most today in the white Christian right. Indeed, in many white Christian groups today, especially those that are evangelical, there is a Christian nationalist story about the US's founding and development in the 1700s that insists the white founders *were* evangelical Christians and that the founding US documents (i.e., the Constitution and Declaration of Independence) are God inspired and grounded in Christian and biblical principles. However, this Christian founding story is largely mythical because neither founding document explicitly mentions Christian or biblical principles, and numerous founders, such as Thomas Jefferson, were deists or otherwise did not identify as Christians. These documents and most founders who crafted them based their political ideas on the secular European tradition, such as the work of John Locke and the tradition of classical liberalism. "It's not that Christian nationalists [today] have a different understanding of American history; it's that they often have an incorrect understanding."[12]

Nonetheless, these elite white founders of the US did work very hard to keep the dominant power and authority at the top of the country's socio-economic hierarchy in the hands of elite white men like themselves. In the eighteenth and early nineteenth centuries many of these famous US founders were authoritarian slaveholders or slavery-associated merchants and professionals who made sure that, politically and legally, most ordinary Americans, especially those enslaved, were submissive to their authority. One difference with today's white Christian nationalists is that these US founders did not need the aggressive validation of mythical Christian symbolism for their authoritarianism and nationalism, such as that of aforementioned Republican leader Patrick Buchanan.

Soon after the country's founding, the white journalist John O'Sullivan coined *Manifest Destiny* for accelerated white nationalism: "Our manifest destiny is to overspread the continent allotted by Providence for the free development of our yearly multiplying millions."[13] Here the white predatory ethic of early colonists is linked by a Catholic Christian to an assertion of a God-given right to take Native American lands—a strong missionary commitment to spread white Christian religion and a Eurocentric nation across the entire continent.

MORE WHITE CHRISTIAN NATIONALISM

The Christian civilization of the US has had an array of discriminatory and other oppressive practices targeting people of color in the name of and for the defense of the "superior white race" from the eighteenth century to the present. Let us now consider the political sphere since the era of 1960s civil rights. Central to white discriminatory practices since then has been the organization and reorganization of what has been called the (white) "southern strategy," the white Republican attempt to preserve white Christian nationalism and hold back the emergence of multiracial democracy in the US. Since well before the 1960s, this pressure for multiracial democracy has been fueled substantially by the demands of the growing number of Americans of color for truly democratic institutions—demands that by the 2040s will definitely be coming from a US population that is a majority not white.

This famous Republican southern strategy (initially called forthrightly "Operation Dixie") began with the 1964 presidential campaign of Senator Barry Goldwater, a vigorous opponent of the 1964 Civil Rights Act who was running on the Republican ticket. Because of his racist political positions, he won just five southern states and lost all but one other state. By 1968, presidential candidate Richard Nixon had reworked this white southern strategy to use somewhat less overtly racist "law-and-order" terminology but for the same purpose of attracting white racist voters in the South and, increasingly, in other states.[14]

Subsequent Republican candidates and presidents like Ronald Reagan also made more use of this barely coded racist law-and-order language, including in famous myths about "welfare queens." A critical racist event for Reagan in the 1980 election campaign, in which he aggressively tried to recruit white voters away from the Democratic Party, was a major speech in Philadelphia, Mississippi, essentially on the graves of civil rights workers murdered in that area during the 1960s civil rights struggles. Reagan thereby accelerated the white southern strategy in his campaign against then southern Democratic president Jimmy Carter. Overall, he made numerous speeches and talks in which he directly appealed to southern white Democrats' racist views. It was clear that Reagan was appealing to white Christian voters in the South (and often elsewhere) who were fearful of the browning of US democracy then emerging from the Black and brown civil rights movements.

Reagan often gave grand political speeches to capture public attention, many with white Christian nationalistic themes linking to earlier eras. At one 1970s conservative political conference he gave a speech underscoring the old Puritan exceptionalism: "Standing on the tiny deck of the *Arbella* in 1630 off the Massachusetts coast, John Winthrop said, 'We will be as a city upon a hill.' . . . Well, we have not dealt falsely with our God. . . . We cannot escape our destiny, nor should we try to do so. The leadership of the free world was thrust upon us. . . . And we are today, the last best hope of man on earth."[15] In this Reagan era, the country saw a repackaging of old American exceptionalism framed with renewed white nationalism, with roots going back to the seventeenth century. Contemporary white Christian nationalism was now strongly established as central to the Republican Party.

In 1976, the majority of white Protestant Evangelicals voted for Democratic Party candidate Jimmy Carter, a "born again" Evangelical. However, because of Carter's liberalism on issues like abortion and women's rights and his lack of support for federal tax exemptions for white religious schools designed to escape desegregation, in 1980 the majority of these moved to support the right-wing Republican candidate, Ronald Reagan. Soon, President Reagan began to orient the Republican Party ever more toward the right-wing goals of white Christian Evangelicals. The 1984 Republican Party platform moved significantly to the right, calling for a "constitutional ban on abortion with no exceptions and the appointment of federal judges who opposed abortion."[16] It also endorsed voluntary school prayer. Jerry Falwell, a prominent Christian leader and founder of the right-wing Evangelical Moral Majority organizatio,n praised that Republican convention for nominating white men who would be "God's instruments in rebuilding America."[17]

THE CONTEMPORARY SOUTHERN STRATEGY: WHITE EVANGELICAL CHRISTIANS AND CHRISTIAN NATIONALISM

This pattern of white Evangelical voters who disproportionately support Republicans has continued to the present. In its basic features, it is clearly not new. For example, in 2004 about eight in ten white Evangelicals were voting for conservative Republican George W. Bush for president, while Black Evangelicals again voted in the majority for the Democratic Party candidate.[18] Today there is still a massive divide between white and Black Evangelical voters, even though they read, teach, and preach from the same Bible. They also assert numerous family and individual values that are similar. Yet, white Evangelicals have voted twice and, overwhelmingly, for the decidedly immoral, irreligious, and openly racist Donald Trump, the largest religious group to do so.

"Through it all," religion scholar Robert P. Jones emphasizes, "Trump has retained the support of white Christians." Exit polls for the 2016 election showed that he got *81 percent* of white Evangelical Protestant voters. Strikingly too, the Pew Research Center "postelection analysis based on validated voters found that strong majorities of white Catholics (64 percent) and white mainline Protestants (57 percent) also cast their votes for Trump."[19] In contrast, Black Evangelicals and other Black Christians have clearly seen and understood Trump's numerous character flaws and racist framing, and voted overwhelmingly for national Democratic political candidates and, specifically, against Donald Trump.

Today, the contemporary Republican Party, including white corporate conservatives and white Evangelical and other Christian conservatives, emphasizes important aspects of a relatively authoritarian framing of society, including routine respect for arch-conservative political authorities and certain traditional folkways. They also tend to link their authoritarian views to socially conservative political policies on issues like abortion.[20]

Furthermore, most conservative whites appear to vote for Trump because they believe that he would, and still will, preserve the white Christian dominance of the US. That is, these Trump voters have been motivated by strong white Christian nationalism. However, as I see it, for this majority of whites, their white Christian nationalism is mainly *white-racist* nationalism with just a superficial veneer of Christian rhetoric. The white-racist dimension is by far the most important part. Indeed, in the Capitol insurrection on January 6, 2021, both the reactionary white leaders and their thousands of white followers made clear that their white Christian nationalism was not mainly religious. Instead, they were using Christian banners and rhetoric to sanitize or camouflage their far-right political goals, in this case an overt attack on US democracy aimed at overturning a legitimate presidential election. As Andrew Whitehead sums up this national reality, white Christian nationalists "see the nation as their own both historically and theologically and so any Presidential election that does not produce the desired result must be illegitimate. True patriots, in this understanding, have the right—the duty, even—to take it back, by force if necessary. . . . Just as the January 6 insurrection and recent voting laws are not aberrations but a reflection of similar events in our nation's history, they too may be a bellwether of events to come if we do not acknowledge and confront Christian nationalism."[21]

Significantly, too, white Christian nationalism is linked to yet other oppressive features of US society. For example, in their 2020 survey, sociologists Gorski and Perry found a strong connection between respondent views of Christian nationalism and their commitment to free-market capitalism but especially for their white respondents. For these whites, "economic self-interest and individualism are not just 'rational' or 'efficient,' they are what 'real Americans' and 'good Christians' value."[22] Why is there a significant racial difference in this relationship of Christian nationalism to free-market capitalism? The main cause likely lies in the fact that both these reactionary economic and conservative religious views are aggressively imbedded and taught in the right-wing cable and social media disproportionately consumed by these arch-conservative whites.

A concrete example of this capitalistic linkage can be seen in the right-wing advocacy organization Council for National Policy (CNP). Created by a white right-wing Christian minister, this policy organization has networked right-wing activists from influential Christian organizations with major right-wing

Republican political operatives. As journalist Jonathan Wilson-Hartgrove has summarized, major political figures who have aggressively defended Donald Trump "from the White House—Steve Bannon, Mike Pence, Kellyanne Conway—have in fact been connected through the CNP for decades to the white evangelicals . . . who have been most eager to praise Trump as a champion of 'religious values.'"[23] There are numerous other important examples of this right-wing political linking with conservative white Christians. One that is also committed to changing contemporary state legislation is the theocratic Christian coalition called Project Blitz. This organization has developed model bills and been successful in getting right-wing state legislators to pass them.[24] Such Christian right groups seek to make the US a country ruled by Evangelical Christians or Evangelical Christian values.

Unsurprisingly, thus, white right-wing Christian nationalists have generally viewed straight white Christians as the most virtuous Americans and the standard for social desirability and appropriate morality, with the negatively framed outsiders and enemies including Black Americans and other people of color, immigrants, as well as LGBTQIA Americans and feminists on occasion.

WHITE CHRISTIAN NATIONALISM, PATRIOTISM, AND VIOLENCE

Building negative racist imagery and delusions among ordinary whites inevitably generates major negative emotions against targeted racial minority groups. Indeed, such white racial framing is often seen by these whites as part of their assertion of national patriotism. Harvard historian Jill Lepore has explained the dangers in this white nationalism hiding behind fake patriotism: "Because it's difficult to convince people to pursue a course of aggression, violence, and domination, requiring sacrifices made in the name of the nation, nationalists pretend their aims are instead protection and unity and that their motivation is patriotism. This is a lie. Patriotism is animated by love, nationalism by hatred. To confuse the one for the other is to pretend that hate is love and fear is courage."[25] This hatred and fear dimension of the white Christian nationalist framing of society has a high emotional valence, one often linked to other such emotions as anger and a sense of threat.

Studies of white nationalism have noted the role of racial fear and threat in its framing of the world, which easily links to right-wing political action.[26] As we have seen frequently in recent years, this emotional nationalism leads to white violence. One observes this in the major insurrectionary attack on the Capitol on January 6, 2021, the first such attack in US history. Unsurprisingly, almost all the several thousand attackers were white and mostly male. Most were not unemployed but were relatively well-off middle-class Americans. The majority were not working class.

This collective type of white violence, and the threat of more such violence, have greatly increased among right-wing whites since the election of Joe Biden as US president in 2020. Since that election, this violent reality has escalated as government investigative and legal actions targeting former president Donald Trump's numerous alleged business and political crimes have increased. For example, after the FBI, a conservative federal policing organization, conducted a legal search of Trump's Florida estate in August 2022 and found various top-secret papers that were there illegally, white Trump supporters went online by the hundreds of thousands to broadcast their anger and threaten violence against the FBI and the federal government generally. So far, one such supporter has attempted a violent attack on an FBI office, and he was killed in the process.[27]

Indeed, journalistic and scholarly analyses over recent years have found major increases in all kinds of public and covert discussions and proclamations, mostly by white men, of violent actions, arming and use of guns and explosives, and revolution against the government on an array of online media. These media have included Twitter (now X), Facebook (now Meta), and TikTok, the latter site probably signaling a younger-age cohort's involvement.[28]

THE NECESSITY OF WHITE BRAINWASHING AND IGNORANCE

In a modern western society, the sustained and widespread perpetuation of this white Christian nationalism requires much historical and contemporary ignorance and misinformation about this country's racial, class, or gender oppression in the minds of millions of whites, most especially those with significant power and influence. Extensive censorship and misinformation efforts have been successful for decades now, even regarding basic empirical information about the country's past and current patterns of racial discrimination. For instance, several recent national opinion surveys have found that white respondents often report that they face as much or more racial discrimination and persecution than Americans of color. In one Public Religion Research Institute survey no less than 57 percent of whites thought that anti-white discrimination was as big a societal problem as anti-Black discrimination.[29] Yet there is no empirical evidence for this widespread white delusion.[30] As scholar Katherine Stewart concludes, most whites "against all reasonable evidence" insist, often quite emotionally, that they are the "most persecuted group in society. . . . It's how a lot of Christian nationalist leaders consolidate the rank and file. It's how they consolidate their base by stoking that persecution narrative."³¹

This white persecution complex does not come naturally. It has been carefully cultivated in the minds of ordinary whites by elite whites for several generations now. Indeed, it is generally linked to a massive con that a large segment of white America has fallen for. The white majority has long been conned into supporting elite white political and economic interests by what the perceptive African American scholar W. E. B. Du Bois once termed the "public and psychological wage of whiteness,"³² that is, the recurring racial privilege and status ordinary whites have received for centuries in this systemically racist society. For centuries now, the white ruling elite has provided most ordinary whites with some racial power and privilege over Americans of color, even as that white elite has greatly exploited these ordinary whites in the form of institutionalized class oppression—such as the suppression of their labor unions, imposing lower wages, and providing them with weak political power under undemocratic elitist leadership.

In addition, as African Americans and other Americans of color have increased their own status and democratic political power since the civil rights movements of the 1960s, elite white men have moved to reduce those democratizing effects by generating yet more ignorance and misinformation about the country's racial group history and contemporary realities, such as what we observed regarding the alleged anti-white discrimination. Over the last decade or two, the powerful white elite has generated numerous attacks on honest research and authentic teaching about this country's racist history. These censorship attacks have often included teachers and administrators in public school systems. For example, even in a relatively liberal northern Virginia suburb, a group of far-right white parents sought to recall school board members because their school district officials sought to require the commonplace teacher training on issues of "systemic oppression and implicit bias."³³

Moreover, even a majority of Republican senators, including the minority leader, in the US Senate have demonstrated this desire for radical censorship of the country's history of racial oppression. Recently, they too condemned honest education (especially the famous 1619 Project led by an African American journalist and scholar) dealing seriously with systemic US racism as just "activist indoctrination." In addition, in various states Republican-controlled legislatures have recently passed legislation that bans public school teachers from teaching the empirical data on how white-imposed racism is systemic in US society. These white right-wing censorship and disinformation efforts are accelerating and widespread: "From school boards to the halls of Congress, Republicans are mounting an energetic campaign aiming to dictate how historical and modern racism in America are taught, meeting pushback from Democrats and educators in a politically thorny clash that has deep ramifications for how children learn about their country."[34] These white elite censorship efforts seem to be necessary for the buildup of yet more virulent white Christian nationalism.

WHITE CHRISTIAN NATIONALISM: SERIOUS DAMAGE TO CHRISTIAN RELIGION

Finally, we need to examine the impact of white nationalism on Christianity in the US. The varying strength in the linkage of a Christian individual's or group's politics and their religious orientation and membership is very important to underscore in making sense of this white Christian nationalism. Adherence to Christianity functions differently for different people. For some Christians, the primary emphasis is on improving their own character and communication with God (termed an *intrinsic orientation*, religion as an *end* in itself), but for other Christians it has been primarily a *means* to relate socially in some fashion (termed an *extrinsic orientation*). Research using scales of intrinsic and extrinsic religion has revealed this pattern for more than a half century, and researchers have found that some people's religious orientation is a strong mixture of these orientations. In addition, some recent researchers have found that the intrinsic orientation needs to be expanded to include the end-oriented "quest" aspect of religion for some Christian believers.[35]

For a majority of Black Christians, the intrinsic aspects of Christianity are more central as they seek to make prayerful contact with God and/or pursue an individual and group religious journey in supporting and sustaining their Christian souls. For example, one 1999 study of religious surveys found that Black Americans showed significantly higher levels of (intrinsic) subjective religiosity than whites. That is, in the surveys they "overwhelmingly indicated that (a) religious comfort and support was extremely helpful in coping with life problems and difficulties, (b) religious and spiritual beliefs were important in their daily lives, (c) they felt close to God, and (d) they considered themselves to be religious."[36] Controls for socioeconomic status and region did not change this pattern by racial group.

This pattern has persisted to the present. Overall, Black and white Christians still have dramatically different approaches to their Christian religious connections. Recently, a large Pew Research Center survey of Black churchgoers again found they are generally more religious than the rest of the US population. One summary of this Pew survey reported that it found Black Americans are more likely "to believe in God, attend religious services, say religion is 'very important' in their lives, and affiliate with a religion." They are also more likely to believe that God talks to them.[37] Nearly three-quarters said it was essential for their congregations to provide spiritual comfort and a sense of community for the congregants. They also indicated that prayer and religious reflection are central in making important life decisions.[38] Additionally, the religious tone and climate within typical Black Protestant church services tends to be different from that in typical white churches. The Pew report found their Black respondents reporting that their church services usually include the congregants calling out, "Amen," as well as frequently dancing or otherwise openly celebrating in their religious fervor.[39] In addition, this Pew survey found that the shared experiences of Black congregants outside their churches had a regular impact on those services. For instance, three-quarters of those surveyed said that opposing societal racism was necessarily a part of their religious faith, and half indicated that their religious services in the last year had included sermons on racism issues.[40] That is, as it has for centuries now, Black Christianity is linked strongly to, and often centered in, a racial equality and fairness framing that is in major ways radically different, *and often resistant to*, much past and present white Christian framing of society.

Particularly significant is the contrast between this Black Christianity and many contemporary white Christians, with the latter being generally less intrinsic and more extrinsic in their overall religious orientation. For many white Christians, indeed for large percentages in many contemporary conservative Evangelical churches, Christianity has been an extrinsic *means* more than an intrinsic *end* in itself. It has been a means of collectively teaching oppressive racial, class, or gender views of other social groups or for socializing for nonreligious (e.g., conservative political) goals. One recent study of Black and white Evangelicals found that the white Evangelicals had a high level of racial resentment—that is, over the mythical notion of most whites facing serious discrimination—that drives them to very conservative political positions, which strongly persists across different political, demographic, and religiosity groups within their group. That is, "White evangelicals hold significantly more conservative political preferences than Black evangelicals . . . and the divide between Black and white evangelicals cannot necessarily be attributed to Black evangelicals' attachment to their racial group. Instead, we do find that white evangelicals' out-group resentment is strongly associated with their political preferences."[41]

CONCLUSION: IS WHITE CHRISTIAN NATIONALISM DESTROYING CHRISTIANITY?

In recent decades, the intensified cooptation of Christian symbolism and white evangelical and other Christian religious organizations for right-wing political purposes—Christian religion as blatantly political means—has been centrally important to the resurgent white Christian nationalist movement of Donald Trump and the now mostly white, far-right Republican Party. Indeed, we should note that this remarkably strong linking of Christian religion and right-wing politics for much of white Christian America has generally done *much damage* to the Christian religion in the US—a story rarely assessed in the mainstream media or, indeed, in academic scholarship. Katherine Stewart is a rare exception. She has emphasized that "this kind of politicized religion is incredibly binary. It demonizes political opponents. And at the [religious] conferences I've attended, I've heard Democrats described as demonic, satanic, like not even as people. . . . It's incredibly dehumanizing language. The targets shift, of course. It could be secularists, liberal Christians, the L.G.B.T. agenda, et cetera."[42]

That is, ultimately this fast-growing white nationalist movement promotes Christian theocratic politics to achieve the distinctive fascistic "strongman" goals of Trump and other leading white Republicans. Stewart underscores the fact that, in turn, Trump has rewarded white right-wing Christian groups with political rewards that signal their *nonreligious* goals, including access to more federal money for their churches and getting far-right-wing Supreme Court justices committed to their religious causes, like ending abortion.[43] In effect, politicization of white Evangelical and other contemporary Christian groups signals that they are no longer principally Christian in the intrinsic religious sense. That is, their Christian symbolism and organization have become much more of an extrinsic means to achieve far-right political goals than to achieve intrinsic soul-supporting religious ends.

NOTES

1. Patrick Joseph Buchanan, "Culture War Speech: Address to the Republican National Convention," *Voices of Democracy*, August 17, 1992, https://voicesofdemocracy.umd.edu/buchanan-culture-war-speech-speech-text/.

2. Quoted in Clarence Page, "U.S. Media Should Stop Abetting Intolerance," *Toronto Star*, December 27, 1991, A27. I summarize here detailed arguments in Joe Feagin and Kimberley Ducey, *Racist America* (New York: Routledge, 2019), chapter 3.

3. Quoted in John Dillin, "Immigration Joins List of '92 Issues," *Christian Science Monitor* (December 17, 1991): 6.

4. Kevin Phillips, *American Theocracy: The Peril and Politics of Radical Religion, Oil, and Borrowed Money in the 21st Century* (New York: Viking, 2006), 1.

5. See Richard Howland Maxwell, "Pilgrim and Puritan: A Delicate Distinction," *Pilgrim Society Note* 2 (March 2003), https://www.pilgrimhall.org/pdf/Pilgrim_Puritan_A_Delicate_Distinction.pdf.

6. John Winthrop, "A Modell of Christian Charity (1630)," *Collections of the Massachusetts Historical Society (Boston, 1838)*, 3rd series, 7: 31–48, http://history.hanover.edu/texts/winthmod.html. I have modernized the spelling and added italics.

7. Deborah Madsen, *American Exceptionalism* (Jackson: University Press of Mississippi, 1998), 8–9.

8. See David D. Hall, "Peace, Love and Puritanism," *New York Times*, November 23, 2010, https://www.nytimes.com/2010/11/24/opinion/24hall.html.

9. Quoted in Robert C. Winthrop, *Life and Letters of John Winthrop*, 2nd ed. (Boston: Little, Brown, 1869), 2:430. For more detail on the Puritan era, see Joe Feagin, *White Party, White Government* (New York: Routledge, 2012), chapter 2.

10. Winthrop, "A Modell of Christian Charity (1630)," 3rd series, 7: 31–48.

11. Robert F. Berkhofer Jr., *The White Man's Indian: Images of the American Indian from Columbus to the Present* (New York: Knopf, 1978), 16.

12. Philip S. Gorski and Samuel L. Perry, *The Flag and the Cross* (New York: Oxford University Press, 2022), Kindle loc 173.

13. John O'Sullivan, "Annexation," *The United States Magazine and Democratic Review* 17 (July 1845): 5–10.

14. Angie Maxwell, "What We Get Wrong about the Southern Strategy," *Washington Post*, July 26, 2019, https://www.washingtonpost.com/outlook/2019/07/26/what-we-get-wrong-about-southern-strategy/.

15. Ronald Reagan, "City Upon a Hill," Conservative Political Action Conference, January 25, 1974.

16. Steven M. Gillon, "Reagan Tied Republicans to White Christians and Now the Party Is Trapped," *Washington Post*, March 22, 2021, https://www.washingtonpost.com/outlook/2021/03/22/reagan-tied-republicans-white-christians-now-party-is-trapped/.

17. Gillon, "Reagan Tied Republicans to White Christians."

18. "Evangelicals, Black and White, Are Divided by Faith, Race and Politics," *The Takeaway*, October 16, 2008, https://www.wnycstudios.org/podcasts/takeaway/segments/6669-evangelicals-black-and-white-are-divided-by-faith-race-and-politics.

19. Robert P. Jones, "Introduction," in *White Too Long: The Legacy of White Supremacy in American Christianity* (New York: Simon & Schuster, 2020).

20. See Bob Altemeyer, *The Authoritarians* (Winnipeg: Department of Psychology, University of Manitoba, 2006), 37.

21. Andrew Whitehead, "The Growing Antidemocratic Threat of Christian Nationalism in the U.S.," *Time*, May 27, 2021, https://time.com/6052051/antidemocratic-threat-christian-nationalism/.

22. Gorski and Perry, *The Flag and the Cross*, 37–39.

23. Jonathan Wilson-Hartgrove, "Who Poisoned Talk Radio?" *Sojourners*, May 2020, https://sojo.net/magazine/may-2020/who-poisoned-talk radio.

24. Frederick Clarkson, "Christian Right Bill Mill, Project Blitz, Hasn't Gone Away, It's Just Gotten More Secretive," *Religion Dispatches*, July 12, 2021, https://religiondispatches.org/exclusive-christian-right-bill-mill-project-blitz-hasnt-gone-away-its-just-gotten-more-secretive/. For much more detail, see Joe Feagin, *White Minority Nation: Past, Present, and Future* (New York: Routledge, 2023).

25. Jill Lepore, *This America: The Case for the Nation* (New York: Liveright, 2019), 23.

26. See Feagin, *White Minority Nation*.

27. Donie Sullivan, "Violent Rhetoric Circulates on the pro-Trump Internet Following FBI Search, Including Against a Judge," *CNN*, August 10, 2022, https://www.cnn.com/2022/08/09/politics/violent-rhetoric-pro-trump-internet-fbi-search/index.html.

28. Abbie Richards, "Examining White Supremacist and Militant Accelerationism Trends on TikTok," Global Network on Extremism and Technology, July 18, 2022, https://gnet-research.org/2022/07/18/examining-white-supremacist-and-militant-accelerationism-trends-on-tiktok/.

29. Vann R. Newkirk II, "The Myth of Reverse Racism," *The Atlantic*, August 5, 2017, https://www.theatlantic.com/education/archive/2017/08/myth-of-reverse-racism/535689/. See also Gorski and Perry, *The Flag and the Cross*, 110–11.

30. See Feagin and Ducey, *Racist America*.

31. Quoted in Jane Coaston, "What's God Got to Do with It? The Rise of Christian Nationalism in American Politics," *New York Times*, August 3, 2022, https://www.nytimes.com/2022/08/03/opinion/republicans-religious-right-the-argument.html?showTranscript=1.

32. W. E. B. Du Bois, *Black Reconstruction in America, 1860–1880* (New York: Harcourt, Brace and Co., 1935).

33. Trip Gabriel and Dana Goldstein, "Disputing Racism's Reach, Republicans Rattle American Schools," *New York Times*, June 1, 2021, https://www.nytimes.com/2021/06/01/us/politics/critical-race-theory.html.

34. Gabriel and Goldstein, "Disputing Racism's Reach."

35. See C. Daniel Batson and E. L. Stocks, "Religion and Prejudice," in J. F. Dovidio, P. Glick, and L. A. Rudman, eds., *On the Nature of Prejudice: Fifty Years after Allport* (New York: Blackwell Publishing, 2005), 413–27.

36. Robert Joseph Taylor, Jacqueline Mattis, and Linda M. Chatters, "Subjective Religiosity among African Americans," *Journal of Black Psychology* (November 1999): 536, https://www.researchgate.net/publication/43117543_Subjective_Religiosity_among_African_Americans_A_Synthesis_of_Findings_from_Five_National_Samples.

37. Jeremy Weber and Morgan Lee, "The Black Church, Explained by Pew's Biggest Survey of African Americans," *Christianity Today*, February 16, 2021, https://www.christianitytoday.com/news/2021/february/black-church-african-american-christians-pew-survey.html.

38. Besheer Mohamed, Kiana Cox, Jeff Diamant, and Claire Gecewicz, "Faith among Black Americans," Pew Research Center, February 16, 2021, https://www.pewresearch.org/religion/2021/02/16/a-brief-overview-of-black-religious-history-in-the-u-s/.

39. Emilee Larkin, "Study Finds That Black Americans Are More Religious Than General U.S. Public," *St. Louis American*, https://www.stlamerican.com/religion/local_religion/study-finds-that-black-americans-are-more-religious-than-general-u-s-public/article_f1c49ca8-0372-11ec-890d-377936ff10ff.html.

40. Mohamed, Cox, Diamant, and Gecewicz, "Faith among Black Americans."

41. Levi G. Allen and Shayla F. Olson, "Racial Attitudes and Political Preferences among Black and White Evangelicals," *Politics and Religion* (April 2022), https://www.cambridge.org/core/journals/politics-and-religion/article/racial-attitudes-and-political-preferences-among-black-and-white-evangelicals/22D575567D953401D9718033F60ED60F.

42. Quoted in Coaston, "What's God Got to Do with It?"

43. Coaston, "What's God Got to Do with It?"

Chapter 6

The Pedagogy of Hegemony
A History of Christian Nationalism, Narrative Wars, and School Dominance

Todd M. Mealy

In 1929, amid the presidential election of Herbert Hoover over the Roman Catholic New York Democrat Al Smith, political historian and editorial writer for the *New York Evening World* Claude Bowers published a book titled *The Tragic Era: The Revolution after Lincoln*. Bowers described how "Negro rule" during Reconstruction led to corruption across different government levels. His thesis centered on explaining how Black freedom following the Civil War resulted in American society's moral degeneration. Largely an uncontested perspective on the post–Civil War period, Bowers proclaimed Black Americans were unfit for freedom, much less to serve in government.

> Freedom—it meant idleness, and gathering in noisy groups in the streets. Soon they were living like rats in ruined houses, in miserable shacks under bridges, built with refuse lumber, in the shelter of ravines and in caves in the banks of rivers. Freedom meant throwing aside all marital obligations, deserting wives and taking new ones, and in an indulgence of sexual promiscuity that soon took its toll in the victims of consumption and venereal disease. Jubilant, and happy, the Negro who had his dog and a gun for hunting, a few rags to cover his nakedness, and a dilapidated hobble in which to sleep, was in no mood to discuss work.[1]

The book, published by Houghton Mifflin, was a bestseller. It went on to enjoy more than a dozen reprintings. When speaking about the book after its publication, Bowers adamantly argued that had Abraham Lincoln survived assassination, he and his states' rights vice president Andrew Johnson would have worked in "moderation" to pull the Union back together. Indeed, he admitted, Lincoln "would have been vilified;" however, with the president of the Union ticket still alive in the Civil War's aftermath, the so-called tragic era "might have been avoided."

Alas, John Wilkes Booth pulled the trigger of his .44 caliber Derringer pistol on the night of April 14, 1865. President Lincoln died the following morning. The resultant tragic period, as coined by Bowers, was marked by the Republican Party's intent "to gain political capital of the South's defeat." To boot, the party of Lincoln had the full support of the formerly shackled Black contingent.[2]

Frankly, Bowers's work on Reconstruction augmented a right-wing, redemptive movement to seize on both formal and informal curricula to implant an idealized version of Confederate history maintaining that white Southerners were inculpable victims of Northern aggression. *The Tragic Era* gave credence to the Dunning School, so named after Columbia University professor William Archibald Dunning, who presented a sanitized version of Reconstruction to students.[3] Broadly speaking, the Dunning School advanced ideas that federal occupation of the South trampled on the enlightenment-era principle of limited government and the American Revolution's offspring, federalism. It also purported that Black Americans were incapable of self-government. Questions asked in classrooms and in real life often circled simplistically around the same frame of reference—justifying segregation, proclaiming Black assault on white women, and validating continued efforts to keep the Black population disenfranchised. These topics were fixations in the first quarter of the twentieth century.

The first indisputable effort to crystalize the people who supported the former Confederacy was a pseudo-historical view of the Southern cause for war—named the Lost Cause, which was a portrayal of white Southern values, slavery, military leadership, and governance as morally pure and righteous; it was a belief that God, Himself, wanted the South to be redeemed of the scourge of Black citizenship. The strange story of the Lost Cause—a term originating in 1867 with a book by Virginian Edward Pollard titled *The Lost Cause: A New Southern History of the War of the Confederates*—unfolds in a subculture many know but in which few grasp the impact on civic participation in national, statewide, and local government. During Reconstruction's redemption period, Southern historians like Pollard began to emphasize constitutional arguments over the morality of keeping people in bondage, especially the claim that a powerful central government and divergent economic systems usurped the doctrine of states' rights as the cause for war.[4]

At the turn of the century, right-leaning Lost Cause sympathizers influenced curricular decisions in schools, especially across the South. They had familiar names, such as the United Daughters of the Confederacy (UDC) and the Sons of Confederate Veterans. Dead set on removing slavery as the cause of the Civil War, this new conservative right, operating in the wake of Reconstruction's failure and while eugenicists emerged as a credible group of academics and scientists basking in public favor for advancing biologically racist ideas, was connected intimately with the effort to establish textbook committees to screen out multiple points of view.

The movement to control education began with Mildred Lewis Rutherford, niece of two Confederate Founding Fathers, Howell and Thomas Cobb. Historian-General of the UDC from 1911 to 1916, Rutherford notoriously pushed Lost Cause textbooks to school boards throughout the South. Her central enterprise, a commission so-called The Rutherford Committee, formed in 1919 with the amalgamation of the UDC, the Sons of the Confederate Veterans, and the United Confederate Veterans, published *A Measuring Rod to Test Text Books and Reference Books in Schools, Colleges and Libraries*. As far as Rutherford was concerned, Northern educators had been "unjust to the south and her institutions," constituting through the misrepresentation of history an "injustice and danger" to the Southern people.[5]

A Measuring Rod did more than merely express grievances. Rutherford offered a rubric to assess textbooks for positive representations of the South and whether Civil War scholars cosigned the Lost Cause narrative. She compelled school boards to hire agents directly from her committee to audit textbooks. If school districts could not afford her team of consultants, *A Measuring Rod* provided the assessment tool for school board members and faculty to measure what she called "truths of history." *A Measuring Rod*'s evaluation metric for a book's inclusion of Lost Cause content depended less on impartial scientific evaluations of school textbooks. She insisted that school boards censure books for the following reasons:

> Reject a text-book that speaks of the Constitution other than a Compact between Sovereign States.
> Reject a text-book that does not give the principles for which the South fought in 1861, and does not clearly outline the interferences with the rights guaranteed to the South by the Constitution, and which caused secession.
> Reject a book that calls the Confederate soldier a traitor or rebel, and the war a rebellion.
> Reject a book that says the South fought to hold her slaves.
> Reject a book that speaks of the slaveholder of the South as cruel and unjust to his slaves.
> Reject a text-book that glorifies Abraham Lincoln and vilifies Jefferson Davis, unless a truthful cause can be found for such glorification and vilification before 1865.

Reject a text-book that omits to tell of the South's heroes and their deeds when the North's heroes and their deeds are made prominent.

Rutherford did more than purely provide a list of reasons to reject a book; she flagged textbooks already in publication. That is to say, she produced a banned books list. The bulk of *A Measuring Rod* features a list of direct quotes by expert authorities, many of whom worked in the Lincoln administration. The quotes, she suggested, should be used as a checklist to evaluate whether historians described the good and proper treatment of the enslaved, why the war was not fought to enslave African people, why the North was responsible for the war, and why secession was not a rebellion.

Like many second-generation Confederates, one of Rutherford's favorite techniques was to appropriate the word *truth*, assuming, quite correctly, that enough supporters would accept the rhetoric as truth, and the masses might control what textbooks on history and literature schools may well have students read. *A Measuring Rod*, then, became the nation's how-to guide on "testing text-books, and endorsing books for libraries."[6] The writing formula of gathering together uncontextualized statements from living witnesses made for widespread consumption.

A year later, Rutherford published a sequel to *A Measuring Rod*. She titled the second volume *Truths of History: A Fair, Unbiased, Impartial, Unprejudiced and Conscientious Study of History*. In addition to basing each chapter on "statements made by men of unquestioned authority," Rutherford believed she had composed a book counterbalancing "falsehoods circulated not only in our country, but now widely circulated in foreign countries."[7] *Truths of History* was a boon to proponents of the Lost Cause. They now had the messaging to seize control over school curricula. *Truths of History* provided the playbook for disdained white Southerners to challenge scholarship that took exception to the Dunning School's filtered view of history and literature.

Why? Because white supremacy was at stake. *Truths of History* spurred parents into pushing back against educators who didn't teach a filtered brand of history. It worked. By 1923, UDC groups in states like South Carolina had purchased enough copies of Rutherford's latest book to supply public libraries.[8] The UDC also prompted many schoolteachers to buy the book. With backing from enough educators in the South, *Truths of History* won the UDC Carter Prize, a hundred-dollar bond bestowed by the national organization, which the Georgia UDC division used to help fund the construction of the Stone Mountain Memorial outside Atlanta.[9]

The two Rutherford guides functioned for many Lost Cause adherents as the great racial conserver, in which the soft-pedaling and veiled recital of Southern heritage displayed racist control over education. The construction of this educational system, one carried out in public schools through school-board-approved curriculum and the other executed through ornamenting public land with monuments to Confederate icons, occurred in the nexus of the country's Black population. In this region, individuals like Rutherford prevented the annihilation of their way of life.

Although not called this yet, the great replacement theory lay behind the work undertaken by Rutherford, Bowers, and Dunning. Alleging a conspiracy among leftists, elitists, and culturally conscious educational leaders to displace whites with people of historically marginalized groups politically and culturally, the great replacement theory has whooped up white anxiety and white rage ever since the Civil War.[10] Beginning with calls to colonize free Blacks to locations along the West Coast of Africa during antebellum, replacementism has a long history. The Dunning School and Lost Cause narratives explain colonization as an effort to provide a place in Africa for free American-born Blacks to live in self-government, fully funded by US Congress. Evidence shows, however, that calls to send the free Black population abroad effectively sustained slavery.[11] Indeed, if no free Black voices actively encouraged enslaved Africans to escape bondage, the institution of slavery could flourish, especially the domestic slave market. Violent resistance to Black freedom prevailed during the Reconstruction period, especially in Colfax, Grant Parish, Louisiana, where, on Easter 1873, a multitude of whites angered about losing the gubernatorial, local sheriff, and judgeship elections took up arms and slaughtered about 150 Black militiamen sheltering inside the parish's courthouse.[12] The violence in Colfax was a response to the burgeoning political influence of the local Black population. In other words, the reaction to Black voters determining elections in Louisiana was mass murder. Three years later, in *United States v. Cruikshank*, the US Supreme Court threw out the murder convictions of the three assailants found guilty for the bloody crime at Colfax.

The Dunning School's redemptive education based in Lost Cause ethos grew in popularity after 1915 due to the release of D. W. Griffith's *The Birth of a Nation*. While presenting white Americans as victims of Black conquest, Griffith's film worked to provide pious cover for symbolic violence (i.e.,, Jim Crow policy) and tragedies like the massacre in Colfax. Under the banner of Christ, Anglo-Saxon Protestant men dressed in white regalia used anti-Black violence to sustain social order. After the release of *The Birth of a Nation*, the Ku Klux Klan experienced a revival under the leadership of its new imperial wizard, William Simmons.

On Thanksgiving, November 25, 1915, Simmons and his followers planted a cross atop Stone Mountain, marking the Klan's rebirth. This time around, Simmons told the *Chicago Tribune* shortly after the Klan's inaugural ceremony, membership was "limited to native born American gentiles," with an emphasis placed on *gentiles*.[13] "Any native-born white American citizen who believes in the Christian religion and who owes allegiance to no foreign government or institution, religious or political, may become a member of the Ku Klux Klan, provided his character is good," the imperial wizard explained.[14] Simmons's key was transforming the Klan into a national Christian movement, a crusade to have nativist white Protestants infiltrate the media, each level of government, and America's schools. The Invisible Empire was no longer invisible; instead, the twenties-era Klan was mainstream with support as far north as Maine and west as Washington. Its members felt that they had a divine right to control the institutions of the US; this was among the earliest forms of Christian nationalism.

> We, the Order of the Knights of the Ku Klux Klan, reverentially acknowledge the majesty and supremacy of the Almighty God. . . . Recognizing our relation to the government of the United States of America, the supremacy of its Constitution, the Union of States thereunder, and the Constitutional laws thereof, we shall ever be devoted to the sublime principles of a pure Americanism. . . . We, the members of this Order, desir[e] to promote real patriotism toward our civil government.[15]

Simmons's notion of "real patriotism" suggests that only a privileged white Christian faction could represent "pure Americanism." All racial, ethnic, and religious Others threatened the social order of that ethnostate. For instance, in Oregon, the Klan, numbering up to fourteen thousand members, including the state's Democratic governor, Walter M. Pierce, successfully led efforts in the early 1920s to absorb private Catholic schools into the public school system so as to preserve Protestant Christian values.[16] The Klan arrived in the Pacific Northwest in 1921, in the wake of the Spanish influenza pandemic and national race riots. The Klan's nerve center ran through Oregon towns of Medford, Klamath Falls, and Tillamook. By 1922, the organization spearheaded a campaign to lobby for the Oregon Compulsory Education Bill, a law requiring every child between eight and sixteen to attend public schools. With the closure of Catholic schools, educators assimilated all children into American and Protestant values. The Oregon Klan supported the bill as a legislative tool to promote hostility toward Catholics, a group characterized as a small but growing religious cabal perceived as a threat to Protestant dominion. In advertisements published in the state's media at the time, the Klan conjectured that the "Catholic organization is attempting to gain control of the country politically for their own selfish benefit."[17] To put it another way, many Oregonians were threatened as much by being replaced by Catholics as Black voting populations threatened American Klansmen and Klanswomen in the Midwest and up and down the East Coast, especially after the ratification of the suffrage amendment granting women the right to vote.

Replacementism equipped racists with a mechanism best utilized by authoritarians in years to come, a system of indoctrination by which the proximity of an apocalyptic event (vis-à-vis replacement) could be precisely ascertained. First in government, then blue-collar positions and amateur and professional sports, Black Americans and other religious minorities might replace white Christians. It was a potent political tactic to inhibit Catholics from disseminating papal values in the education system, as Ku Kluxers halted in the 1920s, or to weaken "black block votes," as George Wallace used to say when campaigning in the 1960s and 1970s.[18]

The tenets of such political and economic maneuvers have constantly beleaguered the American public education system. Indeed, in schools, replacementism by other names has commonly reached a manic zenith among popular support. White fear and anti-Black sentiment obstructed efforts to desegregate schools after the 1954 *Brown v. Board of Education* decision and its 1955 corollary, *Brown II*. White brutality and anti-Black terror permeate the modern Civil Rights Movement's history: the integration of school districts, swimming pools, diners, movie theaters, bowling alleys, and buses. White resentment and anti-Black avoidance defined efforts to diversify the workforce in the 1970s and 1980s. White supervision and criminalization of Blacks in predominantly white spaces have worked to sustain the caste of the Jim Crow days without the apartheid apparatus. This is the twisted history of an eternal problem, a saga of factional interests, the clutching of power, and universal persuasion.

Enslavement, lynching, branding, flogging, and harassment were deterrents designed to maintain order. But each lacks sustainability as a hegemonic mechanism. In contrast, unremitting control over the education system prevails as an indelible machine. As it currently is in the early twenty-first century, we now see thuggish power prevailing on school boards. In rural and suburban school districts, in particular, since fall 2020, the final days of Donald J. Trump's term in office, many white-controlled school boards with enough vocal support from taxpayers within their districts presumed the right to see efforts to make curriculum and pedagogy more culturally inclusive as the cause of division in schools that are supposed to be—on paper at least—designed for the public. Curricular segregation has not only been the best play to mobilize the white masses into a growing authoritarian faction, but history shows us how the relationship between schools and religion can be used to justify irreverent behavior in the name of a white theological absolutism by a contingent of Make America Great Again conservatives.

To attack progressive educational theories, to silence and intimidate educators whose personal beliefs fall left of center, to ban books written by

LGBTQIA+ authors and authors of color, and to obstruct critical evaluation of American history and society, Christian nationalism exists, even matures, inside our schools given the history that school board directors lend themselves to processes of factional interests over those representing culturally diversifying student bodies. During summer 2022, Congresswoman Lauren Boebert (R-CO) went on Fox News's Christian news show, *FlashPoint*, to discuss the state of morality in America after the first eighteen months of the Joe Biden presidency. She buttressed "some sort of legislation that requires . . . biblical citizenship training in our schools." That, she said, good-humoredly or not, is "how we get things turned around."[19]

Boebert revealed to *FlashPoint*'s host, Gene Bailey, that she once enrolled in a course titled "Biblical Citizenship in Modern America." The Christian conservative group Patriot Academy facilitates the class. Patriot Academy educates its students on how to "understand and influence government policy with a [Christian] Biblical worldview."[20] Among the most visible Republican officials in office, Boebert had earlier told people at the Cornerstone Christian Center in Basalt, Colorado, that she thought the church must guide the government. She intimated that if this were the case, the public wouldn't be affected by "so many overreaching regulations." She criticized the church for being complicit in government overreach. Church first, government second is how to rectify moral degradation in society. "The government is not meant to direct the church," she said. "That is not how our founding fathers intended it." Adding moments later, "And I'm tired of this separation of church and state junk, that's not in the Constitution."[21]

Although it is easy to dismiss Boebert as misinformed on the First Amendment, one does not question that much of the US Constitution is a matter of interpretation. All the same, Supreme Court holdings on the First Amendment's "establishment clause" have a long, fixed precedent that prevents government action preferencing one religion over another or over nonbelief. Boebert's remarks, however, posit in this manufactured culture war that Christianity is under siege: Christian holidays, namely whether one can say "Merry Christmas" or "happy holidays" in school, are part of the war on Christians. The 2020 presidential election and the 2022 midterms existed, largely, by the Boebert contingent, as the war on Christians and schools were ground zero.

Several authorities have explored the growing influence of the Christian right. Chris Hedges provides a historical account of the culture wars driven by the Christian church in *American Fascists: The Christian Right and the War on America*. Though written in 2006 during President George W. Bush's second term, Hedges provides illustrative case studies during the turn of the century in how fundamentalists aiming for a Christian nation worked overtly and covertly for their means. It is a war, he contends, centered on public coercion and political strong-arming. Hedges says the Christian nationalist movement depends on ignorance. They seek "to appropriate not only our religious and patriotic language, but also our stories to deny the validity of stories other than their own, to deny that there are other acceptable ways of living and being."[22]

Similar to Hedges, in *Unholy: How White Christian Nationalists Powered the Trump Presidency, and the Devastating Legacy They Left Behind*, Sarah Posner traces the moments when white Christians on the right used religion as a way to slow down, or altogether halt, school desegregation. Historically, race has been used as the cudgel to decelerate the court-ordered "social engineering" project. By the Trump presidency, Posner shows, debates over diversity initiatives were used to destroy the idea of creating and maintaining culturally rich schools by means of incorporating fundamentalist Christian values into schools through curricular objectives and school board control over hiring practices and extracurricular programming. What began as a series of Trump-issued executive orders, followed by a conservative blitz on American school boards, became an assault on the civil rights of taxpaying public school families that included efforts to cancel any talk of race, gender, gay marriage, transgender rights, abortion, and contraception, not just in curriculum, but in school services to ensure academic achievement.[23] Once confined to chat rooms or books read only by the most devoted adherents to a white ethnostate, rural and suburban schools have become the epicenter of contemporary replacement theory rhetoric.

While Hedges and Posner share the disposition that Christianity and nationalism merged into the Christian nationalist movement due to "openly hostile [feelings about] democratic pluralism,"[24] journalist and leading expert on the Christian right Katherine Stewart distinguishes the election of Trump as the movement's inflection point. In *The Power Worshippers*, Stewart suggests Trump's candidacy in 2016 was the moment when the Christian conservative movement fused with advocates of a white ethnostate. The result was a constituency that put Trump and a cabinet of leading proponents of the Christian right in charge of the executive branch. And therein lies the mechanism from which the Christian nationalist movement is powered.[25] In a July 2022 *New York Times* editorial, Stewart says that the movement is "leader-driven" though buoyed by a coterie of Christian conservatives motivated by cherry-picked biblical rhetoric promoting "vigilante justice." Its leaders drive Christian conservative voters to the polls with bluster about morality, inasmuch as sexuality, marriage equality, faith, and law and order are concerned.[26]

It is important to note that not every Christian is a Christian nationalist; in fact, many Christian conservatives are vocal in editorial sections of local newspapers across the country in denouncing Christian nationalism. Stewart is among the first to acknowledge the difference. "Christian nationalism is not Christianity," she says. "It is not a religion." In fact, she emphasizes that Christian nationalism is an "ideology" and "movement" that uses "culture war issues" and "an authoritarian playbook" to drive the right to the polls.[27] To that end, the movement thrives by its ability to persuade Republican politicians to use value differences to further divide the country. Not all, but enough, Christian conservatives enable politicians like Congresswoman Boebert to champion an exclusive, intolerant, and authoritarian movement aiming to deny the existence of historically marginalized groups (e.g., LGBTQIA+, Muslims, Jews) and to ascribe Black Americans, in particular, as a perverted class of people unable to conform to the Christian social order (vis-à-vis non-compliance with law enforcement, insistence on equal rights). Such rhetoric has enraged parental groups at the school-district level across the country.

Boebert's narrative about those who support LGBTQIA+ rights as "groomers" or Muslim representatives in Congress as the "jihad squad" has gone a long way in encouraging partisan divides and culture wars in the US. In my home state of Pennsylvania, the 2022 midterm generated anxiety about what the election might produce. Most notable was the candidacy of Republican gubernatorial nominee Doug Mastriano. Although not self-described as a Christian nationalist, Mastriano, a sitting state senator who went on record calling the separation of church and state a "myth," built a campaign around the Christian nationalist movement's central tenets—that the US is God's chosen nation, established as a Christian nation, with Christianity woven into the fabric of society, and that laws should keep the country Christian. In a word, Mastriano campaigned on the belief that the US is a Christian nation and should be run by Christian leaders prizing power (he was at the Capitol on January 6), domination (he introduced legislation to control a woman's right to choose, and he supports efforts to punish educators who promote gender and racial inclusion), and exclusion (he actively exploited the most vulnerable to improve his chances of election). As Election Day neared, the candidate couldn't escape breaking headlines exposing antisemitic signaling, which included an appearance in *Operation Resist*, a low-budget and fictional movie about the Holocaust. *Operation Resist* espouses messages that abortion and gun control, two turbulent political topics dividing conservatives and liberals, "paved a path to Nazi-like control" reported in the press.[28] In 2019, Mastriano sponsored a "heartbeat" bill in the Pennsylvania legislature preventing abortions when a fetal heartbeat could first be detected at six weeks into pregnancy. The proposed legislation would have levied charges of murder on a woman who chose to have an abortion.[29] He doubled down on that stance for rigid abortion restrictions during the gubernatorial election.

While in defeat, Mastriano was no anomaly within the Republican Party's Christian nationalist faction. In fact, a *Politico* survey of more than two thousand participants carried out six months before the 2022 midterm election shows most Republicans, at a rate of 61 percent, favor declaring the US a Christian country. When broken down by generation, majorities in all but one age group of the Republican Party wished to make the US a Christian nation: 71 percent Silent Generation, 72 percent Baby Boomers, 49 percent Generation X, 51 percent Millennials, and 51 percent among Generation Z.[30] In 2023, the Pew Research Center noted that 99 percent of Republicans in Congress are Christian, and about seven out of ten lawmakers in that delegation identify as Protestant.[31]

Simultaneously, my home county, Lancaster County, played host to a Christian nationalist movement to make the Commonwealth a Christian state. Leaders of the Mid-Atlantic Reformation Society lobbied hard to convince Pennsylvanians that the state's original constitution "called for an explicitly Christian state." Those efforts, like Mastriano's bid at the governor's mansion, failed; yet such attempts to embolden voters through culture wars, underpinned by replacement theory, have had profound implications in local politics. A radically exclusive populist movement (see No Left Turn in Education and Free PA's takeover of school boards in Pennsylvania) to make school boards across the country the fundamental source of muscle for Christian nationalist power—church first, government second—is how to rectify moral degradation in society.

As history shows, the wellspring for the Christian right's *reclaim America* campaign lies at the social engineering plant that fuses local school communities with Christianity. Dating back to Reagan-era televangelist Jerry Falwell, the conservative counterrevolution's first prominent Christian voice, right-wing efforts saw the need to "awaken the religious people" as the nation's "only hope" for redemption. As was intended, the Christian right interpreted Falwell's words as a call to use fundamental Christian doctrine to get people voting for conservatives.[32] With a vitae featuring bestselling books *America Can Be Saved* and *Listen America!*, along with a growing televangelist market, Falwell's message was that the country's survival depended on an Evangelical "Moral Majority." At the outset, Falwell placed public schools at the center of Moral Majority efforts to save the country from a pluralistic takeover. His loathing of public schools had its roots in court-ordered removal of school prayer and abortion rights, cultural pluralism workshops in corporate America, the threat that the Supreme Court might end school religious segregation by removing tax-exempt status from private schools, and efforts by educators to provide an integrated curriculum giving equal attention to value diversity and cultural representation.[33] Falwell said in 1979, "I hope to live to see the day when we won't have any public schools. The churches will have taken them over and Christians will be running them." He added, "Biblically sound textbooks must be written for every school child in every course of study."[34] The goal, of course, was to ensure the Christian faith wasn't diminished by public school teachers proselytizing about values not aligned with the Christian right.

A generation later, Pat Robertson, founder of the Christian Coalition and former presidential candidate, revived Falwell's assertion that any effort to abolish public schools was worthy. He wrote in 1993, "[Democrats] say [school] vouchers would spell the end of public schools in America. To which we say, so what?"[35] Public schools, he said, were "firmly in the grip of fanatical ideologies whose crackpot theories are fast destroying not only the public school system but an entire generation of our young."

À la Congresswoman Boebert's unapologetic formula to shape the government's bureaucratic agencies with a Christian worldview, church first, government second will equal a morally rectified society. Such Falwellian attempts have morphed into contemporary efforts to take back the education system by grooming school board members to shut down programming designed to provide more services for students from historically marginalized communities. Atop the agenda, of course, is to intercept any attempt to integrate school curriculum with more inclusive racial, ethnic, gender, and religious representation.

In his reporting on how the Texas-based conservative Evangelical cellphone company Patriot Mobile helped assert its Christian influence on school boards in the Lone Star State in 2022, Mike Hixenbaugh, senior investigative journalist for NBC News, reminded readers of the Seven Mountain Mandates. A by-product of the Ku Klux Klan's "Kreed" in the 1920s and later the Christian Identity movement of the 1970s but gaining most traction during Falwell's Moral Majority movement, the Seven Mountain Mandates is a doctrine inspiring the Christian right to infiltrate "seven spheres" of American society: family, religion, media, entertainment, business, government, and education.[36] One of Seven Mountain's leading proponents is Donald Trump's former White House spiritual adviser, Paula White.

The Christian nationalist movement, then, marked America's public school boards as ground zero to usurp political power. Why not inflame impressionable conservative Christian parents whose children might attend schools where educators provide support for LGBTQIA+ students and where humanities laboratories might critically discuss the country's troubled history of systemic racism? The Fox News guest who first sparked the parental rights panic in 2020, Christopher Rufo, a senior fellow at the Manhattan Institute, used a nationally syndicated column to tie critical race theory (CRT), an academic legal theory designed to help students view racism as systemic rather than interpersonal, to Marxism. His messaging, in the same manner as 1950s-era anticommunist witch hunts, energized the right. CRT, he suggests, substitutes class categories with racialized categories. He explains, "[CRT's] basic conclusion is the same: In order to liberate man, society must be fundamentally transformed through moral, economic and political revolution."[37] Rufo positioned K–12 public school teachers as the new "Red-ucators." Look out for *Race-ucators* (my word, not his) pushing any model of critical thinking pedagogy. And, thus, all forms of problematizing systems and institutions about the US, which are the duty of the humanities, have been placed under the watchful eye of parental groups on the right. Inevitably, anything deconstructing aspects of US history and contemporary culture has resulted in indictments of anti-Americanism, anticapitalism, and anti-Christianity.

While a winning political strategy, efforts to bully educators into silence are not new. In the same spirit as Rutherford's *A Measuring Rod* and *Truths of History*, Rufo and the Manhattan Institute provide the "Briefing Book" and "Woke Schooling: A Toolkit for Concerned Parents," respectively, to help parents identify critical pedagogy in the form of race, ethnicity, and gender studies courses, as well as educational equity professional development programming, such as social-emotional learning and culturally responsiveness, for administrators and classroom instructors. "Briefing Book" and "Woke Schooling" bred vigilance groups asserting "indoctrination" and "parental rights," such as Florida's Moms for Liberty and Pennsylvania's No Left Turn in Education. These advocacy groups correspondingly secured support from the Trump Republican faction, generating local influence on school boards and in statewide offices.

Moms for Liberty, in particular, built a national profile for establishing a vocal presence at school board meetings across the US. Founded in fall 2021 by former and current Republican school board members in Florida to resist COVID-19 restrictions, the 501(c)(4) nonprofit gained about one hundred thousand members with greater than two hundred chapters in forty states before the midterm election.[38] A rapidly emerging coalition of conservative parental rights advocates pressured school boards to give parents access to classroom materials, with little thought given to an honest balance of instructor professionalism and parental involvement in their children's education.

The politician who saw an opportunity to capitalize on the parental rights coalition's influence was Florida governor Ron DeSantis. In March 2022, DeSantis signed House Bill 1557, Parental Rights in Education, otherwise known by its critics as the "Don't Say Gay" law, prohibiting elementary teachers from reading books or mentioning topics with themes about sexual orientation or gender identity. That same year, he signed House Bill 8422, censuring any teaching that "advances, inculcates, or compels [students] to believe specified concepts constitute discrimination" in the form of CRT. Titled "Stop the Wrongs to Our Kids and Employees Act," or "Stop W.O.K.E. Act" for short, the statute also prohibits "instruction and curricula from being used to indoctrinate or persuade students" to see their country as flawed.[39] Lauded by DeSantis as "the strongest legislation of its kind," the act codifies efforts made by Florida's education department to prohibit teaching CRT in K–12 schools. Moreover, the law prohibits the state's colleges, universities, and corporations from contracting with "woke CRT consultants."[40] In the governor's words, "Florida is where 'woke' goes to die."[41]

This rightward turn toward educational control by the Southern governor happened just as DeSantis faced stiff competition from Democratic challenger Charlie Crist in his 2022 reelection campaign and after witnessing then–Republican gubernatorial candidate Glenn Youngkin successfully use a similar playbook one year prior in Virginia. On the surface, wedging ideological differences over values alone warmed up the far-right and moderate conservatives to reelect DeSantis. But a retracing of the incumbent's footsteps along the campaign trail exposes a novel connection with the Christian right, one that Mastriano failed to execute in Pennsylvania. When delivering stump speeches dating back to the Faith and Freedom Coalition's "Road to Majority" conference during summer 2021, DeSantis regularly invoked Ephesians 6: "Put on the full armor of God," he would sermonize to massive audiences as his political acumen grew in the run up to Election Day. "In addition to this," he said, "take up the shield of faith, with which you can extinguish all the flaming arrows of the evil one. Take the helmet of salvation and the sword of the Spirit, which is the word of God." His speeches typically climaxed with a nod toward public education. While calling for a "renewal" of civics education that should impart knowledge to protect the public from the "devil's scheme" resembling "ideologies like critical race theory," DeSantis, a former high school history teacher, proclaimed, "People need to be taught why America was founded, what the principles that made our country unique were. They need to be taught that your rights do not come from government; they come from God."[42] As a raised Catholic, DeSantis's popularity among conservatives, especially those in the Make America Great Again contingent, share familiar values: family rights, prayer in school, and a belief that the Constitution does not establish a strict border separating church and state. Journalists covering DeSantis's rise among conservatives link his fight against liberal "wokeness" in schools with a broader religious crusade. To DeSantis, and even some respectable academic scholars, wokeness is a religion in and of itself.[43]

Despite pushback from civil liberties groups for academic freedom and free speech violations, the aforementioned regulations are just two among many "memory laws" signed by Republican governors across the US since the founding of Moms for Liberty.[44] Though such measures to control thought tend to resemble actions of the Daughters of the Confederacy of an earlier generation, the implications are different. In the past, for example, Lost Cause efforts to usurp school curriculum were precisely that, coercive displays of populism isolated in one school district or fought from school to school. Today, memory laws are state dictates aimed at suppressing controversial history, diversity of thought, and critical thinking under the shroud of inhibiting white students' discomfort and psychological distress.

Award-winning historian Timothy Snyder identifies two "patterns" of authoritarian control over memory. The first is the effort to write laws that create a rigid climate of fear, causing teachers to "self-censor," that is, to err on the side of state mandates. Second, by nature, such legislation will produce a culture of bullying. State messaging commonly links a specific mode of thinking to anti-Americanism and anti-Christianity. Take, for example, Governor DeSantis's comments in 2021 when encouraging parents to sue school district officials for teaching CRT: "We won't allow Florida tax dollars to be spent teaching kids to hate our country or to hate each other." Similarly, a tip line established by Virginia Governor Youngkin in 2022 encouraged students and parents to anonymously report teachers and administrators for "inherently divisive practices."[45] The result is state control over memory.

Perhaps the best way to think of memory laws is by comparing them to propaganda. In both instances, a communication culture exists between state actors and its polity, functioning to embolden violent action against the political, racial, or religious Other. Snyder says state-issued memory laws "work by asserting a mandatory view of historical events" by using patriotic pride or themes of American exceptionalism to keep educators from discussing ugly parts of history or providing diverse interpretations of the past. Such measures, he critiques, "are meant to protect the powerful, not the victims of past atrocities." Memory laws lead to character assassination efforts by parent groups.[46]

A clear example of state control over memory occurred shortly after DeSantis's election to a second term as governor of Florida. Around the Martin Luther King Jr. Holiday in January 2023, DeSantis announced the Florida Department of Education would not certify the teaching of the College Board's newly created Advanced Placement African American Studies. What was his argument? The governor claimed the course violated the state's Stop W.O.K.E. Act for its inclusion of course texts written by West Indian political philosopher Franz Fanon, journalists Ta-Nehisi Coates and Michelle Alexander, and several authors linked to CRT, which include Kimberlé Crenshaw, Edward Bonilla Silva, bell hooks, and Robin D. G. Kelley. After a predictable public uproar from educators and civil rights groups, DeSantis defended the state action, claiming not only is the law *the law* but also that the course "lacks educational value."[47] While positioning one lesson plan titled "The Black Power Movement and the Black Panther Party" as inappropriate for high school students because teachers would have to discuss anticapitalist ideology, DeSantis levied most complaints upon the curriculum's final unit, which broached issues underpinning many contemporary debates in the culture war he is actively trying to win: reparations, queer theory, intersectionality, prison abolitionism, and the Movement for Black Lives. Such issues, DeSantis and his commissioner of education, Manny Diaz Jr., professed, not only violate the Florida statute but also only serve to brainwash students.

Conservative pundit Rich Lowry defended the actions of Florida's chief executive, stating that the course veers too far to the ideological left. The *National Review* editor-in-chief cited queer theory, intersectionality, and Black feminism as sticking points. While criticisms are warranted in a democracy, this does not invalidate the course's "educational value," nor should it lead to a course's governmental regulatory action. After all, few would argue against the point that activism should remain out of the classroom. And while the aforementioned topics may not be of interest to many in rural and suburban school communities, they are certainly relevant to students, community members, and educators in Florida's urban districts. In fact, Advanced Placement African American Studies is an elective, something students opt into. Furthermore, efforts to ban the course, which never mentioned the use of CRT, are indicative of government overreach. In Black communities, more specifically, discussions on reparations and the carceral state hardly qualify as arbitrary activism; they are foundational in African American history, culture, and life. Actions to remove interdisciplinary discussions on these topics, plus the whitewashing of how members of the LGBTQIA+ community founded the Black Lives Matter movement, only sow distrust and resentment in an education field already predominated by whites.

Two weeks after DeSantis's original denunciation of Advanced Placement African American Studies, the College Board seemingly reversed course. On February 1, 2023, the start of Black History Month, the nonprofit announced significant changes to the pilot while asserting political pressure did not influence the curricular transformation. The course's curriculum designers removed from the original syllabus unit anchor texts featuring the controversial authors flagged by Florida's Department of Education, choosing to instead place them into the curriculum's "Sources for Consideration." The College Board's job "is not to create a canon," explained Head of the Advanced Placement Program Trevor Packer, which is why apparent redlined works by Audre Lorde, bell hooks, Ta-Nehisi Coates, and even the less controversial Henry Louis Gates Jr. were made optional reading material after the pilot.[48] Indeed, the evidence of the revised curriculum supporting Packer's claim shows that teachers are free to choose their anchor texts from the "Sources for Consideration." The move allows teachers to make instructional decisions grounded in state mandates or school board policy.

Furthermore, critics raised similar questions about the College Board's decision to shelve or "water down" learning targets related to Black Lives

Matter, reparations, and other hot-button contemporary culture war issues. When accused of appeasing Governor DeSantis, the College Board issued an affirmative repudiation, claiming curriculum writers had already internally made changes to the course "weeks before Florida's objections were shared."[49] The revised curriculum makes researching any such topic a permissible option for the final assessment paper.

While the College Board's reasons for revising the curriculum are valid, the episode exposes a serious dilemma over the dangers facing the public school system. A linkage between state actors and a complicit constituency creates an acceptable cover for legislative measures influencing curricular offerings, where efforts to control memory at the state level have a sweeping influence across the country. Actions by political favorites like DeSantis overlap with local politics in the form of out-of-control school board meetings, subjective book bans, and defunded local libraries. Such actions only strengthen the growing conservative movement against the *public* part of public schools. Previously noted is the Stop W.O.K.E. Act. In the Sunshine State, there is also House Bill 1467, which went into effect on January 1, 2023. The statute requires school districts "to be transparent in the selection of instructional materials and library and reading materials." While reasonable in theory, a violation of the law imposes third-degree felony penalties upon a noncompliant educator, which include a $5,000 fine and up to five years in prison. (This chapter went to print before the implications of HB 1467 on the Florida school system could be ascertained). Sure, bills protecting children from inappropriate materials are reasonable and proper; however, the air of authoritarian coercion was ubiquitous among the population seemingly targeted by the DeSantis administration and lawmakers in the Florida assembly.[50]

The fight over the College Board's African American Studies curriculum and the threat of felony charges levied upon educators accused of left-wing indoctrination shows that DeSantis has something that neither Mildred Lewis Rutherford nor William Dunning possessed, legislative power. As Edmund Burke said, "The greater the power, the more dangerous the abuse." Time will tell how much the DeSantis movement in Florida will run its course across the US. But we already know memory laws have clear implications: Public schools are not the "people's college" designed to serve all students regardless of class, race, ethnicity, gender, language, religion, or physical status, as William Howard Day, a nineteenth-century educator and probably the nation's first African American school board president, once said. Like the varying degrees of Christian nationalism discussed herein, distorted truths, gaslighting, and Big Lies morph into beliefs that produce dangerous outcomes.

As long as respectable members of American society use schoolchildren to garner political support, democracy in the US will never reach its promise of a functioning multicultural society. One harkens back to Claude Bowers's bestselling publication *The Tragic Era* and the fight over how to remember the legacy of the Civil War. Bowers and Lost Cause redemptionists of yesteryear are still winning the narrative wars. The ability to control how people think about differing values results in policies, practices, language, and rhetoric impacting the lives of every American. Lost Cause champions, who initially went down in defeat with General Robert E. Lee's surrender at Appomattox Court House the morning of April 9, 1865, ultimately won the narrative war: The freedom legacy generated with Union victory gradually perished in the decades after the Civil War. Starting with school-based curricula, by the end of the nineteenth century, Lost Cause adherents generated a culture of voter suppression, mass incarceration, and anti-Black terrorism. Two decades into the twentieth century, monuments to the Confederacy festooned towns in the North and South as Klansmen used God to rally support among the white Christian populace to procure control over political and educational spheres. Jim Crow statutes, forced sterilization policies, and anti-immigration legislation reinforced assimilationist curricula in American schools. Changes to the wording of the Pledge of Allegiance, melting pot schools, and curricular standards that W. E. B. Du Bois suggested "bring more evils on the Negro" licensed some in the majority for bigotry and violence while reeducating generations of marginalized populations with self-defeating thoughts.[51] Then the modern Civil Rights Movement (1955–1965) set up a new vision for inclusion lasting the next two generations, from the passage of the Voting Rights Act in August 1965 to the June 2013 *Shelby v. Holder* Supreme Court holding ending the Voting Rights Act's coverage formula in Section 4(b) and Section 5's requirement for legislative districts to obtain authorization from the Attorney General's office before changing election practices. Here is where the myth of the Lost Cause meets the Moral Majority and where the Moral Majority meets Christian nationalism. Spanning three eras across the twentieth and twenty-first centuries, these movements propagandize salvation through redemptive narratives characterizing marginalized groups as unpatriotic and un-Godly.

Redemptive narratives, as professed by civil rights historian Peniel Joseph, aim to tell a deluded story about American exceptionalism.[52] Its thesis to the people who inhabit the US: The US is a fundamentally good nation blessed by a Christian God. This model of American exceptionalism casts the nation as loyalists versus traitors, the nonviolent versus the violent, and ultimately the pure American against the non-Christian Other. The story of exceptionalism not only perpetuates systemic violence against Black Americans, immigrants, and individuals from the LGBTQIA+ community, but it also, in recent years, serves to silence moderate voices, including Republicans-in-name only (RINOs) as well as liberal allies. The most racially and politically divisive presidential administration in my lifetime concocted a voting base motivated by sharp juxtapositions: The 1776 Commission duking it out with "The 1619 Project," à la the anti-CRT hoax, and the Black crime wave against law-and-order rhetoric. Anti-LGBTQIA+ legislation combined with memory laws in education, school board members banning books, and county commissioners cutting funding for public libraries fed its base, which was starving for fodder that could put moderates and those left of center in their place. These efforts reestablish a redemption-era social order.

As argued by the foremost authority on Christian nationalism, Katherine Stewart, voters are the "root source" of the effort to control schools, though "they are not the source of its ideas." These "foot soldiers of the movement," she writes, come to see schools as the cardinal pillar of American society.[53] As such, Christian nationalist leaders and their political liaisons stir resentment by using what are deemed apolitical biblical issues: gender, sex, and content acknowledging historical and contemporary institutional racism under the guise of teachers placing students into oppressor and oppressed categories.

While conservative Christian leaders contend that efforts to give parents authority over the curriculum are not part of the Christian nationalist movement, such movements result in the whitewashing of non-Christian, nonwhite, and noncritical points of view. The proclamation is one of "pro-freedom," but a freedom limited to a privileged few.

All that is to say, we are at a similar crossroad to what our ancestors bore in the first half of the twentieth century. The way our progenitors managed to lead the country toward civil rights victories, or that of the second reconstruction, was to confront, boldly, the history of this American democratic project. And right now, in places where it matters the most, schools, a faction has gained unmeasurable power by controlling the education system in suburban and rural areas with a cloaked curriculum and a culture of intimidation.

In each era, the zeal of Lost Causers to control the narrative outweighs the enthusiasm of those who support a heterogeneous, inclusive multicultural democratic America. As a result, the country has suffered. There is no be-all and end-all solution to universally extinguish an exclusionary movement like Christian nationalism. Indeed, for as hateful as it is, its speech is protected by the First Amendment. The answer, then, is to not hide from it. For years, leaders in the political, educational, and religious realms have hoped that ignoring the problem won't draw attention to the movement. It is often posited that by giving it more attention, a caucus of voters might elect believers in its doctrine into public office like school boards. If the narrative wars promulgated by the believers in the Lost Cause and American exceptionalism permeated the educational system generations ago, and if the 2022 midterm elections are any indication that a contingent of the Republican Party will continue to nominate candidates that use cultural divides as a way to control how schools educate our children, there has to be a countermovement by a coalition of traditional conservatives, moderates, liberals, and progressives. Those who believe in natural rights for all must do more than just focus on national elections. They need to put serious thought and energy into generating a comprehensive campaign to help those within the minority of a school district to withstand abuses of a majority faction united by a passion not to lose a particular order of society, as James Madison once wrote. The best weapon against hate speech has always been counterspeech, a flood of information to pull people out of ignorance.

A more-speech movement to balance the First Amendment can get people to cross ideological bridges, resulting in a civic culture where people are able to withstand authoritarian efforts to maintain a mythical status that to be white or Christian or straight or English-speaking is the apex of humanity or the defining feature of Americanism. Building more speech coalitions at the local level is the real work of democracy. Though a difficult process of inclusion, of faction disruption, this is a necessary step to overwrite efforts of Christian nationalists who project the marginalized as "deviants," as "unpatriotic" "anti-Americans" predestined to Hell and who don't belong.

NOTES

1. Bowers, *The Tragic Era*, 49.
2. "No More Tragic Eras," *Lexington Herald* (Lexington, KY), May 23, 1956, p. 4.
3. John David Smith, "Introduction," in Smith and Lowery, *The Dunning School*, 3–5.
4. Bowers, *The Tragic Era*, v–vii; Pollard, *The Lost Cause*.
5. Rutherford, *A Measuring Rod*, 4.
6. United Daughters of the Confederacy, "Truths of History," *The Atlanta Constitution* (Atlanta, GA), April 11, 1920, p. 3; Rutherford, *Truths of History*, xi.
7. Rutherford, *Truths of History*, v.
8. "With U.D.C. of this State," *The State* (Columbia, SC), March 25, 1923, p. 31.
9. "Prizes and Medals Given by General Organization, U.D.C., and Rules Governing Contests," *Macon News* (Macon, GA), January 15, 1922, p. 11; "Urges Work for $100 Prize," *Atlanta Constitution*, May 14, 1922, p. 4.
10. See writings of Renaud Camus and the white extinction theory.
11. Forten, "Letters from a man of colour."
12. Lane, *The Day Freedom Died*, 10–14; Keith, *The Colfax Massacre*, 115–17.
13. William Simmons quoted in Ron Grossman "Chicago and the KKK," *Chicago Tribune*, January 25, 2015, p. 17.
14. William Simmons quoted in *Los Angeles Evening Express*, "Ku Klux Klan Denies Acts of Terror in South," November 25, 1920, p. 1.

15. William Joseph Simmons, Imperial Wizard, "The Klu [sic] Klux Kreed," *Albany Democrat-Herald*, August 10, 1921, p. 8.

16. OPB, "Oregon's Klan in the 1920s: The Rise of Hate," YouTube, March 15, 2022, https://youtu.be/jaW6F2aEWic.

17. V. K. "Bearcat" Allison quoted in "KKK Brought Anti-Catholic Message to Albany," *Albany Democrat-Herald*, March 14, 1997, p. 26.

18. George Wallace quoted in Frederick Burger, "Campaign Fails to Stir Public," *The Anniston Star*, June 2, 1968, pp. 1–2.

19. David Weissman, "Lauren Boebert said she wants a biblical citizenship test," Twitter, August 4, 2022. David Weissman on Twitter: "Lauren Boebert said she wants a biblical citizenship test in the US. I'd say knowledge of the United States Constitution should be required before running as a candidate for any position in the United States Government."

20. Patriot Academy, "About," 2022, https://www.patriotacademy.com/about/.

21. Boebert quote in Weisman, "Lauren Boebert said she wants a biblical citizenship test."

22. Hedges, *American Fascists*, 11.

23. Posner, *Unholy*, 6–8.

24. Hedges, *American Fascists*, 19.

25. Stewart, *The Power Worshippers*, 7.

26. Katherine Stewart, "Christian Nationalists Are Excited about What Comes Next," *New York Times*, July 5, 2022.

27. Katherine Stewart quoted in Olivia Warren, "Author and Journalist Discusses Christian Nationalism in Politics," *The Tulane Hullabaloo*, December 9, 2022.

28. Ron Kampeas, "Holocaust Film That Likened Abortion, Gun Control to Nazism," *The Times of Israel*, November 3, 2022, https://www.timesofisrael.com/gop-nominee-had-role-in-holocaust-film-that-likened-abortion-gun-control-to-nazism/.

29. Patrick Damp, "Gubernatorial Candidate Doug Mastriano Said Women Who Get Abortions Should Be Charged with Murder," *CBS Pittsburgh*, September 28, 2022.

30. Stella Rouse and Shibley Telhami, "Most Republicans Support Declaring the United States a Christian Nation," *Politico*, September 21, 2022.

31. Jeff Diamant, "Faith on the Hill," Pew Research Center, January 3, 2023, https://www.pewresearch.org/religion/2023/01/03/faith-on-the-hill-2023/.

32. Jerry Falwell quoted in Russell Chandler, "'Electronic Church' Has Audiences in the Millions," *The Clarion-Ledger* (Jackson, MS), March 15, 1980, pp. 5A–6A; Stewart, *The Power Worshippers*, 9, 186.

33. Stewart, *The Power Worshippers*, 9, 186.

34. Jerry Falwell quoted in Holtz, *Education and the American Dream*, 98; Falwell, *America Can Be Saved!*, 52.

35. Pat Robertson quoted in Apple, *Educating the Right Way*, 161.

36. Mike Hixenbaugh, "How a Far-Right, Christian Cellphone Company 'Took Over' Four Texas School Boards," *NBC News*, August 25, 2022.

37. Christopher Rufo, "What I Discovered about Critical Race Theory Shocked Me," *Knoxville News-Sentinel*, July 11, 2021, p. 5E.

38. Moms for Liberty cited in Zac Anderson and Sommer Brugal, "Moms for Liberty: How a Group of Outraged Parents Battle School Policy," *Florida Today* (Cocoa, FL), December 12, 2021, pp. A1–A5.

39. Florida House Bill No. 7, April 22, 2022, http://laws.flrules.org/2022/72.

40. , "Stop W.O.K.E. Handout," Florida.gov, https://www.flgov.com/wp-content/uploads/2021/12/Stop-Woke-Handout.pdf.

41. Ron DeSantis quoted in Matt Dixon and Gary Fineout, "'Where Woke Goes to Die': DeSantis, with Eye Toward 2024, Launches Second Term," *Politico*, January 1, 2023, https://www.politico.com/news/2023/01/03/desantis-2024-second-term-00076160.

42. Ron DeSantis quoted in Tre Goins-Phillips, "Ron DeSantis Says He Will Put on 'Full Armor of God' to Fight Leftism: 'Our Rights Come from God,'" *CBN*, June 23, 2021, https://www1.cbn.com/cbnnews/us/2021/june/ron-desantis-says-he-will-put-on-full-armor-of-god-to-fight-leftism.

43. Ana Ceballos, "What Message Does DeSantis Send with Religious Rhetoric?" *Miami Herald*, September 13, 2022, pp. A1–A2; McWhorter, *Woke Racism*.

44. See *Pernell, et al. v Florida Board of Governors, et al. Complaint*, American Civil Liberties Union, 2022, https://www.aclu.org/letter/pernell-et-al-v-florida-board-governors-et-al-complaint.

45. Scott Simon, "A 'Tip Line' Championed by Virginia Gov. Youngkin Last Year Has Been Quietly Shut Down," *NPR*, November 5, 2022, https://www.npr.org/2022/11/05/1134514204/a-tip-line-championed-by-virginia-gov-youngkin-last-year-has-been-quietly-shut-d.

46. Timothy Snyder, "The War on History Is a War on Democracy," *New York Times*, June 29, 2021.

47. Stanley Kurtz, "DeSantis: AP African-American Studies Program, as Written, Violates Florida Law," *National Review*, January 18, 2023, https://www.nationalreview.com/corner/desantis-ap-african-american-studies-program-violates-florida-law/.

48. Trevor Parker, "AP African American Studies: An Inside View for the AP Community," Webinar, College Board, February 8, 2023.

49. College Board quoted in Giulia Heyward, "College Board's Revised AP African American Studies Course Draws Criticism," *NPR*, February 1, 2023, https://www.npr.org/2023/02/01/1153434464/college-boards-revised-ap-african-american-studies-course-draws-new-criticism.

50. CS/HB 1467, 2022 Legislature, Florida House of Representatives, https://www.flsenate.gov/Session/Bill/2022/1467/BillText/er/PDF; Jacob Oliva, Memorandum, House Bill 1467, K-12 Education, School District Responsibilities, Florida Department of Education, June 3, 2022, https://info.fldoe.org/docushare/dsweb/Get/Document-9557/dps-2022-83.pdf; Jacob Oliva, House Bill 1467, Call for Workgroup Members to Develop Online Training Program for School Library Media, Florida Department of Education, May 20, 2022, https://info.fldoe.org/docushare/dsweb/Get/Document-9545/dps-2022-76.pdf.

51. Du Bois, "Does the Negro Need Separate Schools?" 328–35.

52. Joseph, *The Third Reconstruction*; Katherine Stewart on Greg Lear, "Bubble-Wrapped in Sanctimony (with Katherine Stewart)," *Prevail* Podcast, November 4, 2022.

53. Stewart, *The Power Worshippers*, 6.

BIBLIOGRAPHY

Apple, Michael. *Educating the Right Way: Markets, Standards, God, and Inequality*. London: Routledge, 2006.

Bowers, Claude G. *The Tragic Era: The Revolution after Lincoln*. Blue Ribbon, 1929.

Du Bois, W. E. B. "Does the Negro need Separate Schools?" *The Journal of Negro Education* 4, no. 3, The Courts and the Negro Separate Schools (July 1935): 328–35.

Falwell, Jerry. *America Can Be Saved!* Murfreesboro, TN: Sword of the Lord, 1979.

Forten, James. "Letters from a man of colour, on a late bill before the Senate of Pennsylvania, ca. 1813."

Hedges, Chris. *American Fascists: The Christian Right and the War on America*. New York: Free Press, 2006.

Holtz, Harvey. *Education and the American Dream: Conservatives, Liberals and Radicals Debate the Future of Education*. New York: Praeger, 1988.

Joseph, Peniel E. *The Third Reconstruction: America's Struggle for Racial Justice in the Twenty-First Century*. New York: Basic Books, 2022.

Keith, Leeanna. *The Colfax Massacre: The Untold Story of Black Power, White Terror, and the Death of Reconstruction*. New York: Oxford University Press, 2008.

Lane, Charles. *The Day Freedom Died: The Colfax Massacre, the Supreme Court, and the Betrayal of Reconstruction*. New York: Holt, 2009.

McWhorter, John. *Woke Racism: How a New Religion Has Betrayed Black America*. New York: Portfolio/Penguin, 2021.

Pollard, Edward. *The Lost Cause: A New Southern History of the War of the Confederates*. New York: E. B. Treat & Co., 1867.

Posner, Sarah. *Unholy: How White Christian Nationalists Powered the Trump Presidency, and the Devastating Legacy They Left Behind*. New York: Random House, 2021.

Rutherford, Mildred Lewis. *A Measuring Rod to Test Text Books, and Reference Books in Schools, Colleges and Libraries*. Athens, GA: United Confederate Veterans, 1920.

———. *Truths of History: A Fair, Unbiased, Impartial, Unprejudiced and Conscientious Study of History*. Athens, GA: United Confederate Veterans, 1920.

Smith, John David, and J. Vincent Lowery. *The Dunning School: Historians, Race, and the Meaning of Reconstruction*. Lexington: University Press of Kentucky, 2013.

Stewart, Katherine. *The Power Worshippers: Inside the Dangerous Rise of Religious Nationalism*. London: Bloomsbury Publishing, 2019.

Chapter 7

"Who Do You Say That I Am?"

Laurie Cassidy

Megyn Kelly's declaration, "Jesus was a White man . . . that is a verifiable fact . . . as is Santa," is a mirror for white Catholics to glimpse how our religious images function in legitimizing and reproducing white supremacy.[1] Kelly identifies herself as a lifelong Catholic, and so do I. Because of the Ku Klux Klan's assertion that being Catholic made us "inauthentic Americans," I have been socialized to view white supremacy as a problem only for white Evangelical Protestants.[2] But this history of anti-Catholicism in America obfuscates the depth to which our white Catholic imagery is an integral part of the formation of the white racial frame in America. The white racial frame is "a way of being . . . that provides the language and interpretations that help structure, normalize, and make sense out of [white supremacist] society."[3] My chapter explores Kelly's equating of white Jesus and white Santa as a door leading down into the collective workings of the racialized white American Catholic imagination, which legitimizes and reproduces the white racial frame.

As white Catholics, we are socialized not to know that Black Catholic theologian Bryan Massingale bluntly states, "'Catholic'='white.'"[4] For many of us who are white and Catholic, it is a struggle to make this equation conscious, let alone acknowledge and understand how our practice of Catholicism in America is white. Kelly's proclamation of the "verifiable fact" of Jesus's historical whiteness can easily be dismissed as comically ignorant, a parody of her claim to be "a straight news anchor . . . not one of those opinion hosts."[5] However, Kelly's comments unintentionally make transparent the connection between Catholic imagination and the white racial frame. She demonstrates what W. E. B. Du Bois describes as "irrational reactions unpierced by reason."[6] To assert as factual that Jesus is white like Santa is patently false. Jesus was a first-century Palestinian Jew, and St. Nicholas was from Asia Minor, which *is* verifiable. Because Kelly's declaration is not historically true, she demonstrates how Jesus's whiteness is not a rational assertion, though she passionately purports it to be, but, rather, indicates the depth to which white supremacy forms the meaning making of Catholic belief in America. Kelly's profession of faith in Jesus's whiteness indicates the radical racialization of Catholic imagination in America. My chapter examines how white images of Jesus function at the intersection of Catholic imagination and the white racial frame.

The title of my chapter, "Who Do You Say That I Am?" is a question posed by Jesus to his disciples.[7] Answering this question is particularly urgent for white followers of Jesus living in America today.[8] Across denominations, Christians are speaking out against the violent perversion of Jesus's message by white Christian nationalists.[9] But who do we, white Catholics—those of us who do not identify as white nationalists—say Jesus is? How do we differentiate our beliefs about Jesus from how white images have formed our internalization of whiteness? Haven't we been surrounded by images of white angels, white saints, and images of God in white since our baptism? These white images are only one element in the white culture we inhabit and reproduce in American Catholicism.[10] Researcher Robert P. Jones gathered data that lays out a profoundly disturbing picture of our situation: "The more racist attitudes a person holds, the more likely he or she is to be identified as a white Christian."[11] For white people, this data makes professing Christian faith an ignominious admission but also requires our soul searching. Do we know how to *dis*identify with the white Jesus?[12] If we are to speak out against white Christian nationalism, and moreover interrupt its violence, white Catholics have to make conscious how we have internalized the white racial frame through our faith in Jesus as white.

To examine how white images of Jesus function at the intersection of Catholic imagination and the white racial frame, my chapter takes three interlocking turns. First, drawing upon the work of Joe Feagin, I demonstrate how the historical amnesia of American Catholicism is a critical epistemic practice of the white racial frame.[13] As an Irish Catholic growing up in the suburbs of Boston, I witnessed the violent reaction of other Irish Catholics against the federally mandated desegregation of Boston city schools in 1974.[14] Boston became known as "the Little Rock of the North."[15] However, the reaction of white Catholics to desegregation was never spoken of at Mass at my parish. In my family, I grew up with the stereotype that those Bostonians were ignorant, "shanty" Irish Catholics; *they* were racist. I did not know that I was living on Nipmuc land and that my Irish immigrant ancestors had settled on stolen Nipmuc land in central Massachusetts. We benefited from the attempted erasure of the Nipmuc from New England history.[16] For American Catholics to resist white Christian nationalism, we need to reclaim these dangerous memories that interrupt the images we have accepted of ourselves and others. As

M. Shawn Copeland explains, in our inability to act against white supremacy and its violence that is rooted in our conspiracy to forget, "[w]e repress and erase; we edit and delete. The result is a peculiar and unsettling, even puerile, ignorance that seeks to pass off as political ignorance."[17] The central practices of our Catholic faith are centered upon memory, remembering Jesus. But as Copeland explains regarding the white racial frame, "[c]ollective *forgetting* is as important as remembering, especially in regard to the prevailing narratives."[18] With this structure to our forgetting, how can white Catholics claim to remember Jesus and not simply our white image of him?

Second, I deconstruct a white image of Jesus titled *Christ in Majesty* located in the National Shrine of the Immaculate Conception in Washington, DC.[19] *Christ in Majesty* is a declaration of our institutional commitment to be white in a nation that was still unsure if Catholics could be American. My analysis demonstrates how the whiteness of Jesus functions within American Catholic imagination. In other words, this white image of Jesus reveals historical, political, and theological connections between white Catholicism and our internalization and reproduction of the white racial frame. To say that the whiteness of Jesus *functions* is to say that our Catholic iconography "is never neutral in its effects, but expresses and molds a community's bedrock convictions and actions."[20] As Copeland has argued, we cannot simply paint over the white images of Jesus.[21] And even if we could paint over the images, this will not necessarily interrupt the radical connection of whiteness and Jesus that has been so deeply imprinted upon American Catholic imagination.[22] To paint over the white face of Jesus is to jettison the process of acknowledging, understanding, and taking responsibility for how our images of Jesus are integral in reproducing the white racial frame. Moreover, this process of deconstructing Jesus as white is an imperative if we are to genuinely engage the question, "Who do you say that I am?"

Third, I will return to Jesus's question that begins my chapter. For white Catholics, Jesus's question holds the possibility of examining the racialization of our faith. Such examination may enable us to shift from our religion being about Jesus, to the religion of Jesus—the first-century Palestinian Jew.[23]

"DO THIS TO REMEMBER ME"[24]

"They have been white, if I may put it, too long."[25]

In this section, I will explore how remembering our history as American Catholics is critical to interrupting the white racial frame. As James Baldwin observed, we have been white too long.

[T]hey have been white, if I may put it, too long: they have been married to the lie of white supremacy too long; the effect on their personalities, their lives, their grasp of reality . . . they are unable to conceive that their version of reality . . . is an insult to my history and a parody of theirs and an intolerable violation of myself.[26]

To remember our repressed history is critical to healing the rupture in remembering Jesus, the first-century Palestinian Jewish man we claim to follow.[27] In addition, exploring this history reveals how the images of Jesus as white function to normalize our whiteness. Amnesia is a disordered condition of memory loss and also "the selective overlooking or ignoring of events or acts that are not favorable or useful to one's purpose or position."[28] As Feagin explains, the promotion of amnesia and selective remembering is a key element of the white racial frame.

Du Bois stated, "The Catholic Church in America stands for color separation and discrimination to a degree equaled by no other church in America, and that is saying a great deal."[29] For example, the Catholic boarding school at Holy Rosary Mission in South Dakota founded in 1888 followed the policy of the US government. For Lakota students, "Long hair was cut, given names were changed and traditional dress was banned."[30] If Catholic doctrine is rooted in the fundamental tenant that all human beings are created in God's image and likeness, how could we justify following the policy of the US government regarding Lakota children? This is not just an ethical or moral scandal. As Willie Jennings writes, "The colonial wound is real and remains largely untheorized within Western Christian theology."[31] We have a language about being human that excludes non-white people and history on this land that makes this wound invisible *to us*.[32] The Catholic origin of justifying colonization and enslavement by defining who is human reaches back much further than our being in America.

The Catholic Church sanctioned colonization and enslavement in a series of papal decrees beginning in 1444.[33] These papal decrees authorized "the Portuguese Royal Crown granting her right of ownership over the territories discovered in her name in Africa as well as empowering her to drive the natives of those territories into perpetual slavery."[34] Pope Nicholas V issued *Dum Diversas* in 1492, which authorized European colonizers to "invade, capture, vanquish, and subdue" non-Christians. Nicholas V went even further to say that colonizers could "take away all their possessions and property" and "reduce their persons to perpetual slavery."[35] In 1492, after Christopher Columbus "discovered" the "New World," Pope Alexander VI "affirmed both Portugal's right to Africa and Spain's right to the people of the 'New World.'"[36] As Sylvia Wynter points out, these papal decrees laid the *theological* foundation to colonize and enslave non-white human beings by defining who is human.

> Wealth expropriated by Western Europe from Non-European peoples was to lay the basis of its global expansion from the fifteenth century onwards, [and] was carried out within the order of truth and the self-evident order of consciousness, of a creed specific conception of what it means to be human.[37]

These horrifying words of papal decree, which "reduce their persons to perpetual slavery," are what Copeland describes as "metaphysical violence."[38] Reduce. Persons. To perpetual slavery. To attempt to "master" reality, by force. To master reality by claiming the power to rename who is human and who is not human and can never attain humanity. This metaphysical violence "eviscerates the central Roman Catholic theological and spiritual claims that all human beings share the divine likeness (*Imago Dei*) within the unity of God's creation."[39]

These papal decrees are a rupture of Christianity from its source in the historical Jesus. Isn't this an attempt to create a new heaven and a new Earth? This racialization of bodies through colonization and in enslavement is "the crossing of a threshold into a distorting vision of creation. This distorting vision of creation will lodge itself deeply in Christian thought, damaging doctrinal trajectories."[40] This lethal belief that we could say "God" is only in creation that resembles us is idolatrous, but is it also an attempt at deicide? On this land, deicide was the experience of the Kiowa. N. Scott Momaday explains that in 1890, US soldiers forbid the Kiowa (without cause) to practice the Sun Ceremony, the essential act of their faith. Momaday's grandmother, "for as long as she lived . . . , bore a vision of deicide [the killing of their god, the end of their faith]."[41]

This series of papal decrees become the theological, anthropological, and legal groundwork that legitimized the Doctrine of Discovery and its enactment in America.[42] Drawing upon this legal and theological history in 1823, Chief Justice John Marshall declared the right of settler colonizers to Native peoples' lands because of "our discovery" of America. Marshall wrote that the US had the right "to extinguish the Indian Title of occupancy either by purchasing or conquest."[43] In America, "[w]hiteness entails 'passionate' belief in one's right to everything and anything."[44]

Marshall's declaration makes America a land where Jesus can only be white. If Jesus were not white, he would remind white Christians of all the colonized and enslaved people whose humanity we have denied. To summarize, "white supremacy is constitutive of US Catholicism."[45] As white Catholics, we must ask ourselves: "Have we *forgotten* the racialized, shattered, and lynched body that lies at the heart of our religious belief and practice?"[46]

CHRIST IN MAJESTY

"[T]o kneel before the racialized idol of whiteness."[47]

These words of M. Shawn Copeland are a disturbing description of our historical and theological situation as white Catholics. We have "attempted to bleach and domesticate the Divine, to make over the Divine in [our] image and likeness."[48] How do we make conscious what Copeland describes to actively disidentify with the white Jesus? In America, the development of Jesus as white is rooted in the abolition of chattel slavery. As Edward Blum and Paul Harvey explain, "The abolition of slavery cut the legal ties between blackness and enslavement and the association of whiteness and freedom."[49] With this legal separation of enslavement and Black skin color, this left white supremacists seeking "new resources to assert their authority."[50]

> The supposed whiteness of Christ was joined to his ethics, words, and actions to symbolize and define white authority. Attaching principles of grace, love, liberty and power to Christ's whiteness, whites could dominate while claiming to be democratic.[51]

Building upon this history in relationship to American Catholicism, I draw upon research of Joe R. Feagin to deconstruct the image of Jesus in the mosaic of *Christ in Majesty* located in the National Shrine of the Immaculate Conception in Washington, DC. Feagin's concept of the "white racial frame" enables us to examine the connection of this image of Jesus and everyday operations of being white and Catholic. For Feagin, the white racial frame is more fundamental to lived experience than defining racism as an ideology. Whiteness, for Feagin, is rather a worldview that encompasses stories, visual images, and affect, and normalizes everyday interactions.[52]

The mosaic of *Christ in Majesty* is located in the upper church of the National Shrine of the Immaculate Conception in Washington, DC, which began construction in 1920.[53] The shrine's geographic location demonstrates the connection of political power and religious imagery at work in representing Jesus as white. The shrine is a place of worship and also American Catholicism's claim to civic space, a church "sunk in tradition yet distinctively American."[54]

> In the United States, with its legally sanctioned diversity, faiths have negotiated political power, constructed denominational identity, and secured public visibility by positioning national churches in the nation's capital.[55]

The physical location of the National Shrine was critical to American Catholicism's staking a claim to the landscape of political power in

Washington, DC, which can be seen in how the shrine is described as it relates to government buildings in the city. The dome of the shrine, which holds the mosaic of *Christ in Majesty*, has been compared in size and shape to that of the Capitol building. In 1960 at the time of the shrine's completion, one commentator declared that one dome honors the "continent-conquering forefathers" and the other shows the "Catholic ecclesiastical forefathers have erected our spiritual capital there."[56]

In the mosaic of *Christ in Majesty*, Jesus is represented as seated with his arms outstretched.[57] A red robe covers most of his body with his left arm and chest exposed, which is youthful and muscular. His skin is a pinkish white, and his blond hair is shoulder length in waves. The face of Christ has arched eyebrows, blue eyes, and an aquiline nose with a short blond beard and mustache. Two halos surround Christ's white head, with flames of fire radiating out in three directions, suggestive of a cross.

By representing the facial features of the risen Christ with blond hair and blue eyes is to erase the memory of Jesus as a first-century Palestinian Jew. Such representation is a critical move in refiguring Jesus as white in American Catholicism, and as Feagin explains:

> What the dominant racial framing ignores or suppresses is critical to the continuation of oppression. Collective *forgetting* is as important as remembering, especially in regard to the prevailing narratives.[58]

The mosaic *Christ in Majesty* is 3,610 square feet with Christ's image spanning 34 feet across, "one of the largest mosaics of Jesus Christ in the world."[59] The enormous scale of this mosaic literally takes up a great deal of space and is suggestive of what philosopher Shannon Sullivan describes as the "ontological expansiveness" of whiteness. Sullivan explains that white people "tend to act and think as if all spaces—whether geographical, physical, linguistic, economic, spiritual, bodily, or otherwise—should be available for them to move in and out of as they wish."[60]

So how could the scale of this image of the white Jesus function as part of the white racial frame? In 2018, the Haudenosaunee hosted a conference on the Doctrine of Discovery. A conference organizer, Betty Lyons, who is an Onondaga tribal member and president of the American Indian Law Alliance, described that the Doctrine of Discovery impacts her on a daily basis.

> Just by going to the local grocery store, or the local gas station or the post office, where we are definitely made to feel unwanted. Or not welcome. It's this sense of entitlement that I see with people not of color. A lot of people who are not of color have this attitude that somehow, they are deserving or have an expectation

that they're going to be treated better than anybody else. And people don't see it from that perspective because they don't have to live it.[61]

Lyons claims that the Doctrine of Discovery has so shaped the consciousness of oppressed and oppressor in America that the patterns of behavior go unquestioned, without awareness of its origin.[62] It may be tempting to say that I am overreaching in my connections between the mosaic and Lyons's experience of colonization. But rather than a retreat from this, let's listen and really hear what Lyons is describing about living on one's own land as an intruder, and remember how our faith legitimized this reality. The white racial frame is an internalization of the status quo and normalizes dominance and subordination in everyday life.

In 2020, Bishop Donald Hying wrote that Catholics may have at times "mistakenly equated 'the fullness of Catholicism with European culture,'" but, Hying notes, Catholics do have multicultural images of Jesus and the saints. Therefore, Hying concludes, "In this context, are white representations of Christ and His Mother inherently signs of white supremacy? I think not."[63] I return to the image of *Christ in Majesty* to understand the relationship of this image to "multicultural images" in the architecture of the National Shrine and how it demonstrates the white racial frame. Because Catholicism does have "multicultural" images of Jesus and the saints does not negate Jesus's signification as white.

Creator of this mosaic Jan Henryk de Rosen (1891–1982) described that the image of Christ was intended to be the culmination of the art in five domes in the upper church of the shrine. De Rosen explains,

> As in St. Mark's in Venice, the chief characteristics of the interior of the Shrine are a succession of decorated domes. Each dome is a unit in itself, leading to the last half dome of the apse of the church, the Christ in Majesty.[64]

In the crypt of the Shrine, diverse communities of Catholics in America are represented, for example, through Our Lady of Antipolo, Our Lay of La Vang, Our Lady of Lebanon, and Our Mother of Africa. What is the significance of this image of Christ as white as the culmination of art in the center of the Shrine while all the non-European images are in the crypt?[65] The juxtaposition of these images reinforces that even when we create "multicultural" images they are always in response to the dominance of Jesus as white.[66]

Bryan Massingale writes of an incident that illustrates the white dominance that is encoded in the architecture of the shrine.

> [A] noted Catholic commentator . . . remarked during Pope Benedict's recent (2008) Mass in Washington, D.C., after a Prayer of the Faithful and Presentation

of Gifts marked by diverse languages and spirited Gospel and Spanish singing: "We have just been subjected to an over-preening display of multicultural chatter. And now, the Holy Father will begin the sacred part of the Mass."[67]

For Catholic theology, our image of the Divine "indicates what it considers the greatest good, the profoundest truth and the most appealing beauty."[68] The whiteness of Jesus is not simply asserting his skin color but moreover attributing to all white skin the characteristics of Jesus. Contemporary social psychological research bears out this seditious connection. A group of social scientists led by Steven O. Roberts of Stanford University documented the concrete consequences for how people conceptualize God. These researchers observed that whether or not a person believes in God, "People are constantly exposed to the image of God as a white man." Their data, published in 2020, found that "when people conceptualize God as a white man, they are more likely to perceive white male job candidates as more fit for leadership than black and female applicants."[69] Roberts explains, "Racism is not about bad apples or people who hate other people. . . . Racism is embedded in our images and in our school systems, it's the air we breathe. We're all affected and infected by it."[70]

This mosaic of *Christ in Majesty* seems to illustrate in stark terms how white Catholics have been induced "to kneel before the racialized idol of whiteness."[71] Briefly, tracing that Jesus signified as white in American Catholic imagination demonstrates the necessity of interrogating our claims about our faith in Jesus.

> The basic theological task in America is not that of establishing the existence of God, but that of discerning the true God from false idols. Today it is no longer meaningful to call one's self a believer; the meaningful thing is to explain in which God one believes. The basic problem is not the existence of God but the presence of God.[72]

"WHO DO YOU SAY THAT I AM?"

"To imagine Jesus as other-than-white would demand a process of unlearning."[73]

If as white Catholics we want to confront the reality of white Christian nationalism, we must confront how our images of Jesus as white function; we can no longer feign ignorance of their lethal legacy. Dylann Roof was a member in good standing at his local ELCA Lutheran parish. His drawings of Jesus as white were used in evidence at his trial for killing nine members of Mother Emmanuel AME Church on June 17, 2015.[74] We must help each other acknowledge that "the white liberal and the white supremacist share the same root postulates. They are different in degree not kind."[75] We have grown up in the same American Christian milieu as Roof. We "grow from the same tree of white dominance."[76]

If you are a white American Catholic, think about the first time we were exposed to an image of Jesus. Industrialization gave Americans the technological ability to mass produce images of the white Christ, and the greatest impact of these images can be seen in Sunday schools and in CCD, "where the whiteness of Jesus became a religious fact in the psyche of children."[77] Through prayer cards, catechisms, song books, illustrated bibles, bookmarks, Christmas cards, and calendars, the whiteness of Jesus was introduced to very young children.

> [V]isual depictions of Christ lodged the idea of his whiteness deep within cultural conventions and individual psyches. Before many children could consider other lessons of faith or morality, they had seen images of white Christs and experienced adults seeming to regard these pictures as authentic. The goal of these pictures was to teach Christianity, but an unintended consequence was to create an often unspoken belief that Jesus was white. This made Christ's whiteness a psychological certainty. It could be felt without thought and presumed without proof. To imagine Jesus as other-than-white would demand a process of unlearning.[78]

We may claim to no longer imagine Jesus as white, but we need to come to grips with the depth to which the white Jesus functions in reproducing the white racial frame. It is worth repeating the observation by Blum and Harvey, "To imagine Jesus as other-than-white would demand a process of unlearning.[79]

"Portraits are potent and can be dangerous."[80] This statement rings true in regard to how we portray Jesus in the United States. Portraits are relational, inviting the viewer to know not just the physical appearance but "something essential about its subject that transcends mere surface likeness."[81] And these portraits of Jesus as white signify power and dominance. Visually representing Jesus is not only "saying" something about his divinity but also his humanity, as well as our own; this visual theology teaches us without words. Contemplating an image of Jesus is risky because we become vulnerable to that which we gaze upon—not words about which we ponder and think critically.[82] As we gaze upon these images of Jesus as white, how do we answer Jesus's question?

It is tempting to distance ourselves from Jesus as white. If you are white and Catholic, there are a variety of strategies to stop the unsettling task of questioning the ways we are complicit in reproducing belief in the whiteness of Jesus. As white Catholics, we have been taught that all we need to do is verbally declare that we do not believe Jesus is white and through this declaration we magically make "null and void" four hundred years of collective socialization into white supremacy in America. Because we say we don't imagine Jesus as white or believe him to be white does not mean his whiteness does not function in our faith—and the way we live. Jesus as white is more than simply describing pigmentation. For example, we can claim Jesus is not white, but in so doing *nothing changes*. More accurately, the patterns of whiteness and the ways in which we relate to other people, to ourselves, and to God stay exactly the same and we remain ignorant of how white supremacy works.

It is also tempting to simply replace these white images with images of Jesus that do not look like us. However, does this act of replacement displace our white racial frame? As white Catholics, we need to collectively examine our consciousness. To answer Jesus's question, "Who do you say that I am?" may hold the possibility of participating in this examination. Rather than answering Jesus's question with abstract Christological formulas, the question can be a probe into who we are as white Catholics.[83] Asking this question can be a way of "flipping the script" and turning our gaze into how we have been socialized as white Catholics in America.[84] Such examination may enable us to shift from our religion being about Jesus, to the religion of Jesus—the first-century Palestinian Jew.[85]

NOTES

1. Megyn Kelly, "Santa Is What He Is,' Which Is White," YouTube, December 12, 2013, https://www.youtube.com/watch?v=7XYlJqf4dLI.

2. See Kenneth C. Barnes, *Anti-Catholicism in Arkansas: How Politicians, the Press, the Klan, and Religious Leaders Imagined and Enemy, 1910–1960* (Fayetteville: University of Arkansas Press, 2016). For a history of anti-Catholicism in America beyond the work of the Ku Klux Klan, see Maura Jane Farrelly, *Anti-Catholicism in America, 1620–1860* (New York: Cambridge University Press, 2018).

3. "[M]uch historical research demonstrates there is in North America and elsewhere a dominant, white-created racial frame that provides an overarching and generally destructive worldview, one extending across white divisions of class, gender, and age." Joe R. Feagin, *The White Racial Frame: Centuries of Racial Framing and Counter-Framing* (New York: Routledge, 2013), 10.

4. Bryan Massingale, *Racial Justice and the Catholic Church* (Maryknoll, NY: Orbis Books, 2010), 81.

5. Massingale, *Racial Justice and the Catholic Church*, 81.

6. W. E. B. Du Bois, *Dusk of Dawn* (New Brunswick, NJ: Transaction, 1984 [1940]), 6. Cited in Feagin, *The White Racial Frame*, 107.

7. "Who do you say that I am?" is a question posed by Jesus to his disciples in Mt 16: 13–16, Mk 8: 27–29, and Lk 9: 18–20.

8. There are many dimensions to the urgency of Jesus's question for Christians in America. For example, how is the Jesus of history related to the Christ of faith? It seems popular culture offers pictures of Jesus that make this distinction ambiguous. Bill O'Reilly's book and movie (coauthored with Martin Duggard) *Killing Jesus* (New York: Henry Holt, 2013) is self-described "Biblical history." Being aired by the National Geographic Channel seemed to authorize this claimed to O'Reilly's work as biblical history. As Brook Wilensky-Lanford comments, to describe this picture of Jesus as biblical history suggests impartiality. See "Killing Jesus: Bill O'Reilly's Film Is Touted as History. But Facts Aren't Sacred to Him," *The Guardian*, March 29, 2015, https://www.theguardian.com/commentisfree/2015/mar/29/killing-jesus-bill-oreillys-film-is-touted-as-history-but-facts-arent-sacred-to-him. But as Jon Sobrino, SJ, makes clear, by obfuscating this distinction we pretend our picture of Jesus has no political stakes or allegiances. *Christology at the Crossroads: A Latin American Approach* (Maryknoll, NY: Orbis Books, 1978).

9. See Catholic News Service, "Fr. Bryan Massingale: White Nationalism Is the Greatest Threat to Peace Today," *National Catholic Reporter*, August 5, 2021, https://www.ncronline.org/news/justice/fr-bryan-massingale-white-nationalism-greatest-threat-peace-today; Carter Heyward, *The 7 Deadly Sins of White Christian Nationalism: A Call to Action* (Lanham, MD: Rowman & Littlefield, 2022); Pamela Cooper-White, *The Psychology of Christian Nationalism: Why People Are Drawn In and How to Talk Across the Divide* (Minneapolis, MN: Fortress Press, 2022); Anthea Butler, *White Evangelical Racism: The Politics of Morality in America* (Chapel Hill: University of North Carolina Press, 2021); Kyle Edward Haden, *Embodied Idolatry: A Critique of Christian Nationalism* (Lanham, MD: Rowman & Littlefield, 2020); Obery M. Hendricks Jr., *Christians against Christianity: How Right-Wing Evangelicals Are Destroying Our Faith and Our Nation* (Boston: Beacon Press, 2021).

10. For example, in American Catholicism we use the term *Black Catholics*. There are good reasons for Black Catholics to identify themselves as such: to resist assimilation into white culture. And it also signifies that the norm is white. To understand this history and theological rationale, see Cyprian Davis, *The History of Black Catholics in the United States* (New York: Herder & Herder, 1995); Diana L. Hayes and Cyprian Davis, eds., *Taking Down Our Harps: Black Catholics in the United States* (Maryknoll, NY: Orbis Books, 1998); M. Shawn Copeland, LaReine-Marie Mosely, and Albert Raboteau, eds., *Uncommon Faithfulness: The Black Catholic Experience* (Maryknoll, NY: Orbis Books, 2009).

11. This quotation of Robert P. Jones is taken from Michael Luo, "American Christianity's White-Supremacy Problem: Story, Theology, and Culture All Contribute to the Racist Attitudes Embedded in the White Church," *The New Yorker*, September 2, 2020, https://www.newyorker.com/books/under-review/american-christianitys-white-supremacy-problem. See Robert P. Jones, *White Too Long: The Legacy of White Supremacy in American Christianity* (New York: Simon & Schuster, 2020).

12. This idea of *dis*identifying with the white Jesus is found in a profound essay by Jennifer Harvey, "What Would Zacchaeus Do? The Case for *Dis*identifying with Jesus," in *Christology and Whiteness: What Would Jesus Do?* edited by George Yancy (London: Routledge, 2012), 99.

13. Feagin, *The White Racial Frame*, x.

14. James Hannon, "The Influence of Catholic Schools on the Desegregation of Public Schools Systems: A Case of White Flight in Boston," in *Population Research and Policy Review* 3 (1984): 219–37; Richard Gribble, "Cardinal Humberto Medeiros and the Desegregation of Boston's Public Schools, 1974–1976," *Journal of Church and State* 48, no. 2 (Spring 2006): 327–53.

15. Ronald Formisano, *Boston against Busing, Race, Class and Ethnicity in the 1960s and 1970s* (Chapel Hill: University of North Carolina Press, 1991), 1.

16. See Jean O'Brien, *Firsting and Lasting: Writing Indians out of Existence in New England* (Minneapolis: University of Minnesota Press, 2010); Thomas L. Doughton, "Unseen Neighbors: Native Americans of Central Massachusetts, a People Who Had Vanished," in *After King Philip's War: Presence and Persistence in Indian New England*, edited by Colin Calloway (Hanover, NH: University Press of New England, 1997), 207–30. I regret there is not enough space here to account for the amazing work that is being done regarding reparations to the Nipmuc and also to celebrate their resilience and resistance to genocide, despite the US government's refusal to acknowledge the Nipmuc's existence.

17. M. Shawn Copeland, "Memory, #BlackLivesMatter, and Theologians," *Political Theology* 17, no. 1 (March 17, 2016), https://politicaltheology.com/memory-blacklivesmatter-and-theologians-m-shawn-copeland/.

18. Copeland, "Memory, #BlackLivesMatter, and Theologians," 17. Emphasis in the original.

19. To view this mosaic and see its location within the basilica, see https://www.nationalshrine.org/art-architecture/.

20. Elizabeth A. Johnson, "Naming God She: Theological Implications," *The Boardman Lecture in Christian Ethics* (October 19, 2000): 1, http://repository.upenn.edu/boardman/5.

21. M. Shawn Copeland, "The (Black) Jesus of Detroit: Reflection on Black Power and the (white) American Christ," in *Christology and Whiteness: What Would Jesus Do?* Edited by George Yancy (New York: Routledge, 2012), 180–95.

22. In 1972 Albert Cleage wrote, "You can take anything and paint it Black, but that does not make it black if it is still serving white interests and if it still comes out of the white experience. . . . A thing is not Black because it is painted Black." Albert Cleage, *Black Christian Nationalism: New Directions for the Black Church* (New York: William Morrow & Company, 1972), 14. Also see Copeland, "The (Black) Jesus of Detroit," 180–95.

23. This distinction comes from the work of Howard Thurman, *Jesus and the Disinherited* (Boston: Beacon Press, 1976), 13.

24. See 1 Cor 11:23–26. This section of Corinthians describes words at the Last Supper that we use as the basis for our celebration of the eucharist.

25. These words of James Baldwin are cited in Robert Jones, *White Too Long: The Legacy of White Supremacy in American Christianity* (New York: Simon & Schuster, 2020), 233.

26. Jones, *White Too Long*, 233.

27. See Kameron Carter, *Race: A Theological Account* (New York: Oxford University Press, 2008), 79–124.

28. Merriam-Webster's Dictionary online.

29. Cited in Jones, *White Too Long*, 65.

30. Maka Black Elk and William Critchley-Menor, SJ, "Atoning for Sins against Indigenous People Begins with Confronting the past. Red Cloud Indian School Is Showing the Way," *America Magazine*, October 8, 2021, https://www.americamagazine.org/politics-society/2021/10/08/indigenous-peoples-day-orange-shirt-culture-jesuits-boarding-school.

31. Willie James Jennings, *The Christian Imagination: Theology and the Origins of Race* (New Haven, CT: Yale University Press, 2010), 115. Jennings points out that the exception to this is Gustavo Gutiérrez.

32. For more on this point, see Laurie Cassidy, "Starting with the Land Under Our Feet," in *What Is Constructive Theology? Methodologies in Constructive Theology*, edited by Marion Grau and Jason Wyman (London: Bloomsbury, 2020), 167–90.

33. There is not space here to adequately account for the deformation of Catholic imagination inaugurated in the transatlantic slave trade and colonization of the "new world." In this section I am indebted to the work of Alex Mikulich, "The Roman Catholic Origins of Coloniality," in *Unlearning White Supremacy: A Spirituality of Racial Liberation* (Maryknoll, NY: Orbis Books, 2022), 53–78.

34. Pius Onyemechi Adiele, *The Popes, The Catholic Church, and the Transatlantic Enslavement of Black Africans, 1418–1839* (Hildesheim, Germany: Georg Olms Verlag, 2017), 250n94. Cited in Mikulich, *Unlearning White Supremacy*, 15n55.

35. See Steve Newcomb, "What Fifteenth-Century Papal Bulls Can Teach Us about Indigenous Identity," *Berkley Forum*, October 21, 2020, https://berkleycenter.georgetown.edu/responses/what-fifteenth-century-papal-bulls-can-teach-us-about-indigenous-identity.

36. Mikulich, *Unlearning White Supremacy*, 76.

37. Sylvia Wynter, "Unsettling the Coloniality of Being/Power/Truth/Freedom: Towards the Human after Man, Its Overrepresentation: An Argument," *CR: The New Centennial Review* 3, no. 3 (Fall 2003): 291. Cited in Mikulich, *Unlearning White Supremacy*, 77.

38. See M. Shawn Copeland, "Anti-Blackness and White Supremacy in the Making of American Catholicism," *American Catholic Studies* 127, no. 3 (Fall 2016): 6. She draws the term *metaphysical violence* from the work of Gianni Vattimo, "Towards an Ontology of Decline," in *Reading Metaphysics: The New Italian Philosophy*, edited by Giovanni Borradori (Evanston, IL: Northwestern University Press, 1988), 64.

39. Mikulich, *Unlearning White Supremacy*, 54–55.

40. Jennings, *The Christian Imagination*, 23.

41. Cited in John Hallwas, "Family Past and the Quest for Identity: N. Scott Momaday," *The McDonough County Voice*, August 15, 2015, https://www.mcdonoughvoice

.com/story/opinion/2015/08/15/family-past-quest-for-identity/33676787007/. See N. Scott Momaday, *The Way to Rainy Mountain* (Albuquerque: University of New Mexico Press, 1969).

42. For an excellent treatment of the intersection of theological and legal issues in the Doctrine of Discovery, see Steven T. Newcomb, *Pagans in a Promised Land: Decoding the Doctrine of Christian Discovery* (Wheat Ridge, CO: Fulcrum Publishing, 2008). See also Mark Charles and Soong-Chan Rah, *Unsettling Truths: The Ongoing, Dehumanizing Legacy of the Doctrine of Discovery* (Downers Grove, IL: InterVarsity Press, 2019); Sarah Augustine, *The Land Is Not Empty: Following Jesus in Dismantling the Doctrine of Discovery* (Harrison, VA: Herald Press, 2021).

43. See Jeanine Hill Fletcher, *The Sin of White Supremacy: Christianity, Racism, and Religious Diversity in America* (Maryknoll, NY: Orbis Books, 2017), 51. This ruling is part of the Marshall trilogy. See Frank Pommersheim, "The Marshall Trilogy: Foundational but Not Fully Constitutional?" in *Broken Landscapes: Indians, Indian Tribes and the Constitution* (New York: Oxford University Press, 2009), 87–124.

44. Ella Myers, "Beyond the Wages of Whiteness: Du Bois on the Irrationality of AntiBlack Racism," *Items: Insights from the Social Sciences*, March 21, 2017, https://items.ssrc.org/reading-racial-conflict/beyond-the-wages-of-whiteness-du-bois-on-the-irrationality-of-antiblack-racism/.

45. James Keenan, "The Color Line, Race and Caste: Structures of Domination and the Ethics of Recognition," *Theological Studies* 82, no. 1 (2021): 75.

46. Copeland, "Memory, #BlackLivesMatter, and Theologians." Italics in the original.

47. Copeland, "Anti-Blackness and White Supremacy," 72.

48. Copeland, "Anti-Blackness and White Supremacy," 72.

49. Edward J. Blum and Paul Harvey, *The Color of Christ: The Son of God and the Saga of Race in America* (Chapel Hill: University of North Carolina Press, 2012), 142–43.

50. Blum and Harvey, *The Color of Christ*, 143.

51. Blum and Harvey, *The Color of Christ*, 142.

52. Feagin, *The White Racial Frame*.

53. To view this mosaic and see its location within the basilica, see https://www.nationalshrine.org/art-architecture/.

54. "Art and Architecture of the Basilica," The Basilica of the National Shrine of the Immaculate Conception, https://www.nationalshrine.org/art-architecture/.

55. Thomas A. Tweed, *America's Church: The National Shrine and Catholic Presence in the Nation's Capital* (New York: Oxford University Press, 2011), 191.

56. Tweed, *America's Church*, 185.

57. This analysis is part of a longer essay; see Laurie Cassidy, "Contemplative Prayer and White Supremacy," in *Desire, Darkness and Hope: Theology in a Time of Impasse*, edited by Laurie Cassidy and M. Shawn Copeland (Collegeville, MN: Liturgical Press, 2022).

58. Cassidy, "Contemplative Prayer and White Supremacy," 17. Emphasis in the original.

59. "A Guide to Basilica Art: Mosaics of the Great Upper Church," The Basilica of the National Shrine of the Immaculate Conception, March 16, 2020, https://www.nationalshrine.org/blog/a-guide-to-basilica-art-mosaics-of-the-great-upper-church/.

60. Shannon Sullivan, *Revealing Whiteness: The Unconscious Habits of Racial Privilege* (Bloomington: Indiana University Press, 2006), 10. Cited in Christina Cleveland, *God Is a Black Woman* (New York: HarperCollins, 2022), 217.

61. Jim Kent, "Haudenosaunee Host Doctrine of Discovery Gathering," *Lakota Times*, August 23, 2018, https://www.lakotatimes.com/articles/haudenosaunee-host-doctrine-of-discovery-gathering/.

62. Kent, "Haudenosaunee Host Doctrine of Discovery Gathering."

63. Jonah McKeown, "'I Cannot Remain Silent': Madison Catholic Bishop Condemns Destruction of Religious Statues," *Catholic News Agency*, June 24, 2020, https://www.catholicnewsagency.com/news/44966/i-cannot-remain-silent-madison-catholic-bishop-condemns-destruction-of-religious-statues#. There is not enough space here to deconstruct this discourse. It is telling that Kelly and Hying are responding to people are calling for change. In both cases their riposte is case in point. Both Santa Claus and the national statues have histories embedded in white supremacy. See Ryan Andrew Newson, *Cut in Stone: Confederate Monuments and Theological Disruption* (Waco, TX: Baylor University Press, 2020); Karen Cox, *No Common Ground: Confederate Monuments and the Ongoing Fight for Racial Justice* (Chapel Hill: University of North Carolina Press, 2021); Lisa Blee and Jean O'Brian, *Monumental Mobility: The Memory Work of Massasoit* (Chapel Hill: University of North Carolina Press, 2019). For a fascinating history of the representation of Santa Claus, see "The Definitive History of Santa Claus," Coca-Cola Company, https://www.coca-colacompany.com/au/news/definitive-history-of-santa-claus.

64. "The 5 Domes of the National Shrine and the Story They Tell," Trinity Dome at America's Catholic Church, May 31, 2017, https://www.trinitydome.org/news/5-domes-national-shrine-story-tell/.

65. *Christ in Majesty* is in the main Church and multicultural images are in the crypt, a place of burial or the basement. It is interesting to consider the connection of "basement" and abasement, which is humiliation or degradation. I am grateful to Br. Martin Byrne, CFC, who shared this insight in personal conversation.

66. For more on this, see Anthony Pinn, "Putting Jesus in his Place," in *Humanism: Essays on Race, Religion and Popular Culture* (London: Bloomsbury, 2015), 76–92.

67. Massingale, *Racial Justice and the Catholic Church*, 81.

68. Johnson, "Naming God She," 1.

69. Melissa De Whitte, "Who People Believe Rules in Heaven Influences Their Beliefs about Who Rules on Earth, Stanford Scholars Find," *Stanford/News*, January 31, 2020, https://news.stanford.edu/press-releases/2020/01/31/consequences-perng-god-white-man/. For more detail on this study, see S. O. Roberts, K. Weisman, J. D. Lane, A. Williams, N. P. Camp, M. Wang, M. Robison, K. Sanchez, and C. Griffiths, "God as a White Man: A Psychological Barrier to Conceptualizing Black

People and Women as Leadership Worthy," *Journal of Personality and Social Psychology* 119, no. 6 (2020): 1290–315.

70. Lila MacLellan, "People Who See God as White Are More Likely to See White Job Applicants as Leaders," Quartz at Work, August 28, 2020, https://qz.com/work/1893701/how-white-depictions-of-god-reinforce-racial-inequality-at-work.

71. Copeland, "Anti-Blackness and White Supremacy," 7. Cited in Mikulich, *Unlearning White Supremacy*, 55.

72. Pablo Richard, "Theology in the Theology of Liberation," in *Mysterium Liberationis: Fundamental Concepts of Liberation Theology*, edited by Ignacio Ellacuria, SJ, and Jon Sobrino, SJ (Maryknoll, NY: Orbis Books, 1993), 155. See also Jon Sobrino, SJ, "Evil and Hope: A Reflection for Victims," *CTSA Proceedings* 50 (1995): 80.

73. Blum and Harvey, *The Color of Christ*, 15.

74. See Jones, *White Too Long*, 137–44. Also see Alexander Jun, Tabatha Jones Jolivet, Allison Asch, and Christopher Collins, *White Jesus: The Architecture of Racism in Religion and Education* (New York: Peter Lang, 2018).

75. These words of Lerone Bennett are cited in Shannon Sullivan, *Good White People: The Problem with Middle-Class White Anti-Racism* (Albany: SUNY Press, 2014), 1.

76. Sullivan, *Good White People*, 4.

77. Blum and Harvey, *The Color of Christ*, 146.

78. Blum and Harvey, *The Color of Christ*, 15.

79. Blum and Harvey, *The Color of Christ*, 15.

80. See Robin Margaret Jensen, *Face to Face: Portraits of the Divine in Early Christianity* (Minneapolis, MN: Fortress Press, 2005), x.

81. Jensen, *Face to Face*, xi.

82. Robin Jensen, *The Substance of Things Seen: Art, Faith, and the Christian Community* (Grand Rapids, MI: William B. Eerdmans Publishing Company, 2004), 19.

83. "To ask a question in this way is not to inform, not to furnish new areas of knowledge. It is rather to probe what is already there inside a human being, even if unrecognized." Michael J. Buckley, SJ, *What Do You Seek? The Questions of Jesus as Challenge and Promise* (Grand Rapids, MI: William B. Eerdmans Publishing Company, 2016), 6.

84. For more on this idea of "flipping the script," see George Yancy, *Look, a White! Philosophical Essays on Whiteness* (Philadelphia: Temple University Press, 2013), 3.

85. This distinction comes from the work of Howard Thurman, *Jesus and the Disinherited* (Boston: Beacon Press, 1976), 13.

Chapter 8

The Theological Irony of White Christian Nationalism

A View from the South

Leah Kalmanson

How is Christianity to address its current entanglement in the US context with white nationalism, xenophobia, and anti-Black racism? A question of such seriousness deserves careful consideration, and I hope to shoulder a small part of this scholarly burden by the end. However, when I was initially asked to contribute to this collection, I hesitated. I am a specialist in East Asian philosophies who is personally, as I discuss, Jewish. Surely, I thought, my views on Christianity are not really relevant here. Nonetheless, I reflected deeply on the ways that I, like all Americans, negotiate the uneasy conflation of "Americanness" with Christianity. This has subtly shaped my scholarly interests, and it has indelibly marked my autobiography. And so, to make this context clear for others, I open this chapter with a personal story.

MY FIRST TRANSLATION PROJECT

I grew up in the small southeastern Georgia town of Swainsboro. It's on the edge of the Canoochee River swamp in the ancestral and unceded territories of the diverse peoples who eventually formed the Muscogee (Creek) Nation. Today, Swainsboro is well over an hour away from any of the larger southeastern Georgia cities like Savannah or Augusta and light-years from the urban center of Atlanta in the north. As of the 2020 census, Swainsboro is home to 7,425 people. About 56 percent are African American, 36 percent are white, most of the remaining percent are Hispanic or Latino/a or identify as mixed race, and right now, there are six Jews. When I lived there, there were eight Jews. By January 2023, there will be four. More on that at the end.

I won't saddle you with all the details of what it was like to grow up Jewish in the Deep South. It was not great. It was also wonderful. There were kids who made fun of the size of my nose, who reminded me *constantly* that I'd be going to hell, who knew *nothing* of my heritage other than that we'd killed Jesus. There were also kids who, now, remain my lifelong friends. And, of course, there's the irreplaceable perspective I gained on American race, religion, and politics having grown up in a predominantly African American town, in the heart of the racially divided South, with a mezuzah on my door.

As soon as they handed me my high school diploma, I left for the big city of Atlanta. I had applied to only one college, which I had selected solely on the basis of a pamphlet I'd received in my gym on college fair day featuring an idyllic campus in an urban setting. When I got there, I found a small liberal arts institution on the north end of Atlanta, populated mainly by wealthy transplants from other large Southern cities in neighboring states. My first clue that I was out of my element came when I noticed people politely suppressing smiles when I spoke. My father may have been a Jewish artist from Brooklyn, but I was born and raised in Swainsboro, and I sounded like it. I had an *accent*, y'all. I still do. This experience at liberal arts college was my first encounter with the demographic differences marking ways of speech. In Swainsboro, I sounded like everyone else. At my liberal arts school, I sounded like a yokel. It was my first time being aware that I was both Jewish and a yokel.

My roommate was one of the handful of students from Atlanta itself, and I fell in with a group of her high school friends. They were the most sophisticated people I'd ever met—urbanites from a Catholic school, suffering from all the existential ailments that you might imagine would befall recovering Catholic youths, as well as all the sad legacies of sexual repression, abuse, and policing of orientation and gender. One evening we drove out to Stone Mountain, a small town with a noted state park and, of course, a noted monument carved into the side of the mountain celebrating the South's role in the Civil War. To my new friends, Stone Mountain was a joke—a backwater full of pick-up trucks, gun racks, and Confederate flags. To me, it just looked like all the rest of Georgia outside the Atlanta bubble.

So, what were we doing out there? We were doing what any kids would be doing at a state park after hours. We were up to no good. As it happened, that evening, we were not alone, and another group of kids, also up to no good, sat in the dark a few yards away from us. These were not urbanite college students from an Atlanta liberal arts school but locals from around Stone Mountain. We didn't immediately hit it off. My new friends (with their black eyeliner, studded chokers, and Doc Martens) and the Stone Mountain locals (with their cowboy boots and crop tops) stayed warily at a distance, up until one group needed to borrow a lighter from the other. I don't remember who approached whom first. But, I do remember, as soon as the young woman from around Stone Mountain opened her mouth and started talking, one of my new friends with his black-lined eyes turned to us aghast and said, "Leah will have to translate."

I felt so bizarrely proud. After all those years of skulking around on the margins of Swainsboro culture, suddenly *I* was the Southern insider. Suddenly, my accent was a mark of experience, of credibility. Don't worry, new city-slicker friends! *I've got this.*

MY LATER TRANSLATION PROJECTS

Let me leave my story there for now, paused at the lighter transfer in Stone Mountain Park, and begin this chapter again. The question of Christianity's entanglement with both nationalist and ethnocentric interests has a long and sad heritage. One of my own areas of philosophical research focuses on the history of the translation of the word *religion* into East Asian languages. This is, in part, a history of the collusion between colonial and missionary aims during the age of European imperialism and, in part, a history of the various attempts of East Asian scholars to negotiate the relation between "religion" and "Christianity" in the European context.

In brief, the word *religion* derives from a Latin root (*religio*), whose precise meaning is debated, although as Jason Josephson-Storm says: "Regardless of its origins, in pre-Christian Roman usage, *religio* generally referred to a prohibition or an obligation."[1] By the fifteenth century, *religio* was used in the Catholic context to refer to "the performance of ritual obligations, especially . . . to describe a state of life bound by monastic vows"; and, accordingly, "the noun 'the religious' referred to monks and nuns."[2] Strictly speaking, these terms are specific to Christian developments in European intellectual history. Or, as Robert Ford Campany says: "Discourse about religions is rooted in Western language communities and in the history of Western cultures. . . . To speak of 'religions' is to demarcate things in ways that are not inevitable or immutable but, rather, are contingent on the shape of Western history, thought, and institutions. Other cultures may, and do, lack closely equivalent demarcations."[3]

By the eighteenth and nineteenth centuries, European scholars were "demarcating things" with a hierarchical schema that tended to include four members. According to Tomoko Masuzawa's 2005 book *The Invention of World Religions*, Christianity served as the paradigm, Judaism and Islam were "almost Christian, or at least would-be Christians," and so-called heathenism was a borderline case described as "idolatry."[4] At stake was the question of whether a tradition was perceived to recognize a unified, transcendent, and universal god in contrast to merely "tribal" gods or local deities. According to this distinction, true religion was "catholic" in the etymological sense (i.e., universal). So, ultimately, there could be only one. Both Judaism and Islam were derided in different ways at different times for following the God of only a certain tribe, culture, or ethnicity, but their theological and textual connections to each other and to Christianity slowly facilitated their admittance into the category "religion," at least as this category was taking shape in the minds of Christian thinkers over time.

What we are left with today is a theologically oriented notion of "religion" latently premised on its opposition to notions such as "idolatry," "heathenism," "paganism," and so forth.[5] As Masuzawa discusses, if we consult any common textbook in "world religions," we will find a collection of chapters on (roughly) Buddhism, Christianity, Confucianism, Daoism, Islam, Hinduism, and Judaism, followed by a catch-all chapter under a heading such as "primal,"[6] "native,"[7] or perhaps "Indigenous."[8] What unites the practices in regions as diverse as the Americas, Oceania, and the whole continent of Africa, such that they should be classified together in a single chapter? As Masuzawa says, this chapter is a descendant of nineteenth-century Europe's hierarchical mapping of so-called world-historical "great" civilizations alongside others "perhaps not so great."[9] The latter "used to be uniformly called 'primitive religions' in the earlier days, but more recently [have] been variously termed 'primal,' 'pre-literate,' 'tribal. . . . The restless shifting of appellations may be a measure of the discomfort felt by contemporary scholars of religion in their effort not to appear condescending to those peoples who used to be referred to as savages."[10] My primary concern as a scholar has been that philosophers such as myself, who work cross-culturally, have a constructive response to this situation. For me, this has required a detour through Jewish theology. This detour, in retrospect, is also the path along which I approach the question of Christian ethno-nationalism.

REVISITING OUR LOCAL GODS

Despite Christianity's status as the paradigmatic member of the category "religion," and despite the collusion between colonial and missionary aims that facilitated European imperialism, nonetheless I have to say that I think it's my *own* people who first theorized adamantly against so-called idolatry. A better historian of religion here could correct me if I'm wrong, but I would trace the philosophical argument, at least, back to the work of the famous scholar Moses ben Maimon ("Maimonides" or "the Rambam," 1138–1204), whose philosophy is rooted in the Jewish tradition but is Aristotelian in form.[11] In the following passage, Maimonides locates the origin of idolatry in the misguided practices of Enosh, identified in Genesis 4:26 as the grandson of Adam via Seth:

> During the days of Enosh, humankind went seriously astray. . . . This was their mistake: They said that since G-d created the stars and the spheres to govern the world, placed them on high, and apportioned them honor so that they would serve before Him as attendants, it would accordingly be fit for us to praise and glorify them and apportion them honor as well. . . . Subsequent to the arising of that thought in their hearts, they began to build temples to the stars, to make offerings to them, to praise and glorify them in words, and to prostrate themselves before them in order to obtain the favor of the Creator, all in accordance with their misconception. This was the essence of idolatry, not that they declared that there was no other god aside from this star.[12]

Here, the original idols were symbolic representations of God's creations, like stars, but they were not themselves alternatives or competitors to the one true God. However, over time, the original relationship with God (capitalized, absolute) was forgotten, and people began to worship the stars themselves as false gods (that is, lowercase, diverse):

> This worship of images, through kinds of service that differed from one to the next, spread throughout the whole world. . . . As the days went on, G-d's glorious and awesome name was forgotten from the mouth and the mind of all beings, and no one knew Him. As a result, all the common people, the women, and the children knew only the image of wood or of stone and the stone temple, for they had been trained from their childhood to bow down to it, to serve it, and to swear by its name. The sages among them, such as their priests and their like, imagined that no other god existed aside from the stars and spheres for which these images had been made and which they were made to resemble. . . . In this way the world continued to unfold until the Pillar of the World was born, our patriarch Abraham.[13]

Maimonides explains that Abraham himself was born into a family of star worshippers but was precocious and philosophical. To hear Maimonides tell it, young Abraham must have been reading up on Aristotle: "After this powerful man was weaned but while still a child, he began to explore in his mind. He began to think day and night and wondered how it would be possible for the heavenly sphere to continually move with nothing impelling its motion. Who is causing it to revolve, since it would be impossible for itself to be the cause of its own rotation?"[14] By the age of forty, says Maimonides, Abraham had reasoned his way to understanding the necessity of a so-called unmoved mover—that is, a single, unified, transcendent God at the origin of all creation.[15]

Notably, for Maimonides, included among the idolators were Christians. As Alon Goshen-Gottstein writes in his introduction to the edited volume *Jewish Theology and World Religions*, "Belief in the Trinity and the Incarnation, along with the worship of statues, leads almost by default to the view that Christianity is idolatry [for Maimonides]."[16] Throughout Jewish history, Jewish scholars and legal experts have debated the status of Christianity and Islam vis-à-vis idolatry and, accordingly, sought to establish appropriate relations between Jews and their possibly idolatrous host cultures. Usually, prohibitions against idolatry are directed toward Jews themselves in the form of legalistic guidelines that facilitate business or civic interactions with non-Jews, while protecting Jews from straying too far into the customs of others and hence too far away from the parameters for ritual mandated via their covenant with God. The existential standing of these other cultures and peoples themselves is much more ambiguous, and diverse opinions abound in the literature, from the earliest halakhic debates to contemporary academic venues such as the edited volume noted. Is God's revelation to Jews the only revelation, or has God given separate revelations to others? Does Jewish particularism imply the falseness of other religions or simply that they play a different, if unknown, role in God's larger plans? Generally, the various approaches to religious diversity in Judaism tend to remain noncommittal: God's business with non-Jews is just that—God's business.

I have been dealing with Jewish perspectives on idolatry because in my current academic work I am engaging those figures that halakhic prohibitions are most keen to ensure I avoid—namely, local and specific deities that may be connected to or identical with natural phenomena. To address the local gods, without resorting to the problematic language Tomoko Masuzawa discusses, we need a shift in perspective as scholars. For me, this shift was only possible after detouring through Jewish theology so as to unearth the various assumptions about idolatry I had absorbed from my tradition. In my visits to local gods, I have met scholars and practitioners from diverse areas who philosophize on issues of cultural appropriation and accommodation (as in the reception of South Asian bodhisattvas among the deities of East Asia), diaspora and displacement (as in those gods who leave their homelands along with diasporic communities and those that do not), and environmental justice and ecological sustainability (as in clashes between colonial agendas and the interests of land-based gods and their peoples).

This research has forced me to face the complex issues that arise when *localities* become *racialized* or *land-based* gods become *nation-based*. In other words, both race as a conceptual construct and the nation-state as a polity are recent developments that take the local gods into new territory.

Thus, for example, to address white nationalist appropriations of neo-pagan lifeways, we need new philosophical resources for navigating cases in which local gods become players in contemporary nation-state politics. Similar resources are needed to understand how the Father, Son, and Holy Ghost of Christianity can operate as a proponent of American exceptionalism and white supremacism.

ETHNO-NATIONALISM AND BAD THEOLOGY

As Goshen-Gottstein goes on to discuss in his survey of Jewish theological approaches to world religions, Judaism is not immune to the vexing questions of religious identity and contemporary ethno-nationalism, especially not with the reemergence of Israel crafted on a nation-state model in the twentieth century.[17] The same can be said for other historical cultural communities, now formed around constitutional governments, that have traditional ties to particular religions and sizeable religious majorities today. For example, Thailand debates the status of Buddhism as its official religion, India negotiates Hindu identity, and Israel fails in balancing its designation as a Jewish state with the constitutional rights and privileges of its non-Jewish citizens. But what of white Christian nationalism in America? Is this just another case of a historical cultural community negotiating its identity as a nation-state with a pluralistic populace?

Various public statements by Protestant institutions, as well as sermons by individual pastors and church leaders, all seem to agree: White Christian nationalism is bad theology.[18] It is a bad theology unmoored from the history of Christian thought on religious diversity, at odds with foundational Christian understandings of God's love and inclusivity, and irredeemably mistaken about the Christian faith's relation to contemporary nation-state politics. Perhaps the theological irony is that white Christian nationalism takes the universal God of the Christians and turns him back into the local god of a specific nation and race. The universalizing theology that wedded Christian missionizing to colonial expansion on the world stage for several hundred years has now arrived back at the position it once rejected—namely, the embrace of the Christian God as the partisan deity of an ethnic community.

Not only is this theology bad, but the ethnocentrism is incoherent. Whiteness is a fluid category deployed differently in different contexts and for different aims. My own status is a case in point. To be abundantly clear, I identify as white in recognition of the white privilege that benefits me daily. But the Jewish "ethnicity" (whatever that means) has sometimes been included and sometimes excluded from the designation "white" both historically and contemporarily. On that note, I feel it's now time to let you in on the other important part of my personal story, which is that I'm not even sure if I'm Jewish.

BACK TO SWAINSBORO

My father is "ethnically" Jewish, or at least suffice it to say that he turns up as 100 percent Ashkenazi on DNA tests. His family immigrated from the Jewish *shtetls* of Odessa to New York City via Ellis Island in the early 1900s. My mother is white and grew up as a Methodist in Tennessee with deeper family roots in Alabama. She converted to Judaism before I was born, I was raised Jewish, and we attended the closest synagogue possible, an Orthodox congregation about forty-five minutes away from Swainsboro in the town of Vidalia (where the sweet onions grow). I also occasionally went to Sunday school at the Methodist church, where I heard things that were confusing to me. My identity was messy, and my upbringing was religiously and culturally mixed. We went to synagogue and church; we cooked both kugel and collards.

So, am I Jewish? As one rabbi once told me over a dinner, "It depends on whom you ask." For some rabbis following Judaism's matrilineal line, the fact that my mother converted before my birth *should* render me Jewish. But conversion is a complex issue here, related to the question of whether Judaism is a religion, an ethnicity, or both. Moreover, my mother converted through a Reform synagogue, and hence, for many Orthodox rabbis, her conversion is in fact not sufficient. The right of someone like me to the Israeli "law of return" has been a subject of debate in the past, and even today I might be asked to go through the full conversion process before relocation would be allowed.[19] Thus, whereas those in my hometown had no doubts about my status as a Jew, this status is much less clear to many in my own supposed religious community.

I tell you all this for a reason: Hybridized and messy identities such as my own are gadflies in the racial ecology of America today, perhaps especially in the South. Telling my story here is not a neutral move; it is a way to shift power. As I knew back on that night in Stone Mountain Park, whether or not I'm white or Jewish, I'm a Southerner. My perspective on the South, ever so slightly, shifts the perspective for others, too.

All that said, claiming my southernness is not the same as claiming the South as my own. There is no national identity for America that escapes the legacies of colonialism and slavery or avoids the complexities of immigration. America is not simply a historical cultural community negotiating its status as a nation-state, just as whiteness is not a cohesive racial or ethnic category. We tell our stories as Americans, in part, because most of us have some explaining to do.

Let me finish my story. I write to you from my current home in Texas on the ancestral and unceded lands of the Caddo and Wichita. Less than a month from now, I will travel back to Swainsboro for what will possibly be the last time. My parents are moving to Texas. After this, there will be just four Jewish people in Swainsboro. I hear two will move to Atlanta to be near their grandkids, and I suspect the other two will leave as well. Soon Swainsboro will have no more Jews, and I'll have no more family in all of Georgia. Sometimes I feel as if severing my last root in Swainsboro is but a natural unfolding of my Jewishness, my heritage of displacement and diaspora. But one thing this writing process has granted me is a better appreciation of the lasting gifts I've taken from Swainsboro, which have shaped me both professionally and personally, and this is where I would like to end.

YOU CAN TAKE THE GIRL OUT OF THE COUNTRY

The historian Jemar Tisby contrasts the incoherence of white Christian nationalism with the integrated vision of patriotism and Christianity he finds in African American communities. As he says:

> While public attention often turns to the absurdities and indignities promulgated by white Christian nationalists, there are other examples of how to demonstrate a commitment to America. Black Christians throughout U.S. history have often hearkened back to the nation's stated commitment to freedom and democracy to fight for greater inclusion. They saw this form of patriotism as a coherent, integrated expression of their Christian faith. While the fusion of faith and public life led white Christian nationalists to an attempted insurrection on January 6, 2021, that left several people injured and dead, it led Black Christians to participate in the Civil Rights Movement, which heralded the end of nearly a century of Jim Crow discrimination. The historic example of Black Christians demonstrates that a Christian commitment to God and country does not always mean making America a white man's country.[20]

Black leadership in Swainsboro helped manage our civic life, our educational institutions, and our industries and retail businesses, all in the face of rampant racism in a highly segregated social context. They usually made space for their small Jewish minority in ways that white evangelical culture often did not. They were good witnesses to Christian values and good stewards of American democracy.

As I said earlier, my Southern childhood afforded me a valuable perspective on race, religion, and politics in the US—namely, I grew up thinking that the US on the whole was just *over* 50 percent African American, just *under* 50 percent white, and *maybe* 0.001 percent Latino/a and Jewish, reflecting roughly the demographics I saw in Swainsboro. It was only when I was much older that I understood that African Americans are a small minority in the US overall and are especially concentrated in southeastern Georgia. So, I had the privilege of growing up in a slightly different America than the one familiar to most people; I grew up in a predominantly Black America. And one of the gifts that Swainsboro has given me is an optimism for the future that stems from spending my formative years assuming that America overall was mostly populated by the patriots and Christians that Jemar Tisby describes.

You might say that I had a skewed perspective on things, and I would say, well, that's just what I'm here in this chapter trying to do—skew the perspective. If someone has to squint to see me as a Southerner or to see America the way I grew up seeing it, then this goes a small way toward dissolving those peripheral assumptions that connect whiteness to Americanness, to southernness, and to Christianity in a vague concept cluster sustained mostly by bad theology and naïve racial essentialism. My story here is only one tiny slice of one perspective on the US from one tiny town, but such a small shift in perspective nonetheless grants a radically different vista. Facilitating these shifts in perspective is part of our collective scholarly work, and, here, it is part of my personal story, too.

NOTES

1. Josephson, *The Invention of Religion in Japan*, 17. The author later publishes under the name Josephson-Storm and is cited accordingly in the notes.
2. Josephson, *The Invention of Religion in Japan*, 16.
3. Campany, "On the Very Idea of Religions," 289.
4. Masuzawa, *The Invention World Religions*, 49.
5. For example, Josephson-Storm, "The Superstition, Secularism, and Religion Trinary: Or Re-Theorizing Secularism."
6. For example, Smith, *The World's Religions*.
7. For example, Bowker, *World Religions*.
8. For example, Partridge, *Introduction to World Religions*.
9. Masuzawa, *The Invention World Religions*, 3.
10. Masuzawa, *The Invention World Religions*, 4.
11. Certainly there are halakhic prohibitions against perceived idolatry or "foreign worship" (*avodah zarah*) that well predate Maimonides, but I refer here to the specific philosophical approach to the question that Maimonides articulates, which prioritizes rational belief.
12. Maimonides, *Mishneh Torah*, "Laws of Idolatry," chapter 1.
13. Maimonides, *Mishneh Torah*, "Laws of Idolatry," chapter 1.
14. Maimonides, *Mishneh Torah*, "Laws of Idolatry," chapter 1.
15. Maimonides, *Mishneh Torah*, "Laws of Idolatry," chapter 1.

16. Goshen-Gottstein, "Toward a Jewish Theology of World Religions: Framing the Issues," 17. Bracketed material is mine.

17. Goshen-Gottstein, "Toward a Jewish Theology of World Religions: Framing the Issues," 2.

18. For example, the excellent essays collected by the Baptist Joint Committee for Religious Liberty in *Christian Nationalism and the January 6, 2021 Insurrection* (Washington, DC: Baptist Joint Committee, 2022), https://bjconline.org/wp-content/uploads/2022/02/Christian_Nationalism_and_the_Jan6_Insurrection-2-9-22.pdf; Jeff Brumley, "Avoiding the Conversation about White Supremacy in Churches Is Dangerous, Jones Warns," *Baptist News Global*, September 15, 2022, https://baptistnews.com/article/avoiding-the-conversation-about-white-supremacy-in-churches-is-dangerous-jones-warns/; Pastor Dave Buerstetta, "Refute and Resist White Christian Nationalism," Pastor Dave's Blog, Woodridge United Methodist Church, September 2, 2022, https://www.woodridgeumc.org/pastor-daves-blog/refute-and-resist-white-christian-nationalism/; Reverend Ryan Dunn, "What Is Christian Nationalism?" The People of the United Methodist Church, https://www.umc.org/en/content/what-is-christian-nationalism; "Churches Uniting in Christ Statement on White Nationalism and White Supremacism," Episcopal Church, August 16, 2017, https://www.episcopalchurch.org/eir/churches-uniting-in-christ-statement-on-white-nationalism-and-white-supremacism/; and Mark Tooley, "Methodism and Christian Nationalism," *Firebrand Magazine* (April 9, 2022), https://firebrandmag.com/articles/methodism-amp-christian-nationalism.

19. For more on the question of conversion through Reform institutions, see Judy Malz, "Does Israel Discriminate against Non-Orthodox Converts When Approving Immigration?" *Haaretz,* February 14, 2017, https://www.haaretz.com/israel-news/.premium-aliyah-does-israel-discriminate-against-non-orthodox-converts-1.5434841. For an Orthodox perspective on patrilineal Jewish descent, see Tzvi Freeman, "To a Child of a Jewish Father," Chabad.org, https://www.chabad.org/library/article_cdo/aid/1014792/jewish/To-a-Child-of-a-Jewish-Father.htm.

20. Tisby, "The Patriotic Witness of Black Christians," 9.

BIBLIOGRAPHY

Bowker, J. *World Religions*. London: DK Press, 2006.
Campany, R. F. "On the Very Idea of Religions (in the Modern West and in Early Medieval China)." *History of Religions* 42, no. 4 (2003): 287–319.
Goshen-Gottstein, Alon. "Toward a Jewish Theology of World Religions: Framing the Issues." In Alon Goshen-Gottstein and Eugene Korn, eds., *Jewish Theology and World Religions,* 1–37. Oxford: The Littman Library of Jewish Civilization, 2012.
Josephson, J. Ā. *The Invention of Religion in Japan*. Chicago: University of Chicago Press, 2012.
Josephson-Storm, J. Ā. "The Superstition, Secularism, and Religion Trinary: Or Re-Theorizing Secularism." *Method and Theory in the Study of Religion* 30, no. 1 (2018): 1–20.

Maimonides. *Mishneh Torah*. "Laws of Idolatry," chapter 1. http://myjli.com/faith/index.php/lesson-1/mishneh-torah-laws-of-idolatry-chapter-1/.

Masuzawa, T. *The Invention World Religions: Or, How European Universalism Was Preserved in the Language of Pluralism*. Chicago: University of Chicago Press, 2005.

Partridge, C. *Introduction to World Religions*. 3rd ed. Minneapolis: Fortress Press, 2018.

Smith, Huston. *The World's Religions*. New York: HarperOne, 2009.

Tisby, Jemar. "The Patriotic Witness of Black Christians." In Baptist Joint Committee for Religious Liberty, *Christian Nationalism and the January 6, 2021 Insurrection* (Washington, DC: BJC, 2022), 7–9. https://bjconline.org/wp-content/uploads/2022/02/Christian_Nationalism_and_the_Jan6_Insurrection-2-9-22.pdf.

Chapter 9

Christian Churches in North America and the Imperatives of the Dialogue of Action toward Restitution and Restorative Justice for Blacks, Latinos/ Latinx, and Native Americans

Marinus Chijioke Iwuchukwu

INTRODUCTION

Following the nationwide protests in many US cities against the murder of George Floyd on May 25, 2020, while in the hands of four Minneapolis, Minnesota, policemen, which in some cases resulted in riots and looting, the sitting president at the time, Donald Trump, addressed the nation from the White House on Monday, June 1, 2020, promising to confront violent protesters with federal troops, as "the president of law and order." After his brief address, the president walked about one block away from the White House to St. John's Church (this church suffered some damage from the rioters earlier that day). The president's visit to the church was primarily for a photo opportunity in the ambience of the church. It was not just about a good photo-op for President Trump, who raised the Bible to pose for pictures in front of St. John's Church in Washington, DC, but also appropriate (in his calculation) for his political gimmicks, to use the opportunity to show how he has craved and successfully used the support of white Christians and their churches for his Machiavellian political maneuvers. His performance, to my mind, conjures up the ghosts of the immoral role Christian churches historically played in perpetuating racism in the US, as well as affirms the active participation of Christian churches in the enslavement of Black people, the appropriation of Indigenous lands and marginalization of Native Americans, the dehumanization and exploitation of Latinx people, and the abuse of children of Native Americans in residential schools and institutions administered by Christian churches.

The history of the US shows that since the first group of African slaves landed in Virginia in 1619, different white Christian groups, along with their cousins in the exploitative business community, used enslaved Africans in their churches, farms, schools, and parsonages. The following historical statements attest to the role to which Christianity is used to accentuate European imperialism and the exploitation of Black and brown labor forces: "Religion and the church . . . played an important role in the social control of Spanish America and in solidifying Spanish authority. . . . Priests preached obedience and compliance with the social rules that governed colonial society. Moreover, they stressed the rewards of an afterlife attained by not challenging the status quo."[1]

It is imperative that Christian churches are actively involved in a comprehensive healing and reconciliation process that includes the victims as well as the offenders of European imperialism and exploitation (today we are, in some instances, talking about descendants of the victims and the offenders). In this chapter, I advocate the concept of dialogue of action toward restitution and reparations for all victims and descendants of victims of the centuries of social injustices and evils Christian churches have been complicit in against Black and brown people in North America.

COMPLICITY OF CHRISTIAN CHURCHES IN THE EVILS OF SLAVERY AND EXPLOITATION OF BLACK AND BROWN PEOPLE IN NORTH AMERICA

I imagine it is no longer news to most people that the evils of slavery, which commoditized Black enslaved persons as labor tools, were at the root of US wealth and "greatness." That evil enterprise, slavery, owes its origin to the persuasive appeal of sixteenth-century Bishop Bartolomé de las Casas to the Spanish Crown. Bishop de las Casas (a Dominican priest) had aggressively campaigned for an end to the use of Indigenous Peoples of the New World as slave workers. Although he himself owned some enslaved Indigenous Peoples of the Caribbean, he became morally and emotionally perturbed by the suffering, trauma, and pain that they experienced and so decided to free them. In 1515, he traveled back to Spain to appeal for an end to the enslavement of Indigenous Peoples. To further convince the Spanish Crown and all those who had benefited economically from their use as slaves, de las Casas argued that they should be replaced by Africans, whom he rated as "more resilient" and "physically stronger." Therefore, although he campaigned to end the enslavement of Indigenous Peoples (or "Native Americans") because it was both inhumane and immoral, he justified the economic advantage and rationale for switching to Africans as the new slave labor force.[2] Thus began the centuries of appropriation and exploitation of Black bodies as business assets/tools to enhance the large plantations in the Americas. During the years of the use of enslaved Indigenous Peoples, the churches and their missionaries, in different parts of the "New World," were major benefactors of the labor provided by those enslaved. So, it was simply a switch of labor force, from Indigenous Peoples to enslaved Black bodies, for the churches and their missionaries. That was the order of the day, not just in the Caribbean, but particularly in the US. Therefore, it is incontrovertible to say that the institutional and structural racism in the US to date is a direct reality of the institutional slavery that began in 1619.

Fast-forward to the twenty-first century, although (in my view) many Christians are genuinely sorry, disappointed, and upset with any form of slavery and human inequality in any part of the world, there is still evidence of racism in both the ranks and the institutions of many Christian churches in the US. It is critically important today that as many Americans as possible, both Black and brown and decent-minded white Americans, crave for an end to the brutality of policing against Black and brown people, the abuse of the humanity of contemporary Indigenous Peoples, and the exploitation of the labor of Latinx people. My argument is that Christian churches come down from their high altars not only to explore solutions but also to be fundamentally part of the solution to the end of institutional and structural racism. It has been convenient for some Christian preachers to speak loudly and eloquently against slavery and deep troubling forms of human inequality. The real question remains: What have Christian churches and their leaders of our age done to ensure that the structural and institutional recrudescence of slavery is effectively ended? There is also the issue of ensuring processes of restitution and restoration. Given the bringing to light of about a century of abuse of Canada's Indigenous children at the hands of Church institutions, there is ongoing approved restitution for these children who suffered abuses in mission-run schools. In 2008, the Canadian government began compensation to families and victims of abuses in residential schools after Prime Minister Stephen Harper issued a public apology to people of the First Nations groups for all the atrocities their children suffered.[3] Furthermore, on December 13, 2021, the Canadian government approved CAN$40 billion as compensation for victims of the mission schools' abuses.[4] On July 25, 2022, while on a pastoral visit in Canada, Pope Francis offered a public apology on behalf of the Catholic Church in Canada to the leaders of the Indigenous Peoples of Canada because of the decades of abuse of their children in the care of Catholic Church institutions in Canada.[5] While the Pope's apology is a welcome development, one is left wondering if his apology suffices. What are the necessary steps toward full reconciliation or even atonement by the Catholic Church and other Christian churches for all the heinous crimes they committed against vulnerable children for so long? Will there be no restitution, reparations, or compensation as some form of restorative justice desirable for the victims and their families? Should Christian churches in Canada not emulate the steps taken by the Canadian government?

60 Minutes on Sunday, June 5, 2022, hosted by Anderson Cooper, reported that such deeply unethical residential school practices were not only in Canada but also in the US. The schools, started in the mid-seventeenth to early twentieth centuries, had the primary objective of assimilating Indigenous children to Western values and culture. In this way, they would be "civilized." One of the surviving victims of a residential school shared with Anderson Cooper that the pains of the brutality and abuse she suffered at the residential school lingers from generation to generation, creating an intergenerational trauma. This cultural genocide, though initiated by the governments of the US and Canada, was effectively executed by the Christian churches that ran the schools. The Christian churches that administered those residential schools should therefore be actively involved in the reparations and restitution for the ensuing cultural genocide.

CHRISTIAN CHURCHES AND SOCIAL JUSTICE IMPERATIVES FOR CENTURIES OF ABUSE AND SOCIAL EVIL AGAINST BLACK AND BROWN PEOPLE IN NORTH AMERICA

Given that the churches in the US are complicit with and perpetrators of social evils against Black and brown people, especially through slavery, exploitation of the labor of Latinx peoples, and the abuse of Indigenous Peoples, it is morally imperative that they adopt pragmatic social justice resolutions toward reparations for the impact of such sustained evils. The churches have historically been part of the institutionalization of racism in the US and remain so in large portion to date. While there have been attempts by different Christian churches to address and end racism in their ranks, it is still running wild in different parts of US society. The structural social evil unleashed by slavery and racism still perdures in this country and Christian churches remain complicit in that structural evil.

Racism today, manifested by the extensive ramifications of slavery and systemic abuse of Black and brown people in North America, is a social evil because it goes against the fundamental theological underpinning of dignity and equality of all people since all humans draw their being and authenticity from the creator. According to Christian theology of creation, all humans are created in God's image (*imago Dei*; Gen 1:27) and God further honored humanity through the incarnation of God's only son in humankind. In the light of this fundamental theological view, every action that dishonors a human person irrespective of their race, gender, religion, sexual orientation, and culture is sinful.

Both restitution and reparations fall under the category of restorative justice. Restorative justice is a form of social justice that is predisposed toward the healing of hurt, pain, and intergenerational trauma and the abolition of the inequity, denigration, and violence caused by social evils like slavery or human exploitation. Restorative justice aims toward restitution or reparations as well as ensuring reconciliation of the offenders with their victims and ultimately attaining peace in society. The social values of restorative justice strive to attenuate and heal the suffering due to slavery and exploitation of human labor experienced by Black and brown people in the US. Restorative justice is also geared toward peace and transformation in society. According to Protonentis, Chordiya, and ObeySumner (2021):

> Restorative Justice is a process that focuses on the restoration of primary victim/s who are most impacted by the harm, as well as secondary victims who are also affected by the harm. These might include family members, friends, witnesses, community members, restorative justice officials and any other individuals or relationships that might have been damaged by the offense.[6]

The concept of restorative justice grew out of the "covenant justice" of the Hebrew Scripture, which seeks to establish *shallom* (peace) and *tikkun olam* (healing) in the community by reconciling offenders and victims to ensure repair of the damaged relationship caused by the evil perpetrated by the offenders against their victims. Therefore, restitution and reparations as grounded in restorative justice are heavily anchored in the theological search for peace and healing (or repair of relationships) in the community—a desire to repair social relationships and transformation of the society to a peaceful enclave of reconciled people. As Thomas Noakes-Duncan explains, in the Old Testament, "Covenant justice was concerned to preserve or restore relationships, and even punishment was oriented to this restorative goal."[7] Given the theological and biblical basis for restorative justice, it is appropriate for Christian churches to be the vanguard for using it to right the wrongs of social injustice that Black and brown people in the US have suffered for centuries under their watch. The dominantly white Christian churches have a moral responsibility to explore ways of engaging the rest of society to ensure healing the relationship between the perpetrators of the social evils of slavery and human exploitation and their victims.

On June 1, 2020, Bishop Mark J. Seitz of El Paso, Texas, took a knee while holding a "Black Lives Matter" sign in solidarity with protesters on the streets of El Paso. In a commentary he submitted to the *National Catholic Reporter*, he said, "We also need to recognize that we are seeing the effects of centuries of sin and violence and rights denied playing themselves out. And frankly, civil rights are not enough. That's the minimum and clearly, we're not there yet."[8]

THE MORAL IMPERATIVE OF THE DOMINANTLY WHITE CHRISTIAN CHURCHES FOR DIALOGUE OF ACTION TOWARD RESTITUTION/REPARATIONS

In his 1972 classic, *God of the Oppressed*, James Cone taps into the revolutionary social justice Gospel of Christianity to call for white Americans to redress the injustice and oppression they are complicit in, especially regarding Black Americans. This work is an attempt to stir the conscience of the dominantly white Christian church leaders to actively seek to restitute and implement restorative justice against all of those they have oppressed in the US. It is imperative for the dominantly white Christian churches to be at the forefront of dialogue of action that will result in restitution and restorative justice for all the victims, survivors, and descendants of the oppressed people.

I have every confidence that Christianity as a religion has the propensity to support its different groups and leaders toward such redeeming repentance, redress, and restitution. The big issue is whether the different Christian churches and institutions are ready to engage in thorough repentance and redress.

In the preface to the 1997 edition of *God of the Oppressed*, Cone laments the absence of dialogue between "most white theologians" and radical Black theologians. He hoped for a better white-Black reconciliation. I submit that what is critically missing from this text is the leadership of the dominantly white Christian churches in the quest for restitution and restorative justice in favor of the oppressed minorities in the US.

Toward a pragmatic social justice response, white-dominated Christian churches must lead in an effective dialogue of action with other religious and social organizations to address the social justice concerns and evils of slavery and exploitation/abuse of Black and brown people. Dialogue of action is a social necessity because it often seeks to achieve common good needs. The

Catholic church recommends dialogue of action (also known as "dialogue of works") as a key form of effective dialogue among religions.[9] Restitution and reparations for such social injustice are indeed common good imperatives, as all people of good will in the society should be invested in them to address generations of injustice and vices perpetuated against Black and brown people who suffered and are still suffering systemic social, economic, and political marginalization and degradation.

Churches must come up with their financial commitments and responsibilities toward the recommended restitution and reparations. Such financial commitment should reflect the economic benefits these churches acquired from engaging in perpetuating slavery.

CONCLUSION

President Trump's decision to photo-shoot his allegiance to a Christian church when Washington, DC, was literally up in conflagration is an eerie replica of Emperor Nero playing his fiddle while Rome was burning in 64 CE. More importantly, Trump knows that his strongest allies are found among white Christian churchgoers, hence raising the Bible after declaring war on protesters was a deliberate form of optics to solicit their usual support and to appear to be one of them. Christian churches were allies with those invested in the purchase of Black bodies, Christian churches have been largely silent regarding the exploitation of Latinx workers, and Christian churches used their various institutions to abuse children of Indigenous Peoples in the US and in Canada for decades, all in the name of missionary evangelization.

As conscientious institutions, Christian churches in the US and their leaders should be at the front line of the campaign and promulgation of legislature that will put in place institutional structures and regulations to mitigate the impact of more than four hundred years of slavery on the great-great-granddaughters and -sons of former slaves. Part of healing the wounds of slavery must entail economic, political, and cultural/social policies. It is simply not enough to reform the police and law enforcement agencies, as those are only the façade of a more deep-seated evil at play, structural and institutionalized racism.

On July 30, 2008, the US House of Representatives officially apologized for slavery and the segregation of Jim Crow laws. But no American president has given an official apology. The US executive arm needs to officially apologize for slavery and restitute descendants of victims.[10] The American presidency can take a cue from the prime minister of the Netherlands, Mark Rutte, who on December 19, 2022, apologized for the Netherlands' slavery past. According to him, "For centuries under Dutch state authority, human dignity was violated in the most horrific way possible, . . . and successive Dutch governments after 1863 failed to adequately see and acknowledge that our slavery past continued to have negative effects and still does. For that I offer the apologies of the Dutch government."[11] Although official apology does not suffice, it is a major official executive step necessary toward restitution and restorative justice. Furthermore, the US needs to borrow a leaf from post-Nazi Germany, which has demonstrated sincere repentance, redress, and restitution to Jews who survived the Shoah, as well as the Canadian government for apologizing to and compensating victims of mission schools' abuses.

Black and brown Americans deserve appropriate US government repentance, redress, and restitution for the evil of slavery. Christian churches and their institutions that directly benefited from slavery need to take a cue from Georgetown University, which has made efforts of repentance, redress, and reparations for the institution's complicity in slavery.[12] While the institution's plan for funding the process of making reparations was criticized, specifically because the institution was going to depend on donations rather than task its own resources to fund the project,[13] its initiative and recognition of its moral complicity and need to restitute for its social injustice are commendable.

Until Black and brown Americans see that day when the dominant white Christian churches and the US government will comprehensively engage to redress and restitute for slavery and the human abuses that they suffered and continue to suffer, we will continue to experience police brutality and racist white people murdering Black and brown people with impunity, as well as continued racial inequality. Toward an effective dialogue of action between Christian churches and other social and religious organizations, white-dominant Christian churches should initiate the redressing of this social justice problem by establishing a network where other organizations complicit in slavery and social injustices against Black and brown people in the US are invited to participate. The success of such a network hinges on Christian churches expressing sincere repentance for their complicity in slavery and the oppression of Black and brown people in the US. The US must be willing to contribute financially toward restitution and necessary restoration of all those who carry the pain, sadness, and negative psychological effects of racism for the centuries of social injustice that the churches participated in.

NOTES

1. "Christianity and Colonial Expansion in the Americas," Encyclopedia.com, https://www.encyclopedia.com/history/encyclopedias-almanacs-transcripts-and-maps/christianity-and-colonial-expansion-americas.

2. Lawrence Clayton, "Bartolomé de las Casas and the African Slave Trade," *History Compass* 7, no. 6 (November 2009): 1526–41. See also Dani Anthony, "Bartolomé de las Casas and 500 Years of Racial Injustice," *Origins—Current Events in Historical Perspective* (July 2015), https://origins.osu.edu/milestones/july-2015-bartolom-de-las-casas-and-500-years-racial-injustice?language_content_entity=en.

3. "The Government Apologizes," Facing History and Ourselves, https://www.facinghistory.org/en-ca/resource-library/government-apologizes?utm_term=&utm_campaign=DSA&utm_source=adwords&utm_medium=ppc&hsa_tgt=dsa-19959388920&hsa_grp=75449327748&hsa_src=g&hsa_net=adwords&hsa_mt=&hsa_ver=3&hsa_ad=333182733493&hsa_acc=4949854077&hsa_kw=&hsa_cam=1635938820&gclid=CjwKCAiAzKqdBhAnEiwAePEjknhbkNUntefdtV_PEOBEUDC6iX138_5HvUnH9ONjBvGuKXNcokRvFBoCVPQQAvD_BwE.

4. Olivia Stefanovich, "Ottawa Earmarks $40B for Indigenous Child Welfare Compensation, Program Reform," *CBC News*, December 13, 2021, https://www.cbc.ca/news/politics/ottawa-indigenous-child-welfare-compensation-offer-1.6283952.

5. Scott Neuman, "The Pope's Apology in Canada Was Historic, but for Some Indigenous People, Not Enough," *NPR*, July 25, 2022, https://www.npr.org/2022/07/25/1113498723/pope-francis-apology-canada-residential-schools-indigenous-children.

6. Adana Protonentis, Rashmi Chordiya, and ChrisTiana ObeySumner, "Centering the Margins: Restorative and Transformative Justice as Our Path to Social Equity," *Administrative Theory and Praxis* 43, no. 3 (2021): 333–54.

7. Thomas Noakes-Duncan, "The Emergence of Restorative Justice in Ecclesial Practice," *Journal of Moral Theology* 5, no. 2 (2016): 1–21

8. Mark J. Seitz, "El Paso's Bishop Mark Seitz: Black Lives Matter," *National Catholic Reporter*, June 4, 2020, par. 9, https://www.ncronline.org/news/opinion/el-pasos-bishop-mark-seitz-black-lives-matter.

9. Secretariat for Non-Christians, *The Attitude of the Church Towards Followers of Other Religions: Reflections and Orientations on Dialogue and Mission*, May 10, 1984, nos. 31–32, https://www.cam1.org.au/Portals/66/documents/Dialogue-Mission-1984.pdf. See also Pontifical Council for Interreligious Dialogue, *Dialogue and Proclamation*, May 19, 1991, nos. 42b and 44, https://www.vatican.va/roman_curia/pontifical_councils/interelg/documents/rc_pc_interelg_doc_19051991_dialogue-and-proclamatio_en.html.

10. There are precedents of official executive apologies in the US for past national social and political wrongs. President Ronald Reagan in 1988 signed into law the Civil Liberties Act, which apologized to all Japanese Americans affected by the internment of Japanese citizens during World War II and awarded them $20,000 each. In 1997, President Bill Clinton rendered an official apology to the victims of the Tuskegee lab experiments and the victims were awarded a $10 million settlement. None of these rank close to the evil and number of people affected by slavery. See Danny Lewis, "Five Times the United States Officially Apologized," *Smart News*, May 27, 2016, https://www.smithsonianmag.com/smart-news/five-times-united-states-officially-apologized-180959254/.

11. Alex Hardie and Sharon Braithwaite, "Dutch Prime Minister Apologizes for the Netherlands' Role in the Slave Trade," *CNN*, December 19, 2022, https://www.cnn.com/2022/12/19/europe/dutch-prime-minister-apologizes-slavery-netherlands-intl-scli/index.html.

12. Stephanie Ebbs, "Georgetown University Announces Reparations Fund to Benefit Descendants of Slaves Once Sold by the School," *ABC News*, October 30, 2019, https://abcnews.go.com/Politics/georgetown-university-announces-reparations-fund-benefit-descendants-slaves/story?id=66642286.

13. Ryan Di Corpo, "Georgetown Reparations Plan for Slaves Sold by University Draws Criticism from Students," *America, The Jesuit Review*, November 4, 2019, https://www.americamagazine.org/politics-society/2019/11/04/georgetown-reparations-plan-slaves-sold-university-draws-criticism?gclid=CjwKCAiAhqCdBhB0EiwAH8M_GvsfXwNsyXb_8GJS7YcLnAsV0U7LbcK6hcIG-nHO1iVXagC_cQHm-xoCq-wQAvD_BwE.

Chapter 10

"Legitimate Political Discourse"
January 6 and the Brutality of White Theodicy

Biko Mandela Gray

January 6 was not an aberration. What happened on that day—the gallows, the armed white supremacist groups, the feces smeared on walls—was exactly who and what whiteness and white people are. If this weren't the case, then we cannot understand the government's response—or lack thereof—on that day. Because despite evidence that *something* was brewing, the government wasn't "ready." Police were "overwhelmed"; the world's largest carceral state "wasn't ready" to apprehend thousands of people who broke the law.

This is the case because, despite all the "melting pot" language, despite calls for multiculturalism and "Diversity, Equity, and Inclusion," this country remains a normatively *white* nation. In the US, whiteness remains a norm. And, at the beginning and end of the day, whiteness and white people are violent. And not just the white supremacists. This country was formed in and through white supremacist violence. And that violence has become normalized. It has become normal. In watching January 6 unfold, we might even say that whiteness is the force that renders such white supremacist violence normal. January 6 wasn't an aberration. For if it were, the police would have been ready. The *government* would have been ready.

Perhaps this is why the Republican Party told us that January 6 was "legitimate political discourse." Because it was. They'd just said the quiet part out loud.

> The Republican Party on Friday officially declared the Jan. 6, 2021 attack on the Capitol and events that led to it "legitimate political discourse," and rebuked

two lawmakers in the party who have been most outspoken in condemning the deadly riot and the role of Donald J. Trump in spreading the election lies that fueled it.[1]

Yes. The Republicans told the truth. White violence is legitimate political discourse. It always has been—at least in the US. White violence, and the legitimation of white violence, founds and sustains this nation. This nation was founded in blood, and it is sustained by blood. But not white blood. Or at least not *primarily* white blood. January 6 wasn't simply about a Big Lie told by a vile and violent egomaniac; it was also a fight for the nation, an attempt to protect "America" from the perversion that nonwhite communities—specifically Black, queer, and non-European immigrant ones—symbolically and politically pose.

With the immigrants closing in, as Black people call for abolishing the police, and as queer and trans communities demand a profound reckoning with the brutal gender normativity of this country, too many white people found themselves yearning for a hegemonic nation of homogenous whiteness that would remain supreme. And make no mistake: This homogenous whiteness is what held them together. Those insurrectionists ran the gamut; whether young or old, straight or queer, cisgender or trans, what those people wanted—what they *want*—is a nation freed of difference.

Though January 6 is a contemporary event, the sentiments undergirding it are as old as the nation itself. And by "nation," I mean the *white* nation, a nation prepared only for white people and their descendants. Understanding themselves as the chosen people for God's mission on Earth, white people sought to form, and still seek to sustain, a nation-state that affirms their chosenness, their blessedness, their *goodness*.

Too many historians of American Christianity have discussed the religious foundations of the "city on a hill" language. In fact, at this point, the idea that the US began as a project in "religious freedom" is a founding myth for the nation itself. The country finds its identity in the Puritans; it sustains itself in a story about a group of people leaving Britain to practice their own brand of Christianity outside of the Anglican Church.

While (some parts of) this story may be true, the truth of that story is not what matters for our purposes here. After all, myths do not derive their power from being historically accurate. It doesn't matter whether Adam and Eve were real, or whether Jesus really turned water into wine. What matters is that these stories give people a sense of orientation, of "how one comes to terms with the ultimate significance of one's place in the world," as historian of religions Charles Long once said.[2] In this regard, the myth of the US—namely, that it is a country founded on religious freedom and white homogeneity—is an orientating device. It is the way that white people make sense of their ultimate significance. It is the way they make meaning of their lives.

But I am not a historian. I'm not a mythologist, either. I'm a philosopher of religion. As such, I'm interested in the logics and effects of these orientating devices. I'm concerned about what logics found these myths; I'm troubled by the effects of these myths. And one such effect—one that we seemingly cannot get away from—is the unyielding commitment to white *goodness*.

It is this historical, widespread, and ongoing commitment to presumed and enacted white goodness that motivates this chapter. Here, I argue that, at least in the US, whiteness is a theodicy.

In the US, white goodness is always presumed and always in need of protection and justification. As such, this country is fueled by a Christian logic of justification, a structure of reason, that cannot help but keep whiteness good in the face of nonwhite "evil." Once the "city on a hill" was constructed, there was no going back; white people have become agents and beneficiaries of divine benevolence, and anything—*anything*—that challenges this benevolence will be dismissed, denigrated, diminished, or denied.

If this isn't a theodicy, I don't know what is.

But let me make it clear.

ON THEODICY AND WHITENESS: OPENING AND ONGOING CONSIDERATIONS

I have written about theodicy and anti-Blackness elsewhere.[3] And I am not alone in this; others have written on it, too.[4] Lewis Gordon, for example, tells us that "blackness is fundamental to the formation of European modernity as it is one that imagines itself legitimate and pure through the expurgation of blackness. It is, in other words, *the theodicy of European modernity*."[5] As Gordon puts it, once "Christendom was transformed into Europe" and "Germanic and Mediterranean Christians were transformed into whites," racial logics and theo-logics coincided, and once this occurred, Blackness became the nothingness to whiteness's plenitude of being; it was, in short, the evil to whiteness's goodness.[6]

I wholeheartedly agree with Gordon here. If we take, for example, the Augustinian argument that evil is the "privation" or "lack" of goodness," or even if we accept the Cartesian/Anselmian claim that existence itself is a good—and perfect existence is the highest good—then to be nothing would amount to being "evil," and as such, Blackness would be the evil that justifies the reality of white goodness. Gordon is right, then: Blackness, as nothingness, is the very evil against which white existence—and therefore goodness—must militate.

But, while I do agree with Gordon, I would also add to his argument. While theodicy requires an interrogation of evil, it also *presumes* the existence of an already-given goodness. If, as Gordon tells us, "the word [theodicy] emerges from a problem forged by *expectations* of a good or benevolent, omniscient, and omnipotent deity,"[7] then theodicy begins with an expectation, a *desire*, that God is *already* good. Theodicy therefore begins, is steeped in, this expectation; it needs *something* to protect, to justify. Without it, theodicy cannot get started.

The theodicean "expectation," and therefore the structures of protection and justification that characterize it, are what motivate my reflections here. As I see it, the US functions on a theodicy of whiteness; in the US, whiteness is *always presumed to be good.* It is whiteness that needs protection from malevolence. And this protection shows up as a profound commitment to absolving—or at least minimizing—the vile actions that white people have enacted throughout history.

This is not mere application. I'm not simply superimposing a theory onto our present-day existential and political realities. In his classic text, *Is God a White Racist? A Preamble to Black Theology*, Black philosopher of religion William R. Jones claims that we must seriously interrogate the possibility that God might actually be a white racist. Drawing from his training in existentialism, Jones suggests that God is the sum of God's acts; the only way we can ascertain God's character is by paying attention to the historical unfolding of our collective lives. And even a cursory glance at US history—replete with scenes of lynching, genocide, mass incarceration, and perpetual political compromise with those who enact such violence—Jones cannot help but conclude that it is at least *possible* that God—or at least the Christian God—might, in fact, be a white racist.[8] In Jones, we find a profound philosophical link between Christianity and white supremacy. "Is God a white racist?" is, therefore, a damning criticism of the theodicean logic of Christianity—a logic that will invite and encourage suffering in the name of a future salvation.

This suffering should, therefore, produce a moment of liberation, of redemption. But here's the twist: If we look at the history of the US, *there is no evidence of such an event for Black people*. Every moment of alleged Black progress can also be understood as a moment of anti-Blackness. Reconstruction and its failures (or successes, depending on one's vantage point) followed emancipation; the wars on crime and drugs followed the Civil Rights Movement; Trump followed Obama. And even within these "successes," there were profound compromises. *There is no redemption event for Black people in the US.*

If this is the case, then I would only add here that there is *ample* evidence of *many* events for white people: the 1776 revolution, the compromise between the North and the South after the Civil War, the refusal to name white supremacy as the primary culprit for January 6.⁹ White people are exalted and liberated on the daily; they move through the world with a sense of nearly unfettered comfort.

In fact, slavery itself—an enactment of disastrous violence with lethal consequences—becomes a liberating event for white people. As Arkansas senator Tom Cotton once stated:

> We have to study the history of slavery and its role and impact on the development of our country because otherwise we can't understand our country. As the founding fathers said, it was the necessary evil upon which the union was built, but the union was built in a way, as Lincoln said, to put slavery on the course to its ultimate extinction.¹⁰

According to Cotton, slavery was a "necessary evil." But the question is—always—*necessary for whom?* The "union" about which Cotton speaks is nothing less than a *white* union, sustained by white normativity and enabled in and through white supremacist structures. When evil becomes "necessary," we are in theodicean territory; Cotton's claims bear this out clearly. And we need not simply think with the politicians. We can also sit with contemporary pastors. Consider, for example, what white pastor Louie Giglio said in the wake of George Floyd's murder: "We understand the curse that was slavery, white people do, but we miss the *blessing* of slavery, that it actually built up the framework for the world that white people live in and lived in."¹¹

In both Cotton and Giglio, we hear the political and theological evidence of a profound desire to protect whiteness from the charges of evil. As Anthea Butler puts it: "While discussing racism in a conversation that was a bit too rosy in tone, Giglio tried to explain how white privilege works. Instead . . . he inadvertently attested to a sentiment held dear by many Christians"—a sentiment that, I would argue, is nothing less than the desire to protect whiteness-as-goodness at any cost.¹² Butler assesses the historical sources for Giglio's claim, but my point here is that Giglio's claim (theo)logically functions to preserve the goodness of whiteness through Christian rhetoric. As Giglio put it, even though slavery was a curse, there was a "blessing" in it—one marked with a metaphysical sign of segregation: Blessings are *for whites only.*

Butler underscores that Giglio's words, which were meant to be a *criticism* of whiteness, not an extolling of it, nevertheless has a historical precedent. The theodicean function of white goodness, the presumption that whiteness must be good, and the entire discursive and analytic sociopolitical structures that set out to protect this goodness, has been working since this nation's inception. It is taught in grade school history classes; it is marked by the hagiography of heinous white men and women like George Washington, Abraham Lincoln, and Susan B. Anthony; and it is sustained by white pastors who bumblingly justify white supremacist violence through discourses of blessedness.

In the US, whiteness is an unquestioned and unquestionable good. Whiteness *is* good. And it is precisely this whiteness-as-goodness that functions as a national theodicy; whiteness-as-goodness is what founds and sustains this nation. It has done so historically, and if Giglio's comments are any indication, that theodicean structure of justification still operates in this current moment. Theodicy is the link between white nationalism and Christianity; it may not be the only one, but it is doubtless a central one.

A PHENOMENOLOGY OF WHITE THEODICY

Theodicy thus operates as a logic of justification and, therefore, as a modality of reason. But this logic isn't merely logical. It isn't mere reason. Which is to say, theodicy is not simply a cognitive enterprise. Theodicy, white theodicy, a theodicy that justifies white goodness in the face unrelenting white brutality *and its effects*, is also *experienced*. It is *felt;* it is seen and heard.

The truth, however, is that we don't always experience theodicy *as* theodicy. More often than not, theodicy, *white* theodicy, shows up in disguise. It shows up as a horizon of reason, as that which operates in the background. Sara Ahmed tells us that whiteness is "a category of experience that disappears as a category *through* experience." It gets "reproduced by being seen as a form of positive residence," wherein "white bodies do not have to face their whiteness; they are not orientated 'towards' it, and this 'not' is what allows whiteness to cohere, as that which bodies are orientated around."[13] In thinking with whiteness, in providing a phenomenology of whiteness, Ahmed discloses how whiteness operates as a phenomenological horizon, a background to experience, a quiet and subtle infrastructure that "describes the very 'what' that coheres a world."[14]

If this is the case, then perhaps the theodicy I've been tracking here, a theodicy of whiteness, a *white* theodicy that justifies white goodness even as white people do horrifying and vile things, also goes unnoticed. Perhaps it also operates as a background. And in so doing, perhaps this theodicy—this vile, heinous white theodicy—distracts us from the violence it causes, obscuring our vision to the point where we are required not to articulate or even see the necropolitical brutality it causes.

Think about it: on January 6, no one was "prepared." And this is because whiteness is always understood as good. In other words, no one was "prepared" because *there was nothing to be prepared for*. The people who stormed the Capitol were *perceived* as "good people"; or, as Ahmed might put it, their bodies conformed to the institutional space they sought to inhabit. They sank into the space, Ahmed might say; and in so doing, they failed to rise to the level of visibility—let alone threatening or malicious visibility. Though there was ample evidence that *something* was brewing, that *something* was white, and, as such, it was not threatening to the public. It was not *perceived* as threatening; it wasn't experienced as threatening. It was, as the Republican Party reminded us, "legitimate" action. If, as Ahmed tells us, whiteness shows up through its disappearance, which is to say, if whiteness emerges through its *not* showing up—through the surreptitious and subtle way it normatively structures space—then the white bodies who showed up that day couldn't be *perceived* as a problem. They were—which is to say, they were *perceived as*—embodiments of goodness; they couldn't have been—which is to say, they couldn't have been *perceived as*—anything else. Smearing shit on the walls and erecting gallows in the name of what they (and by extension, the nation) understood as "legitimate political discourse"—or what we might call justifiable ethical action—that swarm of white people found comfort and (en)courage(ment) in their whiteness.

Somehow, this militarized, overpoliced, and overincarcerating nation was "unprepared."

But we, we who know, already knew what was the case.

And yet, it seems Congress still needed to "investigate."

CONCLUSION: JANUARY 6, THEODICY, AND WHITENESS

I brought up Congress because I have one last philosophical point to make regarding white theodicy. Whiteness is not perceived as evil; this is the phenomenological structure of white theodicy—a nation hangs on to its inability to perceive white evil in real time.

Sometimes, however, white vileness and white violence can be perceived in the aftermath. But there is a twist here. Consider, for example, the following excerpt from the congressional committee investigating January 6:

> On October 31, 2022, in a Federal courthouse in Washington, DC, Graydon Young testified against Stewart Rhodes and other members of the Oath Keepers militia group. The defendants had been charged with seditious conspiracy against the United States and other crimes related to the January 6, 2021, attack on Congress.
>
> In his testimony that day, Young explained to the jury how he and other Oath *Keepers* were provoked to travel to Washington by President Donald Trump's tweets and by Trump's false claims that the election was "stolen" from him.

Prosecutor: And so how do you feel about the fact that you were pushing towards a line of police officers?

Young: Today I feel extremely ashamed and embarrassed.

Prosecutor: Looking back now almost two years later, what would that make you as someone who was coming to D.C. to fight against the government?

Young: I guess I was [acting] like a traitor, somebody against my own government.

Young's testimony was dramatic, but not unique. Many participants in the attack on the Capitol acknowledged that they had betrayed their own country.[15]

Pay close attention. Don't miss the details. By highlighting how "many participants in the attack . . . acknowledged that they had betrayed their own country," the report rhetorically sets up a pathway to redemption. Moreover, the executive summary makes a moral distinction: By laying nearly *all* the blame at the feet of Donald Trump, the report distinguishes Trump's actions from the people he called to enact that violence. Beneath the written words of this chapter is an ethical and moral sentiment: *These people might have done a bad thing, but they have come to their senses. They might have done a bad thing, but, at the end of the day, they are good people.*

In other words, despite the violence these people enacted, they are nevertheless perceived as *redeemable*. In producing this report, and in refusing to name whiteness and white supremacy as the *primary* motivating factor for the attack, the committee redeems whiteness and, therefore, sanctifies it, renders it *good*.

Even as the committee sought to make a case for decrying the violence of that day, their report is nevertheless an enactment of justification. This committee, wittingly or not, rhetorically protected whiteness from charges of malevolence. *Not all white people are bad*, so the logic goes. *And even the ones who did bad things can come to their senses.* These sentiments—sentiments that undergird this report—are precisely what keeps the goodness of whiteness in place; they are what keeps the game of whiteness going, and they maintain the normativity of whiteness in service of maintaining *the nation itself.*

These defendants might go to prison. They might be convicted. And many of them were—and some are still being tried. But—*but*—what this report rhetorically, even if unwittingly, allows for is the refusal of calling *whiteness* out, of calling white people out *for enacting violence in the name of whiteness*.

This isn't intentional. But that's my point. What occurred on and after January 6 is nothing less than this world, this *nation*, seeing a mass of white bodies as *taking up* the "positive residence" of which Ahmed spoke earlier;

refracted through the lens and language of theodicy, that positive residence looks like unquestioned and unquestionable goodness. Sure, those bodies did violence. Sure, they did a "bad" thing. But the "badness" of the thing wasn't perceived as "bad" in real time. And though it *was* perceived as bad in retrospect, such "badness" did and does not hinder these bodies—*white* bodies—from being capable of redemption. Which is to say, even when they'd done "bad"—*if* they could do "bad" at all—white people *could still do good*.

This is a white theodicy at work.

This is how it is experienced.

And it is precisely this kind of (theo)logic that continues to sanction white supremacist violence.

January 6 was not an aberration.

We must remember this.

But, chances are, given the theodicy of whiteness that sustains this nation, "we" won't.

And we know who that "we" is.

NOTES

1. Weisman and Epstein, "G.O.P. Declares Jan. 6 Attack 'Legitimate Political Discourse,'" *New York Times*.

2. Long, *Significations*, 7.

3. I have written about theodicy in a host of places, but the following essays and public pieces of scholarship are perhaps the most succinct treatments: "Unwilling Sacrifices: Anti-Blackness, Religion, and the Clearing" and "A Theodicy of the Unliving, or, Why I Won't Teach My Black Lives Matter Class Anymore." Those are public pieces, but I have also written, with Stephen Finley, "God Is a White Racist." I also speak to theodicy explicitly—albeit in more expansive ways—in *Black Life Matter*, particularly in the first and second chapters.

4. I will discuss Lewis Gordon in more detail in just a bit, but for a robust discussion of theodicy and anti-Blackness, see Pinn, *Why Lord?*; Gordon, *Bad Faith and Antiblack Racism*; Jones, *Is God a White Racist?*; and An Yountae, "On Violence and Redemption: Fanon and Colonial Theodicy," in *Beyond Man*, edited by Yountae and Craig, 204–25.

5. Gordon, "Race, Theodicy, and the Normative Emancipatory Challenges of Blackness," 729.

6. Gordon, "Race, Theodicy, and the Normative Emancipatory Challenges of Blackness," 729.

7. Gordon, "Race, Theodicy, and the Normative Emancipatory Challenges of Blackness," 725.

8. See Jones, *Is God a White Racist?*, 1–23, my emphasis.

9. I'll have more to say about this later.

10. Cole, "Tom Cotton Describes Slavery as a 'Necessary Evil' in Bid to Keep Schools from Teaching 1619 Project."
11. Butler, *White Evangelical Racism*, 13.
12. Butler, *White Evangelical Racism*, 13.
13. Ahmed, "A Phenomenology of Whiteness," 156.
14. Ahmed, "A Phenomenology of Whiteness," 150.
15. US Congress House of Representatives Select Committee, *Final Report of the Select Committee to Investigate the January 6th Attack on the United States Capitol*, 1.

BIBLIOGRAPHY

Ahmed, Sara. "A Phenomenology of Whiteness." *Feminist Theory* 8, no. 2 (2007): 149–68.
Butler, Anthea. *White Evangelical Racism: The Politics of Morality in America*. Chapel Hill: University of North Carolina Press, 2021.
Cole, Devan. "Tom Cotton Describes Slavery as a 'Necessary Evil' in Bid to Keep Schools from Teaching 1619 Project." *CNN*, July 27, 2020. https://www.cnn.com/2020/07/27/politics/tom-cotton-slavery-necessary-evil-1619-project/index.html.
Gordon, Lewis. *Bad Faith and Antiblack Racism*. New York: Humanity Books, 1995.
———. "Race, Theodicy, and the Normative Emancipatory Challenges of Blackness." *South Atlantic Quarterly* 112, no. 4 (Fall 2013): 725–36.
Gray, Biko. *Black Life Matter: Blackness, Religion, and the Subject*. Durham, NC: Duke University Press, 2022.
———. "A Theodicy of the Unliving, or, Why I Won't Teach my Black Lives Matter Class Anymore." *The Immanent Frame*, January 7, 2021. https://tif.ssrc.org/2021/01/07/a-theodicy-of-the-unliving/.
———. "Unwilling Sacrifices: Anti-Blackness, Religion and the Clearing." Georgetown Berkley Center for Religion, Peace, and World Affairs. https://berkleycenter.georgetown.edu/responses/unwilling-sacrifices-anti-blackness-religion-and-the-clearing.
Gray, Biko, and Stephen Finley. "God Is a White Racist: Immanent Atheism as a Religious Response to Black Lives Matter and State-Sanctioned Anti-Black Violence." *Journal of Africana Religions* 3, no. 4 (2015): 443–53.
Jones, William R. *Is God a White Racist? A Preamble to Black Theology*. Boston: Beacon Press, 1986.
Long, Charles. *Significations: Signs, Symbols, and Images in the Interpretation of Religion*. Aurora, IL: Davies Group Press, 1995.
Pinn, Anthony. *Why Lord? Suffering and Evil in Black Theology*. New York: Continuum Books, 1994.
US Congress House of Representatives Select Committee. *Final Report of the Select Committee to Investigate the January 6th Attack on the United States Capitol*. December 22, 2022. https://www.govinfo.gov/collection/january-6th-committee

-final-report?path=/gpo/January%206th%20Committee%20Final%20Report%20and%20Supporting%20Materials%20Collection/Final%20Report.
Weisman, Jonathan, and Reid J. Epstein. "G.O.P. Declares Jan. 6 Attack 'Legitimate Political Discourse.'" *New York Times*, February 4, 2022. https://www.nytimes.com/2022/02/04/us/politics/republicans-jan-6-cheney-censure.html.
Yountae, An, and Eleanor Craig, eds. *Beyond Man: Race, Coloniality, and Philosophy of Religion.* Durham, NC: Duke University Press, 2021.

Chapter 11

Philosophical Ends and Theological Beginnings

The Logos, the Nigger, and Whiteness in American Christianity

Timothy J. Golden

I

Philosophy aims for rational explanation at high levels of abstract theory. In contrast, Christian theology aims for love demonstrated through the crucified, bloody mess of deliverance, redemption, and salvation. The end, or the telos, of philosophy is the mere *archē*, or the beginning for Christian theology, which has its telos in the flesh (*sarx*) of embodiment. In this chapter, I argue that if the end of Christian theology is understood as the philosophical end of rational explanation rather than as the theological end of embodiment, then both philosophy and Christian theology are corrupted, with at least three tragic consequences. First, philosophy produces a pseudo-knowledge of that which lies beyond the bounds of experience, such as the white god *imago hominis*, while Christian theology maintains this idol by ignoring its moral imperative of embodiment in favor of relentless abstract justifications of the pseudo-knowledge that philosophy has produced. I make this argument in the second section of this chapter. Second, I argue in the third section that such a white god *imago hominis* does not bring deliverance, but oppression; it both creates and justifies the concept of the *nigger*, which I address through a discussion of James Baldwin's question of why a "nigger" was necessary "in the first place." I address Baldwin's question as a philosophical question that demands an ontological account of the nigger and that demands a modal account of the necessity of the nigger. To provide such an account, I turn to Aristotle's discussion of "origin" (*archē*) in Book Delta of *Metaphysics*, concluding that the idolatrous god of white Christian nationalism demands both the legislation of "the nigger" into the American political order and its incorporation into the *archē* of Christian theological order. And third, with the nigger thus ensconced in American Christian theology, law, and politics, I aim to show in the fourth section that the deployment of a weaponized logos in Christian theology also occurs in both American law and political theory and against the backdrop of a philosophy of history dogmatically understood as culminating in the vindication of white supremacy. The final tragic consequence of corrupting philosophy and Christian theology is an evisceration of hope for racial progress that generates a perpetual struggle for justice, a struggle that demands relentless resistance to American racism despite its permanence, and a struggle requiring the intestinal fortitude prescribed by Derrick Bell and the deep Christian spirituality endorsed by Howard Thurman, which I take up in fifth section. I conclude in the sixth section.

II

When the abstractions of philosophy are applied to Christian theology, both undergo severe moral deterioration. Philosophy deteriorates because reason, which is essential to human life and dignity, becomes disingenuous and mischievous, as it applies the logos beyond its rational boundaries, intruding on the realm of Christian theology, which is then degraded because humanity creates a god in its image (*imago hominis*), which replaces the biblical model of a God who creates human beings in His image (*imago Dei*). The biblical God of deliverance becomes a human idol of oppression because, through a perverse act of reverse mimesis, this idol is a mere act of self-transcendence that moves beyond appearances to posit itself as the *Ding-an-Sich*. Kant's transcendental idealism and Heidegger's critique of "Onto-Theology" warned of this moral deterioration of philosophy and theology, and here I want to give some sense of what this god *imago hominis* may resemble and of how this god *imago hominis* appears in the service of maintaining an oppressive, racist, theologically supported status quo essential for the thriving of white Christian nationalism.

Kant's Transcendental Idealism and Heidegger's Critique of "Onto-Theology"

Both Kant and Heidegger demonstrate an appreciation for how reason ensnares humanity in epistemic conundrums. For Kant, this happens through what I shall call "reason's dilemma," which is the uniquely human phenomenon of human nature demanding answers to theological questions that its very same human nature prevents us from answering. And for Heidegger, humanity is always already in "danger" because of "enframing" (*Gestell*). Heidegger's notion of *Gestell* describes a condition in which the essence of technology exposes itself through a revealing of all beings as a sort of standing reserve that is ready at hand for our use. In this way, nature becomes a resource, forests become lumber, rivers become hydropower, and so forth. I want to extend Heidegger's point here and argue that human bodies, Black bodies, become a sort of disposable standing reserve, as evidenced by the eighty-year practice of the penalties of the corrupt legal systems of Jim Crow, which provided a standing reserve of Black bodies to work in steel mills of the post-Reconstruction American South.[1] Considering the wide variety of theological justifications for slavery that migrated easily into the racist logic of the post-Reconstruction South, one sees a rational enframing, a *Gestell*, that both Heidegger and Kant use to expose the dangers of an unchecked, weaponized logos as applied to *theos*: It is conducive to the development of a social and political system with theological underpinnings that demands unquestioned loyalty of Black bodies to a white god, *imago hominis*. I begin with an analysis of Kant's transcendental idealism.

Kant's transcendental idealism is designed to protect the integrity of both philosophy and Christian faith by preventing philosophical reason from overtaking—and thus degrading—both itself and Christian theology. Hence, Kant's explicit objective in the *Critique of Pure Reason* was to "deny reason in order to make room for faith."[2] Preserving the integrity of both reason and faith is important for Kant because he is trying to reconcile the reality of Newtonian physics with the dignity of human personhood. How is it that human beings can abide in a world of deterministic natural laws and still be free? And what do we make of God and of the soul in light of the scientific world around us? Does science take precedence over theology? Does theology take precedence over science? These are the principal questions confronting Kant; questions concerning the integrity of philosophy and Christian theology, as Kant vigorously argued in defense of the integrity of each.[3] Compounding the difficulty of these philosophical and theological questions is a challenge endemic to human reason that Kant acknowledges in the beginning of the *Critique of Pure Reason*: "Human reason has this peculiar fate that in one species of its knowledge it is burdened by questions which, as prescribed by the very nature of reason itself, it is not able to ignore, but which, as transcending all its powers, it is also not able to answer."[4] In other words, human reason is confronted with a dilemma in which it naturally raises questions that it is naturally unable to answer. To deal with this dilemma, Kant develops his transcendental idealism, which imposes restrictions on our ability to attain knowledge in rational theology. Without the restrictions of the cognitive faculty that Kant calls the "understanding," philosophy would become mischievous and disingenuous, as would Christian theology. Philosophy would apply the rigors of deductive and inductive logic to matters beyond experience and purport to have "knowledge" of them, while Christian theology would neglect moral concerns because of its preoccupation with defending the pseudo-knowledge that philosophy has produced, thus paving the way for oppression; for if Christian theology is not tending to moral concerns because of its interest in defending the bogus knowledge that philosophy has produced on its behalf, then it is engaged in acts of oppression, not deliverance. This has been the case throughout Western thought, as oppressive religious regimes have assumed social and political control in the name of Christian theology. From the pseudo-religious "knowledge" of the Inquisition to that of the Ku Klux Klan, philosophical explanation as a replacement for Christian theology has been oppressive.

To avoid this state of affairs, Kant's transcendental idealism eschews an objective knowledge of God in favor of an authentic, subjective moral and religious practice. Although one cannot know God as an object of possible experience, one can practice one's moral faith in ways that are good for oneself and for the neighbor. Philosophy, then, despite its natural inclination toward metaphysical speculation, must deny knowledge of God to make room for a personal faith in God. Philosophy has its place, which is the realm of empirical cognition, and Christian theological ideas have their place, which is the realm of subjective moral and religious life—not as dishonest idols of reason but rather as honest, unknowable ideas that foster Christian faith. It is in this way that Kant paves the way for Søren Kierkegaard, who, on the other side of G. W. F. Hegel, will proclaim that "Christianity is an existence communication"[5] and that "truth is subjectivity."[6] Space limitations prevent this extended discussion here, but I have presented this discussion elsewhere.[7]

Martin Heidegger warned in his essays "The Onto-Theological Constitution of Metaphysics," "The Question Concerning Technology," and "The Word of Nietzsche: 'God Is Dead'" that philosophy runs the risk of creating a god of philosophy that is fundamentally nihilistic and, thus, socially, politically, and culturally destructive. Heidegger's notion of the onto-theological is compelling, as it implicitly hearkens back to Aristotle's *Metaphysics*. For Heidegger, Western philosophy is engaged in the search for a ground of being, which makes Aristotle's "god" an ontological placeholder in the interest of human reason. Being needs a ground of rational explanation, hence the "onto" of *ontology*. And it is this ontological quest for a ground of being that becomes theological insofar as Aristotle refers to this being as "God." But this god, as Heidegger points out, is not the God of the Bible. Instead, it is an ersatz version of the Judeo-Christian God before whom no one, in Heidegger's words, can "dance or sing." At bottom, the problem with Aristotle's god is that it is a product of a finite, rational imagination that overcomes the God of the Bible and repackages Him as a Greek aristocrat desperately trying to solve the intellectual problem of motion inherited from Parmenides and Zeno on the one hand and Heraclitus on the other. God, then, is recast into the social and political identity of the thinker. Evidence of this is found in a particularly dense passage of Aristotle's *Metaphysics*, in which he points out that God is apparently a philosopher much like himself in that "God's thinking is a thinking on thinking."[8] This god is a far cry from the word of God made flesh in the Gospel of John. The contrast is striking.

Heidegger takes up this contrast further in his essay "The Question Concerning Technology." There, he points out the dangers of a philosophical god that result from intellectual, Aristotelian-styled, causal/metaphysical thinking:

> Thus where everything that presences exhibits itself in the light of a cause-effect coherence, even God can, for representational thinking, lose all that is exalted and holy, the mysteriousness of his distance. In the light of causality, God can sink to the level of a cause, of a *causa efficiens*. He then becomes, even in theology, the god of the philosophers, namely, of those who define the unconcealed and the concealed in terms of the causality of making, without ever considering the essential origin of this causality.[9]

So it is that the quest for metaphysical first principles, if left unchecked, results in the idol-making of reason in which God is reduced to an Aristotelian efficient causality. Heidegger takes up this point even further in his essay "The Word of Nietzsche: 'God Is Dead,'" in which his principal interest is to interrogate the essence of nihilism. There, he writes of philosophical thinking about God:

> The heaviest blow against God is not that God is held to be unknowable, not that God's existence is demonstrated to be unprovable, but rather that the god held to be real is elevated to the highest value. For this blow comes precisely not from those who are standing about, who do not believe in God, but from the believers and their theologians who discourse on the being that is of all beings most in being, without ever letting it occur to them to think on being itself, in order thereby to become aware that, seen from out of faith, their thinking and their talking is sheer blasphemy if it meddles in the theology of faith.[10]

Here, Heidegger points to the idol-making of philosophy: Reason, motivated by its incessant demand for explanation—the logos—transforms even God into a product of its philosophical reflections. One hears an echo of Kant with Heidegger on this point. Notice in this passage that placing the limitations on the knowledge of God—as does Kant's transcendental idealism—is not the nihilistic move coming from a dangerous "secular Enlightenment" philosopher in Kant. Alvin Plantinga's accusations against Kant notwithstanding, Heidegger, rightly understood, can be read as endorsing the view that Kant is actually doing a greater service to Christianity than what might otherwise be thought because Kant's transcendental idealism is denying reason to "make room for faith" in such a way as to respect the integrity of both philosophy and Christian theology, which is precisely what Heidegger is calling for when he writes of a meddling of reason in the "theology of faith."

Perhaps the worst example of reason "meddling" in the theology of faith is the following passage, taken from the Reverend Buchner Payne, a nineteenth-century thinker from Tennessee who argued that Black people were inferior and had no souls.[11] Payne's move in the following passage is both philosophical and theological and thus the quintessential example of the philosophical and theological corruption at the core of my thesis in this chapter, as Payne, through the use of the logos as applied to Christian theology, deifies white people and demonizes Black people:

> Now as Adam was white, Abraham white and our Savior white, did he enter heaven when he arose from the dead as a white man or as a negro? If as a white man then the negro is left out; if as a negro then the white man is left out. As Adam was the Son of God and as God is light (white) and in Him is no darkness (black) at all, how could God then be the father of the negro, as like begets like? And if God could not be the father of the blacks because He was white, how could our Savior, "being the express image of God's person," as asserted by St. Paul, carry such a damned color into heaven, where all are white, much less to the throne?[12]

This passage presents an argument that is theological in content yet philosophical in form; its theological content is its claims about Christianity. Its philosophical form has two aspects. First, the logical form of the argument is that of the disjunctive syllogism. And second, the argument presupposes that God is the Being who is the ground of all beings. Such an argument, then, is based on a sort of Western metaphysics that posits God as the principal and universal ground of all beings, and is thus ontological. And it posits this Being as the ultimate ground, even of itself, and is thus theological. Again, philosophically—ontologically—speaking, the argument is a disjunctive syllogism of the following abstract form:

1) $P \lor Q$
2) $\sim P$
$\therefore Q$

It may be restated thus: Jesus entered into Heaven after the resurrection either as a Negro or as a white man (P v Q). Jesus cannot be a Negro because there is "no darkness" (no Negro) in Him (~P). Therefore, Jesus entered into Heaven as a white man, excluding all Negroes from Heaven because God can have no companionship with darkness (∴Q). That this passage is logically valid in its form is not surprising, as Payne "was once considered to be the greatest logician in the South."[13] But there is a difference between validity and soundness. An argument is deductively valid if its conclusion follows out of necessity from its premises, but a deductive argument is sound if and only if it is valid and its propositions—both its premises and conclusion—are true. Here, then, we have an argument that is logically valid but unsound. Much work must be done—work that is, epistemologically speaking, impossible to do—to prove the truth of its propositions, especially if we take Kant and Heidegger seriously. Again, Payne's logically valid and racist thinking exemplifies the philosophical and theological problem I am addressing in this chapter, which is how the totalizing tendencies of abstract philosophical thinking—the logos—transgress the limitations of reason, intrude upon the theological, and through a process of abstraction, reduce God to an idol of a corrupt philosophical and theological imagination for the sake of corrupt human interests. In other words, Payne's racist logic is where, for Heidegger, the Onto-Theological—a product of reason's natural interest in a metaphysically and epistemologically justified totality according to the logos and, in Kantian terms, its resulting dilemma of being naturally unable to comprehend such a totality—reduces God's transcendence to immanence and produces a morally corrupt logic of a white god that produces an abundance of valid arguments but little truth. Such is the white god *imago hominis* of white Christian nationalism. Indeed, Payne's arguments were so influential that they philosophically justified American chattel slavery and logically vindicated the whiteness of god all at once.

To summarize, based on my interpretation of Kant and Heidegger, I have argued thus far that both philosophy and Christian theology are corrupted when the end of philosophy is conflated with the end of Christian theology. The former is corrupted because of its production of a pseudo-knowledge, whereas the latter is corrupted because of its illicit relationship with such pseudo-knowledge in the interest of maintaining a pseudo-religion with a white racist god *imago hominis* as its morally corrupt centerpiece. This god is now thoroughly prepared, as Reverend Payne has shown, to justify all manner of evil; in particular, it is able to be the god of white Christian nationalism, the god who emerged in all its ignominious "glory" on January 6, 2021, to proclaim its racist gospel of both the necessity and the perpetuity of the nigger, which I take up in the next section.

III

On May 24, 1963, Dr. Kenneth Clark interviewed James Baldwin, the twentieth-century literary giant and political activist. Throughout the interview, they discussed major issues of the day concerning the status of race relations in America, including the import of Dr. Martin Luther King Jr.'s commitment to nonviolence. Toward the end of the interview, Dr. Clark asked Baldwin about the future of America. This was Baldwin's response:

> What white people have to do is try to find out in their own hearts why it was necessary to have a nigger in the first place, because I'm not a nigger. I'm a man. But if you think I'm a nigger, it means you need him. And the question you've got to ask yourself, the white population of this country's got to ask itself, north and south because it's one country and for a Negro, there's no difference between the north and the south, there's just a difference in *the way they castrate you*. But the fact of the castration is the American fact. If I'm not the nigger here, and you invented him, you, the white people invented him, then you've got to find out why. And the future of the country depends on that; whether or not it's able to ask that question . . . to have the moral strength simply to face that question, to face that question.[14]

Here, I am interested in the philosophical nature of Baldwin's remarks as they relate to his point that white people must have the "moral strength" to confront the question of why it was "necessary to have a nigger in the first place." Two philosophical points are, I think, significant. First, the problem of induction, which is that there is no guarantee that the future will resemble the past, would seem to preclude Baldwin from answering a question about the future based on the past, and yet that is precisely what Baldwin does when Clark asks him about the future of America: He answers the question by arguing that whites must have the moral strength to ask themselves about why a nigger was necessary "*in the first place*." Baldwin addresses the end, or the future, of America from its beginning. For an epistemological skeptic, such an approach would prove futile, as there is always the possibility that the future could be otherwise, that claims about the future are based not on any present observations but, rather, on past experiences. But Baldwin is not a skeptic in the Humean tradition of skepticism. Puzzles and thought experiments do not concern him. As an African American acquainted with American history, Baldwin understood that ordinary philosophical problems like induction are subject to certain exceptions when it comes to Black people in America; with Black people, Baldwin understood that the future does indeed resemble the past, which is why when asked about America's future, he addressed the question by referring to America's past. The second philosophical point about Baldwin's question is that it is a question of origins, of beginnings; it is a metaphysical question, an ontological question about the first principles of the nigger. Baldwin tells white people that the question they must have the moral strength to confront is the question of why it was necessary to have a nigger in the first place. Here, I want to focus on the words *why* and *in the first place*. These words are philosophical words demanding metaphysical answers related to explanations (*why* a nigger) and origins (why a nigger *in the first place*), as well as a modal answer (why the nigger was *necessary*). Since I take Baldwin's question seriously, I turn to Aristotle, the consummate metaphysician, for an ontological investigation of the nigger. I do so, however, with two caveats.

First, I recognize that Baldwin is not demanding that I, a Black scholar, answer his question. He is instead asking that whites have the moral strength to simply confront the question. Whites should thus be doing this work, not me. In fact, in facing the question, whites can do more than I could ever do in providing an answer to the question, precisely because as the perpetrators of slavery's legacy through privilege, facing the question signals a gesture toward their infinite responsibility. I can always—and have always—articulated Black pain in my philosophical and theological work. But white accountability has not been likewise articulated. In merely having the courage to face the question, whites can cross the Rubicon and do the hard work of addressing the damage done in the legacy of what Douglass called that "peculiar institution" that curiously turned persons into property. And second, the answer to Baldwin's question that I provide in this chapter is in no way intended to absolve whites from having the moral strength to simply face the question. I answer this question as a Black scholar with a keen interest in the abiding problem of racism in American Christianity, and I think that Baldwin's question is an attractive point of departure to help elucidate the idolatry of white Christian nationalism. Whites must still do the work. With these caveats in mind, I now turn to Aristotle's account of origins as applied to the nigger.

Aristotle on Origins

Chapter 1 in Book Delta of Aristotle's *Metaphysics* presents a brief but nuanced discussion of the term *origin* (ἀρχή). We use the word *origin*, writes Aristotle, in at least six different senses.[15] To answer Baldwin's question about the necessity of the nigger in the first place, I turn to the third sense of the word *origin* from Book Delta of Aristotle's *Metaphysics*, which is that *origin* is used to indicate "that from which, as an immanent part, a thing first comes to be," as in the foundation of a building is its origin.[16] The nigger was both "necessary" and "in the first place" because it is an origin in the same sense that a foundation is the origin of a house; the house may be said to have its origin in its foundation, which is immanent to itself and without which it could not be, and America may be said to have its origin in the nigger, which was immanent prior to America's formal political organization and without which it could not be. In light of this political necessity, the white god *imago hominis* of white Christian nationalism demands the creation of the nigger, who was an immanent part of America prior to is formal political founding, by legislating the nigger into America's founding political documents, especially the Constitution, which, although ratified 168 years after the first slaves arrived in Jamestown, Virginia, did nothing to free the slaves. In fact, through a series of political compromises among whites and in which no Black people participated, the Constitution ensured the continuation of American chattel slavery at least for the foreseeable future; a future that would erupt in a civil war, the failure of Reconstruction because of another compromise between only whites that affected Black people, and state-sponsored white racist terrorism that many would argue continues even today. Not only was the creation of the nigger essential politically, but it was also necessary theologically, so a white Christian nationalist theology could be used to justify American chattel slavery, Jim Crow, and lynching, and which regrettably persists even today to justify certain forms of white racial violence against Black people.

Consider, then, the results of the idolatry of white Christian nationalism. Through a conflation of the telos of philosophy with the mere *archē* of Christianity, philosophy produces a corrupt pseudo-knowledge that justifies a corrupt white god *imago hominis*. This god then produces the nigger as its first act of creation and then, through its weaponization of the logos within white Christian nationalism, posits the nigger as the first principle—the *archē*—of America itself, resulting in a profane but accurate rearticulation of John 1:1, stated as follows: "In the beginning was the nigger, and the nigger was with America, and the nigger was America." This pseudo-gospel is not far-fetched, for at the core of the American historical beginning was the desire to maintain chattel slavery. Indeed, aside from the debates and literature surrounding the Philadelphia Convention of 1787, historian Gerald Horne points out that, contradicting the most celebrated narrative of the Revolutionary War as a war fought in the interest of human freedom, there is evidence indicating that the Revolutionary War was actually a counterrevolution of conservative whites who were fighting an opposition to chattel slavery from the British and Africans residing in the colonies. Horne argues, then, that America's framers actually fought the Revolutionary War to protect the institution of chattel slavery. Horne's insights thus imply that the Revolutionary War was not about the protection of human liberty but, rather, its degradation.[17] The philosophical and theological underpinnings of Horne's argument are significant because at the core of Horne's claim about the Revolutionary War is a deep need to found America on the subhuman status of the nigger, understanding niggers to be, in both politics and theology, the creation of a racist white theology that today is white Christian nationalism.

IV

With the social and political orders of America having been established and justified by a racist theology, the next phase in the development of white Christian nationalism is that it must maintain the subordinate status of the nigger that its white god has created. Such maintenance demands two interrelated chronic conditions, the first of which furthers the second: first, a chronic invisibility of the nigger, and second, chronic injustice toward the nigger. An effective way to accomplish this subordination is through the power of abstraction—the weaponizing of the logos—in American Christian theology, political theory, and law. Abstraction dispatches America's history of anti-Black racism, thus causing a chronic invisibility of history—completely at odds with the Gospel of Jesus Christ, which is thoroughly interested in history—which is then used to perpetuate injustice. I argue in this section that the chronic invisibility and injustice maintain the status quo against the backdrop of a philosophy of history that posits a teleology of white supremacy in the interest of the white god *imago hominis* accompanied by its correlate of Black subordination—the subordination of the nigger—that occurs in a frightening repetition of the history that its chronic invisibility ignores. In what follows, I present a discussion of the weaponization of the logos in American law and political theory, attempting to show not only their essential role in the chronic conditions of invisibility and injustice but also how a white supremacist philosophy of history is attentive only to those historical events that vindicate its racist white god *imago hominis* in the interest of maintaining notions of Black inferiority, or the nigger.

American Law and Political Theory

Abstraction—the weaponization of the logos—is operative in American law and political theory as much as it is in Christian theology and with similar results of a chronic invisibility that ignores the concrete realities of Black life and a chronic injustice resulting from that invisibility that almost always leads to Black death. Although this death at the hands of an oppressive anti-Black regime is often physical, it can be said that Black people die twice; their physical death is but a belated pronouncement of a prior social and political demise ensured by abstract American legal doctrine and political theory. One sees this social and political death in abstract legal notions in

American law such as "equality," which eclipse more just notions of fairness. Indeed, the juridical commitment to the abstraction of equality leads to the absurd result of a doctrinal account of equal protection jurisprudence that, despite notions of original intent, deprives Black descendants of newly freed slaves the benefit of public policy initiatives that end up benefiting whites and thus maintaining the subordinate position of Black people through American law. Despite contemporary caricatures of critical race theory (CRT), the phenomenon of abstract reasoning—what I am calling here the weaponization of the logos—is CRT's principal target, for it is through abstraction in jurisprudence that the American legal system vindicates rather than eliminates white supremacy, despite the best efforts of American civil rights activism. Derrick Bell, a leading founder of CRT, put it this way: "Even those herculean efforts we hail as successful will produce no more than temporary 'peaks of progress,' short-lived victories that slide into irrelevance as racial patterns adapt in ways that maintain white dominance."[18] It is this maintenance of white dominance that interests me here, as I try to show the weaponization of the logos in American law.

The development of Bell's work in CRT takes place within a much broader tradition of Black social and political thought going back at least as far to the works of Lewis Woodson and Martin Delany in the nineteenth century[19] and through the twentieth-century work of political theorist Ralph Bunche. Bell draws from Bunche's work in his magnum opus, *Race, Racism, and American Law*. Bunche, in his 1935 essay "A Critical Analysis of the Tactics and Programs of Minority Groups,"[20] is critical of Supreme Court adjudication in the area of voting rights. Bunche writes, "Perhaps no better example of the tendency of the Supreme Court to detach itself from political reality when questions involving Negro rights are concerned and to resort to legal fictions can be afforded . . . the recent Texas Primary case."[21] Bunche is referring to *Grovey v. Townsend*, in which the Supreme Court unanimously upheld the race-based exclusion of Blacks from voting in the Texas state Democratic Party primary on the grounds that the Equal Protection Clause of the Fourteenth Amendment and the Fifteenth Amendment's guarantee of the right to vote only applied to actions of the state, not to voluntary, private political associations. The problem was that Texas was what was called a "primary state," meaning that the general election was practically insignificant, as the winner of the primary won the general election. So, the inability to vote in the primary is de facto disenfranchisement. Bunche writes of this decision, pointing out how it exemplifies the height of abstraction in that rather than engaging the concrete political reality of Black people on the ground in Texas, Court instead "sought refuge in the dialectical stratosphere,"[22] that "the decision is especially ironical in view of the fact that the Court invoked the Fourteenth Amendment—the most important section of the Negro's charter of liberty—as the sanction for thus denying him the franchise,"[23] and that the Court is thus able "to avoid delicate issues by hiding behind legal technicalities."[24] Bunche then offers his considered assessment of the American legal system as a vehicle for Black liberation: "Such . . . political tactics, while winning a minor and too often illusory victory now and then, are essentially inefficacious in the long run. They lead up blind alleys and are chiefly programs of escape."[25]

Bell, drawing from Bunche's insights on the Supreme Court, developed his thesis of racial realism, which is that American anti-Black racism is permanent, and despite its permanence, one must struggle against it. I have written extensively on Bell's thesis of racial realism elsewhere. Here, however, I want to briefly discuss the first part of racial realism, which I call the "permanence thesis." I take up the thesis about resistance in the fifth section. In his landmark book *Faces at the Bottom of the Well*, Bell discusses how the language of the Supreme Court, ostensibly just and fair in the abstract, is, beneath the surface, fundamentally unjust. To support this view, Bell discusses the difference between legal formalism and legal realism, two prominent theories of adjudication that predominate much of twentieth- and twenty-first-century jurisprudence. Legal formalism theorizes that when judges decide cases, they turn to an abstract, a priori notion of "the law" and then formulaically apply it to a set of facts to reach a conclusion. American legal realism, in contrast, argues that when judges decide cases, they are, first and foremost, stimulated to their decision by the facts and then resort to the law as a post-hoc justification for a decision motivated by factual considerations. Legal realism finds its support in empirical accounts of cases pending on appeal, in which the ability to justify a decision with multiple legal rules is an indication of legal indeterminacy in adjudication. Bell argues that a realist account of adjudication will consider social and political factors rather than merely resorting to a formalistic application of the law, which can, and often does, lead to unjust results. Bell argues that one such unjust result is *Coppage v. Kansas*, a Supreme Court decision ruling that a state law that prohibited "yellow dog" contracts—contracts in which workers agreed not to participate in union activities—was an unconstitutional infringement of employers' rights under the Due Process Clause of the Fourteenth Amendment. Of this decision, Bell writes:

> The Court adhered to formalistic thinking even during the Great Depression, when any realistic analysis of the state of affairs would have included some recognition of the desperate need for state intervention. People were starving, and for at least half of the population, the economy held little hope of future employment. . . . [T]he Court insisted on venerating grand rules that had little to do with the modern context of poverty and misery.[26]

Likening the realist assessment of the *Coppage v. Kansas* decision to adjudication in cases involving race, Bell continues:

> The realist attack on short-sighted and stubborn judicial formalism is quite like the realistic assessment we're making of formal civil rights policy. My position is that the legal rules regarding racial discrimination have become not only *reified* (that is, ascribing material existence and power to what are really just ideas) . . . but *deified*. The worship of equality rules as having absolute power benefits whites by preserving a benevolent but fictional self-image, and such worship benefits blacks by preserving hope. But I think we've arrived at a place in history where the harms of such worship outweigh its benefits.[27]

The logos, then, weaponized in American law generates an abstract idol of justice in the form of a theory that demands a chronic neglect of concrete social and political realities affecting Black people, rendering them chronically invisible and chronically subject to injustice in American law. And one must not miss the theological dimensions of this philosophical abstraction. Notice Bell's use of theological terms such as *deified* and *worship*. This is, I would argue, the worship of the white racist god *imago hominis* as operative in American law and legal theory.

As it is in American law, so it is in American political theory: Abstraction—the philosophical logos—reigns supreme in an oppressive regime that, in the name of ideal theory and conceptual stipulation, chronically ignores racial injustice toward Blacks and thus makes them chronic sufferers of that same injustice. Consider John Rawls's political theory in his magnum opus, *A Theory of Justice*. There, Rawls purports to take traditional social contract theory to "a higher level of abstraction."[28] Classical social contract theory begins with a thought experiment referred to as the "state of nature" in which people are hypothetically situated and then the need for government is theorized from that ideal situation. For Rawls, this ideal situation takes the form not of a "state of nature," but rather an "original position." In this original position, people exist behind a "veil of ignorance," meaning that no one knows their racial, religious, or gender identity, has no sense of their socioeconomic status, personal networks, or natural endowments. According to Rawls, it is only from this original position that people can discern the principles of justice needed for an ideally just society.

Charles Mills has been one of the most outspoken critics of Rawlsian political theory.[29] Referring to it as "ideal theory," he argues that Rawls ignores the historical realities of racial oppression in the interest of theorizing and that, in doing so, not only fails to address injustice against marginalized groups such as Black Americans but also, because of this neglect, perpetuates it. Here one sees chronic invisibility, an unseen-ness, accompanied by chronic injustice.

Even as the weaponization of the logos maintains the subordinate status of the nigger in the theology of white Christian nationalism and in its legal theory, it also happens in the context of political theorizing that has the same result. In my recent monograph, I liken the abstractions of analytic theism's reformed epistemology to the notions of invisibility that Mills delineates in his critique of Rawlsian political theory as ideal theory.[30]

Philosophy of History

The chronic invisibility and chronic injustice of an abstract Christian theology and abstractions in American law and political theory resulting from the weaponization of the logos occur against the backdrop of a philosophy of history dogmatically considered teleological, with the maintenance of white supremacy as its end. The white god *imago hominis* must dogmatically posit such a teleology to maintain its own superiority and the perpetual oppressive subordination of the nigger. To this end, white Christian nationalism embraces a philosophy of history that first dispenses with any critical view of history in favor of a dogmatic claim to ultimate American white racial progress at the expense of Black people, and second, through its neglect of history to prevent justice, repeats history to maintain injustice. The philosophical framework for my account of history as presented here is Kant's philosophy of history. I choose Kant for consistency, as previously in this chapter I discussed Kant's transcendental idealism as a means for protecting the integrity of both philosophy and Christian theology. I strive to maintain continuity with the implications of Kant's transcendental idealism as related to protecting philosophy and Christian theology, as I argue here that the conclusions of Kant's transcendental idealism also affect his philosophy of history.

According to Kant, the true nature of history is unknowable. History is, for Kant, either a random series of meaningless events or a teleological progression that moves us toward the improvement of humanity. One cannot, however, have any knowledge of the nature of history in either of these ways because such a knowledge claim demands a transcendent insight that humanity is fundamentally lacking. In his essay "Idea for a Universal History from a Cosmopolitan Perspective," Kant argues, consistent with the conclusions of his transcendental idealism, that human will is determined in its appearances, but that as it is, in itself, it is free. But of course, since Kant concludes that one can never have synthetic a priori knowledge of things in themselves, humanity must see itself as part of an order of beings capable of the spontaneous causality of moral freedom that is independent of the causal relations of nature. Thus it is that Kant constructs his moral philosophy around the a priori nature of the categorical imperative. Kant takes a similar approach to his philosophy of history. He writes that, on the one hand, "however deeply concealed" the causes of appearances of the freedom of the will may be, "History . . . allows us to hope that . . . if we consider the free exercises of the human will broadly, we can ultimately discern a regular progression in its appearances. History further lets us hope that, in this way, that which seems confused and irregular when considering particular individuals can nonetheless be recognized as a steady progressing, albeit slow development of the original capacities of the entire species."[31]

In contrast, Kant points out that because humanity neither follows the causal laws of natural instinct, as animals do, nor does humanity "proceed in accordance with a previously arranged plan, it does not seem possible to present a systematic history of them (as could be given for bees or beavers, for instance). One cannot but feel a certain disinclination when one observes their activity as carried out on the great stage of the world and finds it ultimately, despite the occasional semblance of wisdom to be seen in individual actions, all to be made up, by and large, of foolishness, childish vanity, and, often enough, even of childish wickedness and destructiveness."[32] Kant goes on to argue that because neither of these perceptions is definitive, one may view history according to the *als ob* (as if) and conclude that based on nine principles, history may be viewed teleologically, but only heuristically, not metaphysically.[33]

Akin to how the logos transgresses its boundaries to corrupt both philosophy and Christian theology, creating a pseudo-knowledge vindicated by a racist idol *imago hominis*, philosophy moves beyond its bounds to produce a pseudo-knowledge of history. Such a movement of philosophy is essential if the chronic invisibility and chronic injustice are to make sense to the racist imaginary of white Christian nationalism, for the weaponization of the logos in Christian theology and American law and political theory is nonsensical unless, at a minimum, the telos of history is metaphysically and dogmatically understood as culminating in the maintenance of white supremacy. Interestingly, this philosophy of history must not only engage in chronic instances of injustice and invisibility but also do so in a manner that mirrors historical events in some uncanny and frightful ways. In other words, the chronic invisibility and chronic injustice occur in a world where history ceaselessly repeats itself.

Consider the events of January 6, 2021. Fueled by rage and widespread deception that the 2020 election had been "stolen" from President Donald Trump, an angry white mob stormed the US Capitol as Congress was engaged in the somewhat perfunctory task of certifying the results of the November presidential election of 2020. Something had to be wrong, reasoned the mob, as there were five states that President Trump won in 2016 that he was winning late on Election Day but ultimately lost over the next few days as mail-in votes, which favored the Democratic Party, were counted. These five states were Arizona, Georgia, Pennsylvania, Michigan, and Wisconsin, and the major cities in each of these states—Phoenix, Atlanta, Philadelphia, Detroit, and Milwaukee—were cities with high concentrations of Black voters, the overwhelming majority of which voted for Biden rather than Trump. Scapegoating Black people in each of these five major American cities as agents of political mischief, a false narrative emerged that there was widespread voter fraud and that it was concentrated in these five cities. It is this narrative that, in part, at least, became the motivation for the mob convening at the Capitol building on January 6, 2021, in an attempt to prevent, through mob violence, the certification of the 2020 election results.

As the mob moved closer and closer to the Capitol building and was on the verge of breaching it, US senators were inside the building—in the Senate chamber—indulging the false narrative of voter fraud. The racism here is compelling: An angry white mob is assembling because of a false belief that Black people in Detroit, Philadelphia, Milwaukee, Atlanta, and Phoenix had done something untoward to "steal" the election from their preferred candidate. And while this was happening and despite the claims of voter fraud having been litigated, adjudicated, and rejected in courts across the country more than sixty times, the Senate was actually engaged in "debate" about certifying the results of the 2020 election. During this debate, Senator Ted Cruz, a Harvard-educated lawyer and former Supreme Court law clerk to Chief Justice William Rehnquist, said two things that were remarkable. The first was remarkably foolish, and the second was remarkably immoral.

First, Senator Cruz indulged the nonsense that the Arizona electoral votes should not be certified. He made this claim despite the democratic operation of the judicial process that had consistently and emphatically dismissed the bogus claims of widespread election fraud. To argue in support of claims that the legal system has resolved and that Congress is constitutionally powerless to entertain is indeed foolish.

Senator Cruz's second move was much more troubling. In the interest of refusing to certify Arizona's electoral votes, Cruz appealed to the presidential election of 1876. He claims that in 1876, an election commission was formed to review the electoral college results of certain states (South Carolina, Florida, and Louisiana). He continued that Congress should do the same in the present historical moment. As he spoke these words, I was initially stunned that he would make an appeal to disenfranchise voters in the twenty-first century based on an electoral commission that ultimately led to the disenfranchisement of newly freed slaves for nearly a hundred years, from 1877 to 1965, despite the ratification of the Fifteenth Amendment in 1870. This appeal to such a political catastrophe was problematic, to say the least. As my shock gave way to anger, I remembered that Senator Cruz's education and culture do not make him moral. I recalled the words of Kant, who once said, "To a high degree we are, through art and science, cultured. We are civilized—perhaps too much for our own good—in all sorts of social grace and decorum. But to consider ourselves as having reached morality—for that, much is lacking."[34]

And then, as my anger gave way to disappointment, I wanted to jump through my television screen and remind Cruz that he was making an appeal to a history that, if we were not careful, would repeat itself; that even as the Hayes-Tilden compromise of 1877 ended Reconstruction and disenfranchised Black voters for nearly a century, his proposed electoral commission would disenfranchise Black voters in Milwaukee, Detroit, Philadelphia, and Atlanta, and Black and Latino voters in Arizona, who voted in states in which he wanted to challenge the electoral vote count. I so wanted to tell Senator Cruz about the danger of repeating this history where angry white mobs used intimidation and murder to overrun the rule of law in favor of mob rule in the post-Reconstruction South and that his proposed course of action would cause this history to repeat itself. As it turns out, I did not have to jump through my television screen to do this. The angry, white mob that was attacking the Capitol building did it for me.

For these reasons, there is a deep connection between the overwhelming sense of white racial and theological entitlement on January 6, 2021, and the white racial and theological entitlement that characterized a veritable reign of state-sponsored racial terrorism on newly freed slaves from the end of Reconstruction until deep into the twentieth century and remains ongoing today. So it is that the white god *imago hominis* dogmatically claims a metaphysical knowledge of a history that repeats itself, supporting abstraction as the weaponization of the logos in the interest of chronic invisibility of Black people and chronic injustice toward them.

To conclude this section of the chapter, I point to two cruel, ironic twists amid this moment of white Christian nationalism's overwhelming sense of racial entitlement and white supremacy on January 6, 2021. The ironies of this incident bolster my claim about the chronic invisibility and chronic injustice toward Black people within the logic of a racist, repetitive, philosophy of history. The incident is the story of a Black man named Eugene Goodman ("Good," "Man"), a Black Capitol police officer who saved wealthy white senators from an angry white mob. Goodman was doing his job on January 6, 2021, when he was under siege and at the mercy of the deranged white mob who had, according to many statutory definitions of burglary, burglarized the Capitol building by breaking and entering with the intent to commit crimes therein. Goodman's interaction with the mob reveals two harsh realities of American anti-Black racism that demonstrate the chronic invisibility and chronic injustice toward the nigger. The first is that the white, "Christian" mob, despite seeing Goodman in full police uniform, gun on hip, did not see a police officer. Despite Goodman's training and experience, the chronic invisibility of white supremacy—cultivated by centuries of philosophical, theological, and political abstraction—only saw a nigger, so they disregarded his show of authority and charged him. The tragedy here is awful, for not only do Black civilians have ample reason to fear the police, but uniformed Black police also have ample reason to fear white civilians.

The second irony is that even as Officer Goodman led the mob away from the Senate chamber to protect the senators from physical harm, twelve of those same senators benefiting from his protection were doing political harm to him as they sought to disenfranchise large numbers of voters in Milwaukee, Detroit, Philadelphia, Atlanta, and Arizona—Black voters who share Officer Goodman's ethnic and racial heritage. Whereas the first aspect of Officer Goodman's interaction with the white mob demonstrated his chronic invisibility despite his show of legitimate authority in the face of illegitimate and racist political and legal claims, the second aspect of Officer Goodman's encounter with the white mob demonstrates that despite how whites benefit from the protection of Black people, Black people are nevertheless subjected to chronic and ironic instances of injustice. Ironic though these instances may be, they show how the white god *imago hominis*, through a dogmatic philosophy of history that posits a progressive teleology, furthers the weaponization of the logos and its abstractions, and thus has more of a regressive, oppressive teleology attained through the repetition of history to maintain white supremacy.

V

The picture thus far is grim: The chronic invisibility of Black people and the chronic injustice toward Black people, both as niggers, seems inescapable insofar as white Christian nationalism has created the nigger, American law and political theory have maintained the nigger, and a racist philosophy of history has ensured the perpetuity of the nigger. What can combat this, especially when attempts at racial justice in America are either met with resistance from existing institutional structures, or, if such resistance gives way, it only does so because some further, white interest is also served?[35]

I want to briefly sketch a possible answer to this question in this final phase of my argument by drawing from the works of Derrick Bell and Howard Thurman. Bell argued forcefully that the permanence of racism ought not prevent protest and resistance to racism, and Thurman pointed out the need for a deep sense of spirituality to face the difficult times that so many Black people must survive in America. While it may be argued that Bell demands resistance against external forces, Thurman prescribes a deep sense of spirituality that makes such resistance possible. In my view, both are essential to resist the onslaught of chronic invisibility and chronic injustice.

Of protests, Bell writes that "while a cliché, speaking truth to power can discourage those who hope to act against the public's interest and convince most people to support them."[36] The seeming futility of a protest or its unpopularity can still make a difference. Bell continues: "Articulating our differences publicly may not win individuals or groups any popularity awards, but protests and the expression of opposition are forms of power we can enlist in campaigns for reforms, including those not recognized by courts or of interest to those individuals we helped elect."[37] The protester(s) can thus effect change but, at the same time, must recognize that any meaningful, systemic change is unlikely. I believe this is what Bell means when he points out: "We must recognize and acknowledge (at least to ourselves) that our actions are not likely to lead to transcendent change and despite our best efforts, may be of more help to the system we despise than to the victims of that system we are trying to help."[38] But despite these challenges, Bell points out that protests can engender a sense of dedication that "can lead to policy positions and campaigns that are less likely to worsen conditions for those we are trying to help, and that can serve as reminders to the establishment that they must contend with strong opposition."[39] And this is not the only benefit of continued struggle, according to Bell, for he writes that beyond reminding the establishment of strong opposition, "continued struggle can bring about unexpected benefits and gains that in themselves justify continued endeavor."[40]

Bell continues, rejecting the possibility of hope in the face of the abstractions of the logos in American law when he writes that "I am convinced that America offers something real for black people. It is not though, the romantic love of integration—though, like romance, we may seek and sometimes experience it. It is surely not the long-sought goal of equality under law."[41] Again, despite the failure to attain justice through an abstract notion of racial equality under law, Bell emphasizes that "we must maintain the struggle against racism lest the erosion of rights become even worse than it now is. The pragmatic approach that we must follow is simply to take a hard-eyed view of the racism as it is, and of our subordinate role in it."[42] Bell concludes with the importance of struggle, regardless of the outcome: "We must realize with our slave forebears that the struggle for freedom is, at bottom, a manifestation of our humanity that survives and grows stronger through resistance to oppression even if we never overcome that oppression."[43] Bell's message is sobering but inspiring: Victory is in the struggle, not the outcome.

Whereas Bell enables a resistance to external forces, it is Howard Thurman's deep spirituality that enables the inner workings of human fortitude to neutralize the relentless assault from without. Thurman writes of the day-to-day: "But the child of the disinherited is likely to live a heavy life. A ceiling is placed on his dreaming by the counsel of despair coming from his elders, whom experience has taught to expect little and to hope for less."⁴⁴ The conditions that Thurman describes here are consistent with those attending the chronic invisibility and chronic injustice of the nigger, and it is in this context that Thurman inspires to see beyond one's condition to overcome fear: "Nothing less than a great daring in the face of overwhelming odds can achieve the inner security in which fear cannot possibly survive. It is true that a man cannot be serene unless he possesses something about which to be serene. Here we reach the high-water mark of prophetic religion, and it is of the essence of the religion of Jesus of Nazareth."⁴⁵ Thurman here invokes Scripture when he writes, "Of course God cares for the grass of the field, which lives a day and is no more, or the sparrow that falls unnoticed by the wayside. He also holds the stars in their appointed places, leaves his mark in every living thing. And he cares for me!"⁴⁶ For Thurman, it is this reminder that "becomes the answer to the threat of violence—yea, to violence itself. To the degree to which a man knows this, he is unconquerable from within and without."⁴⁷

VI

Both philosophy and Christian theology are corrupted when the end of philosophy is taken to be the end of Christian theology. The telos of philosophy and the telos of Christian theology are different. The former ends in abstract reason, which is merely the *archē*, or the beginning of Christian theology. The telos of Christian theology is *sarx*, implying the flesh and embodiment. With these differences ignored, philosophy, which ought to result in knowledge and truth, produces a bogus version of the truth in Christian theology through an abstract understanding of an ersatz god *imago hominis*, which corrupts Christianity because rather than being the transcendent God of the Judeo-Christian tradition made immanent in the *sarx*, or the flesh, of Jesus Christ, it is the immanent made transcendent through an anthropomorphized projection of whiteness, becoming the god of white Christian nationalism.

Once created by the white racist imaginary, this god establishes a regime of oppression that endeavors several acts of creation, the first of which is the creation of the nigger, a metaphysical first principle and a modal necessity for the oppressive regime. The nigger is thus both legislated into the political and theological orders of white Christian nationalism at the origin of America. Even as origin implies a starting point from that which is immanent to a thing, for example, the foundation of a house, the nigger is the origin, the starting point, indeed the foundation of America, and the foundation of the idolatry of white Christian nationalism, which blasphemously transforms the Gospel of

John's opening to include the nigger as the *archē*, or first principle of America. Thus installed as a metaphysical first principle of white Christian nationalism, the nigger, attentively created, must now be chronically ignored, except for the purpose of maintaining the oppressive status quo. Such is achieved through a self-executing system of law and political theory, which weaponizes the logos as an agent of abstraction through a philosophy of history that must protect the white god *imago hominis* at all times. Hence the permanence of American anti-Black racism. Resistance to such a regime of oppression demands both relentless moral fortitude and deep spiritual renewal.

NOTES

1. See Douglas A. Blackmon, *Slavery by Another Name: The Re-Enslavement of Black Americans from the Civil War to World War II* (New York: Anchor Books, 2009).

2. Immanuel Kant, *Critique of Pure Reason*, trans. by Norman Kemp Smith (New York: St. Martin's Press, 1929).

3. Kant argues in favor of the integrity of philosophy as science in the "Transcendental Aesthetic" and "Transcendental Analytic" of the *Critique of Pure Reason*, and he argues in favor of the integrity of religion (Christianity) in both the *Critique of Practical Reason* and *Religion within the Limits of Reason Alone*.

4. Kant, *Critique of Pure Reason*, A:vii.

5. See Søren Kierkegaard, *Concluding Unscientific Postscript to Philosophical Fragments*, ed. and trans. by Howard V. Hong and Edna H. Hong (Princeton, NJ: Princeton University Press, 1992).

6. Kierkegaard, *Concluding Unscientific Postscript to Philosophical Fragments*.

7. See my monograph *Frederick Douglass and the Philosophy of Religion: An Interpretation of Art, Narrative, and the Political* (Lanham, MD: Lexington Books, 2022), especially pp. 54–67.

8. Aristotle, *Metaphysics*, 1074b, 32–34.

9. Martin Heidegger, "The Question Concerning Technology," *The Question Concerning Technology and Other Essays*, trans. by William Lovitt (New York: Harper and Row, 1977), 26.

10. Heidegger, "The Word of Nietzsche: 'God Is Dead,'" in *The Question Concerning Technology and Other Essays*, trans. by William Lovitt (New York: Harper and Row, 1977), 105.

11. *The Morning Astorian* (Astoria, Oregon), June 3, 1883, p. 4.

12. Thomas F. Gossett, *Race: The History of an Idea in America* (Dallas, TX: Southern Methodist University Press, 1963), 96.

13. *The Morning Astorian*, June 3, 1883, p. 4.

14. James Baldwin, "James Baldwin Interview with Kenneth Clark, May 24, 1963," 18:53 to 19:53, YouTube, https://www.youtube.com/watch?v=Ua2Rb7vVsMY.

15. Aristotle points out each of the six senses of the term *origin* as follows. First, he writes that we use it to indicate a starting point, as in the beginning of a journey. Second, *origin* implies a starting point which is not the origin proper but, rather, a point from which it is easiest to begin learning something. For example, it may be easier to understand a text by beginning in the middle rather than at the start. Third, *origin* is used to indicate "that from which, as an immanent part, a thing first comes to be," as in the foundation of a building is its "origin." Fourth, *origin* means that from which something comes to be that is external to the thing itself, for example, as parents are the origin of children or as harsh, abusive words are the origin of a fight. Fifth, *origin* implies the choice of one who moves that which is moved and changes that which is changed. Here, Aristotle gives political examples such as magistrates and rulers, whose decisions are origins insofar as they set things in motion and cause change. Lastly, Aristotle writes that something can be an origin in the sense that it is a cause of something else. *Metaphysics*, 1012b33–13a22.

16. Aristotle, *Metaphysics*, 1013a, 4–7.

17. See Gerald Horne, *The Counter-Revolution of 1776: Slave Resistance and the Origins of the United States of America* (New York: New York University Press, 2014).

18. Derrick Bell, *Faces at the Bottom of the Well: The Permanence of Racism* (New York: Basic Books, 1992), 12.

19. See Bill E. Lawson, "Frederick Douglass and African-American Social Progress: Does Race Matter at the Bottom of the Well?" in *Frederick Douglass: A Critical Reader*, ed. by Bill E. Lawson and Frank M. Kirkland (Malden, MA: Blackwell, 1999), 365–91, and Floyd J. Miller, "The Father of Black Nationalism: Another Contender," *Civil War History* 17, no. 4 (December 1971): 310–19.

20. Ralph Bunche, "A Critical Analysis of the Tactics and Programs of Minority Groups," *Journal of Negro Education* 4, no. 3 (July 1935): 308–20.

21. Bunche, "A Critical Analysis," 319.

22. Bunche, "A Critical Analysis," 319.

23. Bunche, "A Critical Analysis," 319.

24. Bunche, "A Critical Analysis," 319.

25. Bunche, "A Critical Analysis," 319–20.

26. Bell, *Faces at the Bottom of the Well*, 100.

27. Bell, *Faces at the Bottom of the Well*, 101, emphasis original.

28. John Rawls, *A Theory of Justice* (Cambridge, MA: Harvard University Press, 1971), 3.

29. See Charles Mills, "Rawls on Race/Race in Rawls," *The Southern Journal of Philosophy* XLVII (2009): 161–84, and "Ideal Theory as Ideology," *Hypatia* 20, no. 3 (2005): 165–84.

30. See my monograph *Frederick Douglass and the Philosophy of Religion*, pp. 28–37. It is also important to point out that Tommy J. Curry takes the critique of abstraction even further by arguing that what Mills has called "non-ideal" theory engages in its own form of abstraction. Curry writes, in his recent essay "Must There Be an Empirical Basis for the Theorization of Racialized Subjects in Race-Gender

Theory?" *Proceedings of the Aristotelian Society* CXXI, no. 1 (2021): 21–44, that his critique of non-ideal political theory

> is not intended to refute the aims of non-ideal theory, but merely to show that while Mills celebrates the generalizable categories one can abstract to examine the subordination of real groups, other non-idealist theorists have completely different, if not antagonistic, accounts of the roles racism and white supremacy have in Black oppression. Philosophers are told to prefer non-ideal theory for its analysis of group subordination over idealist theory, which ignores the centrality of race-gender subordination, but non-ideal theory offers no way to guarantee the quality and accuracy of the generalizations abstracted from the oppression of Black groups. (32)

In support of this assertion, Curry points to what he understands to be the abstractions of nonideal theory in the works of Elizabeth Anderson and Shannon Sullivan, arguing that neither of them "provides any justifications of why the generalizations produced by their perception of the groups are the correct generalizations that most accurately explain the subordinate position of the group in question" (32). Curry's point about the abstractions of nonideal theory is well taken, as so much effort in public policy must be grounded in empirical data about the actual experiences of Black people, which, Curry argues, nonideal theory simply does not do. Curry points out that ideological considerations about what is offensive to one group or another determine the efficacy of developing liberation strategies based on ideal theory precisely because "there is *no method* being deployed that can justify or insist upon one description of racism more than the other within non-ideal theory" (32). Although well intended, nonideal theory, is, for Curry, still beholden to abstraction. It seems, then, that both ideal and nonideal theory fall short of the necessary concreteness to offer relief in matters of racism and public policy. Interestingly, whereas the empirical methodologies of the social sciences are nonstarters in Christian theology, they are a necessity for justice in the realm of public policy. Even as in Kant's transcendental idealism, one must not extend reason beyond the boundaries of experience but must do so for the sake of practical reason; in the Black American struggle for justice, one must not deploy empiricism in Christian theology, but one *must do so* in the analysis of actual Black life, the quest for a more just understanding of Black people, and a more just public policy.

31. Immanuel Kant, "Idea of a Universal History from a Cosmopolitan Perspective," in *Toward Perpetual Peace and Other Writings on Politics, Peace, and History*, ed. by Pauline Kleingeld and trans. by David L. Colclasure (New Haven, CT: Yale University Press, 2006), 3.

32. Kant, "Idea of a Universal History," 4.

33. Kant, "Idea of a Universal History," 4–16.

34. Kant, "Idea of a Universal History," 12.

35. Here I am referring to Bell's notion of interest convergence, which I discuss in the introduction, titled "I Want My Ham," in my book *Racism and Resistance: Essays on Derrick Bell's Racial Realism*, edited by Timothy Joseph Golden (Albany: State University of New York Press, 2022).

36. Derrick Bell, *Silent Covenants:* Brown v. Board of Education *and the Unfulfilled Hopes for Racial Reform* (New York: Oxford University Press, 2004), 192.
37. Bell, *Silent Covenants*, 192.
38. Bell, *Silent Covenants*, 192.
39. Bell, *Silent Covenants*, 192.
40. Bell, *Silent Covenants*, 192.
41. Bell, *Silent Covenants*, 192.
42. Bell, *Silent Covenants*, 192.
43. Bell, *Silent Covenants*, 192.
44. Howard Thurman, *Jesus and the Disinherited* (Boston: Beacon Press, 1996), 44.
45. Thurman, *Jesus and the Disinherited*, 45.
46. Thurman, *Jesus and the Disinherited*, 45.
47. Thurman, *Jesus and the Disinherited*, 46.

Chapter 12

Misogyny and the Stench of White Supremacist Christianity

Traci C. West

White supremacy has infused the history of Christianity in the US with a relentless sense of political purpose. It is like a stench that will not go away in spite of Christian attempts to cover it up with sweet-smelling claims about Christ's love for all. Misogyny must be understood as a vital part of that stench because it lends staying power to the drive for political domination that is found within Christian white supremacist aims.[1]

I refuse to acquiesce to timid characterizations of misogyny as incidental and ancillary in critical narratives of historical Christian white supremacist practices, or in their more contemporary reiterations in Trumpist politics and white nationalist extremism. Whether articulated through tolerance of sexual abuse or support for rigid regulation of gender roles in white racist Christian prescriptions for moral life, the aggressiveness of misogynist thinking and practices begs for more attention. Misogyny can lurk in seemingly benign understandings of gender in Christian mission activities. Or it may be quite obvious in public and private displays of Christian entitlement to brutalize women and girls that enforce the structural power and control of whites. Especially when this violence is sexualized, Christian misogynistic practices can also sometimes contribute an inviting sense of titillation. Through such dynamic, hydra-headed tactics, misogyny serves the will to dominate, which is at the heart of Christian white supremacist objectives, with tremendous effectiveness. Helpfully discomfiting knowledge about the nature of these tactics can be found in certain historical patterns of white Christian misogyny in the nineteenth-century US—for example, the torment visited upon enslaved Black women and Indigenous girls in Christian boarding schools. Because misogyny continues to evolve and adapt, a more contemporary, critical grasp of its coercive capacities must attend to new configurations and gendered complexities such as those found in twenty-first-century Christian targeting of brown and Black transgender girls and women.

In order to highlight *how* misogyny functions, I explore the meaning of its strategic role in advancing white supremacist Christianity. I stress select historical examples that are embedded in broader societal public practices. We need to etch the historical details of racist misogyny's tactics and the lessons they offer into our collective memories, refusing to allow them to be trivialized as inconsequential, discounted as aberrations, or rendered inaccessible by twenty-first-century state-imposed bans on teaching and reading about them.[2] I am seeking out starting points for increasing our sensitivity to how the stench of white supremacist Christianity retains its vitality.

FAMILY VALUES: HOW TO SMELL THE STENCH OF WHITE SUPREMACIST CHRISTIANITY

Stench provides an apt metaphor for understanding white supremacy as a cultural process that pervades Christianity in the US, particularly white supremacy's drive for political dominance. Like a hideous stench that saturates everything, white-dominance-oriented Christianity has defined faith-filled living in terms of both the choices that individual Christians make and their collective decision-making in churches, state agencies and governing bodies, businesses, schools, and elsewhere in community life. A standard expectation lingers within this definition of Christian faithfulness of an easy companionability between one's Christian identity and the reinforcement of white superiority in mundane daily habits and social interactions. As with foul odors that fill our nostrils and actively alter our sensory perceptions of all that surrounds us, white racist perceptions have determined Christian understandings of human worth and dignity and the capacity to differentiate between virtuous and heinous acts. How has this process been lived out? White racist Christian commitments have spread through some of the most basic means of cultural formation in the US—in the expression of, for instance, traditional family values, especially those related to how children are nurtured. Understandings of gender within traditional Christian family values, established throughout the US history of white racism, contribute foundational underpinnings to our misogynist sensibilities.

These well-worn, formative patterns are illustrated in deeply perverse everyday community activities. They occur in the late nineteenth- and early twentieth-centuries when white Southern Christian families had picnic outings or their community leaders organized special gatherings of children to watch the lynching of Black people by white Christians as a form of entertainment.³ As journalist and ardent antilynching advocate Ida B. Wells documented, white children were sometimes let out of school to view lynchings. She notes how in Paris, Texas, in 1893—alongside excursions offered by the railroads—"the mayor of the town gave the children a holiday so that they might see the sight" of a Black man, Henry Smith, being tortured to death with hot irons shoved down his throat as he was burned alive.⁴ In another case, a white newspaper in 1915 reported on the crowd of whites gathered for a Fayette County, Tennessee, lynching, noting that "women and children were there by the score. At a number of country schools the day's routine was delayed until the boy and girl pupils could get back from viewing the lynched man."⁵ It seems to have been particularly important to white Christian community leaders and parents that their children absorb a sense of communal enthusiasm in witnessing brutal mob murders of Black men like Henry Smith. The association of pleasurable excitement with the torture and murder of Black people helped to instill in white children an appreciation of lynchings as a Christian family/communal value they should savor.

One core heteropatriarchal aspect of this racist education was imbued with the message that killing Black men served to protect Southern Christian white womanhood. This frequently repeated rationale created a means for ensuring that white Christian male social and political power prevailed.⁶ Misogynist control of white women coexisted with the elevation of white women's status. Both were reinforced through public messages about the supposed need for their protection and became inextricably attached to the white Christian mob murders/family outings. Paying attention to this core dimension of misogyny—control—reminds us to note an essential aspect of the political purpose advanced in these acts of racist Christian terror. That is, it reveals how rhetoric about a concern for protecting white women furthered the interests of heteropatriarchal control by white Christian men over white women through the lynching of Black men.

But often neglected in contemporary understandings of this gendered white racist history is any consideration of the circumstances surrounding the lynching of Black women by white Christians. Although much less frequent than the lynchings of Black men, Black women were also targeted. As Ida B. Wells declared when two Black women, Mahala Jackson and Louisa Carter, were lynched in Mississippi in 1893 after they had been found innocent by the courts of poisoning a well, the law did little to "protect the women from the demands of Christian white people."⁷ I do not want Wells's compact, matter-of-fact tone here to allow us to miss the import of her analysis. White supremacist Christians fomented an insistent demand for hate violence. They did so even when, in this instance, the white racist state apparatus of nineteenth-century Mississippi courts found the Black women innocent. Her words "protect," "women," and "Christian white," in the context of the horror of these lynchings, ought to sting the nostrils of our collective conscience and memory. She proves the falseness in any generalized narrative asserting that the protection of women was a nineteenth-century culture of domesticity and communal Christian value. In a concerted, public act of racist murders, local white Christian men made clear that control over the Black women's lives belonged to them, not to the state judicial system. Their lynching of the women was not just authorized but, indeed, as Wells articulated it, demanded by Christian white people.

A sharp grasp of how misogynistic values involve historically embedded notions of womanhood, domestic family relationships, and the inculcation of Christian white supremacist family values in children has to be expansive. It must include a wider range of US practices beyond the history of lynching, and an attendant focus on the nurturing of white children in these values. The imprint of Christian white supremacy also proliferated in the systematic destruction of families in nineteenth-to-twentieth-century (1880s–1970s) policies of the western US government of kidnapping Indigenous/Native American children by removing them to Christian boarding schools. Christian missionaries and civic groups launched these schools with a mandate from Congress in the 1880s and made them compulsory for Native Americans by authorizing the Bureau of Indian Affairs to punish parents who resisted sending their children to the boarding schools.[8] In these schools, children were tortured through food deprivation, forced labor, unsanitary conditions, and harsh physical punishments, all of which were overseen by Christian school officials.[9] The girls were taught on a daily basis that they needed to be lifted to civilization through Christianity and to reflect the model of white motherhood when they were heterosexually married. The girls were to learn how to emulate a "white life," as Philena Johnson, one 1890s white Christian woman leader, racially expressed as the intent of this school system targeting Indigenous children.[10] American Indian Studies scholar Brenda Child describes how Johnson included in her public advocacy a white supremacist definition of the role of matrons in the lives of the girls. In Johnson's description, the white Christian boarding school matron would easily serve as a more wholesome replacement for the girls' darker and supposedly immoral natural mothers. According to Child, Johnson explained that the white matron was "to the Indian girl what the white mother is to her child."[11] The presence of the colonizing misogyny in this white supremacist Christian project may seem negligible and temptingly easy to ignore, in part, because of the agency exhibited in white Christian women's leadership.

Misogyny blossoms, however, in the gendered nature of the white Christian racist shaming here. The female identity of these children is shamed based on their racial and national heredity as progeny of Indigenous mothers. White Christian women functioned as enforcers of this misogynist shaming that demeans and removes the worth of Indigenous femaleness and mother-daughter family bonds. For some of the girls, the resulting anguish they must have experienced was also accompanied by sexual abuse perpetrated by male school officials. Feminist American Studies scholar Laura Briggs reports that although we do not have access to a comprehensive study of the history of sexual abuse at these US boarding schools for Indigenous children, "a 2012 survey of boarding school attendees found that nearly 30 percent reported that they had been sexually abused at their school."[12] While I do not know the specifics of the individual experiences of the girls (or of the victimized boys), the varied forms of trauma they endured resulted from methodical collaborations between church and state, with broad implications for how racist misogyny masquerading as family values shaped US cultural and political values.

I want to underscore the patterns of reproductive politics generated in this racist history. Recognizing these patterns can hone our perceptions of the politics of reproduction, enabling us to better understand them as defined by coercive social control of the bodies, mothering, and gendered selfhood—that is, moral worth—of Indigenous girls and women. White racist misogyny insinuates itself as a supposed restoration of traditional family values through a unique, systemic form of reproductive-parental replacement practices. Although individual white matrons functioned as on-site enforcers, the church and state orchestrated the policies establishing and governing the boarding schools. White racist family values became naturalized as the girls were shamed for being products of mothers who are cast as innate reproducers of immorality. Specifically, in a colonizing reproductive-replacement process, the whiteness of white mothering must be reproduced by literally removing Indigenous mothers from the lives of the girl children and an accompanying effort to sever and replace the girls' emotional and spiritual bonds to their mothers. Christian indoctrination into whiteness attempted to transform the Indigenous girls' self-understandings through coerced reproduction. They could only regain self-worth as reproducers of civilizing whiteness. Though, of course, this was a goal they could never actually achieve.

Another method of targeting and removing children occurred in one of the most well-known US historical examples of the widespread institutionalization of white supremacist Christian family values. White Christian slave masters took Black enslaved children from their mothers in order to sell them and maintain their bondage. This was a common practice of the US chattel slavery system for centuries, and its practitioners relied upon Christian theology and leadership for its moral acceptance by most whites. As womanist theologian Kelly Brown Douglas summarizes with regard to the foundational Christian theological arguments undergirding the system of US chattel slavery, "Freedom itself is seen as a sin when held by certain races, namely those who don't possess the property of whiteness. Proslavery proponents of natural law attempt to make it clear that God did not make all humans equal, and God did not intend for all humans to be free."[13] In accord with pro-slavery Christians, whose views held sway for centuries, the political distribution of freedom and inequality for the benefit of whites reflected God's intentions as creator of humankind. Thus, routine white slave owner practices such as selling off young Black children and permanently severing them from any parental bonds were rendered a natural and faithful white Christian activity.

Both of these historical examples of mainstream traditional Christian family values convey how, for many white Christians, the bond between parents and children who were Indigenous/Native/Indian or Black had to be destroyed, whether purportedly for civilizing the children or for capitalist profit made from the sale of the children.[14] The reproduction of supposed white Christian virtuousness demanded a systematic destruction of nonwhite family bonds. The women who birthed the abused or commodified kidnapped children were seen as useful tools in generating material and moral advantages for white Christians.

In the dynamic push toward political and cultural white dominance in white supremacist Christianity, whether misogyny functions within the justification of lynching as a means of maintaining white heteropatriarchal control or as a reproducer of shame attached to Indigenous mothering, it transforms our moral sensibilities. Focusing on its function invites us to notice not only the understandings of gender that are revealed in who is misogynistically targeted, but also the broader political and cultural processes that cultivate and embolden the stench of white supremacist Christianity.

HOW CHRISTIAN MISSION COVERS UP THE STENCH OF WHITE SUPREMACIST CHRISTIANITY

During the mid-nineteenth century in Alabama, white surgeon James Marion Sims, today hailed by many as the father of gynecology, conducted experimental surgeries on enslaved Black women's vaginas and uteruses without the use of anesthesia. He acquired eleven enslaved Black women from their masters in order to conduct those experiments.[15] Through these surgeries, he perfected gynecological treatment of vesicovaginal fistulas, for which he received accolades when he later moved his medical practice to New York and began treating white women patients (with whom he used anesthesia).[16] In Alabama, the enslaved Black women—including Anarcha, Lucy, and Betsey—upon whom he conducted experiments had needed health care for emergency complications related to pregnancy or vesicovaginal fistulas. He noted the pain and agony that the Black women suffered during his surgeries in a comparison with the experiences of a few white women who voluntarily sought his medical services during the same time. In his notations, he explained how the Black women were able to bear more pain with much less complaining than the white women, thus enabling his success as he chose to keep his focus on the Black enslaved women, conducting surgical experiments on their vaginas and uteruses for four years.[17] Sims was a Christian slave owner who understood his professional accomplishments in the context of Christian morality. As he later wrote from New York in an 1850s letter to his wife, he had "a high and holy mission to perform, that his [God's] blessing has already crowned my efforts."[18]

This example of the Sims medical experimentation on enslaved Black women offers us lessons on how Christian white supremacy and misogyny can function together without any outward expressions of white racial malice or animosity. It shows how easily practices of white Christian supremacy can masquerade as a "holy mission" to help those in need, thereby creating a false sense of virtuousness and impunity from responsibility for causing harm. The coercion and suffering of the enslaved women during the experiments can be construed as part of the blessing that God intends for white Christians such as Sims and the white women he subsequently treated in New York. In Christianity-dominated US society, certainty of the Christian God's blessing and crowning confers unearned white social and political status.

In the practices of Sims, misogyny represents one element among others in the preservation of Christian white supremacist social order. When attempting to discern the role of misogyny, we must remember that hatred does not always form the context and motivation. The framework of Christian mission enables our grasp of what constitutes the healing and the torture of the Black women's bodies to blur together until they become morally indistinguishable and any impetus toward seeking accountability for harm fades away. The blurring of Christian harm and healing of their bodies carries implications for reproductive politics well beyond this nineteenth-century moment, as misogynist assumptions about basic health care for Black women's vaginas and uteruses continues to beget gendered restrictions on human entitlement to moral agency. This process illustrates how white Christian supremacist logic makes ownership of, decision-making about, and control of Black women's sexual/genital organs by others in power seem like a natural, necessary part of a well-ordered society, and even a good expression of public health. Historically, in an almost mutual interplay, misogyny also functions as an enabler of the white Christian supremacy so evident in the system of chattel slavery. In turn, misogynist naturalizing of gendered control of vaginas and uteruses aids Christian white supremacist constructions of reality by blunting our recognition of the harmful structural context of the Sims example: the systemic coercion of the Black enslaved women, particularly when they were so desperate for vaginal and pregnancy-related medical care.

Racist misogynist or misogynoir[19] understandings of ethical conduct that dull our perception of how vulnerable Black women were exploited in this medical context also diminish our capacity as interpreters of this history of influential white Christian medical leadership. These constraints on our perception of the depth of Black women's vulnerability can guide us to reduce the harm they experienced to a judgment about one individual's questionable ethics and conduct. Or, perhaps we may be tempted to focus on the benefits that the Sims experiments produced for gynecological care. This trajectory of minimizing the importance of the harm to the enslaved Black women narrows what we can know about the meaning of misogyny itself. Racist misogyny entices us by seeping into the role of analytical tool. It can persuade us to cling to some rigid, universal definition asserting that misogyny always references vicious hatred of all women, meted out and supported only by men in exactly the same form to all women. If such universals were accepted in the Sims case, we would not recognize any form of violence against women in the unique, dehumanizing, supposedly medical assessment of the enslaved Black women as being unable to experience pain like the white women did since white suffering was more legible to Sims. A more universalistic, relativizing analytical approach grants impunity to us as interpreters of the historical legacy of these acts, freeing *us* from responsibility to account for the harm it perpetuated.

But sometimes my pestering about avoidance is not at all relevant to the misogyny problem. It would be a mistake to conclude that avoidance and erasure of harm monopolize the role misogyny plays in its service of white supremacist Christianity in the US. Christian lessons taught through misogynist acts have also sometimes more simply conveyed a direct message: Harming women is good. Examples can be found in the writings of former slave and public intellectual Frederick Douglass, perhaps the foremost chronicler of Christian white supremacy as it was manifested in the system of US chattel slavery. He details the cruelty of one of his Christian slave owners, Thomas Auld. Auld was an especially zealous Methodist Christian convert-believer who, with intense missionary fervor, converted many in his community to Christianity.

A particularly unambiguous instance of the role of misogynist support in Christian white supremacy emerges in the acts of Christian violence against women that Douglass describes in his 1845 memoir, *Narrative of the Life of Frederick Douglass, an American Slave*. His slave master Auld often beat the physically disabled enslaved woman, Henny, because of her inability to work. According to Douglass, this white Christian slave master quoted a specific Scripture passage aloud each time he used "a heavy cowskin upon her naked shoulders, causing the red blood to drip."[20] There seems to be an element of titillation in the almost ritualistic beating of the partially clad "lame young woman" and the recitation of Scripture commending beatings of those who refuse to do their master's will. Disability produced by her initial injury and the continuing brutal physical impairment by Auld add another dimension of lurid fascination to this Christian racist routine.[21] In a calculated manipulation, the uselessness of Henny's body for the work her owner demanded becomes its utility as the target of Auld's violence that is placed on the display for spectators. Her increasingly disabled body is objectified as if in a coerced performance of combination circus act and Christian morality play. This was not an intemperate act of hate-filled rage by Thomas Auld.

Rather, Douglass reports that this Christian master would carry out the beatings at deliberate intervals, keeping "this lacerated young woman tied up all day," returning to whip her again, and "cutting her in places already made raw."[22] The role of misogyny in Auld's cruelty comes to the surface in his invitation to other enslaved persons in that household (as well as the text's white abolitionist readers and us) to observe the horror of the violence he wreaked on her partially exposed body in accord with Christian Scriptural directives to not to look away from it. The particular recipe of sexualized public assaults on her already disabled body enlivens the desire to gawk, enticing the moral imagination to rehearse its sadistic incursions on her human dignity. In this iteration of white supremacist Christianity illustrated in Douglass's narrative, the luring role of misogyny in the brutality helps to convey that *stench* is not stench, but appealing. Inhale deeply.

I find all of these historical details in the legacy of Christianity deeply painful to recall. But forgetting only allows the pain-inducing tactics to flourish.

SNIFFING OUT THE STENCH

The driving Christian mission in contemporary community life to maintain white racial superiority benefits from a combination of the misogynist historical patterns that I have highlighted, even as it invents fresh adaptations. Currently, for example, misogyny may function as an effective repressive resource in responding to open disobedience, specifically by transgender girls and women, of coercive, exclusionary norms of cisgender binaries. A Connecticut civil court case in the early 2020s demonstrated how past remnants of white supremacist Christian reasoning can join with misogyny in the targeting of Black transgender teenage girls for discrimination and humiliation in the public setting of the courts.[23] This tactic was on display as part of a broader judicial and legislative drive by the Alliance Defending Freedom (ADF), an extremist Christian right-wing legal group dedicated to systemically enforcing the subjugation of LGBTQIA people.[24] Their mission, described on their website, reflects the vision of their founding white evangelical Christian cisgender leaders: "Our faith also instructs us that God created man and woman as complementary equals and that sex is binary and biologically determined."[25]

This Connecticut case targeting the Black girls helped to galvanize a national movement of legalizing discriminatory practices against transgender youth.[26] Two transgender Black teen girls were taken before the court by the Christian legal organization for participating in the self-affirming, embodied, and fun activities of public sports practice and competition. "Running has been so important for my identity, my growth as a person, and my ability to survive in a world that discriminates against me," Andraya Yearwood, one of the two transgender runners at the center of the case, wrote to the court.[27] One especially dramatic moment in the court proceedings occurred when the Christian right evangelical legal organization's lawyers continued to deliberately misgender these Black girls, insisting on referring to them as boys. The maliciousness in how this tactic used by the ADF lawyers in their treatment of the Black children was so aggressive, even the judge felt it necessary to call a halt to it, in part, he asserted, for the sake of "human decency."[28]

These legal campaigns in US courts by white Christian leaders showcase misogyny in their regulation of the meaning of girlhood, echoing past white racist projects as they do so. This strategy coheres with familiar historical patterns of gendered racism, for instance, as the ADF lawyers' repeated misgendering of the targeted teens as Black males served to further characterize the teens as a threat to the cisgender white teenage girl who was cast as in need of protection. Though, the ADF also added in their discussion of this case on their website that a student of color was included among the cisgender girl plaintiffs the organization represented (even as the white plaintiff was featured in most of the photographs and narrative).[29] The misogynist harm of this Christian transphobic strategy might escape our notice since several cisgender females advocated for their own protection and seemingly embraced both the limitations placed on their expression of gender and the status of being models of God's human creation. But if we look closely, the problematic implications of this embrace may become more discernable as we take into account how this Christian evangelical legal strategy bears the legacy of past Christian racist misogynist tactics that deliberately trained us to be indifferent to moral harm. Those past trajectories of white racist misogyny reverberated in this contemporary case through the combination of the several tactics: cruel targeting of children for humiliation, coerced restrictions on how Black femaleness can access moral agency and affirming embodiment, and a perniciously targeted claim of a holy mission to preserve God's supposed design of cisgender superiority.

Far from being a confusing or mysterious dynamism behind such a relentless and comprehensive historical process, this US-honed Christianity has the intentional aim of preserving white cultural and political dominance. As religious studies scholar Anthea Butler notes in her historical study of white Christian evangelicals, "Why have evangelicals and their leadership made choices over and over again to embrace racism? Because it is what has allowed them to attain and hold political power."[30] Our twenty-first-century ethos provides ever-evolving and abundant means of supporting brash, no-need-to-hold-your-nose efforts at sustaining Christian white dominance and the misogynist tactics that uphold it. Whether in the form of systemic policy initiatives, legal cases, or political leadership choices, expressions of these commitments and tactics in US public life may vary, but they are centrally informed by historically rehashed themes of protection and indifference to targeted violence.

To analytically hold onto the stench of misogyny in both historical and fresh contemporary patterns of Christian white supremacy, we need an approach that ensures that its presence will neither be taken for granted nor oversimplified. Misogyny involves intense regulation of certain female identities and embodiment, but we mistakenly truncate its impact if our analysis only remains there. The proliferation of white racist misogynist strategies across public spheres demands that we also focus on the rituals of obedience in which we participate. They nurture our tolerance of those strategies as they take the forms of reproductive erasures and replacement, sexually violent titillation, and ciswoman-facilitated, family-oriented, Christian holy mission deceptions, among many others. Moreover, discernment of these explicitly Christianity-sanctioned historical patterns can help, for example, contemporary gender justice advocacy related to reproductive coercion and justice continue to expand its focus beyond much-needed abortion rights. For instance, efforts to end reproductive coercion must also be informed by sociopolitical contexts, moral messages, and a critical understanding of legacies of Christianity's colonizing misogyny such as reproductive-parental replacement practices of Christian boarding school system for Indigenous/Native children.

Although I am hesitant to do so, in my story-of-stench description of how Christian white supremacy and misogyny constitute a deliberate social process, I should at least acknowledge the presence of resistance. As with some parts of the body that react with an intensely intolerant physiological reaction to a stench (e.g., watering eyes, gagging), multiple forms of cultural resistance and political rebellion against repression will always occur, no matter how all-encompassing that repression is. Revolts, especially by the people most directly targeted for racist, misogynistic devaluation, may take any form of brazen defensive violence, subtly hidden circumvention, innovative communal networking, articulate rebuke, or just persistent obstinacy. In every instance, resisters counter the white supremacist Christian dehumanization that seeks to destroy their mental, bodily, and spiritual thriving. But I am wary of the unintended support for avoidance I might stoke as I note the vitality of this kind of struggle. It might aid in offering permission to those of us who primarily experience more indirect costs of racist misogynist repression to remain passive, to treat those who do the resistance labor of sniffing out the stench as proxies for us.

Across our genders, racial/ethnic/national backgrounds, and migrant/immigrant/citizen status, US/American Christian faith and influence disciplines us in what we know and sense about measuring human dignity and worth. This disciplining process dissuades us from taking up the tasks demanded by antiracist conceptualizations and practices that center on gender analysis. As we steadily acclimate to ongoing, innovative evolutions of the stench of white supremacist dominance and its misogynist tactics that teach us not to notice it, I know that it can be quite confusing for most of us to be asked, in the ways in which I am doing here, "Don't you smell that?"

NOTES

1. I wish to thank Sarah Williams, Nicole Hoskins, Paola Marquez, Dani Hobbs, and Althea Spencer-Miller for their insights in crucial conversations with me about the notions of misogyny that I explore here.

2. See news articles such as Sarah Schwartz, "Lawmakers Push to Ban 1619 Project," *Education Week*, February 3, 2021, https://www.edweek.org/teaching-learning/lawmakers-push-to-ban-1619-project-from-schools/2021/02; also see the summary report "#TruthBeTold: Legislative Attacks on Racial and Gender Justice Education," *African American Policy Forum*, March 20, 2021, https://www.aapf.org/truthbetold.

3. For a discussion of the role of Christianity for whites and the picnic-style rituals that they involved, see Philip Dray, *At the Hands of Persons Unknown: The Lynching of Black America* (New York: Random House, 2002), 80–82; Dora Apel and Shawn Michelle Smith, *Lynching Photographs* (Berkeley: University of California Press, 2008), 5, 31. A 1935 photo captures a group of white girls and boys at the front of a crowd as they look up at the lynched Black man Rubin Stacy.

4. Wells describes this prelude to the white mob actions against a Black man accused of killing a white child. The white leaders entertained the crowd by slowly murdering him as they "burned his eyes out and ran the red-hot iron down his throat, cooking his tongue." In Jacqueline Jones Royster, ed., *Southern Horrors and Other Writings: Anti-Lynching Campaign of Ida B. Wells, 1892–1900* (Boston: Bedford Books, 1997), 203.

5. As quoted in Leon F. Litwack, *Trouble in Mind: Black Southerners in the Age of Jim Crow* (New York: Alfred A. Knopf, 1998), 286–87.

6. Crystal Nicole Feimster, *Southern Horrors: Women and the Politics of Rape and Lynching* (Cambridge, MA: Harvard University Press, 2011), 158. Feimster writes: "Desperate to control white women's sexual behavior and maintain sexual control over black women, southern white men, reasoned Wells, had created a scapegoat in the figure of the black rapist." Feimster's otherwise comprehensive study seems to understate the emphasis on criticizing white Christianity that Wells incorporated in her antilynching writings.

7. As quoted in Feimster, *Southern Horrors*, 159.

8. Laura Briggs, *Taking Children: A History of American Terror* (Berkeley: University of California Press, 2020), 52–53.

9. Mary Annette Pember, "Death by Civilization," *The Atlantic*, March 8, 2019, https://www.theatlantic.com/education/archive/2019/03/traumatic-legacy-indian-boarding-schools/584293/.

10. Brenda J. Child, *Boarding School Seasons: American Indian Families, 1900–1940* (Lincoln: University of Nebraska Press, 1998), 79.

11. As quoted in Child, *Boarding School Seasons*, 79.

12. As cited in Briggs, *Taking Children*, 56; see the study that Briggs cites: Teresa Evans-Campbell, Karina L. Walters, Cynthia R. Pearson, and Christopher D. Campbell, "Indian Boarding School Experience, Substance Use, and Mental Health among Urban Two-Spirit American Indian/Alaska Natives," *American Journal of Drug and Alcohol Abuse* 38, no. 5 (September 2012): 421–27.

13. Kelly Brown Douglas, *Stand Your Ground: Black Bodies and the Justice of God* (Maryknoll, NY: Orbis Books, 2015), 58.

14. In another, very different example, white Christian clergy have colluded in government-initiated policies to purportedly protect the economic interests of white families. In his study of the legal enactment of racial segregation in the US, economic policy researcher Richard Rothstein documented how white clergy led twentieth-century housing discrimination efforts to keep African American families from moving into white neighborhoods in northeastern and midwestern communities such as Philadelphia, St. Louis, Buffalo, and Chicago. As one Detroit white pastor, Reverend Dzink, argued against housing desegregation, "It would jeopardize the safety to many of our white girls." In Richard Rothstein, *The Color of Law: A Forgotten History of How Our Government Segregated America* (New York: Liveright Publishing, 2017), 105.

15. In her study of these events, Harriet A. Washington writes: "Sims acquired a total of eleven women slaves with vesicovaginal fistula from their masters by promising to lodge, board, and treat them, and he built a spartan wooden building, where he conducted surgical experiments on them for the next four years." Washington, *Medical Apartheid: The Dark History of Medical Experimentation on Black Americans from Colonial Times to the Present* (New York: Doubleday Books, 2006), 64.

16. Washington, *Medical Apartheid*, 65.

17. Seale Harris and Frances Williams Browin, *Woman's Surgeon: The Life Story of J. Marion Sims* (New York: Macmillan, 1950), 109; Washington, *Medical Apartheid*, 65. Also see Dineo Khabele, Kevin Holcomb, Ngina K. Connors, and Linda Bradley,

"A Perspective on James Marion Sims, MD, and Antiblack Racism in Obstetrics and Gynecology," *Journal of Minimally Invasive Gynecology* 28, no. 2 (2021): 153–55.

18. J. Marion Sims, *The Story of My Life* (New York: D. Appleton and Company, 1894), 392. This quotation is from a letter to his wife. After Sims's death, his son added to his father's autobiography the letters written to his mother.

19. For discussions of the term *misogynoir*, see Moya Bailey, *Misogynoir Transformed: Black Women's Digital Resistance* (New York: New York University Press, 2021); Denise Noble and Lisa Amanda Palmer, "Misogynoir: Anti-Blackness, Patriarchy, and Refusing the Wrongness of Black Women," in *Palgrave Handbook of Critical Race and Gender*, edited by Shirley Anne Tate and Encarnación Gutiérrez Rodríguez (New York: Palgrave Macmillan, 2022), 227–45; Kalima Young, *Mediated Misogynoir: Erasing Black Women's and Girls' Innocence in the Public Imagination* (Lanham, MD: Lexington Books, 2022).

20. Frederick Douglass, *Narrative of the Life of Frederick Douglass, an American Slave* (1845; repr., *Autobiographies*, New York: Library of America, 1994), 52–53; also see Robert T. Jones, *White Too Long: The Legacy of White Supremacy in American Christianity* (New York: Simon & Schuster, 2020), 86–87; David W. Blight, *Frederick Douglass: Prophet of Freedom* (New York: Simon & Schuster, 2018), 59.

21. Jenifer L. Barclay, *The Mark of Slavery: Disability, Race, and Gender in Antebellum America* (Urbana: University of Illinois Press, 2021), 117–18.

22. Douglass, *Narrative*, 53.

23. *Soule et al. v. Connecticut Association of Schools, Inc. et al.*, Docket No. 3:20-cv-00201 (D. Conn. February 12, 2020); *Soule v. Connecticut Association of Schools*, Docket No. 21–01365 (2d Cir. May 26, 2021). I am grateful to Imara Jones, a Black transgender woman activist leader, for her analysis of the misogynist implications of this case.

24. For a discussion of ADF's work with white nationalists, see Hélène Barthélemy, "In Romania, Alliance Defending Freedom Works with Allies Tied to Far-Right Christian Nationalism and White Supremacy," *SPLC Hatewatch*, June 11, 2018, https://www.splcenter.org/hatewatch/2018/06/11/romania-alliance-defending-freedom-works-allies-tied-far-right-christian-nationalism-and.

25. Alliance Defending Freedom, "Who We Are," *ADF Legal*, https://adflegal.org/about-us/who-we-are.

26. The political and legal movement targeting transgender youth for discrimination has included a range of restrictions, including access to bathrooms in schools, medical care, and athletic programs, mentioned here. For a summary discussion of some of these efforts, see M. Killian Kinney, Taylor E. Pearson, and Julie Ralston Aoki, "Improving 'Life Chances': Surveying the Anti-Transgender Backlash, and Offering a Transgender Equity Impact Assessment Tool for Policy Analysis," *Journal of Law, Medicine & Ethics* 50, no. 3 (2022): 489–508.

27. As quoted in Pat Eaton-Robb, "Judge Hears Arguments in Lawsuit Over Connecticut Transgender Athletes," *Connecticut Public Radio*, February 26, 2021.

28. Case 3:20-cv-00201-RNC Document 94, Filed April 22, 2020: "THE COURT: All right, thank you. Let me raise a point that undoubtedly will cause some consternation for you, Mr. Brooks, and your colleagues, but I exercise my prerogative

as the presiding judge in this instance and I hope you will forgive me. I don't think we should be referring to the proposed intervenors as 'male athletes.' I understand that you prefer to use those words, but they're very provocative, and I think needlessly so. I don't think that you surrender any legitimate interest or position if you refer to them as transgender females. That is what the case is about. This isn't a case involving males who have decided that they want to run in girls' events. This is a case about girls who say that transgender girls should not be allowed to run in girls' events. So going forward, we will not refer to the proposed intervenors as 'males'; understood?" (26). See also: "THE COURT: Okay, thank you. I'm not asking you to refer to these individuals as 'females.' I know that you don't want to do so. What I'm saying is you must refer to them as 'transgender females' rather than as 'males.' Again, that's the more accurate terminology, and I think that it fully protects your client's legitimate interests. Referring to these individuals as 'transgender females' is consistent with science, common practice and perhaps human decency. To refer to them as 'males,' period, is not accurate, certainly not as accurate, and I think it's needlessly provocative; and, for me, civility is a very important value, especially in litigation. So if you feel strongly that you and your clients have a right to refer to these individuals as 'males' and that you therefore do not want to comply with my order, then that's unfortunate. But I'll give you some time to think about it and you can let me know if it's a problem. If it is, gosh, maybe we'll need to do something. I don't want to bully you, but at the same time, I don't want you to be bullying anybody else" (29–30).

29. Alliance Defending Freedom, "Track Athletes Taking a Stand to Defend Women's Sports," accessed November 2022, https://adflegal.org/selina-soule-track-athlete-story.

30. Anthea Butler, *White Evangelical Racism: The Politics of Morality in America* (Chapel Hill: University of North Carolina Press, 2021), 140.

Chapter 13

"Where Is the Love?"

Christian Nationalism and the Politics of Exclusion

Kathy Glass

On January 6, 2021, pro-Trump insurrectionists stormed the Capitol, shattering windows, defacing walls, brutalizing police officers, and ransacking lawmakers' offices; meanwhile, other protestors lingered on the Capitol grounds, waving signs bearing Confederate imagery and Christian symbolism. This religious imagery could rightly be called ironic, as the rioters' violence contradicts Jesus's basic teachings on love, mercy, and compassion. Indeed, the protesters' rampage raises urgent questions around race, religion, and Christian nationalism, a divisive ideology spreading across the nation.

The long and complicated history of race and religion in the US emerges starkly in slave narratives, shedding historical light on the present. Nominally Christian ministers in Harriet Jacobs's *Incidents in the Life of a Slave Girl* (1861) routinely espouse racist rhetoric, reinforcing slavery's racial hierarchies. Under the guise of "religious instruction," in the narrative Reverend Pike preaches a perverse Christianity on Sunday evenings, for instance, urging enslaved congregants to obey their masters. In one memorable sermon he warns listeners, "If you disobey your earthly master, you offend your heavenly Master. You must obey God's commandments."[1] Conflating corrupt earthly "masters" with the Almighty, Pike's gospel casts white men as God's representatives, justly exercising unrestrained power over Black bodies. But Jacobs and her fellow congregants reject this insidious teaching as a ludicrous performance; indeed, when the sermon ended, they "went home, highly amused at brother Pike's gospel teaching, and . . . determined to hear him again."[2] If their amusement stems from the crude, heavy-handed teaching of a racist mouthpiece, Jacobs draws sharp distinctions between his corrupt theology and the beliefs of the enslaved, whom Jacobs describes as "sincere" and "nearer to the gate of heaven than sanctimonious Mr. Pike."[3]

More than a decade prior, Frederick Douglass, too, exposed the perverse practice that he called "slaveholding religion" of the South.[4] Rejecting it as "bad, corrupt, and wicked," Douglass embraced its opposite—"Christianity proper"—as "good, pure, and holy."[5] This critical distinction allows Douglass to condemn nominally "religious" masters who torture enslaved Blacks, while maintaining his faith in the "pure, peaceable, and impartial Christianity of Christ."[6] As racist scriptural exegesis transcends borders, Douglass also denounces "religion of the north," which was "by communion and fellowship" aligned with the South.[7]

A bloody civil war culminated in slavery's official demise, but racist scriptural practices endured. Proslavery ministers had routinely identified Blacks as Ham's children, whom Noah had cursed, to justify their enslavement (see Gen. 9:18–29). In the same vein, misguided exegesis provided cover for postbellum racism; Christian minister Henry Ward Beecher, for instance, published "the first American biography of Jesus" in 1871, containing "five depictions of the perfect God-man named Jesus" as white.[8] As Ibram X. Kendi puts it, Ward aimed to "reunite White northerners and southerners through Christian Whiteness."[9] In so doing, he revised Jesus's Middle Eastern origins, centering whiteness as normative in scripture. Well into the twentieth century, white supremacists recycled regressive "religious" rhetoric to cast segregationist policy as God ordained.[10]

History offers key insights into race and religion, but a tangle of sociopolitical forces caused the chaos at the Capitol. Researching religious aspects of January 6, scholars and journalists foreground "Christian nationalism," the belief that "America is God's chosen nation and must be defended as such."[11] It further "seeks to merge Christian and American identities," while "demand[ing] Christianity be privileged by the State and implies that to be a good American, one must be Christian."[12] Notably, Christian nationalism "often overlaps with and provides cover for white supremacy and racial subjugation."[13] These disturbingly unconstitutional and undemocratic tenets conflating Americanness and Christianity—troubling as they are—cannot be dismissed as fringe religious views. On the contrary, recent surveys "fin[d] that close to half of the country supports the idea of fusing Christianity and civic life."[14]

Referencing historians, philosophers, and theologians, this chapter examines how racism, sexism, and violence fuel Christian nationalism, endangering Christianity and the nation alike. Highlighting white evangelical Protestantism promoting nationalist beliefs,[15] this chapter first engages the social, cultural, and historical implications of Christian nationalism; it concludes by examining alternative possibilities animating a Presbyterian church in Pittsburgh. In this case study, I survey the mission and structure of an urban house of worship committed to antiracist communion. No organization is immune from systemic oppression, but this church—what I will term an "insubordinate space"[16]—fosters antiracist inclusion designed to bridge racial divides.

UNTANGLING ELEMENTS OF WHITE CHRISTIAN NATIONALISM

While Catholic and Anglican leaders were also complicit with slavery's evils, this chapter highlights racism within US Protestant traditions, exemplified by whites perverting religion to justify Black oppression. Jacobs's and Douglass's individual testimonies against proslavery Christians thus implicate broader misuses of religion throughout the nineteenth century. Religious studies scholar Anthea Butler argues, "Slavery in America enabled white Christian nationalism by asserting that enslaved Africans were not human."[17] Rather than citing biblical values such as loving one's neighbor and liberating the captive to eradicate the inhumane institution, "Southern slaveholder pastors and elected officials justified slaveholding, even if the enslaved embraced Christianity."[18] To protect white power, proslavery pastors and politicians drafted arguments depicting Blacks as inferior and uniquely suited to serve as slaves. These treatises helped alter the course of religious history, fostering an environment in which "Baptists, Methodists, and Presbyterians would split over the issue of slavery."[19] As history shows, this definitive religious split paralleled a broader fracture within the national body.

The US Constitution purportedly ensures the welfare of "we the people," but prejudiced nineteenth-century Christians failed to conceive a truly inclusive "we." In his 1861 address on slavery, influential South Carolina Presbyterian clergyman James Henry Thornwell observes, "There are, no doubt, many rights which belong . . . to Englishmen, to Frenchmen, to [the slave's] master, for example[,] which are denied [the slave]. But is he fit to possess them? Has God qualified him to meet the responsibilities which their possession necessarily implies?"[20] Casting enslaved men as "the other," Thornwell's litany of questions implies Blacks are of a different type—unlike and unequal to the English, French, and their masters. Questioning their worthiness to enjoy basic human rights, he endeavors to *confirm* Black unworthiness. Endorsing racial difference and perpetuating white supremacy, Thornwell and other Presbyterian leaders bolstered insidious ideologies that endure today.

Yet we must examine both race and gender as factors driving the events on January 6. In *Jesus and John Wayne: How White Evangelicals Corrupted a Faith and Fractured a Nation*, for example, Kristin Kobes Du Mez examines white evangelicals' "embrace of militant masculinity," which celebrates "patriarchal authority and condones the callous display of power."[21] This militant model, which relies on aggressive male behavior and female submission in the household, reinforces long-standing American gender roles.[22] Christian nationalists have historically clung to traditional gender ideals in times of sociopolitical change. As Du Mez writes, the evangelical media promotes "comfort and courage in symbols of a mythical past," including "a rugged, heroic masculinity embodied by cowboys, soldiers, and warriors to point the way forward."[23] Inspired by this worldview, violent January 6 protesters sought to resist change—the certification of electoral votes for a legally elected Democratic president—through a "callous display of power." For some, the "way forward" resulted in crushing a police officer in a doorway and dragging another into an angry crowd that beat him unconscious.[24] Inhumane practices prevailed that day, exemplifying the aggressive rhetoric of Christian nationalist adherents. Such violence cannot be delinked from white evangelical masculinity, which "serves as the foundation of a God-and-country Christian nationalism."[25] Flaunting their Christian faith and battlefield mentality that day, for example, members of the white extremist Proud Boys organization—some of whom were armed and "dressed for combat"—erected a large red cedar cross at the Michigan State Capitol.[26] Meanwhile, members of the same Proud Boys group were celebrated as "God's Warriors" at the Capitol.[27]

In a similar vein, Republican Senator of Missouri Josh Hawley, vocal proponent of the January 6 protestors, normative gender roles, and Christian nationalist rhetoric,[28] has "deep ties to evangelical Christianity."[29] A desire to reverse the clock on cultural change underlies his 2021 speech at the National Conservativism Conference, where he lamented,

> the deconstruction of America begins with and depends on the deconstruction of American men.
>
> The Left want to define traditional masculinity as toxic. They want to define the traditional masculine virtues—things like courage, and independence, and assertiveness—as a danger to society. . . .
>
> [T]he problem with the Left's assault on the masculine virtues is that those self-same qualities, the very ones the Left now vilify as dangerous and toxic, have long been regarded as vital to self-government.[30]

Denouncing the "deconstruction of American men," Hawley's divisive language portrays besieged Republican men as unwarranted victims of progressive forces. De-historicizing traditional forms of masculinity, Hawley de-links gender norms from gender inequities reinforcing women's sociopolitical subordination. Yet bell hooks reminds us, "Feminist struggle to end patriarchal domination should be of primary importance to women and men globally . . . because it is that form of domination we are most likely to encounter in an ongoing way in everyday life."[31] Hawley, however, prefers male "assertiveness"—against whom?—which he claims is "vital to self-government." This uncritical call for "masculine virtues" raises the specter of Raewyn Connell's "hegemonic masculinity," which can include "toxic practices—including physical violence—that stabilize gender dominance in a particular setting."[32] Within this framework, Hawley's embrace of "toxic" qualities cynically discounts victims of male aggression. Indeed, his rallying cry strives to stabilize traditional roles underpinning male dominance. Indelibly captured in a photo facing January 6 protesters with his raised fist in the air, Hawley signifies the masculine aggression he valorizes, demonstrating solidarity with violent political actors.

Undoubtedly, such aggression contradicts biblical teachings on compassionate Christian behavior. Ephesians 4:2–3 states, "Conduct yourselves with all humility, gentleness, and patience. Accept each other with love and make an effort to preserve the unity of the Spirit with the peace that ties you together."[33] Yet rioters, including Christian nationalists, opposing the vice president performing his constitutional duty called for his hanging.[34] Hostility toward Mike Pence percolated in a toxic brew of murderous rage even for those trying to protect the Capitol. Many self-identified Christians mercilessly attacked police offers that day, leading to permanent injury and even death. While not permanently maimed, Black officer Eugene Goodman, who lured an "aggressive" crowd away from the Senate floor, was attacked with bear spray and "jabbed" at three times with a Confederate flag.[35] Nor did journalists attempting to report the day's events escape protestors' vitriol.[36] Far from gentle, patient, and loving, these protestors—some of whom gathered in prayer throughout the day—objectified and brutally attacked their fellow human beings.

Christian nationalism materialized explicitly in Christian flags, prayers, and imagery on January 6. Police Officer Daniel Hodges, for instance, reported seeing Christian and pro-Trump flags displayed as he navigated angry rioters at the Capitol. In his estimation, "It was clear the terrorists perceived themselves to be Christians," based on their flags proclaiming, "Jesus is my savior, Trump is my president," and "Jesus is King."[37] These very protestors, Hodge testified, "ignored [the officers'] commands and . . . assault[ed] [them]." Insurrectionists further displayed their Christian affiliation on the Senate floor, where trespasser Michael Roche led a crowd in prayer: "Jesus Christ, we invoke your name, Amen!"[38] Rioter Jacob Anthony Chansley, who would also invoke "Christ's holy name," offered an extended prayer, thanking God for "allowing the United States of America to be reborn."[39] Conflating religion, politics, and violence, the rioters cast America as a "reborn" nation over which Christ would reign and Trump would again preside. Like a sinner rediscovering its religious footing, a reborn America would be an overtly Christian America.

Leaving little room for ambiguity, the rioters' words and actions confirm their Christian nationalist affiliation. From the Senate floor, for instance, Chansley thanked God "for this opportunity to stand up for our God-given unalienable rights," implying that God condoned their actions.[40] Espousing hallmark Christian nationalist rhetoric in a "'post-insurrection interview,'" trespasser Roche explained that those on the Senate floor "all started praying and shouting the name of Jesus Christ, and inviting Christ back into our state [sic] capitol."[41] Despite the constitutional separation of church and state, they envisioned an essentially Christian country whose religious values could be restored, in part, through prayerful petition. But who counts as American in this narrative? In his Senate floor prayer, Chansely rejects "all the tyrants, the communists, and the globalists," as "this is our nation, not theirs."[42] Invoking a widely recognized antisemitic slur (the "globalists"),[43] Chansely demonstrates anti-Jewish sentiment and general intolerance for those unlike himself—be they Democrats or secularists. Conjuring a world in which "true" Americans are Christian, conservative, and white, he rhetorically banishes nonconforming groups from the body politic.

WHITES UNITED: EVANGELICAL CHRISTIANITY AND ITS OTHERS

Apparently unmoved by appeals to Christian unity, some white Evangelicals privilege racial identity over religious values, making more urgent the need to distinguish between Jesus's love-based teachings and race-centered worship. Translations of the Bible using the term *race* often refer to the "human race," thus underscoring "the unified origins of our common humanity."[44] Yet sociology professor Michael O. Emerson's extensive research shows that many worshippers care more about "whiteness" than Christian unity with nonwhite believers. As he observes,

> White practicing Christians differed from Christians of other racial groups and from non-Christian whites whenever the topic was race. For example, white practicing Christians are twice as likely as other whites to say "being white" is important to them and twice as likely as other whites to say they feel the need to defend their race. Through extensive statistical analyses, we found that

two-thirds of practicing white Christians are following, in effect, a religion of whiteness.[45]

While both the hard sciences and social sciences understand that race is socially constructed, Emerson's respondents nevertheless expose its continuing sociopolitical power in society. In effect, they demonstrate what George Lipsitz would call a "possessive investment in whiteness," meaning they invest in whiteness "like property."[46] But rather than "divest themselves of their investment in white supremacy" and "develop antiracist identities,"[47] Emerson's subjects believe they "need to defend" and protect their whiteness, as though policing their property's perimeter or protecting national borders. With demographic changes marking a declining white population, these Christians have constructed a white supremacist "imagined community" privileging phenotype over principles of faith.[48] Such racist views find safe harbor among Christian nationalists who believe nonwhites pose a threat to America.[49]

Yet, as the Bible makes clear, Christians are called to love, not segregate from, their neighbors in racial enclaves. Proclaiming a key commandment of the faith, Jesus says, "You must love your neighbor as you love yourself."[50] But how do we love at this level? Jemar Tisby affirms, "This love animates the call for racial justice,"[51] while Cornel West contends, "Love is what justice looks like in public."[52] Together, these moral appeals invoke the love-driven politics championed by hooks and Dr. Martin Luther King Jr., each offering paths toward equitable futures. In its concluding section, this chapter considers how love-driven politics shapes reparative Christian efforts in Pittsburgh.

CONCEPTUALIZING PLACE AS "INSUBORDINATE SPACE"

No institution dwells in a pristine site "beyond" race and inequity, but Eastminster church represents an "insubordinate space" where "defiance, disobedience, and intractability can have transformative and redemptive power when mobilized as weapons against exploitation and hierarchy, when they fuel resistance to unjust and illegitimate authority."[53] Unlike Christian nationalist practitioners, the Eastminster community resists white supremacy and promotes "insubordinate" boundary-crossing, love-driven behavior. Rejecting racism as sinful, it strives to implement a racially redemptive social justice model within its very walls.

The most segregated hour for much of US society may indeed be "high noon on Sunday," but Eastminster Presbyterian identifies as "a Christ-Centered and

Intentionally Cross-Cultural Church Family."[54] During my conversation with the church's senior pastor, Paul Roberts, who is white, he elaborated on the church's ethos:

> Take a look at the Gospel. In Acts and the birth of the church, especially the Antioch church. It was a commitment to racial reconciliation. It was Jews and Gentiles saying, "Guess what? We have to learn to live with each other. We need to lead this whole different concept of humanity."[55]

In Roberts's view, twenty-first-century Christians can learn from the Antioch church, an international faith community where multiethnic believers worship together in Christ. His emphasis on *learning to live with each other* suggests that this process requires consistent, sincere, and intentional practice. In this view, Christian faith is a practice rather than simply a belief.

Roberts and like-minded theologians earnestly seek biblical guidance for their racial justice initiatives. Similarly applying Christian values to questions of difference, Tisby writes, "The Bible does not talk about race in the same way we commonly use it today, [but] it still has plenty to say about how people should relate to one another across cultural and ethnic differences."[56] Describing those gathered when the Holy Spirit descended upon the apostles, Tisby observes that worshippers "spoke in languages representing more than a dozen different nations and people groups including Parthians, Medes, Elamites, Mesopotamians, and Cretans."[57] As the Bible "regularly records interactions between different people groups,"[58] Tisby concludes that "from beginning to end, from Genesis to Revelation, God has planned for a racially and ethnically diverse church."[59] Aligned with this biblical model of unity across difference—and Jesus's call to love one's neighbor—Pastor Roberts works with Black and white believers to sustain a diverse, culturally aware congregation.

Yet simple awareness of racial and ethnic difference is insufficient. For Roberts, reckoning with the past and fostering racial reconciliation remain critical to the church's work. As he explains, "Racism is the sin of America. . . . We are founded on the principle that there are two deep sins: one is the genocide against Native Americans and the second . . . is that we decided that slavery was okay." Centering indigenous peoples, racism, slavery, and the legacy of Jim Crow, Roberts believes the clergy must actively address structural racism and work to undo it. Unlike Christian nationalist churches that deny oppression exists,[60] Roberts insists pastors face and address these realities. "We have to admit the church was in it; we weren't idle bystanders," he reflected, adding that the truth may be "too scary for a lot of people to admit," but "the church needs to take a deep look at that."[61] Reflecting on Christian nationalists, in particular, he laments: "With the patriotism and nationalism of the evangelicals, we don't even want to admit . . . what our part was in slavery, in segregation, in Jim Crow, in the lynching. As an evangelical, I'm willing to admit it all, because I believe in the Bible." Since white Christian churches have historically promoted racism and perpetuated oppression, Roberts believes Christians must do what the Bible says: confess and address the problem. For him, the path to reconciliation requires churches to admit the sin of racism, acknowledge their role in it, and work to "rectify the problem."

As a model, Roberts references the "constant Barrier-Breaking Jesus," who defied social norms, forging new ways of being in the world. Citing Jesus's revolutionary practices, Roberts recounts that Jesus interacted with a Samaritan woman at the well and challenged listeners to expand their loving through the good Samaritan parable. Rather than reject social outcasts, Jesus recognized their humanity. "The person you racially hate is the one God loves," Roberts reflected. "I see Jesus's whole ministry as constantly breaking down racial stereotypes and male-female stereotypes. God loves these people that you are separating yourself from."[62]

Christian nationalists cynically cite biblical verses to justify sexual and racial hierarchies, but Roberts wants believers to be "menders of the breach," removing barriers dividing humanity and seeking justice for marginalized communities. *Mending* implies a healing and the righting of historical wrongs, a goal that retired senior Presbyterian pastor Nibs Stroupe amplifies in his recommendation that "church judicatories . . . designate parts of [their] budgets to supply floors of income to descendants of people held as slaves."[63] Acknowledging the church's historical role in perpetuating racism combined with meaningful action are critical steps toward rectifying injustice.

Eastminster's reparative work includes a six-point plan backed by its multicultural vision statement.[64] Invited to help integrate the church more than sixteen years ago, Roberts committed to removing racial barriers and created six points for change in the areas of hiring, worship styles, education, organizational structure, artistic representation, and music. "If we're intentionally cross-cultural," Roberts explains, "we're also going to change the power structure." For him, change includes hiring a diverse staff (including deacons and elders), embracing various worshipping styles, playing culturally diverse music, and privileging multicultural aesthetic representation. While these changes have not appealed to all congregants, some of whom realized they felt uncomfortable in an intentionally diverse church, those who remain are committed to fulfilling the intentionally inclusive mission statement, which, Roberts says, "produces accountability."

CONCLUSION

Roberts believes building an intentionally diverse church is biblical and finds "barrier-breaking" books throughout scripture. "Once you open up to it," he advises, "you'll see it everywhere." This expansive optic, sustained by agape love, emphasizes connection across difference. Alternatively, fear drives the Christian nationalists Du Mez describes: "Generations of evangelicals learned to be afraid of . . . feminists, liberals, [and] secular humanists," she writes.[65] They "look[ed] to a strong man to rescue them from danger, a man who embodied a God-given, testosterone-driven masculinity," a man much like Donald Trump.[66] Fear-driven nationalists in this camp demonize rather than love, yet scripture says, "There is no fear in love, but perfect love drives out fear."[67] This loving foundation animates Roberts's racial justice work and drives Reverend William Barber's Poor People's campaign, which insists that "real social change has come when those most impacted by social injustice have joined hands with allies of good will to stand together to transform and better society."[68] Citing struggles for abolition, women's rights, labor rights, and civil rights, Barber's campaign wisely notes these multiracial movements knew that "in the end, love is the greatest power to sustain a fight for what is right."[69] Rather than merely stand against or succumb to fear, Christians can likewise choose love by reckoning with America's history, practicing *parrhesia*,[70] and actively working to fight oppressive structures. Oppositional at its core, such love seeks justice-oriented solutions countering the oppression Christian nationalism champions.

NOTES

1. Harriet Jacobs, *Incidents in the Life of a Slave Girl*, 2nd ed., edited by Frances Smith Foster and Richard Yarborough (New York: W. W. Norton and Company, 2019), 62.
2. Jacobs, *Incidents in the Life of a Slave Girl*, 62.
3. Jacobs, *Incidents in the Life of a Slave Girl*, 62.
4. Frederick Douglass, *Narrative of the Life of Frederick Douglass*, 2nd ed., edited by William L. Andrews and William S. McFeely (New York: W. W. Norton and Company, 2017), 79.
5. Douglass, *Narrative of the Life*, 79.
6. Douglass, *Narrative of the Life*, 79.
7. Douglass, *Narrative of the Life*, 82.
8. Ibram X Kendi, *Stamped from the Beginning: The Definitive History of Racist Ideas in America* (New York: Bold Type Books, 2017), 251–52.
9. Kendi, *Stamped from the Beginning*, 251.

10. See Tisa Wenger, "Discriminating in the Name of Religion? Segregationists and Slaveholders Did It, Too," *The Washington Post*, December 5, 2017, https://www.washingtonpost.com/news/made-by-history/wp/2017/12/05/discriminating-in-the-name-of-religion-segregationists-and-slaveholders-did-it-too/.

11. Kristin Kobes Du Mez, *Jesus and John Wayne: How White Evangelicals Corrupted a Faith and Fractured a Nation* (New York: Liveright Publishing Corporation, 2020), Kindle Format, page 4.

12. See Christians against Christian Nationalism, "Statement," https://www.christiansagainstchristiannationalism.org/statement.

13. Christians against Christian Nationalism, "Statement," https://www.christiansagainstchristiannationalism.org/statement.

14. Kathryn Joyce, "Christian Nationalism Drove Jan. 6: Now It's Embraced the Big Lie, and Wants to Conquer America," *Salon*, February 11, 2022, https://www.salon.com/2022/02/11/christian-nationalism-drove-jan-6-now-its-embraced-the-big-lie-and-wants-to-conquer-america/

15. As Du Mez explains, "evangelical" connotes a specific identity within Christian community. For conservative white Evangelicals, "the 'good news' of the Christian gospel has become inextricably linked to a staunch commitment to patriarchal authority, gender difference, and Christian nationalism" (6).

16. See Barbara Tomlinson and George Lipsitz, *Insubordinate Spaces: Improvisation and Accompaniment for Social Justice* (Philadelphia: Temple University Press, 2019). Police officer Michael Fanone was beaten unconscious.

17. Anthea Butler, "What Is White Christian Nationalism?" In *Christian Nationalism and the January 6, 2021 Insurrection*, Baptist Joint Committee, https://bjconline.org/wp-content/uploads/2022/02/Christian_Nationalism_and_the_Jan6_Insurrection-2-9-22.pdf, 5.

18. Butler, "What Is White Christian Nationalism?" 5.

19. Butler, "What Is White Christian Nationalism?" 5.

20. James H. Thornwell, "Address by the General Assembly to All the Churches of Jesus Christ Throughout the Earth," Teaching American History, December 31, 1861, https://teachingamericanhistory.org/document/address-by-the-general-assembly-to-all-the-churches-of-jesus-christ-throughout-the-earth/.

21. Du Mez, *Jesus and John Wayne*, 3.

22. See Barbara Welter, "The Cult of True Womanhood: 1820–1860," *American Quarterly* 18 (1966): 151–74.

23. Du Mez, *Jesus and John Wayne*, 12.

24. Rosa Sanchez, "Police Release Photos of Suspect Who 'Assaulted' Capitol Officer Daniel Hodges While He Was Crushed in Doorway," *ABC News*, January 16, 2021, https://abcnews.go.com/US/police-release-photos-suspect-assaulted-capitol-officer-daniel/story?id=75292063.

25. Du Mez, *Jesus and John Wayne*, 301.

26. Edward Lempinen, "Crisis of Faith: Christian Nationalism and the Threat to U.S. Democracy," *Berkeley News*, September 20, 2022, https://news.berkeley.edu/2022/09/20/crisis-of-faith-christian-nationalism-and-the-threat-to-u-s-democracy/.

27. Andrew L. Seidel, "Attack on the Capitol: Evidence of the Role of White Christian Nationalism," in *Christian Nationalism and the January 6, 2021 Insurrection*, Baptist Joint Committee, https://bjconline.org/wp-content/uploads/2022/02/Christian_Nationalism_and_the_Jan6_Insurrection-2-9-22.pdf, 35.

28. See Kathryn Joyce, "'Without the Bible, There Is No America': Josh Hawley Goes Full Christian Nationalist at Nat Con," *Salon*, September 13, 2022, https://www.salon.com/2022/09/13/without-the-bible-there-is-no-america-josh-hawley-goes-full-christian-nationalist-at-natcon/.

29. Katelyn Fossett, "Why Republicans Can't Stop Talking about Masculinity," *Politico*, November 11, 2021. https://www.politico.com/news/magazine/2021/11/21/josh-hawley-madison-cawthorn-jd-vance-masculinity-523136.

30. For full text of Hawley's speech, see Josh Hawley, US Senator for Missouri, "Senator Hawley Delivers National Conservatism Keynote on the Left's Attack on Men in America," November 21, 2021, https://www.hawley.senate.gov/senator-hawley-delivers-national-conservatism-keynote-lefts-attack-men-america.

31. bell hooks, *Talking Back: Thinking Feminist, Thinking Black* (New York: Routledge, 2015), 21.

32. Raewyn Connell and James Messerschmidt, "Hegemonic Masculinity: Rethinking the Concept," *Gender and Society* 19, no. 6 (2005): 840.

33. *Common English Bible*.

34. See Seidel, "Attack on the Capitol," 28.

35. See Stephanie Lai, "Eugene Goodman, Capitol Police Officer, Recounts How He Held Off Mob on Jan. 6," *New York Times*, June 13, 2022, https://www.nytimes.com/2022/06/13/us/eugene-goodman-capitol-riot.html.

36. See Seidel, "Attack on the Capitol," 28.

37. See C-SPAN, "DC Police Officer Daniel Hodges Full Opening Statement on January 6th Attack on US Capitol," YouTube, https://www.youtube.com/watch?v=Z0OT3hnle14.

38. See Seidel, "Attack on the Capitol," 33.

39. Seidel, "Attack on the Capitol," 34.

40. Seidel, "Attack on the Capitol," 34.

41. Seidel, "Attack on the Capitol," 33.

42. Seidel, "Attack on the Capitol," 34.

43. For more on globalist conspiracy discourse, see Ben Zimmer, "The Origins of the 'Globalist' Slur," *The Atlantic*, March 14, 2018, https://www.theatlantic.com/politics/archive/2018/03/the-origins-of-the-globalist-slur/555479/.

44. Jemar Tisby, *How to Fight Racism: Courageous Christianity and the Journey toward Racial Justice* (Grand Rapids, MI: Zondervan, 2021), 23. Tisby writes that a second use of the term *race* refers to "the difference between those who believe in Jesus Christ as the Messiah and those who do not" (23).

45. Michael O. Emerson, "What Happens When White Identity Comes before Christian Faith?" *Sojourners*, July 2022, https://sojo.net/magazine/july-2022/what-happens-when-white-identity-comes-christian-faith.

46. George Lipsitz, *The Possessive Investment in Whiteness: How White People Profit from Identity Politics* (Philadelphia: Temple University Press, 1998), vii, viii.

47. Lipsitz, *The Possessive Investment*, viii.
48. See Benedict Anderson, *Imagined Communities* (New York: Verso, 2006).
49. For more on the perceived threat of nonwhite non-Christians with white Christian nationalist discourse, see Philip Gorski, "White Christian Nationalism: The Deep Story behind the Capitol Insurrection," Berkley Center for Religion, Peace, and World Affairs, January 22, 2021, https://berkleycenter.georgetown.edu/responses/white-christian-nationalism-the-deep-story-behind-the-capitol-insurrection.
50. Mt 22: 39, *Common English Bible*.
51. Tisby, *How to Fight Racism*, 143.
52. See "Reverend Cornel West speaks to crowd of 300 at Stamp Student Union," *The Diamondback*, August 12, 2016. https://dbknews.com/2016/08/12/article_141e1a90-7989-11e2-9ceb-0019bb30f31a-html/.
53. Tomlinson and Lipsitz, *Insubordinate Spaces*, 6, 7.
54. See the Eastminster Presbyterian Church (Pittsburgh, PA) website.
55. Pastor Paul Roberts, in discussion with the author, August 2022.
56. Tisby, *How to Fight Racism*, 24.
57. Tisby, *How to Fight Racism*, 24.
58. Tisby, *How to Fight Racism*, 24.
59. Tisby, *How to Fight Racism*, 26.
60. A number of studies show a correlation between white Christian nationalist beliefs and "a much greater likelihood of embracing racist attitudes." See Andrew Whitehead and Samuel Perry, "What Is Christian Nationalism," in *Christian Nationalism and the January 6, 2021 Insurrection*, Baptist Joint Committee, https://bjconline.org/wp-content/uploads/2022/02/Christian_Nationalism_and_the_Jan6_Insurrection-2-9-22.pdf, 3.
61. Roberts, August 2022.
62. Roberts, August 2022.
63. Nibs Stroupe, "Making Amends for Wrongs Is a Spiritual Issue," *Presbyterians Today*, April 29, 2020, https://www.presbyterianmission.org/story/pt-0520-hungering/.
64. In particular, I refer to the bullet point describing Eastminster as "a Christ-Centered and Intentionally Cross-Cultural Church Family."
65. Du Mez, *Jesus and John Wayne*, 13.
66. Du Mez, *Jesus and John Wayne*, 13.
67. 1 Jn 4:18, *Common English Bible*.
68. See "Our Demands: A Moral Agenda Based on Fundamental Rights," Poor People's Campaign: A National Call for Moral Revival, https://www.poorpeoplescampaign.org/about/our-demands/.
69. "Our Demands."
70. See George Yancy, "Being 'Anti-Racist' Isn't Enough. The Violence of Whiteness Must Be Exposed," Truthout, April 5, 2021. https://truthout.org/articles/being-anti-racist-isnt-enough-the-violence-of-whiteness-must-be-exposed/.

Chapter 14

The Life and Death of Queen Elizabeth II

Defender of the Faith, Supreme Governor of the Church of England, and Manifestation of the White Colonial Gaze

Kimberley Ducey

INTRODUCTION

In 1947, the heir presumptive to the British throne, Princess Elizabeth, accompanied her parents on a leisurely tour of the southern African dominions of the British Empire—South Africa, Southern Rhodesia, Swaziland, Basutoland, and the Bechuanaland Protectorate. To mark her twenty-first birthday, the princess recorded in Cape Town what would become a much-celebrated speech. It was screened in cinemas across the Commonwealth and regularly rebroadcast during her lifetime. "I welcome the opportunity to speak to all the peoples of the British Commonwealth and Empire, wherever they live, whatever race they come from, and whatever language they speak," she said. "I . . . make my solemn act of dedication with a whole Empire listening. . . . I declare before you all that my whole life whether it be long or short shall be devoted to your service and the service of our great imperial family to which we all belong."[1] Elizabeth proudly claimed that the British Empire had "saved the world" two years earlier and reflected on "the anxieties and hardships that the [Second World War] . . . left behind for every nation of [the] commonwealth."[2] She said nothing of the war as an impetus for the liberation of colonial peoples. For many of her white "subjects," the speech remains a moment of collective reflection on the righteous sacrifices of a queen, who lived and died in service to and in defense of her nation's colonial ideals.

In 1952, in her inaugural Christmas message as queen—but before she was anointed with chrism (holy oil) at her investiture, a symbol that she was bound to God and the divine—Elizabeth referred "to the British Commonwealth and Empire" as "that immense union of nations with our home set in all the four corners of the earth."[3] A year later, she again waxed poetically about the empire, referring to white colonials, conquerors, and genociders as "adventurous heroes" and "pioneers," and her imperial kinfolk as "a world-wide fellowship of nations." She admired and panegyrized as grand and sublime British colonial "settlements," as if no one lived in white settler societies before the British Crown took possession of these lands.[4] She indirectly referred to the "doctrine of discovery," which granted "explorers" the legal right to claim "vacant land (*terra nullius*)" for their monarch. Only places *not* occupied by Christians were considered *newfound land* and vacant; thus, only their sovereignty, dominion, title, and jurisdiction could be legally claimed.[5]

During her 1953 coronation speech, Elizabeth again presented a whitewashed version of the British Empire and the white elite's colonial ambitions. The "thousand years" plus that she described as "splendid" were marked by the barbaric transatlantic slave trade and the conquest, colonization, and appropriation of foreign lands in the name of white predatory capitalism.

> I have behind me, not only the splendid traditions and the annals of more than a thousand years, but the living strength and majesty of the commonwealth and empire, of societies, old and new, of lands and races different in history and origins, but all, by God's will, united in spirit and in aim. Therefore, I am sure that this, my coronation, is not the symbol of a par and a splendor that are gone, but a declaration of our hopes for the future and for the years I may, by God's grace and mercy, be given to reign and serve you as your queen.[6]

At the time of her death in 2022 at ninety-six, she remained devoted to the "imperial family." Referring to Elizabeth as "the number one symbol of white supremacy," the scholar Kehinde Andrews argues that the problem with the narrative she spun is that the "outcomes for those in the 'imperial family' have always been based on the logic of white supremacy."[7] Alternatively put, Elizabeth saw the world through the white gaze, "a site of lived sedimentation of white power and privilege that perpetuates violence upon Black [and brown] bodies" and assumes "a fundamental site of what is called 'suturing,' an embodied white practice that involves fleeing the ways in which we are, in these terms, un-sutured."[8] During her seventy-year reign, she failed to "develop specific socio-ontological un-suturing practices, ones that refuse to cover over the festering reality of white lies and white attempts at self-master."[9]

I refer to *the white colonial gaze*, adding to the esteemed US philosopher George Yancy's original interpretation of the white gaze, as a focus on Black and brown bodies in the British Empire and the British Commonwealth, which officially became the Commonwealth of Nations in 1949. Intimately connected to the white colonial gaze is the *colonial countergaze*. It celebrates Black and brown bodies and cultural identities and identifies and marks whiteness and white colonialism as the problem, particularly whites who see themselves as unsullied by racism and colonialism, as the queen's most loyal supporters saw her and she likely saw herself.

This study's specific contribution lies in analyzing the ideology of whiteness, its connections to Elizabeth's interpretation of Christianity, and the implications for Black and brown lives. However, it does not speak for all Black and brown bodies. It relates to personal experiences borne by the individuals of color cited throughout the chapter, which correspond to white racism experienced by other Black and brown bodies as they are forced to maneuver racist and colonial spaces.[10]

The story I tell is of Black and brown resistance and identity. Subverting the white colonial gaze behind the theatrics surrounding Elizabeth's death, the people of color cited in the chapter acknowledge the historical reality and influence of white supremacy while defying the discursive and social practices that reinforce white hegemony.[11] Inspired by these courageous voices, who uncompromisingly stared down the white colonial gaze in the aftermath of Elizabeth's death, I tell a story of a queen who failed to confront the evils of white supremacist domination and ignored calls to acknowledge centuries of slavery, Indigenous genocide in white settler nations, and other racial violence and exploitation.[12] This is a story of a queen who refused to concede that her great wealth was directly accumulated through international systems of exploitation. As the writer-activist Lisa Sharon Harper puts it, "The queen closed her eyes, shut her mouth and laid hold of the scepter and the story of divine election, ordination to rule and inherent nobility. She played her part in the pageant."[13]

The story I tell is premised on the theologian Mark Lewis Taylor's distinction between "a human-in-the-world" and "a follower of Jesus." I contend that Elizabeth's faith did not contradict her embrace of the white hegemonic colonial gaze because she saw herself as "a follower of Jesus" first and not as "a human-in-the-world."[14] She was not necessarily cognizant of the racist patterns informing her inactions or the framing of herself, her family, and her nation as "pure, civilized, [and] innocent."[15] Nevertheless, her global influence began with colonialism and remained embroiled in it. No measure of white denial or commiseration over her death can change this.[16]

In light of Taylor's dichotomy, I examine Elizabeth's annual Christmas messages, 2020 Easter message, long-standing association with white Evangelicalism, and failure to acknowledge racism within the church, even after her bishops did so. I also examine links among the monarchy, the Church of England, and the British Empire. I briefly discuss the Mau Mau Uprising in Kenya and the Nigerian-Biafran War, which occurred during her reign. I conclude with an examination of the National Day of Mourning at the University of Winnipeg, where I teach, which coincided with Elizabeth's state funeral and signified the end of the official mourning period in Canada.

A FOLLOWER OF JESUS VERSUS A HUMAN-IN-THE-WORLD

In 2012, Taylor shared with Yancy that he sees himself as a human-in-the-world *first* and a follower of Jesus *second*.[17] "This means I have to reckon with the kind of human I am," he explained, "with a personal history and . . . a political, racial, social, economic way of being in the world. . . . All this is part of resisting Christian supremacy."[18] While it is regularly claimed that Elizabeth remained politically neutral throughout her reign, it is widely agreed that she was vocal about her faith in Jesus. While framing Jesus's message as antithetical to greed, division, retribution, and violence, she maintained her dominant position in a white-privileging racialized social system.[19]

"HER MAJESTY'S MOST GRACIOUS SPEECHES" (AKA "THE QUEEN'S CHRISTMAS MESSAGES")

The historian Catherine Pepinster explains that while Defender of the Faith is a hereditary title, Elizabeth increasingly embraced it and publicly framed herself as a dedicated follower of Jesus.[20] Pepinster observes:

> Her early Christmas Day broadcasts were platitudinous—the holidays as an occasion for family was a frequent theme. In 2000, however, she spoke of the millennium as the 2,000-year anniversary of the birth of Jesus Christ, "who was destined to change the course of our history." She went on to speak very personally and frankly about her faith: "For me the teachings of Christ and my own personal accountability before God provide a framework in which I try to lead my life. I, like so many of you, have drawn great comfort in difficult times from Christ's words and example."[21]

Pepinster notes that such sentiments were a constant refrain in the queen's Christmas messages after 2000. In 2012, for example, she described the holidays as "the time of year when we remember that God sent his only son 'to serve, not to be served.' He restored love and service to the centre of our lives in the person of Jesus Christ."[22]

In 2014, Elizabeth described herself even more overtly as "a follower of Jesus." In the following excerpt, her reference to Jesus as the "Prince of Peace" is noteworthy for at least two reasons. One, it inadvertently distances white hegemony, which is based on power, from Jesus's so-called earthly kingdom, which was, in her view, based on peace. Two, Jesus, the Prince of Peace, and Jesus, the "counter-imperial, political insurrectionist," are in direct and unequivocal opposition.[23]

> For me, the life of Jesus Christ, the Prince of Peace, whose birth we celebrate today, is an inspiration and an anchor in my life. A role model of reconciliation and forgiveness, he stretched out his hands in love, acceptance and healing. (2014)[24]

Capturing well the late queen's beliefs is Taylor's description of liberal and conservative Christians who favor traditional "grand scenarios" in understanding Jesus's death. "They intone . . . the grander themes," he explains, "he came to forgive sins, to make expiation for human sin, to satisfy on the cross God's wrath, to pay [the] ransom with his death on the cross to appease an angry God, to die intentionally to show self-sacrificing love, and so on."[25] Consider the following excerpts from Elizabeth's 1981 and 2011 Christmas messages, which reflect the traditional grand scenarios Taylor describes.

> Christ not only revealed to us the truth in his teachings. He lived by what he believed and gave us the strength to try to do the same—and, finally, on the cross, he showed the supreme example of physical and moral courage. (1981)[26]

Notably, from 1963 to 1980—a mere year before she spoke these words—her government and the white settlers in East and Central Africa contested the "physical and moral courage" of Indigenous Black Peoples who fought for majority rule. Her annual Christmas messages continued to be framed through the white colonial gaze, including in 2011.

> Although we are capable of great acts of kindness, history teaches us that we sometimes need saving from ourselves—from our recklessness or our greed. God sent into the world a unique person—neither a philosopher nor a general (important though they are)—but a Saviour, with the power to forgive.[27]

She cautions her "subjects," including Black and brown bodies in the Global South—a region that primarily represents the former colonies and many of today's Commonwealth nations, such as Antigua and Barbuda, Belize, Ghana, Lesotho, and Sierra Leone—against "recklessness" and "greed." Yet, between 1970 and 2015, the Global South transferred resources estimated at $242 trillion to the former colonizers and their allies in the Global North.[28] Compare this to Elizabeth's investments, art, jewels, and real estate, estimated in 2022 at approximately £370 million ($426 million).[29] Andrews aptly sums up this white supremacist absurdity: "Queen Elizabeth II's Legacy Keeps the White World Rich and the Black World Poor."[30]

In her 2015 Christmas message, Elizabeth remarked:

> For Joseph and Mary, the circumstances of Jesus' birth in a stable were far from ideal. But worse was to come as the family was forced to flee the country. It is no surprise that such a human story still captures our imagination and continues to inspire all of us who are Christians, the world over. Despite being displaced and persecuted throughout his short life, Christ's unchanging message was not one of revenge or violence but simply that we should love one another.[31]

Her message minimizes humanitarian concerns such as forced displacement and persecution with the blissful illusion that *all we need is love*. Intentionally drawing on Jesus's message to his disciples, "This is my commandment, That ye love one another, as I have loved you," her message inadvertently evokes Karl Marx's adage, "Religion is the opium of the people."[32]

THE QUEEN'S EASTER MESSAGE AND HER LONG HISTORY OF SILENCE IN THE FACE OF WHITE RACISM

Taylor observes that modern-day Christians tend to favor the grand scenario interpretations of the crucifixion and death of Jesus rather than recognizing Jesus as a "counter-imperial, political insurrectionist who met a torturous death."[33] In 2020, amid the coronavirus pandemic and for the first time in her then-sixty-eight-year reign, Elizabeth recorded an Easter message. Akin to her 2014 and 2015 Christmas messages, her words reflect the grand scenario of which Taylor speaks.

> This year, Easter will be different for many of us but by keeping apart we keep others safe. But Easter isn't cancelled; indeed, we need Easter as much as ever. The discovery of the risen Christ on the first Easter Day gave his followers new hope and fresh purpose, and we can all take heart from this. We know that coronavirus will not overcome us. As dark as death can be—particularly for

those suffering with grief—light and life are greater. May the living flame of the Easter hope be a steady guide as we face the future.[34]

If Elizabeth rejected the grand scenario and accepted Jesus as a counter-imperial, political insurrectionist, would she have publicly acknowledged the Church of England's culpability in enslaving Black and brown bodies? Would she have conceded that the monarchy and the church elite pocketed huge profits from slavery? Would she have apologized for the slave trade—arguably, the monarchy's most infamous link to racism?[35] Would successive Canadian governments, which ruled in her name, have removed and isolated Indigenous children from their loved ones, traditions, and cultures to forcibly assimilate them into the dominant white culture via the "Indian Residential School" system?[36] Would she have used the parliamentary procedure known as "Queen's consent" to acquire an exemption from antidiscrimination legislation and bar "immigrants or foreigners" of color from holding clerical positions at Buckingham Palace until at least the late 1960s?[37] Would she have publicly addressed her grandsons' (William and Harry) attendance at a 2005 "Colonials and Natives" costume party, and the latter donning a World War II German Afrika Korps uniform? Would she have openly condemned the racist comments her grandson (Harry) made while training at the Sandhurst Military Academy in 2008? Would she have candidly commented on so-called racist "gaffes" by her husband, mother, and favorite son (Philip, the Queen Mother, and Andrew)? Would she have addressed her heir and eldest son's (Charles) multiple racist performances, including in 2017 when he and his wife, the future Queen Consort, Camilla, hysterically laughed at an Inuit katajjaq performance? Would she have addressed the 2018 incident when the future King Charles III found it difficult to believe that a Black writer hailed from Manchester, a major city in northwest England?[38] Would Elizabeth have ignored claims that one of Britain's highest honors, which she bestowed on ambassadors, diplomats, and senior Foreign Office officials, is "highly offensive" given that it contains an image of a white angel (Saint Michael) standing on the neck of a chained Black man (Lucifer)? Would she have offered understanding and compassion to the many Black Britons who said the award's insignia resembled the murder of George Floyd, the forty-six-year-old practicing Christian who mentored Black youth and opposed gun violence?[39] Would she have stood in solidarity with Harry when he defended his then-girlfriend Meghan Markle against a series of gendered racist media stories, including one that implied her hometown was "gang-scarred" and "(almost) straight outta Compton"? Would she have responded to Markle's claims of racism in the royal family by declaring, "Some recollections may vary . . . and will be addressed by the family privately"?[40]

Detractors will argue that Elizabeth possessed no real power to effect laws or policies because Parliament is the supreme legislative body in a constitutional monarchy, and as monarch, she was forced to remain rigidly neutral concerning political affairs. Nevertheless, as Harper explains, Elizabeth had "the soft power of the bully pulpit. As head of the Church of England and protector of the U.K. constitution, she had the ability to raise her voice."[41]

THE QUEEN AND WHITE EVANGELICALISM

The queen's links to white Evangelicalism were aligned with the grand scenario. In 2001, she bestowed Honorary Knight Commander of the Order of the British Empire (KBE) on the prominent US Evangelical Christian figure Billy Graham. He was the first clergyperson outside the Commonwealth to receive an honorary knighthood. "Elizabeth had a long connection to White evangelicals," explains the *Washington Post* columnist Karen Attiah.[42]

Writing for *Christianity Today*, Dudley Delffs describes how fond Graham was of his royal "friend and confidant."

> Graham attested to the Queen's love for the Bible, as well as the strength and depth of her Christian faith, in his autobiography, *Just As I Am*. "No one in Britain has been more cordial toward us than Her Majesty Queen Elizabeth II," Graham wrote. "Almost every occasion I have been with her has been in a warm, informal setting, such as a luncheon or dinner, either alone or with a few family members or other close friends." They rarely publicized their meetings or leveraged their relationship professionally, but the two enjoyed a friendship that endured for more than 60 years until Graham's passing in 2018.[43]

Upon her death, Graham's son Franklin remarked that his father viewed the queen as "a woman of rare modesty and character."[44] He also said that his

> father had the privilege of meeting with the Queen more than a dozen times, and she was a gracious host, inviting my parents to visit Buckingham Palace on several occasions. My father . . . made a pledge to pray for her and her family every day. He also appreciated how she often talked about Jesus Christ during her public addresses—there was never any question about where she placed her faith. Queen Elizabeth once said, "I draw strength from the message of hope in the Christian gospel." The Queen was a friend to my father, but more importantly, she was a true friend of the Christian faith.[45]

Owen Strachan, provost and research professor of theology at a conservative US Evangelical Christian seminary, refers to the late queen as "an example of decorum, duty, dedication to traditional principles, toughness, womanhood, and British classiness."[46] He also decries "wokeness" as an existential threat to Christianity and a "once-in-a-lifetime crisis."[47] Al Mohler, the president of one of the world's largest Baptist theological seminary institutes, describes Elizabeth as a foil to the depravity that accompanies liberalization. She is a "symbol of stability" in the face of undesirable "moral revolution and cultural convulsion," Mohler contends, including "divorce, premarital sex, abortion, homosexuality, the entire LGBTQ spectrum of issues, but . . . also the general liberalization that came home in [her] own family."[48]

AN UNCOMFORTABLE RELATIONSHIP: THE MONARCHY, THE CHURCH OF ENGLAND, AND THE BRITISH EMPIRE

Crucified for insurrection against the state, Jesus would assuredly oppose the contemporary white supremacist elite and the white colonial gaze. However, as a follower of Jesus who did not rock the boat or genuinely address racism, Elizabeth belonged to this elite and routinely operated out of the white colonial gaze.[49] Attiah explains:

> Elizabeth willingly took on the role of representing British power and wealth. She willingly adorned herself with jewels plundered from former colonies. Her image is on the currencies of many former colonies; by stewarding the British Commonwealth, she willingly took on the symbolic, patronizing role of "white mother" to the darker peoples of the former empire. All while reportedly banning "coloured immigrants or foreigners" from serving in royal clerical roles until the 1960s.[50]

With her passing and the commemorative ceremonies and state funeral that followed, the British Australian biblical scholar and clergyman Michael F. Bird remarked on the "uncomfortable" relationship between the monarchy, the Church of England, and the British Empire. Bird cited an Australian Baptist clergyman who lamented the Church of England's "complicity" with the British state. This included religious leaders who use "Christian language, images and symbols to celebrate the monarchy, military and empire and consecrate the status, pomp and power, which Jesus was expressly, repeatedly and implacably opposed to."[51] Elizabeth's state funeral certainly fit the bill: "The congregation in St. George's Chapel at Windsor stood in silence as the instruments of the Queen's earthly power—the orb, scepter and imperial state crown—were removed from the coffin and placed on the high altar."[52]

The imperial state crown is ornamented with stones, including the 317-carat Cullinan II diamond. It is one of several cut from the three-thousand-plus-carat

Cullinan Diamond that was excavated in South Africa in 1905 when the nation was a British colony. The principal stone is the 530.2-carat Cullinan I diamond, also referred to as the Star of Africa. It rests on top of the monarch's scepter. There have been regular calls to return the diamonds to their countries of origin. Following Elizabeth's death, a representative for the African National Congress (ANC)—the social-democratic political party in South Africa—said: "The minerals of our country and other countries continue to benefit Britain at the expense of our people. The Cullinan Diamond must be returned to [South Africa] with immediate effect."[53] Prominent voices were not alone in calling for the jewels' return. Alongside Elizabeth's official coronation portrait, @Qban_Linx tweeted:

> Pictured here, in Elizabeth's crown and sceptre, are shards of the Star of Africa diamond. The stone was stolen from South Africa in 1905, and is worth $400M. These fragments alone could cover the cost of higher education for nearly 75,000 South African students.[54]

The Royal Collection Trust—the charity primarily responsible for the jewels—opposes reparation, saying the Cullinan stone "was presented to Edward VII in 1907 as a symbolic gesture to heal the rift between Britain and South Africa after the Boer War."[55] This argument encapsulates the white colonial gaze through which the crowns and scepters are characteristically viewed. Edward's and Elizabeth's reginal stories are "not the way of brown colonized Jesus—the conquered one."[56] Instead, as Harper explains:

> We see jewels scavenged from the lands of the conquered. We do not see the conquered. We see the prizes of war sitting atop the brows of ivory-toned men and women. We do not see the shattered families, the gutted resources, [or] the bloodied brown and Black bodies. We see the pomp and circumstance of ceremonies, not the mayhem of the massacres and concentration camps required to pluck emeralds from the hands of rightful heirs and place them in imperial scepters. Set in the crowns and scepters that have bejeweled the kingdom, itself united by force, the spoils of war reinforce England's story. The diamonds in the . . . crown no longer mean carnage. They mean "ordained to rule."[57]

WHITE DENIAL VERSUS UN-SUTURING: ELIZABETH AND HER BISHOPS

During her reign, Elizabeth was content to play the role of white matriarch—unsullied by racism and colonialism—to the Black and brown bodies throughout the Commonwealth. In 2020, in the wake of the Archbishop of Canterbury Justin Welby's public admission that the Church of England is "still deeply institutionally racist" and that he is "ashamed" of its history of racism, her silence continued to legitimize white power and privilege.[58] In contrast, the admission of white racism by the representative of the global Anglican Communion, including churches in more than 165 nations, was momentous. Two years earlier, the Church of England's bishops voted to apologize for "the conscious and unconscious racism experienced by countless Black, Asian and minority ethnic (BAME) Anglicans in 1948 and subsequent years" when they sought spiritual homes in local British churches or parishes.[59] The bishops committed themselves to root out "all forms of conscious or unconscious racism," and named the many other ways whites within the church harmed people of color, including the Windrush Generation.[60]

In 2022, the Windrush Generation—migrants from Jamaica and other Commonwealth countries in the West Indies who arrived in the UK in the 1940s, 1950s, and 1960s to help rebuild postwar Britain—was finally honored with a national monument. Despite headlines like "Queen Elizabeth II, Prince William Highlight Racism Faced by Britain's Caribbean Migrants," the queen said nothing about the racism the Windrush Generation endured. She merely penned a statement that read: "The new statue was a 'fitting thank you to the Windrush pioneers and their descendants, in recognition of the profound contribution they have made to the United Kingdom over the decades.'"[61] At the unveiling, her grandson William remarked: "Discrimination remains an all too familiar experience for Black men and women in Britain in 2022."[62] That William and not the queen made such a statement is a reminder that Elizabeth was a follower of Jesus first as opposed to being a human-in-the-world *first*. To the very end of her life, she squandered the many opportunities presented to her to become "un-sutured," to renounce her illusory white innocence, and to practice "white courageous listening."[63] Yancy explains:

> Being un-sutured is a powerful concept as it implies, especially for whites, the capacity to tarry with the multiple ways in which their whiteness is a problem, and to remain with the weight of that reality and the pain of that realization. Being un-sutured is a site of openness, loss, and great discomfort. It is a site of suffering, a form of suffering that is necessary for white people. . . . For white people to tarry within such a space is dangerous. It is dangerous because it is demanding; dangerous because it refuses to play it safe, which is another way of remaining sutured. Whites will find themselves in a process of alienation as they struggle to undo white racial parasitism. As they go in search of themselves, Black [and brown] bodies will no longer function as props.[64]

Elite whites becoming un-sutured is "the exception rather than the rule," while the dearth of such allies among the establishment is emblematic of "the hegemonic forces of White supremacy."[65] Sadly, Elizabeth represented the latter.

BLACK BODIES, WHITE QUEEN: A SYMBOL OF THE RACIST ILLS OF AN EMPIRE

Mau Mau Uprising

White settlers soon displaced large numbers of Indigenous Peoples who had worked the land as migratory farmers for centuries when Kenya was declared a British colony in 1920. Limits on Indigenous land ownership and agricultural practices were instituted. In February 1952, Elizabeth was in Kenya on a Commonwealth tour when her father, King George VI, died, and she succeeded him to the throne. The same year, Mau Mau fighters—mainly from the Kikuyu ethnic group—rose against the colonial regime demanding political rights and land reforms. In October 1952, "Her Majesty's Government" declared a state of emergency and established internment camps, which continued until the Mau Mau were defeated in 1960. During this period, the African Home Guard was recruited by the colonials and led by British soldiers. Together they systematically pillaged, starved, tortured, castrated, sexually assaulted, and murdered the insurgents.[66] Officially the number of dead Mau Mau and other insurrectionists was estimated at 11,000, including 1,090 people hanged by the British administration. Thirty-two white settlers died as a result of the eight-year state of emergency. Survivors among the insurgents eventually sued Her Majesty's Government, which paid compensation of approximately £3,000 per living victim. But the queen never apologized for being a benefactor, beneficiary, or bystander to this brutal moment in colonial history.[67]

In the aftermath of Elizabeth's death, the Cornell University professor Mũkoma wa Ngũgĩ, who is Kenyan, criticized the histrionics surrounding her passing and her failure to make an act of contrition. "If the queen had apologized for slavery, colonialism and neocolonialism and urged the crown to offer reparations for the millions of lives taken in her/their names, then perhaps I would do the human thing and feel bad," he said. "As a Kenyan, I feel nothing. This theater is absurd."[68] An angry line of white faces soon besieged Ngũgĩ on Twitter.

The Atlantic's Jemele Hill also courageously stared down the white colonial gaze. She confronted a long line of angry white faces on her Twitter thread. "Journalists are tasked with putting legacies into full context," she tweeted, "so it is entirely appropriate to examine the queen and her role in the devastating impact of continued colonialism."[69]

Typically, whites respond with digressive maneuverings that reject or debunk the claims people of color make about racism. The angry whites Ngũgĩ, Hill, and other Black and brown voices encountered after Elizabeth died were no different. The white voices assumed an air of authority that prevented the sincerity necessary for genuine self-reflection. As Yancy explains: "When it comes to the complexity and depth of their own racism [whites] possess the capacity for absolute epistemic clarity and [presume] that the self is transparent [and] fully open to inspection."[70]

Nigerian-Biafran War

To protect British oil interests, late in the 1960s, Her Majesty's Government clandestinely provided the Nigerian government with military hardware to facilitate the defeat of the Biafran secessionist movement, ultimately leading to the Igbo Genocide. Approximately three million people perished, mostly civilians of Igbo descent.[71]

When Elizabeth died, the Nigerian President Muhammadu Buhari—a retired army major general who served in the Nigerian-Biafran War and later as the nation's military head of state following a military coup d'état—fondly recalled his nation's "very close ties with the monarchy," referred to the queen as "a very strong ally even in the midst of our difficult time during the Biafran war," and commended her for supporting the "indivisibility of the Nigerian state."[72]

While the media uncritically reported Buhari's commendation of Elizabeth, the Nigerian-born scholar Uju Anya—whose family members were murdered during the genocide—posted a tweet wishing the queen "excruciating pain" and describing her as "the chief monarch of a thieving and raping genocidal empire." Twitter removed the post for violating its rules, while Carnegie Mellon University, a private research university in Pittsburgh, Pennsylvania, where Anya works, condemned her statements.[73] In response, Anya tweeted:

> If anyone expects me to express anything but disdain for the monarch who supervised a government that sponsored the genocide that massacred and displaced half my family and the consequences of which those alive today are still trying to overcome, you can keep wishing upon a star.[74]

Similarly, the British Nigerian social media coordinator Kelachi Onyebuchi said she "felt a sense of victory" upon learning of the queen's death. "Slowly, the very institution that signifies years of slavery, colonialism, pain, suffering is crumbling down," she explained, "and for that very reason it will be extremely pretentious of me to mourn her death. . . . I don't and never will mourn my colonisers. I will never mourn the people that facilitated starvations and massacres . . . of my people. Never."[75]

CONCLUSION

The story I tell "is not what . . . a Christianity that fights in the name of parrhesia, social justice, or in the name of a beloved community looks like."[76] Nevertheless, following the death of Elizabeth, her life was celebrated globally, including via the following communiqué that appeared on my university's website.

> The University of Winnipeg community mourns the loss of Her Majesty Queen Elizabeth II. In her honour, the University's campus flags will be lowered to half-mast. As Canada's longest serving head of state, Queen Elizabeth reigned with grace and compassion for 70 years. She visited our province six times, most recently in 2010, when she dedicated a cornerstone of the Canadian Museum for Human Rights. We will always remember and honour Queen Elizabeth's life of selfless service. Her unwavering belief in the power of education and the potential it provides to the world's youth was inspirational. Although it is hard to imagine the world without her, we look to continue her legacy by building a brighter future together.[77]

The communiqué led me to question how the university could simultaneously frame Elizabeth's legacy so uncritically and undo Indigenous invisibility; challenge white supremacy, white nationalism, and transnational whiteness; oppose coloniality and neo-coloniality; condemn imperialism; share and affirm the distinct histories of communities of color; honor the legacy of resistance to colonization and white supremacy; actively examine disparities and injustices; and center healing and transformative justice. The university prides itself on "providing high-quality post-secondary education with a strong emphasis on accessibility, especially for non-traditional students—including adult learners, war-affected youth, First Nations, Métis and Inuit students and new immigrants."[78] I pondered how Indigenous students, who comprise approximately 12 percent of the student body, and the 25 percent of students who identify as "visible minorities" felt about this uncritical framing of Elizabeth's legacy.[79] I wondered how to reconcile the fact that only four years previous, the University of Winnipeg President declared "diversity" to be "our biggest strength."[80] Our main goal, she explained, is "to create . . . a university-bound identity for everyone."[81] These claims contradict the white colonial gaze through which the queen's life and death were later framed.

Almost without exception, self-identifying white students in my fall 2022 classes supported, were apathetic toward, or thought the communiqué and the National Day of Mourning benign. In contrast, students of color were mostly confounded, offended, outraged, or hurt by the university's uncritical framing of the queen. The differing reactions bring to mind Yancy's contention that the subjugated "possess a level of heightened sensitivity to recognizable and repeated occurrences that might very well slip beneath the radar of others who do not have such a place and history in a white dominant and hegemonic society."[82]

NOTES

1. Windsor, "A Speech by the Queen on Her 21st Birthday, 1947."
2. Windsor, "A Speech by the Queen on Her 21st Birthday, 1947."
3. "The Queen's Christmas Broadcast 1952 Transcript."
4. Queen Elizabeth II, "Christmas Broadcast 1953."
5. "Indigenous Title and the Doctrine of Discovery."
6. "The Queen's Coronation Day Speech June 2nd, 1953 Transcript."
7. Andrews, "Queen Elizabeth II's Legacy."
8. Yancy, "White Embodied Gazing," 243.
9. Yancy, "White Embodied Gazing," 243.
10. Yancy, "Elevators, Social Spaces and Racism," 869.
11. Yancy, "Elevators, Social Spaces and Racism," 848.
12. Newman, "Racism, White Supremacy and the British Royal Family."
13. Harper, "After Elizabeth."
14. Yancy, "Christianity Is Empty."
15. Yancy, "Elevators, Social Spaces and Racism," 19.
16. Busari, "Cloud of Colonialism."
17. Yancy, "Christianity Is Empty."
18. Yancy, "Christianity Is Empty."
19. Bonilla-Silva, *Racism without Racists*.
20. Pepinster, "Elizabeth II."
21. Pepinster, "Elizabeth II."
22. "10 Surprising Things."
23. Yancy, "Christianity Is Empty."
24. "10 Surprising Things."
25. Yancy, "Christianity Is Empty."
26. Yancy, "Christianity Is Empty."
27. Yancy, "Christianity Is Empty."
28. Andrews, "Queen Elizabeth II's Legacy."
29. Kiderlin, "Corgis, Castles and Handbags."
30. Andrews, "Queen Elizabeth II's Legacy."
31. Jones, "Queen Elizabeth II Speaks."

32. Jn 15:12; see also Jn 13:34–35; Moroni 7:46–48; Yancy, "Christianity Is Empty."
33. Yancy, "Christianity Is Empty."
34. Davies, "'New Hope.'"
35. Archbishops' Anti-Racism Taskforce, "Update."
36. Goldsmith, "Queen Elizabeth Sends Message."
37. McGee, "Britain's Royals Have Denied."
38. Ducey and Feagin, *Revealing Britain's Systemic Racism*, 232–39.
39. Friel, Hosie, and Mitchell, "The British Royal Family."
40. Friel, Hosie, and Mitchell, "The British Royal Family."
41. Harper, "After Elizabeth."
42. Attiah, "What Queen Elizabeth Meant."
43. Delffs, "Died."
44. Ross, "Why Was Queen Elizabeth II."
45. Graham, "Facebook"; Garrett, "Womanhood."
46. Strachan, *Christianity and Wokeness*, 26.
47. Strachan, *Christianity and Wokeness*, 26.
48. Mohler, "Moral Revolution."
49. Yancy, "Christianity Is Empty."
50. Attiah, "We Must Speak."
51. Bird, "The Death of Queen Elizabeth II."
52. de Souza, "The Strikingly Christian Funeral of Queen Elizabeth II."
53. Onyanga-Omara, "Imperial State Crown."
54. qaomene at TikTok, Twitter post, September 8, 2022, 1:27 p.m.
55. Onyanga-Omara, "Imperial State Crown."
56. Harper, "After Elizabeth."
57. Harper, "After Elizabeth."
58. Haynes, "Church of England. "
59. Moughtin-Mumby, "Windrush Commitment and Legacy."
60. Haynes, "Church of England."
61. Hui, "Queen Elizabeth II."
62. Hui, "Royals Thank Caribbean Migrants."
63. Yancy, "White Suturing,"
64. Yancy, "White Suturing."
65. Spanierman and Smith, "Confronting White Hegemony," 730.
66. Rios, "Queen's Death."
67. "Mau Mau Torture Victims to Receive Compensation."
68. Ngugi, Twitter post, September 8, 2022, 1:55 p.m.
69. Hill, Twitter post, September 8, 2022, 1:05 p.m.
70. Yancy, "Elevators, Social Spaces and Racism," 76.
71. Curtis, "How Britain's Labour Government."
72. Sabastine, "Queen Elizabeth's Britain."
73. Rios, "Queen's Death."
74. Anya, Twitter post, September 8, 2022, 12:51 p.m.
75. Katsha, "For Black Brits."

76. George Yancy, email with the author, May 17, 2022.
77. University of Winnipeg, "UWinnipeg Mourns the Loss."
78. University of Winnipeg, "Diversity."
79. University of Winnipeg, "Diversity."
80. University of Winnipeg, "Diversity."
81. University of Winnipeg, "Diversity."
82. Yancy, *Black Bodies, White Gazes*, 23.

BIBLIOGRAPHY

"10 Surprising Things the Queen Said about Jesus." *Haven Today*. September 8, 2022. https://haventoday.org/blog/10-surprising-things-queen-says-jesus/.

Andrews, Kehinde. "Queen Elizabeth II's Legacy Keeps the White World Rich and the Black World Poor." *Scientific American*. October 28, 2022. https://www.scientificamerican.com/article/queen-elizabeth-iis-legacy-keeps-the-white-world-rich-and-the-black-world-poor/.

Anya, Uju. Twitter post. September 8, 2022, 12:51 p.m.

Archbishops' Anti-Racism Taskforce. "Update from the Anti-Racism Taskforce." *The Church of England*. February 26, 2022. https://www.churchofengland.org/news-and-media/news-releases/update-anti-racism-taskforce.

Attiah, Karen. "We Must Speak the Ugly Truths about Queen Elizabeth and Britain's Empire." *Washington Post*. September 10, 2022. https://www.washingtonpost.com/opinions/2022/09/10/britain-colonial-brutalities-queen-elizabeth-death-commentary/.

———. "What Queen Elizabeth Meant for White Christianity." *Washington Post*. September 16, 2022. https://www.washingtonpost.com/opinions/2022/09/16/queen-elizabeth-white-christianity/.

Bird, Michael F. "The Death of Queen Elizabeth II and the Ghost of Christian Nationalism." *Word from the Bird*. October 5, 2022. https://michaelfbird.substack.com/p/the-death-of-queen-elizabeth-ii-and?r=ilx28&utm_campaign=post&utm_medium=web.

Bonilla-Silva, Eduardo. *Racism without Racists: Color-Blind Racism and the Persistence of Racial Inequality in America*. Lanham, MD: Rowman & Littlefield, 2017.

Busari, Stephanie. "Cloud of Colonialism Hangs over Queen Elizabeth's Legacy in Africa." *CNN*. September 10, 2022. https://www.cnn.com/2022/09/10/africa/colonialism-africa-queen-elizabeth-intl/index.html.

Curtis, Mark. "How Britain's Labour Government Facilitated the Massacre of Biafrans in Nigeria—To Protect Its Oil Interests." *Daily Maverick*. April 29, 2020. https://www.dailymaverick.co.za/article/2020-04-29-how-britains-labour-government-facilitated-the-massacre-of-biafrans-in-nigeria-to-protect-its-oil-interests/.

Davies, Caroline. "'New Hope': Queen Reassures Nation in First Easter Message." *The Guardian*. April 11, 2020. https://www.theguardian.com/uk-news/2020/apr/11/new-hope-queen-reassures-nation-in-first-easter-message.

Delffs, Dudley. "Died: Queen Elizabeth II, British Monarch Who Put Her Trust in God." *Christianity Today*. September 8, 2022. https://www.christianitytoday.com/news/2022/september/obit-queen-elizabeth-ii-personal-faith-christian-bible.html.

de Souza, Raymond J. "The Strikingly Christian Funeral of Queen Elizabeth II." *National Catholic Register*. September 19, 2022. https://www.ncregister.com/commentaries/the-strikingly-christian-funeral-of-queen-elizabeth-ii.

Ducey, Kimberley, and Joe R. Feagin. *Revealing Britain's Systemic Racism: The Case of Meghan Markle and the Royal Family*. New York: Routledge, 2021.

Friel, Mikhaila, Rachel Hosie, and Taiyler Simone Mitchell. "The British Royal Family Has Turned a Blind Eye to Its Racist Past." *Insider*. September 8, 2022. https://www.insider.com/british-royal-family-racist-history-black-lives-matter-2020-8.

Garrett, Greg. "Womanhood, White Christian Nationalism and Queen Elizabeth." *Baptist News*. September 12, 2022. https://baptistnews.com/article/womanhood-white-christian-nationalism-and-queen-elizabeth/.

Goldsmith, Annie. "Queen Elizabeth Sends Message to Canadians on National Day of Truth and Reconciliation." *Town & Country*. September 30, 2021. https://www.townandcountrymag.com/society/tradition/a37808784/queen-elizabeth-canada-national-day-of-truth-and-reconciliation-message/.

Graham, Franklin. "Facebook." Accessed October 23, 2022.

Harper, Lisa Sharon. "After Elizabeth: The Spiritual Implications of Imperial Succession." *Religion News Service*. September 15, 2022. https://religionnews.com/2022/09/15/queen-elizabeth-king-charles-on-spiritual-implications-of-imperial-succession/.

Haynes, Suyin. "Church of England 'Still Deeply Institutionally Racist,' Says Archbishop." *Time*. February 13, 2020. https://time.com/5782904/church-of-england-institutionally-racist/.

Hill, Jemele. Twitter post. September 8, 2022, 1:05 p.m.

Hui, Sylvia. "Queen Elizabeth II, Prince William Highlight Racism Faced by Britain's Caribbean Migrants." *USA Today*. June 22, 2022. https://www.usatoday.com/story/entertainment/celebrities/2022/06/22/queen-elizabeth-prince-william-racism-caribbean-migrants/7699308001/.

———. "Royals Thank Caribbean Migrants for Contribution to the UK." *AP News*. June 22, 2022. https://apnews.com/article/queen-elizabeth-ii-politics-caribbean-cb98c2889afe6b09a39998c4e94d90d3.

"Indigenous Title and the Doctrine of Discovery." Indigenous Corporate Training Inc. January 26, 2020. https://www.ictinc.ca/blog/indigenous-title-and-the-doctrine-of-discovery.

Jones, Morgan. "Queen Elizabeth II Speaks about Jesus Christ in Christmas Message." *Deseret News*. December 30, 2015. https://www.deseret.com/2015/12/30/20579554/queen-elizabeth-ii-speaks-about-jesus-christ-in-christmas-message.

Katsha, Habiba. "For Black Brits, the Queen's Death Is Raking up Conflicted Feelings." *Huffington Post*. November 9, 2022. https://www.huffingtonpost.co.uk/entry/black-british-conflicted-reactions-to-queen-death_uk_6319f25ce4b082746bdcb1cb.

Kiderlin, Sophie. "Corgis, Castles and Handbags: What Happens to Queen's Wealth after Her Death?" *CNBC*. September 16, 2022. https://www.cnbc.com/2022/09/16/what-happens-to-queens-money-now-corgis-castles-and-handbags-in-the-mix.html.

"Mau Mau Torture Victims to Receive Compensation—Hague." *BBC*. June 6, 2013. https://www.bbc.com/news/uk-22790037.

McGee, Luke. "Britain's Royals Have Denied Being a Racist Family. Archived Papers Reveal Recent Racist Past." *CNN*. June 3, 2021. https://www.cnn.com/2021/06/03/uk/queen-racist-employment-policy-intl-cmd-gbr-analysis/index.html.

Mohler, Al. "Moral Revolution and Cultural Convulsion but One Great Symbol of Stability: Queen Elizabeth's Legacy." *The Southern Baptist Theological Seminary*. September 9, 2022. https://albertmohler.com/2022/09/09/briefing-9-9-22.

Moughtin-Mumby, Andrew. "Windrush Commitment and Legacy." *General Synod of the Church of England*. January 2020. https://www.churchofengland.org/sites/default/files/2020-01/GS%202156A%20Windrush%20Commitment%20and%20Legacy.pdf.

Newman, Brooke. "Racism, White Supremacy and the British Royal Family." *Spiegel International*. December 3, 2021. https://www.spiegel.de/international/world/the-queen-s-silence-racism-white-supremacy-and-the-british-royal-family-a-d4475024-943b-4ecc-bf13-9cecc76c936d.

Ngugi, Mukoma Wa. Twitter post. September 8, 2022, 1:55 p.m.

Onyanga-Omara, Jane. "Imperial State Crown and Royal Scepter Glimmer, but Some Say on Back of Colonialism." *USA Today*. September 16, 2022. https://www.usatoday.com/story/entertainment/celebrities/2022/09/16/imperial-state-crown-atop-queen-elizabeth-iis-coffin-colonialism/10389746002/.

Pepinster, Catherine. "Elizabeth II, Longest to Rule Britain and Church of England, Dies at 96." *Religion News Service*. September 8, 2022. https://religionnews.com/2022/09/08/elizabeth-ii-longest-to-rule-britain-and-church-of-england-dies-at-96/.

qaomene at TikTok. Twitter post. September 8, 2022, 1:27 p.m.

Queen Elizabeth II. "Christmas Broadcast 1953." *The Royal Household*. December 15, 1953. https://www.royal.uk/christmas-broadcast-1953.

"The Queen's Christmas Broadcast 1952 Transcript." Rev. https://www.rev.com/blog/transcripts/the-queens-christmas-broadcast-1952-transcript.

"The Queen's Coronation Day Speech June 2nd, 1953 Transcript." Rev. https://www.rev.com/blog/transcripts/the-queens-coronation-day-speech-june-2nd-1953-transcript.

Rios, Edwin. "Queen's Death Intensifies Criticism of British Empire's Violent Atrocities." *The Guardian*. September 10, 2022. https://www.theguardian.com/us-news/2022/sep/10/queen-death-colonies-atrocities-british-empire.

Ross, Larry. "Why Was Queen Elizabeth II Friends with the Evangelist Billy Graham for More Than 40 Years?" *allisraelnews*. September 12, 2022. https://allisrael.com/why-was-queen-elizabeth-ii-friends-with-the-evangelist-billy-graham-for-more-than-40-years-as-a-long-time-aide-to-graham-i-got-to-see-this-remarkable-friendship-for-myself.

Sabastine, ThankGod. "Queen Elizabeth's Britain Strongly Supported Nigeria during Biafra War: Buhari." *People's Gazette*. September 11, 2022. https://gazettengr.com/queen-elizabeths-britain-strongly-supported-nigeria-during-biafra-war-buhari/.

Spanierman, Lisa B., and Laura Smith. "Confronting White Hegemony: A Moral Imperative for the Helping Professions." *The Counseling Psychologist* 45, no. 5 (2017): 727–36.

Strachan, Owen. *Christianity and Wokeness: How the Social Justice Movement Is Hijacking the Gospel—and the Way to Stop It*. Hackensack, NJ: Salem Books, 2021.

University of Winnipeg. "Diversity Is UWinnipeg's Strength." December 14, 2016. https://news.uwinnipeg.ca/diversity-is-uwinnipegs-strength/.

———. "UWinnipeg Mourns the Loss of Queen Elizabeth II." September 9, 2022. https://news.uwinnipeg.ca/uwinnipeg-mourns-the-loss-of-queen-elizabeth-ii/.

Windsor, Elizabeth. "A Speech by the Queen on Her 21st Birthday, 1947." *The Royal Household*. April 21, 1947. https://www.royal.uk/21st-birthday-speech-21-april-1947.

Yancy, George. *Black Bodies, White Gazes: The Continuing Significance of Race in America*. 2nd edition. Lanham, MD: Rowman & Littlefield, 2016.

———. "Christianity Is Empty If It Doesn't Address the Racist Carceral State." Truthout. September 26, 2021. https://truthout.org/articles/christianity-is-empty-if-it-doesnt-address-the-racist-carceral-state/.

———. "Elevators, Social Spaces and Racism: A Philosophical Analysis." *Philosophy and Social Criticism* 34, no. 8 (2008): 843–76.

———. "White Embodied Gazing, the Black Body as Disgust, and the Aesthetics of Un-Suturing." In *Body Aesthetics*, edited by Sherri Irvin, 243–60. New York: Oxford University Press, 2016.

———. "White Suturing, Black Bodies, and the Myth of a Post-Racial America." *Society for the Arts in Religious and Theological Studies*. 2018. https://www.societyarts.org/white-suturing-black-bodies-and-the-myth-of-a-post-racial-america.html.

Chapter 15

"The Order" of the Day

Lessons, Philosophical and Otherwise, from *Childhood* at the *Heart* of American Christian Nationalism

James Garrison

Just the other day, I was doing some work in a local middle school. We were engaged in a get-to-know-you icebreaker activity with the teenage students. To the extent that I claim being a philosopher though, I'm compelled to ask: How can I get to know you, before I get to know me, after all? After all, I still ask myself all the time "What am I, really?" And race, the focus of this chapter, is only but one of the domains in which I'm uncertain of myself.

Maybe with my middling skills at self-reflection, I shouldn't be the one leading exercises in self-introduction. Better to approach self-conscious identity in a college classroom on a theoretical level with a bunch of entry-level Descartes, right? Is this not the very meaning of the phrase "those who can't do, teach"? Well, despite myself, I had one of those from-the-mouths-of-babes moments, at least when it comes to race and knowing who and what I am. And as so often happens, it was a mildly petulant middle schooler who helped to snap things into focus for a bit.

Anyways, we all wrote down somewhat secret (but not too secret) facts about ourselves, crumpled up the pieces of paper, and threw them to the front of the room for everybody else to retrieve before guessing the secret (but, again, not too secret) identity of the writer. So far, this was a fairly benign activity.

And so, I wrote, or rather scrawled, a trivial "secret" about myself (namely, that I studied martial arts, which is only barely technically true but meant to grab the attention of bored teenagers). It was not my barely existent martial-arts background that was of interest to the students, but, rather, they were intrigued by my mangled handwriting. The student who obtained my crumpled note card commented, before reading my hieroglyphic script aloud, that "apparently this person has kindergarten handwriting." In that moment the answer to "What am I, really?" was apparently "shit."

Later in class though, the subject of my kindergarten handwriting came up again, and I had more chance to respond. I informed the students that the comment was accurate (from the mouths of babes, after all) and that it had a basis in my biography. I pulled up a map of the US and then focused in on Washington state in the Pacific Northwest. However, rather than focusing on Seattle, the city of my birth and the object of most people's attention when it comes to the region, I directed them to look at probably the most often overlooked area of the state—Metaline (pronounced "meh-tah-leen"), which lies just a few miles from both Idaho and Canada in the far northeastern corner of the state.

I told them that, having moved there because of my father's work and remaining there for reasons that I still don't comprehend, I attended kindergarten and first grade there. I told them that this meant living in what was one of the most racist places in the country, where I was probably the only Black kid in at least an hour in any direction. I told them (without getting into specifics, as I'm about to do) that Metaline was the origin of a lot of the ideology behind the modern white power movement. I told them that I encountered resistance from my teacher when it came to learning how to read and write. I told them that I taught myself how to write by awkwardly holding my pen/pencil in my own ungainly way, resulting in what, despite various attempts over the years at retraining myself, remains horrific penmanship to this day. And I told them that the result of all of this is the horribly illegible script that attracted mockery in their classroom in the waning days of 2022.

The students of the classroom, mostly students of color, were taken aback by this major childhood confessional by this mostly unknown part-time volunteer professor-type leading the class, especially as these revelations were coming in the last minutes of my time on the last day before holiday break. The student who had, sensing weakness in the honed manner of middle schoolers well practiced in the arts of close-quarters social Darwinism, lightly goaded me for my scratched-out writing seemed to change in countenance, perhaps having learned some small lesson about making presumptions of others just for laughs—I don't know. In any case, this student, more attentively and with genuinely curious engagement, did ask me if I'd go back to Metaline. Remembering that I was in a middle school classroom and halting myself from using the word *shithole*, I took a barely perceptible moment before responding, "No."

What I didn't say was more particular though, and not for eighth graders, at least in the last five minutes before lunch. I didn't get into memories of feeling like less than shit when older kids screamed, "Die, n-----, die!" while beating on me. That's not for them, at least it wasn't at that moment. I also didn't get into the more specific history of this remote place, Metaline, and the relevance of this past to our present condition and future prospects for both American and world citizens.

So why does the history of this tiny town of Metaline matter? Well, aside from being the ancestral home of the Kalipsel Tribe and the current host to a few hundred people amid the towering mountains and old-growth evergreens, Metaline is also the origin point of a still-influential movement in the development of modern confluence of white power and Christian nationalism. It is the site of the founding of "The Order."[1]

If you're familiar with The Order in any way, it's likely through their numeric quasi-code and slogan "1488," which, as a shibboleth for shitheads, is popular among white power gangs and their neo-Confederate confederates. Here "88" is a reference to "Heil Hitler" (with "H" being the eighth letter of the alphabet, so HH=88).[2] Meanwhile and very much in line with this horrific sentiment, the preceding "14" is *the* singular contribution from my one-time hometown to our shared discourse, and it refers to the so-called "Fourteen Words," which are the operating credo of The Order.

How do these infamous Fourteen Words from Metaline go then? Simply put, the first version is "We must secure the existence of our people and a future for white children," and the secondary phrase is "Because the beauty of the White Aryan woman must not perish from the Earth."[3]

This isn't exactly Christian in the sense of most mainstream interpretation of Scripture, but it is the one offered by Richard Butler, reverend of the Church of Jesus Christ Christian-Aryan Nations, one of the most visible exponents of the idea of a white homeland in the Northwest of America.[4] Butler, having moved not that far away from Metaline into neighboring Idaho, would profoundly influence the growth of far-right American Christian nationalism in the region, setting the tone for a number of groups in the region operating on the precept of his Christian Identity movement "that whites have the God-given right to reclaim Canada and the United States for white people."[5]

With all of that out of the way, I hasten to mention that, by the time that I got there, The Order, which in previous years had committed armed robbery and murdered outspoken left-wing, Jewish, Denver-area radio host Alan Berg, already broke under the strain of federal interdiction and prosecution.[6] That doesn't mean, though, that the basic hostility of The Order's Fourteen Words disappeared from the hearts of a worrying number of people in this highly isolated area. Despite a reputation for lily-white demographics, the more urban corridor west of the Cascade Mountains has long been too liberal and too friendly to minority populations for more conservative folks out east. This remains the case to this day with movements like the "Liberty State" movement, which "wants eastern Washington to secede and form a [fifty-first] state called Liberty embodying his style of Christian values" and, while certainly operating on the fringes, is championed, on a national level, by figures "attracting wide attention in far-right and white supremacist circles."[7]

It was this long-enduring political and, frankly, demographic climate with few to no liberals and/or people of color that led to people like The Order's founder Robert Jay Matthews descending on the area. And these trends didn't just go away magically in 1984 when Matthews met his violent demise.[8] After all, with far less violence, but certainly some sympathy to this way of "thinking," one of my first teachers refused to teach me how to write, as mentioned. Moreover, not that far away, in 1992, US Marshals and FBI agents seized the well-armed compound of Aryan Nations member Randy Weaver, resulting in a flurry of national news coverage of his death and leading further to what passes for martyrdom in his circle.[9]

My own presence in the region was sandwiched by these events. I arrived a few years after The Order was in operation in Metaline and beyond, and my family left for Seattle before the events of Ruby Ridge. I was there for just a couple of years, which my mental filing system records as kindergarten and first grade—ages five and six—though I suppose that a more reliable narrator might call them 1987 and 1988. It wasn't unremitting hostility, true. It wasn't even complete isolation out there. I remember playing with friends and visits with people around town. There were neighborhood kids who'd ride bikes with me in the summer and play in the snow in the winter, with all the normal traffic between houses that happens when little kids play in small towns. There were neighbors who grew morel mushrooms in abundance, there was the nice next-door neighbor lady who taught at the high school, and there were even an ambitious man and woman on a major back-to-nature kick who built their own dome house over several years while camping on site (and the woman in question remains a friend to this day).

However, even if there were friendly neighbors and neighborly friends, this was the exception and not the rule. The response that I recall from way back when was overwhelmingly hostile, though this hostility was usually cut with a mix of brusque, restrained politeness and seething curiosity (especially as concerned my white mom when out and about with her Black husband and Black-ish children).

After all, this was super-remote eastern Washington, and to this day, the area remains a haven for people seeking to eliminate from their lives what they perceive to be the ills of "the city," which according to rhetoric seems to be some mix of Seattle, Portland, Hollywood, New York, DC, with maybe a little Chicago thrown in, depending on how right-wing media outlets are framing things at the moment (especially if it's proximate to an election, which past data indicate is when the usual right-wing media suspects curiously amplify their coverage of "urban" crime).[10]

This was before the twenty-four-hour cable news cycle, the internet, and social media. This was years ahead of anybody having the lizard-brain genius to issue the imperative "Make America Great Again" from a red baseball hat. This was, indeed, about a more basic American Christian nationalism, which, out in the proverbial middle of nowhere, was cut off from communication with a great deal of the contemporary world (indeed, unless one had a satellite dish, the few scraps of television we had relied on clear weather). This was unlike the new Christian nationalism, which, despite still preferring remote locales away from Democratic power structures with visible racial minorities, is nowadays quite well plugged into a coordinated and increasingly empowered apparatus networking a not-so-silent not-quite majority in small towns throughout the nation. Nonetheless, political coverage in the charmingly quaint media of the time still pierced my six-year-old consciousness, leading me to process the experience of my racial trauma in Metaline against an incongruous and almost humorous backdrop—the Democratic Party's 1988 presidential primary election.

Though my grasp on the peripheral context was admittedly dim, I vividly remember watching some long-lost news report talking about the democratic candidates, Michael Dukakis and Jesse Jackson. A great deal might've been uncertain for me, but I did know, though, that my mom was white and my father was Black, just like Dukakis was white and Jackson was Black.

Against the background of my early, sometimes traumatic experiences, I was just beginning to understand that Blacks existed on a second tier in America as a "race" subjected to what I'd eventually learn to call treatment like mine—"racism." Drawing this little bit of nascent factual content together, it was then from some combination of racial trauma and imagination that I cobbled together what my six-year-old mind took to be a completely plausible narrative to help me figure out the apparent opposition between the two contenders for the presidency, which I knew was a pretty big deal.

I told myself that these men were fighting to see who was going to control the country, even if I couldn't possibly understand what that meant. However, I didn't think that it would be just one of these men—Jackson or Dukakis—in charge of America. Rather, I thought that it was going to be one of these *races* calling the shots. I thought that if Jackson won, Black people like my father and his family would be in control and would no longer be in a position of inferiority. I thought that if Dukakis won, then the status quo of white superiority would remain (and to think that my six-year-old imagination reached such conclusions without even factoring in Republicans).

In any case, I immediately became worried. I didn't know what I was. What would happen if Jackson won? What if Dukakis won? Would I win either way since I had parents and blood on both sides? Or would I be excluded because I was neither Black nor white in a full and complete way? I needed to know who I was, so that I would know where to situate myself in the great impending social upheaval of which I was all too certain.

After expressing these fears, my mother explained to me, how shall I say, the intricacies of American politics (on a level that I could comprehend). In any case, even though the extravagant imagined danger of a race war started by executive order faded away, the question of my identity remained. I had only exaggerated the immediate importance of the question of my racial identity in my make-believe situation, but the question itself had basis in reality. My place within this thing called *race* was not clear to me, which in some regards remains true today.

Even though I've since become accustomed to American society and its rule that one drop of Black blood means that a person *is* Black, I for myself, cannot deny that my mother and her whiteness are a part of me, even if an unsettling number of her white family members more specifically and white compatriots more generally do like W. E. B. Du Bois's "tall newcomer" and refuse me "peremptorily, with a glance."[11] Just like Du Bois, I also experience a strange "double consciousness," seeing myself one way and seeing others see me another way, and having to reconcile the two views while struggling my way through new adventures in cognitive dissonance in the course of living life.[12] So even today, the question "What am I, really?" haunts me in all those situations that pull at the tension between how the public and I differ on how we regard race as a whole and my race more personally.

So, what's the takeaway from these remembrances of things past supposed to be? Is the foregoing nothing more than pseudo-academic navel-gazing? Or is there something worth learning from all of this?

Well, there was, in fact, a lesson for me and, I'd submit, something to be learned more broadly here. As regards my own personal lesson, I didn't realize it at the time, but the racist children of this Christian nationalist backwater who assaulted me were teaching me some real philosophy, particularly as regards the finer points of Hegel's master-slave dialectic in concurrence with Frantz Fanon. How so?

I learned from my assailants that, despite the fig-leaf rhetoric, white separatist and white supremacist strands within Christian nationalism are really just a cover. What I learned in fits and starts with fists and snarls, Fanon articulates with proper words in a searing critique of Hegel's famous master-slave narrative:

> I hope I have shown that here the master differs basically from the master described by Hegel. For Hegel there is reciprocity; here the master laughs at the consciousness of the slave. What he wants from the slave is not recognition but work.
> In the same way, the slave here is in no way identifiable with the slave who loses himself in the object and finds in his work the source of his liberation.
> The Negro wants to be like the master.
> Therefore he is less independent than the Hegelian slave.
> In Hegel the slave turns away from the master and turns toward the object. Here the slave turns toward the master and abandons the object.[13]

A full analysis of Hegel's fascinating yet confounding dialectic isn't needed here; the basics are as follows. For Hegel, writing on an abstract level about nonspecific human spirit from early 1800s Prussia, those in control (collectively "the master") eventually lose themselves in seeking validation from those whom they control as mere objects (collectively "the slave"), while those who are controlled or enslaved eventually find a truer, freer sense of themselves through laboring on objects (a view that seems to anticipatorily endorse the Nazi *Arbeit macht frei* credo). Meanwhile, Fanon, a Martinican psychotherapist active in the middle part of the 1900s, sought to diagnose the madness of racism over a century later by using practical observation to correct and extend the valuable yet often misguided theories of white philosophers and psychologists to account for the Black condition. For Fanon, Hegel has it wrong and real-world white folk in control neither require nor seek approval of the Black folk whom they control, while Black folk continually seek validation, not in objects, but in the eyes of the white subjects who control them.

I learned this lesson too. I learned that, at its heart, extreme American Christian nationalism of the sort I saw on display in Metaline, and which we can all see in the more diffuse variety prominent nationwide nowadays, doesn't want validation from people like me. With a variety of mechanisms in place preventing the kind of subjection experienced during slavery and in Jim Crow days, Black people are of little use to the kind of white people who are invested in exercising control (which thankfully is far from all white people). For these would-be controllers, Black people who no longer fulfill a desire, like the slaves or indentured sharecroppers of yore, just need to go away. These people want me and people like me eliminated one way or the other. Most of the time this means simply wanting all people with melanin and their cultures gone somewhere else not near. This desire to eliminate me is largely manifest in exclusionary calls ("Go away, n-----," said a potential neighbor to me while I was house hunting in Cleveland's city limits in 2020) and/or visible consternation with me dating white people (i.e., relatives of the consternated). But every so often this isn't enough, and I hear a call like the "Die, n-----, die!" I remember from Metaline from someone who wants to eliminate me by any physically violent means necessary simply for having the temerity to exist.

This situation is, in microcosm, what's going on with the widespread phenomenon known as "eliminationism." This term was popularized by Daniel Jonah Goldhagen in *Worse Than War: Genocide, Eliminationism, and the Ongoing Assault on Humanity*. In unpacking the term, Goldhagen establishes that eliminationism underlies a variety of phenomena like genocide, where "the desire to eliminate peoples or groups should be understood to be the overarching category and the core act."[14]

My experiences, first in Metaline and then usually in more subtle forms elsewhere, show me that this desire to eliminate groups, to eliminate the Other is real. This desire often peaks when the ability to fulfill other desires ceases to be a possibility (how many men, now going under the name "incel," give into violent hatred of *all* women after one or a few experiences of being rejected by individual women?). This desire is seldom coherent, not necessarily settling on a single mode of eliminating this Other perceived as useless.

Goldhagen details how eliminationism encompasses a number of different approaches, different means, laying out a fivefold classification composed of transformation, repression, expulsion, prevention of reproduction, and extermination, which are all "different technical solutions to the perceived problem of dealing with unwanted or putatively threatening groups, to fulfilling the most fundamental desire of somehow getting rid of such groups."[15]

Extending this paradigm in light of "Goldhagen focus[ing] almost solely on the Holocaust and the virulently anti-Semitic form of eliminationism that took root in Europe prior to World War II,"[16] long-time documenter of Pacific Northwest extremism David Neiwert examines how eliminationism is prevalent in many facets of American life generally. To help make this claim, Neiwert sets forth a narrow definition of eliminationism, noting that two factors distinguish it from other hyperbolic political speech, namely:

1. [Eliminationism] is *focused on an enemy within*, people who constitute entire blocs of the citizen populace.
2. [Eliminationism] advocates the excision and extermination of those entire blocs by violent or civil means.[17]

Now, I might have been a child, and my reading of the situation may have been imperfect, but I did correctly perceive eliminationism in the air in Metaline. I did pick up on the threat of elimination with racialized elections in America, even if I misconstrued the details and interpreted the

Jackson-Dukakis primary as portent of a coming race war. However, I had the excuse of being six and scared in the aftermath of physical harm. That doesn't mean that I'm the only one coming to such conclusions, as Neiwert lays out in a survey of views of people attending a pro-McCain (anti-Obama) rally in the weeks before 2008's decisive election, with actual grownups likely to vote, who freely voice their own twisted version of my traumatized, immature fear. To wit:

> I'm afraid if he wins, the blacks will take over. He's not a Christian! This is a Christian nation! What is our country gonna end up like?[18]

Admittedly, this is just an individual's view. Or is it? My past, with of those raised voices and raised fists, instilled a *justifiable* fear of being eliminated by American Christian nationalists who *unjustifiably* see themselves as under attack and therefore warranted in striking first to eliminate the misperceived threat. This perverse way of thinking, which I once thought confined to obscure stretches of the America like Metaline, is now trafficked in both darker corners of the internet and under bright lights on Fox News.

As such, eliminationism has answered for me part of the question of who/what I am. I'm the sort of person who is targeted for elimination, and I can't eliminate that fact from me, no matter how much I might want to. Accordingly, the eliminationism of my youth and of today helps to settle, for me at least, a philosophical debate concerning the reality of race, where ultimately I am compelled to take a stand against philosophical positions that seek, out of good intentions, to eliminate talk of racial identity as being counterproductive. The very real threat of eliminationism means that I cannot stomach eliminativism. "What am I, really?" indeed.

Eliminativism is an awkward (though apt) label used to describe philosophical paradigms that deny the reality of race as a phenomenon and seek to eliminate talk of racial identity due to the harm that it brings on balance. Eliminativists oppose the unforgivably antisocial and sometimes violent nature of racist eliminationists; they share a label only by way of coincidence. Eliminativists tend to come from the other part of the political spectrum, where a commitment to left-wing ideals and a future beyond the harms of race as we currently know it motivates a well-intentioned resistance to engaging talk of racial identity at all, especially when race has no biological basis and is instead constructed and often incoherent (as mixed-race identity makes painfully clear). Such eliminativist reasoning is at work where prominent mixed-race philosopher Naomi Zack argues that "race resembles astrology in this way. If you know someone's birth date and the place and hour of her birth, she can be astrologically classified," before ultimately casting aspersions on both fields by concluding that "race shares with astrology the absence of justification for its typology."[19]

This general view leads perhaps the most well-known eliminativist working in the area of philosophy of race in the early decades of 2000, K. Anthony Appiah, to cast doubt on the efficacy of talk of racial identity. Paul C. Taylor, perhaps most prominent in applying the label to Appiah, whom he directly calls "a racial eliminativist," notes that Appiah "believes that races do not exist, that acting as if they do is metaphysically indefensible and morally dangerous, and, as a result, that eliminating 'race' from our metaphysical vocabularies is an important step toward the right, or a better—that is to say, a rational and just—world-view."[20]

Appiah is not a fool and, thus, is careful in not rejecting race outright, especially since racial identity needs to be employed to analyze and explain how history has unfolded into the here and now. However, while conceding this point, he cautions that "there is a danger in making racial identities too central to our conceptions of ourselves; while there is a place for racial identities in a world shaped by racism," arguing that "if we are to move beyond racism we shall have, in the end, to move beyond current racial identities."[21]

Appiah is quite insistent that racial identity can easily become confining and, thus, a hindrance to the kind of world beyond present-day racial injustice that he seeks. Racial identities, which are already incoherent, can go beyond describing people to setting forth normative expectations, which are likely to lead to disagreement—after all, what's the one right way to be Black?[22] He follows up by observing,

> What demanding respect for people as blacks or as gays requires is that there be some scripts that go with being an African-American or having same-sex desires. There will be proper ways of being black and gay: there will be expectations to be met; demands will be made. It is at this point that someone who takes autonomy seriously will want to ask whether we have not replaced one kind of tyranny with another.[23]

Appiah thus ends up showing his clear disdain for collective identities that "'go imperial,' dominating not only people of other identities but also the other identities, whose shape is exactly what makes each of us what we individually and distinctively are."[24]

However well intentioned and well reasoned such an eliminativist approach may be, my issue is this: The child's fist that attempts to make good on that "Die, n-----, die!" threat doesn't care one iota what academics might say about my status as "n-----" being a social construct into which I've been thrown. The child's punching fists from my 1980s horror-show care about the fine points of eliminativist racial antirealism about as much as that same grown-up assailant's still-childish mind likely does nowadays, which is to say not one damn bit. Though I very much subscribe to the premise that race is a pervasive construct, the childhood lessons in applied philosophy of race that I received upside my head from a playground mob who wanted to eliminate me resulted in me being unable to make the leap from that premise to the conclusion that race should be eliminated from discourse.

Christian nationalism, at least as I experienced it in a small yet overly influential part of America, is part of who I am. I am my travels as well as my travails. My experiences, though fleeting and immaterial, have a real-world material effect. As such, these experiences of race in America, like my bodily limbs, cannot be cut from me without a great deal of pain. Does this mean by implication that making peace with myself means making peace with my time in Metaline and the specter of its eternal recurrence, as Nietzsche's Zarathustra would bid?[25] To put it another way, reiterating the words of that eighth-grade student: Would I go back there?

Well, no, but that's simply because I don't need to. It's not necessary for me to define my identity in terms of resistance and resentment of past Christian nationalism. Everything from that time that would weigh me down, what Nietzsche's Zarathustra might rue as the spirit of gravity continues to confront me, with a twist. What Nietzsche calls the eternal recurrence of the same is well captured by the phrase "the more things change, the more they stay the same," where the challenge is to make peace with repetition of the "now" and thereby affirm this present moment and all of the horrible past that led to it as necessary. This challenge is what vexes me every time that I end up running into my past when I actually want to cross the threshold of "now" into a novel future of new values.

Wherever I go (in America, at least), Metaline is already there. I keep running into the bullies of my childhood from Metaline, but in a different guise. Sometimes, it's a voice on the television bleating about how books like mine should be banned, eliminated from discourse. Sometimes, it's some white woman's dad trying to drive a wedge lest we reproduce, eliminating reproductive possibility. Sometimes, it's a voice wanting to eliminate my proximity as a possible neighbor. And sometimes, usually at places serving alcohol, it's somebody threatening everything from an ass-kicking to a straight-up killing, so as to eliminate me from the claimed spaces of rural/suburban America. Usually, things are toned down and more subtle than this last example, but it doesn't take an especially keen ear to hear howling calls for elimination recurring just the same.

With all this talk of race and elimination, feeling like an actual eliminated bowel movement because of skin color and its aftermath is not something I'm willing to abide. So, what might I offer as a path to something less shitty, if I'm committed to some variety of racial realism against eliminativist antirealism regarding race? Well, I similarly believe that race is demonstrably an absurd and harmful construction, as mentioned. I believe that it is also very much materially effective in our social reality—in the geography of where we live, in the health and educational conditions inexorably tied to that racial geography, in the intergenerational wealth, or lack thereof, that springs from the real conditions of real estate. Race, as an operative concept over and above anything given, in this regard is little different from gender, from class, from nation. Racism and hierarchical classification based on visual cues is a tool that extends the body politic, and it's not so easy to remove even a vestigial part of our collective body. What we're ultimately talking about is human nature, and we're naturally artificial, and this very much includes the artifice of race. Hence, while I agree on the diagnosis that humanity's afflicted by the unreality of race, I disagree with my humanities doctor colleagues on the prescription.

My goal is not to endlessly relitigate the past of racial eliminationism. However, I'm not, on that basis, inclined to live my life in terms of a future which may well never come, and, thereby to shed my messy, incoherent, and sometimes harmful racial identity, as eliminativists seem to wish. I reckon that, with race, as it is with most things, the challenge is living in the present. Thanks to a child's insight, I have slightly more clarity as to what that means. I likely won't go back to Metaline, true, but neither will I expend good energy trying to escape it.

That said, my disagreement is partial and mitigated. My grimly pragmatic view on confronting, rather than denying, the constructed reality of race must concede the point that a variety of strategies need to be deployed over the long term to bring about some kind of change. It may be that, for me, a world beyond race remains nothing more than a regulative ideal, and that's okay. The motive force of this ideal is significant if it makes people do something rather than nothing, even if that "something" might not make demonstrable conceptual sense to me personally (which is why philosophers distinguish between ideals and concepts anyway).

A child asking if I'd go back to Metaline led me to realize that it's not necessary to set aside the past to focus on racial injustice here and now. Focusing on racial injustice here and now will, inevitably, bring the eternally recurrent past to the fore as needed. Metaline's not going anywhere; it's embedded in America after 2016. I'm not going anywhere either, and that means that I'm certainly not retreating into either a painful past or an imagined future. I might still not be perfectly clear on what I am really, but thanks to a child's question and the reflection it occasioned, I have newfound certainty of the general finding that race as we now know it cannot be eliminated. Moreover, I know on a personal level in a way that I didn't before that I need to deal with the question of what *I am* as it's given, which means in the present tense.

NOTES

1. Carter, "Resurgent Hate Groups Have Long History in Washington State, Northwest."
2. Chan and Ventura, *White Power and American Neoliberal Culture*, 28.
3. Chan and Ventura, *White Power and American Neoliberal Culture*, 32, 42.
4. Carter, "Resurgent Hate Groups Have Long History in Washington State, Northwest."
5. Martz, "Klan Marching Staunchly to Ultra-Right."
6. Carter, "Resurgent Hate Groups Have Long History in Washington State, Northwest"; "The Murder of Alan Berg in Denver."
7. Read, "In Eastern Washington, State Rep. Matt Shea Faces Backlash against White Nationalism."
8. Carter, "Resurgent Hate Groups Have Long History in Washington State, Northwest."
9. Carter, "Resurgent Hate Groups Have Long History in Washington State, Northwest."
10. Bump, "What's the Non-Obvious Reason Fox News Is Talking about Crime More?"
11. Du Bois, *The Souls of Black Folk*, 8.
12. Du Bois, *The Souls of Black Folk*, 8.
13. Fanon, *Black Skin, White Masks*, 172n8; Hegel, *The Phenomenology of Spirit*, 111–19 [§178–96].
14. Goldhagen, *Worse Than War*, 14.
15. Goldhagen, *Worse Than War*, 14–19.
16. Neiwert, *The Eliminationists*, 14.
17. Neiwert, *The Eliminationists*, 12.
18. Neiwert, *The Eliminationists*, 5; *cf.* "Misconceptions of Obama Fuel Republican Campaign."
19. Zack, *Philosophy of Science and Race*, 108.
20. Taylor, "Appiah's Uncompleted Argument," 103.
21. Appiah, "Race, Culture, Identity," 32.
22. Appiah, "Race, Culture, Identity," 92, 97.
23. Appiah, "Race, Culture, Identity," 99.
24. Appiah, "Race, Culture, Identity," 103.
25. *Cf.* Nietzsche, *Thus Spake Zarathustra*.

BIBLIOGRAPHY

Appiah, K. Anthony. "Race, Culture, Identity: Misunderstood Connections." In *Color Consciousness: The Political Morality of Race*. Princeton, NJ: Princeton University Press, 1998.

Bump, Philip. "What's the Non-Obvious Reason Fox News Is Talking about Crime More?" *Washington Post*. October 26, 2022. http://www.wapo.com/politics/2022/10/26/crime-midterm-elections-news-coverage-fox-news/.

Carter, Mike. "Resurgent Hate Groups Have Long History in Washington State, Northwest." *Seattle Times*. August 24, 2017. https://www.seattletimes.com/seattle-news/law-justice/resurgent-hate-groups-have-long-history-in-washington-state-northwest/.

Chan, Edward K., and Patricia Ventura. *White Power and American Neoliberal Culture*. Berkeley: University of California Press, 2023.

Du Bois, W. E. B. *The Souls of Black Folk*. Edited by Brent Hayes Edwards. Oxford: Oxford University Press, 2007.

Fanon, Frantz. *Black Skin, White Masks*. Translated by Charles Lam Markmann. London: Pluto Books, 2008.

Goldhagen, Daniel Jonah. *Worse Than War: Genocide, Eliminationism, and the Ongoing Assault on Humanity*. New York: PublicAffairs, 2009.

Hegel, Georg Wilhelm Friedrich. *The Phenomenology of Spirit*. Edited by A. V. N. Miller. Oxford: Oxford University Press, 1977.

Martz, Ron. "Klan Marching Staunchly to Ultra-Right." *Atlanta Journal-Constitution*. March 17, 1985. https://www.ajc.com/news/state--regional/klan-marching-staunchly-ultra-right/gb4KdOXWWS8211Hi28TLAM/amp.html.

"Misconceptions of Obama Fuel Republican Campaign." *Al Jazeera English*. October 13, 2008. https://www.youtube.com/watch?v=zRqcfqiXCX0.

"The Murder of Alan Berg in Denver: 25 Years Later." *Denver Post*. May 6, 2016. https://www.denverpost.com/2009/06/17/the-murder-of-alan-berg-in-denver-25-years-later/.

Neiwert, David. *The Eliminationists: How Hate Talk Radicalized the American Right*. London: Routledge, 2016.

Nietzsche, Friedrich. *Thus Spake Zarathustra*. Translated by Graham Parkes. Oxford: Oxford University Press, 2008.

Read, Richard. "In Eastern Washington, State Rep. Matt Shea Faces Backlash against White Nationalism." *Los Angeles Times*. November 27, 2019. https://www.latimes.com/world-nation/story/2019-11-27/matt-shea-spokane-washington-white-nationalism.

Taylor, Paul C. "Appiah's Uncompleted Argument: W. E. B. Du Bois and the Reality of Race." *Social Theory and Practice* 26, no. 1 (2000): 103–28.

Zack, Naomi. *Philosophy of Science and Race*. New York: Routledge, 2002.

Chapter 16

Victims of the Cross

Violence and Apocalyptic Discourse in *Christian Nationalism*

Sheldon George

On August 3, 2022, the Christian banner became the first and only religious flag to be flown in the Plaza of Boston City Hall, the seat of Boston city government. Five years earlier, in 2017, Camp Constitution, an organization with a mission to "enhance understanding" of America's "Judeo-Christian moral heritage" (Camp Constitution, "Mission," par. 1), was refused permission by the City of Boston to fly the flag in commemoration of Constitution Day, September 17. The hoisting of the flag for two hours high above the Boston City Hall Plaza in 2022 was mandated by a unanimous US Supreme Court ruling. Though the flag is now the only religious banner ever allowed to fly over City Hall, the court ruled that Camp Constitution had been victims in 2017 of "Boston's come-one-come-all practice," which approved flags—including the LGBTQ+ Pride flag—without exception, "except, that is, for [this] petitioners' flag" (US Supreme Court, 3). The court found that the City of Boston had "exclud[ed] private speech based on 'religious viewpoint'" and Camp Constitution had therefore been a victim of "impermissible viewpoint discrimination" (3).

Whatever the validity or fairness of the court's ruling, what interests me in this case is its relation to the pervasive notion of white victimhood that inflames Christian nationalist movements. The court's decision lends credibility to Camp Constitution's argument that "every viewpoint was permissible to go on this public forum flagpole except a Christian viewpoint," and that it was "because of one word in the application" that their request was denied, "the word 'Christian' that preceded the word 'flag'" (Camp

Constitution, "Christian Flag Raising Symbolizes Freedom," par. 5). Recent scholarship has pointed to notions of white victimhood as an activating factor catalyzing and "strengthen[ing] the tie between religious ideology and support for violence" (Armaly et al., 944). Of course, we have seen this violence in such incidents as the storming of the Capitol on January 6, 2021. The insurgent crowd included Christian nationalists who believed they were called to the Capitol by both President Donald Trump and God, with figures such as presidential spiritual adviser Paula White describing "demonic plans and networks" working on Joe Biden's behalf, and author and radio host Eric Metaxas stating that "this is God's battle even more than our battle" (Manseau, par. 6).

Christian nationalism in and of itself does not directly lead to violence. What generates this violence is an apocalyptic rhetoric produced, as Armaly and others have argued, by influential social figures who help exacerbate "perceived victimhood," reinforce "racial and religious identity," and promote "conspiratorial information sources" (938). I wish to approach a psychoanalytic understanding of Christian nationalism as an exaltation of whiteness that deploys apocalyptic rhetoric to establish violence as a means of bringing white victimhood to an end. My suggestion is that it is not primarily religion that today binds together violent members of Christian nationalist groups but an apocalyptic sense of the death of whiteness itself in our contemporary moment. While Christian nationalism merges "American and Christian group membership" around a "set of political-theological beliefs" (938), the apocalyptic, racist, and conspiratorial rhetoric that often surrounds the movement has allowed for racial unification across religious lines. Just as Camp Constitution celebrates the Judeo-Christian heritage of the nation, Trump supporters held Jericho Marches in Washington in December 2020 that were aimed at imitating the biblical story of the Israelite army that surrounded the walled city of Jericho and blew the shofar as God destroyed its defenses. It is these biblical final battles and the apocalyptic rhetoric of Christian nationalism that allow us to understand its move toward violence.

Pervasive around white identity today is not only a sense of victimhood but also a sense of loss. The violence of our contemporary moment is agitated by the perceived loss of whiteness as what Lacanian psychoanalysis would call an ego ideal or a representation of a unified self. Lacanian theory shows that the psyche avoids the traumatic fact of its own fragmentation. Far from seeing ourselves as split subjects, with an unconscious and a conscious mind, we fantasize the kind of wholeness promoted by the Cartesian cogito: "I think therefore I am." Where much of Western philosophy has been rooted in the notion of a unified thinking subject whose being is united with his conscious mind, psychoanalysis recognizes an unconscious that often thinks in the place of the subject, an unconscious that intrudes on consciousness through acts such as parapraxis that insist upon the existence of a subjective self that is elided from active cognition.

Whiteness, I argue, seeks to mask the loss of this elided subjectivity. But what constantly threatens our current moment is an unveiling of whiteness as pure discourse, as a fantasy construct with binding psychic import. The discourse of whiteness has secured psychic fantasies of wholeness for "white subjects" for centuries. The very concept of racial identity as marked by skin color is bound to a Christian religious past emerging during the Holy Crusades, which began in 1095 when Pope Urban II called the devout to take up arms against Turkish Muslims. This was an apocalyptic war. The popular belief of the period was that the judgment day would soon arrive: After being bound for a thousand years, Satan would be set loose upon the earth, and the antichrist's final defeat by Jesus would bring about the end of the world; simultaneously, the death of nonbelievers would hasten the coming of Jesus's kingdom. The ensuing Crusades against brown-skinned nonbelievers marked a transition when the blackness of one's skin came to be equated with the darkness of one's soul (Dalal, 142) and, additionally, "resulted in Europe starting to define itself as Christian and white" (151).

Soldiers of the Crusades fought for the same cross that is featured on the Christian flag flown by Camp Constitution. The Christian flag is a white banner with a blue square at its top-left corner, at the center of which is a red cross. Created in the early 1900s as a symbol for all Christians, the flag repurposes the colors of the American flag, aligning whiteness with "purity and peace" while symbolizing "fidelity" through the color blue and invoking "Christ's blood sacrifice" through the red cross (Coffman). The more conservative adherents to the flag make the following pledge: "I pledge allegiance to the Christian flag, and to the Savior for whose kingdom it stands; one Savior, crucified, risen, and coming again with life and liberty to all who believe" (Coffman). What the flag and its cross thus promise is the remanifestation of a lost divinity and the return of lost liberty. This remanifestation allows for a kind of forestalled homecoming, a full emergence of a purified whiteness that is longed for in Christian nationalist discourse. Accordingly, Camp Constitution, after winning its case, celebrated a reacquired communal sense of national and racial identity similar to that granted by the Crusade's production of whiteness. From the perspective of Camp Constitution, the Supreme Court's ruling ensured that "the Christian community, the community of faith, across this whole country are not constitutional orphans" but "full heirs" to the nation and its constitution ("Christian Flag Raising Symbolizes Freedom," par. 9).

This rhetoric of a white-striving against homelessness has been a constant part of American national discourse. It has aligned itself in seminal historical moments with a rhetorical construction of white Americans as a dying race, a construction that supplants Native American genocide with a figuring of the death of the true modern natives of America, white men. While the initiating language of the Naturalization Act of 1790 restricted national citizenship to whites of "good standing," the establishment of American national identity as a white identity depended upon the discursive and literal death of Native Americans. In the realm of discourse, we see this in the novels of seminal American writers like James Fenimore Cooper, whose popular novels in the early 1800s seem to mourn the passing of the *Last of the Mohicans* but truly celebrate their replacement with white American society. By the 1960s, the Native American had been subjected to a discursive death, and authors like Ken Kesey, in *One Flew Over the Cuckoo's Nest*, could depict American society as an insane asylum run by women nurses and Black orderlies. Here, it became no longer necessary to mourn the Native American, for it is a Native American patient who flies from the asylum while the white protagonist dies from a lobotomy. This death of whiteness is the true tragedy of the modern world, it would seem, and it is what contemporary authors like the Trump-backed winner of the 2022 Ohio Senate election, J. D. Vance, bemoans in his book *Hillbilly Elegy*.

The power of whiteness has always been its ability to define reality. Lacanian psychoanalytic theory allows us to see this. Lacanian theory describes the human psyche as composed of three intersecting "registers." The register of the Symbolic coincides with the world of language, where it is language that grants subjects a conscious and discursive sense of self, literally providing access to the "I" of subjectivity. The register of the Real is where all that escapes language finds a place for itself in the subject's psyche. It is the register of our psychic lack, to which the traumas of our lived lives are relegated, the exclusions that must be excluded for the psyche to maintain itself. The Imaginary is the register of our fantasies, which allow us to dream our invulnerability to loss and lack while also plaguing us with a constant psychic sense of fragmentation and inadequacy. What whiteness creates, I argue, is a suturing of the registers of the Symbolic and the Imaginary over the Real, such that the fantasies of wholeness generated by the Imaginary are reinforced for white subjects by the Symbolic discourses of whiteness in ways that ensure white people's superiority, their ostensive lack of lack.[1]

This suturing is what we see in slavery, where slave masters claimed exclusive right to define reality for slaves and themselves. But something changed during Reconstruction, as slaves gained their freedom and asserted a right to define their own identity. Whiteness was now overtly threatened in its ability to mask lack, and whites responded with an aggression that Lacan may call *aggressivity*, the aggression that emerges upon a subject's recognition of the fracturing of their ego image. It is this fracturing of whiteness that justified the wide-scale lynchings that occurred in this era, which, by one estimate, amounted to more than one hundred per year in the 1880s and 1890s (Wells-Barnett, 3). These lynchings brought a new symbolic meaning for the cross that was extolled in the Crusades. As Klan members burned crosses along with Black bodies, African Americans took on a status that the scholar James H. Cone has urged us to see as paralleling that of the sacrificed Jesus.

Cone aligns the cross with "the quintessential symbol of black oppression in America," the lynching tree (xiii). He argues that "until we can see the cross and the lynching tree together, until we can identify Christ with a 'recrucified' black body hanging from a lynching tree, there can be no genuine understanding of Christian identity in America, and no deliverance from the brutal legacy of slavery and white supremacy" (xv). Cone acknowledges whiteness's masking of its own brutality and violence, a drive for destruction that is veiled by the suturing of the Imaginary and the white Symbolic. This violence positions African Americans as the historical bearers of the cross. Since the biblical Simon of Cyrene—"the African"—took up Jesus's cross when Jesus was too weak to carry it on the path to Calvary, Blacks have continued to "carry the crosses of slavery, segregation, and lynchings" (48). And they do so while subjected to the free rein of whites' destructive psychic drives.

Freud himself came to recognize the presence of these drives in the psyches of white men after witnessing the violence of the First World War. Freud divulges, "We were . . . quite ready to believe that for some time to come there would be wars between primitive and civilized nations and between those divided by color," but "we expected that the great ruling nations of the white race, the leaders of mankind . . . would find some other way of settling their differences" (*Reflections*, 4–5). The violence that Freud now saw was not limited to "primitives" who forced him to acknowledge a drive toward death in all subjects, a drive that makes even the proximity called for in Christian cries for the love of one's neighbor a catalyst to violence. Such proximity, shows Freud, "tempts" subjects to "satisfy their aggressiveness" on their neighbor, to "exploit his capacity for work without compensation, to use him sexually without his consent, to seize his possession, to humiliate him, to cause him pain, to torture and to kill him" (*Civilization*, 69).

Such aggressiveness is what whiteness both expresses and masks. And Christianity has long facilitated this masking for many whites. Freud is again useful when he reads Christianity as a means of guilty "atonement," through the figured death of the son, Jesus, for man's oedipal desires to kill the father (*Totem*, 191). Freud's theory ties modern civilization to a "great crime" committed at the psychic level of our desires (186), a crime that causes us to erect civilization and its "laws of prohibition" out of guilt over wishes that ever threaten to drive us toward new patricidal and transgressive acts (178). It is such a transgressive act that unified the mob as they marched in unison into the Capitol. But, contra Freud, the factor of guilt does not emerge when the chant of the insurrectionists is, "Whose house? Our house!" The unifying factor of race makes this transgression an act of homecoming, echoing the experiences of the members of Camp Constitution, who are reclaimed from their orphanage through the ruling of the Supreme Court.

Here it is not Freud, but Lacan's understanding of religion that is most illuminating of our current moment. Lacan's focus in addressing religion is not on the cross but, more precisely, on the image of the crucifixion. For Lacan, the crucifixion is the divinization of an act of atrocity, and it has been "crucifying man in holiness for centuries" (*Ethics*, 262). Lacan's suggestion is that the crucifixion stagnates man's desires, fixing desire at the limit of an unimaginable beyond that we both crave and dread. This beyond, in which Christians position their God, represents the impossible state of completion and wholeness we each long for at the psychic level. For Lacan, it is this longing that allows the atrocity of the crucifixion to dominate desire. The subject is fixated at the place of the crucifixion, suggests Lacan, and although their desires are thus crucified in holiness, the subject remains at a protective distance from the beyond. But what racial violence involves, I suggest, is a breaching of the limit of the atrocious, an attempt at attaining to the beyond itself.

We sense something of this grasping toward the beyond in the apocalyptic rhetoric of Christian nationalists and other Trump supporters. During a December 2021 Prayer Rally, the radio personality Alex Jones declared, "Jesus Christ is king, not David Rockefeller, not Bill Gates, not Barack Obama, not Joe Biden, but Jesus Christ is king! And God gave us and rose up Donald Trump to stand against the enemy and draw out the enemy. So as dark as some of these days are, understand this is the beginning of the great revival before the Antichrist comes" (Badash, pa.r 5). Not only does this rhetoric echo the religious discourse of the Crusades, with its talk of the antichrist, but it modernizes this discourse through the presentation of a new savior in the figure of Trump. Jones proclaims, "Christ's crucifixion was not our defeat, it was our greatest victory!" (par. 11), and though Trump is not Jesus, "with Trump [as president], it [was] as close as it got" (par. 16). Here Trump takes on a similar function to Jesus, catalyzing the desires of Christian nationalists while remaining distinct from Jesus. Jones declares, "So we hold up President Trump before the creator of the universe. And we say, 'Thank you for trying to send us a deliverer, though he's unperfect as we are. But we pray for him. And we pray for America, and we hold him up in this hour of peril'" (par. 26).

At the level of discourse, what Trump allows is not the stagnation of desire created by a Jesus who crucifies Christians in holiness, but a victimhood that calls for transgression of all established limits to apocalyptically manifest the beyond. Rather than stagnate desire, Trump agitates it in ways that are psychically destructive. Jones proclaims that "the state has no jurisdiction over any of us" because "our relationship with God is sacred and is eternal" (Badash, par. 13). This freedom from the law places Christian nationalists in a fraught relation to psychic lack. As the discourse of the Symbolic sutures over the Real with Imaginary fantasies of racial whiteness, the white Christian nationalist is dominated by racial fantasies. He fanaticizes a superiority that is belied by the violence he brutally exercises on his neighbor. When the object that determines desire directs us to the beyond, all moral limitations can be breached. And when an Archbishop of the Catholic Church, one Carlo Maria Viganò, can assert to a crowd of Trump supporters at the Jericho March, "We are the silent army of the children of Light, the humble ranks who overthrow evil by invoking God," we are back at the Crusades of the Dark Ages that gave free rein to the darkest of drives (par. 6).

Whiteness unleashes man's destructive psychic drives, the ones that Freud identified beyond the homeostasis of the pleasure principle. Our drive to destroy is aimed as much at the other as it is at the self. The destructive drive breaches the limits of our pleasures to introduce pain as the true motivator of our actions. Lacan describes the transgressive pleasure of the drive as "evil," noting that it "involves suffering for my neighbor" but also for me (*Ethics*, 184). A subject can achieve only personal suffering when they cannot access and express their drives in the sublimations of culturally appropriate expressions, when the fantasies that comprise their Symbolic mask the true nature of their lack. The other becomes the scapegoat, fueling fantasies of a victimhood that steers the subject clear of both their social and their psychic realities. Such fantasies are what generate the conspiracies of a discourse that defines democrats as satanic pedophiles and pushes a man like twenty-eight-year-old Edgar Maddison Welch to enter a pizza restaurant with an assault rifle intent on investigating rumors that the owners run a pedophile ring from the store basement with the help of Bill and Hillary Clinton (Samuelson).

The Christian defense of Trump has subjected Christian nationalists to massive delusional realities in which Trump stands as the last line of defense against the Satanists, and his supporters become soldiers in God's army. These delusions are what root the violence of a January 6, in which insurrectionists sought to "stop the steal." What was stolen from these insurrectionists was a glorious whiteness that rooted fantasies of white psychic wholeness. Perhaps most visibly through the presidency of Barack Obama, whiteness had lost track in its claims to superiority, and Trump was the savior whose election could bring dignity back to a form of white masculinity that asserted its own beliefs and opinions with utter contempt for others and their views. But what Christian nationalism has achieved in positioning Trump as its savior is an unleashing of a self-destructive drive that is as willing to embrace the Capitol as its reclaimed "house" as it is to ransack and destroy this national home. Here Christian nationalists who saw themselves as victims of a governmental system that no longer prized their heritage could free themselves of the burden of holiness and moral propriety through which their Christianity attempts to crucify them with its restrictions upon their most base desires and drives. Freeing themselves of the burdens of a Christ who preaches love, these supporters unleashed an atrocious violence that, like the crucifixion itself, displayed the true evil at the heart of men's souls.

NOTE

1. See my *Trauma and Race* for a fuller analysis of this suturing.

REFERENCES

Armaly, Miles T., et al. "Christian Nationalism and Political Violence: Victimhood, Racial Identity, Conspiracy, and Support for the Capitol Attacks." *Political Behavior* 44, no. 2 (January 4, 2022): 937–60. https://doi.org/10.1007/s11109-021-09758-y.
Badash, David. "Before the Insurrection, Alex Jones Told MAGAites Biden Is a 'Slave of Satan' Who 'Will Be Removed One Way or Another.'" *Rawstory.com*. February 9, 2021. https://www.rawstory.com/alex-jones-old-magaites-biden-is-a-slave-of-satan-who-will-be-removed-one-way-or-another/.
Camp Constitution. "Christian Flag Raising Symbolizes Freedom from Viewpoint Discrimination in Boston." *Campconstitution.com*. August 4, 2022. http://camp-constitution.net/christian-flag-raising-symbolizes-freedom-from-viewpoint-discrimination-in-boston/.
———. "Mission Statement." *Campconstitution.com*. http://campconstitution.net/mission-statement/.
Coffman, Elesha. "Do You Know the History of the Christian Flag?" *Christianitytoday.com*. August 8, 2008. https://www.christianitytoday.com/history/2008/august/do-you-know-history-of-christian-flag.html.
Cone, James. *The Cross and the Lynching Tree*. Maryknoll, NYk: Orbis Books, 2013.
Dalal, Farhad. *Race, Colour and the Processes of Racialization: New Perspectives from Group Analysis, Psychoanalysis and Sociology*. New York: Routledge, 2002.
Freud, Sigmund. *Civilization and Its Discontents*. Translated by James Strachey. New York: W. W. Norton & Company, 1989.
———. *Reflections on War and Death*. Translated by Dr. A. A. Brill and Alfred B. Kuttner. New York: Moffat, Yard, 1918.
———. *Totem and Taboo*. Translated by James Strachey. New York: Norton, 1989.
George, Sheldon. *Trauma and Race: A Lacanian Study of African American Identity*. Waco, TX: Baylor University Press, 2016.

Lacan, Jacques. *The Seminar of Jacques Lacan, Book VII: The Ethics of Psychoanalysis*. Translated by Dennis Porter. New York: W. W. Norton, 1997.

Manseau, Peter. "Some Capitol Rioters Believed They Answered God's Call, Not Just Trump's." *Washington Post*. February 11, 2021. https://www.washingtonpost.com/outlook/2021/02/11/christian-religion-insurrection-capitol-trump/.

Samuelson, Kate. "What to Know about Pizzagate, the Fake News Story with Real Consequences." *Time*. December 5, 2016. https://time.com/4590255/pizzagate-fake-news-what-to-know/.

US Supreme Court. *Shurtleff et al. v. City of Boston et al*. Supremecourt.gov. October term, 2021. https://www.supremecourt.gov/opinions/21pdf/20-1800_7lho.pdf.

Viganò, Carlo Maria. "Abp. Viganó at Jericho March: We Must Pray 'Truth Will Triumph over Lies, Justice over Abuse and Fraud.'" Online transcript of speech. Lifesitenews.com. March 14, 2020. https://www.lifesitenews.com/opinion/abp-vigano-speech-to-jericho-march/.

Wells-Barnett, Ida B. *On Lynchings*. New Hampshire: Ayer Company, 1991.

Chapter 17

White Solidarity on Campus and the Sin of Neutrality

Elisabeth Vasko

White progressives like me have a hard time making the connection between what happened on January 6, 2021, at the Capitol and what we do in our day-to-day lives.[1] Most White people are only comfortable engaging the problem of race at a distance when there is someone else to blame, Amy Cooper, Donald Trump, Derek Chauvin, or Dylann Roof. We like to see ourselves as exempt in the face of the worst kinds of evil. It is much easier to look away. Sometimes we pretend to be outside observers, neutral parties who can evaluate or judge the merits of good and evil from afar. Yet, this guise of neutrality is not innocent. It is complicit in holding up a system of values and practices that encircle White supremacy.

Ta-Nehisi Coates writes that Trump's presidency and its aftermath were less about Trump himself than "what people would rather not see": a country built on White supremacy.[2] As many have pointed out, Trump won not only the White vote across all classes but also the White Christian vote in 2020. According to the Pew Research Center, approximately seven-in-ten White, non-Hispanic Americans who regularly attend religious services cast a ballot for Trump in 2020.[3] As Isabel Wilkerson notes, numbers like these tell a story about the power of White solidarity. Writing in response to the 2016 election, Wilkerson highlights how White women "disregarded the common needs of women and went against a fellow white woman to vote with their power trait, the white side of their identities to which Trump appealed, rather than help an experienced woman, and themselves, make history."[4] White solidarity, a form of racial bonding, involves White people using their power to protect their station in life and their resources.

Yet, the political arena is hardly the only or even the most common place where White people fail to hold one another accountable in the face of White supremacy, protecting White interests. As Robin DiAngelo illustrates, White solidarity is commonplace in social settings, the workplace, and at home.[5] In educational settings like my own, racial bonding involves networking; it's how you get on the right committees and have your ideas heard in meetings. White solidarity plays a role in determining whether your work is considered credible. White solidarity can also play a role in hiring, promotion, tenure, grant funding, and curriculum design.[6] For students, it plays out on the athletic field, in the classroom, and in the social life on campus. Sometimes, White solidarity determines whether you are seen at all.

To illustrate this phenomenon, I describe a few recent patterns that I have noticed, drawing from my teaching and lived experience at a predominantly White Catholic institution in the midwestern part of the US. Though the stories shared are based on my experience as a White Catholic cisgender female theologian, I do not find them unique to my institution or the individuals involved. (I have removed identifying details.) I share these stories because of their ability to illustrate how Whiteness is performed and encoded within the fabric of normalcy at a predominantly White institution (PWI). In other words, the stories I share are not newsworthy or noteworthy, which is precisely the point. The purpose of this chapter is to further critical theological reflection upon what many might see as ordinary at a PWI. While I write to primarily White educators, I also hope to be in conversation with my Black, Asian, Latine, and Indigenous colleagues so that we can find new ways together toward substantive change.

THE PERFORMANCE OF WHITENESS

Several weeks into the semester, a White male undergraduate student lost self-control during one of my classes in a discussion about systemic racism. The class had been reading a chapter out of Miguel de la Torre's *Reading the Bible from the Margins* to unpack the role of social identity in biblical interpretation. In the text, de la Torre discusses racism in terms of societal norms and gives the following example:

> White privilege makes all whites racist not because of their possible beliefs of superiority but because they benefit from the present social structures; in the same way, I must confess my racism when in Miami because those structures are designed to benefit me. This does not make all whites evil, wicked people; it simply reveals who benefits in society because of race.[7]

The notion that all White people are racist provoked and enraged this student. Raising his voice, he disputed the fact that racism is systemic. Speaking rapidly and forcefully, he professed that affirmative action policies are unfair to White people and that racial profiling does not exist. He pontificated that race does not matter and that White supremacy has nothing to do with hate crimes. Academically, this student's engagement with the course material was problematic on several counts, including failure to support claims with evidence, going outside of the scope of course material, and lack of professional conduct in the classroom. Instead of engaging others, he shut down the conversation through a politics of interruption. Reminiscent of Trump during the 2016 debates with Hillary Clinton, he interrupted the class so many times that we could not continue. When I tried to remind the students of our covenant for learning, I could not do so because he interrupted me so many times that I could not get a word in edgewise. Since it was impossible to continue with a discussion, I prematurely ended the class. I asked to speak to the student afterward.

In the back of the classroom, this student was surrounded by his friends, many of whom shared his belief system. While he "spoke up," some of them nodded in agreement, arms crossed. Others looked down at their phones. After class, I told the student his behavior was unacceptable. He contested this and continued to argue, raising his voice, and following me around the classroom and invading my personal space. He wanted to know where my dean and department chair were so that he could report my teaching. Reflecting on the incident, I knew in advance of the session that the readings would upset a number of the students in the class. I also acknowledge that I continue to grow and learn as an educator when it comes to teaching about race in the classroom. Yet, this was hardly the first time I had taught this material to students of diverse backgrounds who held a range of beliefs. As an educator, I am committed to teaching my students about the intersection between race and Christian tradition. Doing so requires dealing with a fair amount of resistance and discomfort in the classroom on a regular basis. It is common for White students to feel uncomfortable when discussing race and racism. I do not change my syllabus because I am afraid of student backlash. At the same time, learning spaces need ethical, physical, and emotional boundaries.[8] These boundaries need to be supported by university policy.

After the session, I reported the incident. Staff were not available to speak to me for three days. I was deeply concerned. Seventy-two hours is a long time to wait. If this student was willing to "get up in my space," what was happening outside the classroom? Part of the challenge is that higher education often views academic space as distinct from the environment of student life. An abundance of scholarship has demonstrated this is a false dichotomy because the same racialized, sexualized, and gendered bodies enter the classroom space as the rest of campus.[9]

I reached out to a few students in my class to see how they were doing. Eventually, I received an email confirming a meeting time. An administrator assured me they were taking the matter seriously, and several parties were looking into it, including campus marketing. Several hours later, an administrator asked if any students from the class had reached out, and if I could please forward any email communications. While I was in contact with students from the class that day, I did not have email communications from students regarding the incident. Later that afternoon, I received another email stating that my case had been passed off to another administrator and that I should follow up with them. At this point, I was confused and frustrated. I wanted to speak to someone in person. It was difficult to get a clear picture of what was going on, as everything was being handled via email. I did not want to go back to class without further details on how the case was being addressed. Had members of the administration contacted the student in question? Was he coming back to class? If he was coming back to class, would there be a set of expectations for his engagement in the course? How was this going to impact students of color in my class?

I made a call and was told unofficially that it was decided that "the incident had not risen to the level of misconduct or bias." I never received a written response to my incident report. Instead, I was told that given the heightened nature of the political climate, "we have to allow everyone to share their opinions." Rather, the situation was being treated as a matter of classroom management, and I could be provided additional resources from campus staff. I stated that I did not feel comfortable with this decision, especially since no one in the administration, to my knowledge, had told the student that his conduct was not "acceptable."[10] I was apprehensive that his staying in the class would further incite his rage, as this material was foundational for the rest of the course. His behavior in and after class demonstrated a lack of boundaries and emotional control. After ten days, the student "voluntarily" withdrew from the course. I did not know whether he would return to class during those ten days. The lack of transparency and communication made it difficult to process the incident with the students in my class.

Educational philosopher Barbara Applebaum points to the tension that many White social justice educators face: It is not just that White students are "woefully uneducated in their understandings of racism," a problem that has gotten worse in recent years given legislation regarding the teaching of race in the classroom, but that White students "willfully protect their innocence."[11] Educators reinforce this behavior by prioritizing White student comfort, and even marking it as a sign of teaching excellence. In so doing, we ignore the harm done to students of color. While I want students to feel welcome and included in my classroom space, there is a profound difference between comfortability and inclusivity. You cannot have radical inclusion when violence is authorized on campus. Inclusivity demands establishing ethical boundaries for communal discussion and a willingness to learn from feelings of discomfort. White discomfort is only possible when White people are willing to see themselves in racialized terms. This does not mean centering Whiteness. It means looking at the bigger picture.

The student from my class is not unique. There is nothing special about his perspective on race.[12] Other White students have responded similarly. They have written letters to my dean and department chair and thrown furniture when they did not receive the grades they wanted and explicitly told me to stop teaching about race and "get back to the real syllabus." I am not the only professor who has received a similar response from an institution when addressing student conduct in a classroom. I say this with confidence, as *The Chronicle of Higher Education* has an entire teaching platform dedicated to the problem of classroom conflict.[13] Caroline Mehl and Jonathan Haidt describe their work as helping to "prevent the type of blow-ups that faculty members and administrators are all eager to avoid."[14] Yet, such programs contribute to the mentality that "the blow-ups" are individual incidents instead of being seen as connected to cracks within the foundation itself. These programs do not name the problem as connected to racism or the performance of Whiteness on campus.

WHITENESS AND THE SIN OF HIDING

> Whiteness confers knowable, quantifiable privileges, regardless of class—much like "manhood" confers knowable, quantifiable privileges, regardless of race. White supremacy is neither a trick, nor a device, but one of the most powerful shared interests in American history.[15]

As the quote by Ta-Nehisi Coates illustrates, Whiteness is not passive. It is an active force in history and one of America's most potent forms of solidarity. This is because of how Whiteness is performed.

Applebaum interprets Whiteness as "less a property of skin than an enactment of power reproducing its dominance in both explicit and implicit ways."[16] It is performative because "it produces a series of effects."[17] In this way, Whiteness shapes who White people are. The performance of Whiteness is formative. Drawing on the work of Judith Butler, Applebaum points out that norms are not stable because they can be resisted and subverted. Theologically speaking, this framework is helpful in talking about human agency. As I have argued elsewhere, Christians tend to think about violence in binary terms: perpetrator and victim.[18] In White spaces, such a mentality reinforces White fragility (denial and discomfort) and White solidarity (silence). That is, it reinforces the tendency to individualize human violation and for perpetrators to deny complicity and shut down the conversation.[19]

Recall, White solidarity "requires both silence about anything that exposes the advantages of the white position and tactic agreement to remain racially united in the protection of white supremacy."[20] Moreover, White people often internally justify White solidarity by telling themselves, "At least I am not the one who made the joke and therefore I am not at fault." This silence "protects and maintains the racial hierarchy" and, therefore, is not innocent.[21] In theological language, such actions or inactions would be considered sinful because they break the relationship with God, oneself, and others. The concept here is that hiding behind a wall of ignorance or denial breaks one's capacity for relationality.

To talk about Whiteness as performative and, thereby, constitutive, it means that the complicity question cannot be ignored. White people are responsible for the ways that we habitually reenact norms. Complicity may be different according to context, but all White people are involved. This is not to deny the individual responsibility of those who have done harm, but it is to explicitly acknowledge that White people are not passive bystanders. We are active contributors in the making of history. When we ignore Whiteness, we do so with agency. There is accountability in this decision.[22] White people are accountable for reflecting on the norms that our bodies replicate. Such an understanding of Whiteness opens the door for participation in social change. Yet, White people cannot begin to speak about social change until the problem of Whiteness is acknowledged in the first place.

When White institutions, faculty, and administrators fail to address racism at a systemic level, we willfully authorize White supremacy and anti-Blackness on our campuses. While it is important to address individual acts of violence, prejudice, and discrimination, institutions must also address "logics that everyday denials or habits of evasion . . . serve and maintain unjust systems, both at the individual level and the institutional level."[23] White people and White institutions cannot attend to racism at a systemic level if (a) one does not understand Whiteness to be part of the problem and (b) one does not truly value Black, Asian, Latine, and Indigenous Peoples and what they have to offer. Educational institutions cannot remain neutral. Neutrality does not exist within the Gospels, as the Christian God is a God who is always *for* justice and the flourishing of human beings. If PWIs that are also Catholic are to live out their missions in today's context, things are going to become uncomfortable.

White solidarity is not the solidarity of which the Gospels speak. In the Christian and Jewish Scriptures, to know God is to do justice. The God of the Hebrew and Christian Scriptures is not a God of "all sides." In Isaiah 58: 6–11, this is a God who proclaims that knowing and praising God is fulfilled through works of justice. In the Gospels, Jesus reveals Godself through acts of justice, healing, and loving-kindness.[24] This is a God who takes sides in the face of violence, poverty, and oppression.

I was met with silence, denial, and avoidance of discomfort by most White faculty and administrators. No one actively took steps to publicly affirm the link between Catholic identity as an institution and racial justice. Instead, people asked: "Why did you let this happen?" "Is this the first time you taught the material?" "Why did he do that?" Through uncritical, selective silence, staff and administrators affirmed the student's actions as "acceptable student conduct." In so doing, they implicitly upheld that statements like "talking about racism only makes it worse," "color has no meaning," and "racial profiling does not exist" do not rise to the level of bias. Through selective silence, staff and administrators used their power to protect White people. Regardless of intent, the practical effect of their actions was encoding White aggression into the fabric of the institution's lived culture of acceptable student conduct. Naming the student's behavior as misconduct or bias would require acknowledging how Whiteness is operative on campus and White complicity within it at a systemic level. Instead, White comfort was prioritized, and I was told we needed to hear all sides.

In a press conference following a violent White nationalist rally in Charlottesville, Virginia, in 2017, Trump remarked: "You had some very bad people in that group, but you also had people that were very fine people, on both sides."[25] A lot of White people were disgusted with this statement, indicating that Trump did not distance himself enough from White supremacists. However, I think it's worth asking whether there is a substantive difference between this statement by Trump and the insistence by moderate White liberals that "we have to listen to all sides." Yes, Trump was talking about White nationalists in response to the work of antiracists in removing Robert E. Lee's statue. When administrators, students, or faculty insist that professors ought to be neutral within contexts marked by racialized violence and racial microaggressions, they are affirming Whiteness in a classroom context. Student bodies are racialized, sexualized, and gendered. Their lived experiences we carry go beyond the classroom. This call for neutrality sets the stage for doing Whiteness as White solidarity. Is it not best read as an expression of White solidarity? In other words, when White people say, "We have to listen to all sides," they foreground White ways of knowing and White ways of being.

When White people are serious about valuing Black and brown wisdom, we create real opportunities for leadership, and lots of them. When White people are serious about valuing Black and brown wisdom, we create healthy work environments that monetarily value and sustain Black and brown talent.

When White people are serious about valuing Black and brown wisdom, we act in ways that demonstrate accountability. When White people are serious about valuing Black and brown wisdom, we step aside. If White people listened to all sides, as in *everyone*, including Black, Latine, Asian, and Indigenous wisdom, the world would not function as it does. PWIs would not exist.

To be clear, I am not innocent in this case. As a White faculty member who works at a PWI, I am intrinsically allied with Whiteness.[26] There have been times when I have chosen to comply with White solidarity because I am too tired to say something or I want to fit in. For example, I could have done more to draw attention to the problem in this case. I could have insisted that my department address the issue with the administration. I did not do this because I did not think I would have the backing. Yes, some people would have allied with me. Yet, the costs would have been great in a department with few resources and a small budget. Getting everyone on board would have been difficult. People who participate in White solidarity are rewarded with social and monetary capital. They are seen as team players, easy to work with, and fun. They are brought into decision-making circles. Resisting White norms is not an individual or one-time effort. It requires the ongoing work of the community.

In a polarized society, I know many do not like the idea of taking sides. I suspect this language is off-putting to some. Yet it's time to get past the pleasantries and get to work. For White people and White institutions, this is going to mean taking sides with those who are dehumanized and subjected to violence. For Christians, neutrality isn't an option.

NOTES

1. I have not capitalized the "w" in previous works on Whiteness. I do so now because it reminds the reader and me that the ways in which Whiteness shapes institutions and communities must be interrogated. Whiteness is the cultural norm, and it always risks invisibility. See Eve Ewing, "I Am a Black Scholar Who Studies Race. Here's Why I Capitalize 'White," *ZORA*, July 2, 2020, https://zora.medium.com/im-a-black-scholar-who-studies-race-here-s-why-i-capitalize-white-f94883aa2dd3, and Kristen Mack and John Palfrey, "Capitalizing Black and White: Grammatical Justice and Equity," MacArthur Foundation, August 26, 2020, https://www.macfound.org/press/perspectives/capitalizing-black-and-white-grammatical-justice-and-equity.

2. Ta-Nehisi Coates, "Donald Trump Is Out. Are We Ready to Talk about How He Got In?" *The Atlantic*, January 20, 2021, https://www.theatlantic.com/politics/archive/2021/01/ta-nehisi-coates-revisits-trump-first-white-president/617731/.

3. Justin Nortey, "Most White Americans Who Regularly Attend Worship Services Voted for Trump in 2020," Pew Research Center, August 30, 2021, https://www

.pewresearch.org/fact-tank/2021/08/30/most-white-americans-who-regularly-attend-worship-services-voted-for-trump-in-2020/.

4. Isabel Wilkerson, *Caste: The Origins of Our Discontents* (New York: Random House, 2023), 328.

5. Robin DiAngelo, *White Fragility: Why It's So Hard for White People to Talk about Racism* (Boston: Beacon Press, 2018), 57–58. Also see Beverly Tatum, *Why Are All the Black Kids Sitting Together in the Cafeteria?* Revised edition (New York: Basic Books, 2017).

6. For example, see Willie James Jennings, *After Whiteness: An Education in Belonging* (Grand Rapids, MI: Eerdmans, 2020).

7. Miguel A. de la Torre, *Reading the Bible from the Margins* (Maryknoll, NY: Orbis Books, 2002), 22.

8. See Stephanie M. Crumpton, "Trauma-Sensitive Pedagogy," in *Teaching Sexuality and Religion in Higher Education: Embodied Learning, Trauma-Sensitive Pedagogy, and Perspective Transformation*, edited by Darryl W. Stephens and Kate M. Ott (New York: Routledge, 2020), 30–43.

9. The scholarship is too numerous in this area to cite. However, the works of Derald Wing Sue and Beverly Tatum are foundational resources in exploring the cross-sectional experiences of students on campuses.

10. In my opinion, *acceptable* is not a strong enough word. However, it is the language in the university student handbook.

11. Barbara Applebaum, "Ongoing Challenges for White Educators Teaching White Students about Whiteness," *Studies in Philosophy and Education* 40 (2021): 433.

12. In June 2020, eight in ten White Republicans said the biggest problem concerning race was seeing an issue where it did not exist. Travis Mitchell, "Amid National Reckoning, Americans Divided on Whether Increased Focus on Race Will Lead to Major Policy Change," Social and Demographic Trends Project, Pew Research Center, May 25, 2021, https://www.pewresearch.org/social-trends/wp-content/uploads/sites/3/2020/10/PSDT_10.06.20_race.update.fullreport-1.correx.pdf.

13. Caroline Mehl and Jonathan Haidt, "Advice: How to Defuse a Classroom Conflict: Make It More Complex," *The Chronicle of Higher Education*, November 30, 2022, https://www.chronicle.com/article/how-to-defuse-a-classroom-conflict-make-it-more-complex.

14. Mehl and Haidt, "Advice: How to Defuse a Classroom Conflict."

15. Ta-Nehisi Coates, "The Enduring Solidarity of Whiteness," *The Atlantic*, February 8, 2016, https://www.theatlantic.com/politics/archive/2016/02/why-we-write/459909/.

16. Barbara Applebaum, "Comforting Discomfort as Complicity: White Fragility and the Pursuit of Invulnerability," *Hypatia* 32, no. 4 (Fall 2017): 868.

17. Applebaum, "Comforting Discomfort as Complicity," 869.

18. Elisabeth T. Vasko, *Beyond Apathy: A Theology for Bystanders* (Minneapolis, MN: Fortress Press, 2015), 14.

19. See Sharon Lamb, *The Trouble with Blame: Victims, Perpetrators, and Responsibility* (Cambridge, MA: Harvard University Press, 1996), chapter 1.

20. DiAngelo, *White Fragility*, 58

21. DiAngelo, *White Fragility*, 58.

22. There is a great deal of literature on White ignorance. In this essay, I have used the work of Barbara Applebaum, "The Call for Intellectual Diversity on Campus and the Problem of Willful Ignorance," *Educational Theory* 70, no. 4 (2020): 445–61. Also see Sharon Sullivan and Nancy Tuana, eds., *Race and Epistemologies of Ignorance* (Albany: State University of New York Press, 2007).

23. Applebaum, "Willful Ignorance," 460.

24. For example, Lk 4: 16–21.

25. Ayesha Rascoe, "A Year after Charlottesville, Not Much Has Changed for Trump," *NPR*, August 11, 2018, https://www.npr.org/2018/08/11/637665414/a-year-after-charlottesville-not-much-has-changed-for-trump.

26. See George Yancy, *Black Bodies, White Gazes: The Continuing Significance of Race* (Lanham, MD: Rowman & Littlefield, 2008), 235. For Yancy, to be White within the context of a world predicated on White privilege, power, and hegemony is to be implicated in White racialized power.

Chapter 18

Can White Christian Nationalists and Donald Trump Be Overcome?

Josiah Ulysses Young III

Donald Trump doesn't come across as an Evangelical, and he appears to be as theologically illiterate as he is politically unscrupulous. Nonetheless, he radiates the racism that has been foundational to pro-white evangelism since the 1700s. White Christian nationalists have perched on his toxic vow to "make America great again" because they think he'll turn back the clock to when Blacks were more marginalized than they are now.[1] But these Evangelical Trumpsters needn't rule the nation. Let me flesh out those assertions by exploring some of the antecedents of white Christian nationalism, thus delving a bit more into why these Evangelicals and Trump are birds of a feather. Finally, I'll discuss how humane Christians undermine Trumpism and white Christian nationalism, thus answering the question I pose in my title.

ANTECEDENTS OF WHITE CHRISTIAN NATIONALISM

Since the eighteenth century, white North American Evangelicals have envisioned a time when Christ would judge their civilization upon his arrival. The postmillenarians hoped the republic would be evaluated favorably. The premillenarians, the dispensationalists, expected apocalyptic devastation and the rapture of those justified by faith alone. Both views of the future have held that their Americanness signified "God's" favor. Given their abusive treatment of African Americans, it's evident that "God's" grace wasn't as salvific for Blacks as it was for whites. Blacks' second-class justification depended on their obedience to Jim Crow laws, their absolute capitulation to racist authority. The distinction between Black and white Christians in the US has thus been the difference between castes. Appealing to the Bible's sanctioning of slavery and seemingly oblivious to the hamartiological significance of their racism, bigoted white Evangelicals have been Black folk's nemesis.

The roots of this enmity stretch to the Great Awakening, the series of massive revivals in the eighteenth and nineteenth centuries. These revivals appealed to the unlettered masses who were ill-equipped to process the supralapsarian writings of John Calvin and his ancient predecessor Augustine of Hippo. The Puritan theologian Jonathan Edwards (1703–1758) and the Anglican theologian George Whitefield (1714–1770) were the premier revivalists of the first Great Awakening. Edwards, the first president of what became Princeton University, and Whitefield, a close associate of John Wesley, Methodism's founder, compellingly stressed the affective facets of Christ's atoning work and thus unleashed effusive responses from their hearers. Edwards writes, "That idea . . . God hath of Himself is absolutely Himself. This representation of the Divine nature and essence is the Divine nature and essence again: so that by God's thinking . . . the Deity must certainly be generated. Hereby . . . is another person begotten . . . another Infinite Eternal Almighty and most holy and the same God, the very same Divine nature."[2] Far more essential than the masses' understanding of the Christological line "the Deity must certainly be generated" is Christ's crucifixion and resurrection. Those whom He saves must know He's "God." In fear and trembling, they must bend the knee to him, for his human nature died for those who must suffer their dire need for repentance and forgiveness lest they burn in hell. As Edwards puts it in his famous sermon "Sinners in the Hands of an Angry God": "Now undoubtedly it is, as it was in the days of John the Baptist . . . that every tree which brings not forth good fruit, may be hewn down and cast into the fire. Therefore, let everyone out of Christ, now awake and fly from the wrath to come."[3]

In his sermon "Christ the Only Preservative Against a Reprobate Spirit," Whitefield holds that hamartiology is but an abstraction if the Holy Spirit doesn't move one to repent and receive "Jesus, who died for all those who believe in him."[4] Without repentance, one would suffer "torments, of which there will be no end."[5] Unrepentant sinners "cannot be saved: Nothing short of the blood of Jesus applied to [their] souls, will make [them] happy to all eternity." The people "must be born again, and become new creatures, and have the spirit of Christ within [them]."[6] According to one scholar, Whitefield's oratory stirred enslaved Blacks. He, in turn, resolved to build them a school while decrying their inhumane treatment in the Southland.[7] When the authorities in Georgia prohibited slavery in 1747, Whitefield took steps to protect an orphanage he established in the state.[8] He acquired land and enslaved people in South Carolina to turn a profit to keep the orphanage in Georgia going. He also used his influence to make slavery legal in the orphanage's location.[9]

Edwards imagined that a born-again America would become a righteous nation before the Parousia, Christ's eschatological arrival. In the meantime, enslaved people were to obey the Scriptures: *"Slaves, you must obey your earthly masters. Show them great respect and be as loyal to them as you are to Christ"* (Ephesians 6:5). *"Slaves, you must always obey your earthly masters. Try to always please them, and not just when you think they are watching. Honor the Lord and serve your masters with your whole heart"* (Colossians 3:22).[10] Upholding the *sola scriptura* (scripture alone) axiom with a clear conscience, Edwards opposed the transatlantic trade but didn't free "his" Blacks.[11] One wonders, *Were their enslavement and humiliation worth it because of the alleged freedom to come?* A new heaven and Earth are unlikely. Edwards allowed his enslaved household to worship in his church. He wasn't a Simon Legree, but he was complicit in maintaining a racist system that punished and maimed multitudes of African Americans so that elite whites could grow wealthy and enjoy the finer things in life.

No matter how sympathetic one is to Whitefield and Edwards as men of their times, and despite the possibility that they didn't know better, their faith in the resurrection of the body was better for them than for the Blacks they owned. That goes for all Evangelicals who enslaved African people. According to the writer Frances FitzGerald, "the southern Baptists and Methodists—with a combined total of three million members—broke away from their denominations" in 1844, "the Methodists to form the Methodist Episcopal Church, South, and the Baptists to form the Southern Baptist Convention."[12] Those "southern evangelicals mounted a comprehensive defense of slavery based squarely on the idea of racial inequality," thus separating themselves from their abolitionist-minded northern counterparts.[13] They thought white supremacy was "God's" will since whites controlled the US.[14] Given the Reformation's *sola scriptura* axiom and the notion of the Bible's inerrancy, white southern fundamentalists argued that the Bible's legitimation of enslavement couldn't be immoral. Therefore, many deemed Blacks' enslavement respectable.

In her book *The Power Worshippers: Inside the Dangerous Rise of Religious Nationalism*, Katherine Stewart discusses the legacy of Robert Lewis Dabney (1820–1898), a nineteenth-century Presbyterian minister and theologian. According to Stewart, "the most important aspect of the proslavery theology that Dabney so ably embodied—or at any rate the one that far outlasted its explicit support for the enslavement of human beings—was its fusion of religion with a racialized form of nationalism."[15] Dabney holds that slavery "in both Testaments is not always essentially unrighteous, since they legitimate it under suitable circumstances, and declare that godly masters may so hold the relation as to make it equitable and righteous."[16] Dabney also holds that "Britain has demonstrated . . . that freedom among the whites is ruinous to the blacks." He thinks their manumission led to the ruin of England's "finest colonies, of the lapsing of fruitful plantations into the bush" and "the return of the slaves, lately an industrious and useful peasantry, to savage life."[17] According to Dabney, manumitted northern US Blacks behave similarly without whites' enslaving but sanctified guidance. Where enslaved southern Blacks are "cheerful, healthy, progressive, industrious, and multiplying rapidly in numbers," freed Blacks up north are "a social nuisance, depressed by indolence and poverty, decimated by hereditary diseases, and tending rapidly to extinction."[18] White supremacism and mendacity flock together.

White Christian nationalists like Jerry Falwell, Sr. (1933–2007) and Bob Jones Sr. (1916–2001) cherished Dabney's archaic views.[19] Jerry Falwell, the onetime head of Liberty University—and the Moral Majority leader who helped make the Republican Party synonymous with "family values" during Ronald Reagan's presidency—vehemently opposed *Brown v. Board of Education* (1954). Falwell asserted in his 1958 sermon "Segregation or Integration, Which?" that the "facilities should be separate" because "God has drawn a line of distinction we should not attempt to cross. . . . The true Negro does not want integration. . . . He realizes his potential is far better among his own race. . . . [Integration] will destroy our race eventually."[20] In an Easter Sunday sermon delivered in 1960, Bob Jones Sr., founder of Bob Jones University, declared that "God Almighty" made one human race but fixed "the bounds of . . . habitation." If whites had adhered to God's orders of creation, Africans wouldn't have "arrived" in the Americas. "But God," Jones avows, has made lemonade from lemons:

> He turned the colored people in the South into wonderful Christian people. . . . Sometimes we have a little trouble, but then we adjust everything sensibly and get back to the established order. . . . If we would just listen to the Word of God and not try to overthrow God's established order, we would not have any trouble. God never meant for America to be a melting pot to rub out the line between the nations. That was not God's purpose for this nation.[21]

For Jones, segregation ensured that Blacks and whites would live amiably in their God-appointed spaces.

It became politically incorrect to espouse such views blatantly in the wake of legislation like the 1964 Civil Rights Act and the 1965 Voting Rights Act. It was savvier to push the Christian nationalist agenda via a Trojan horse, namely the 1973 *Roe v. Wade* decision federally legalizing abortion. In her book *Unholy: How White Christian Nationalists Powered the Trump Presidency, and the Devastating Legacy They Left Behind*, Sarah Posner unveils that the pro-life imperative wasn't what moved Falwell and others like him to form the Moral Majority and its obligation to family values.[22] Katherine Stewart agrees: "Jerry Falwell and many of his fellow southern, white, conservative pastors were closely involved with segregated schools and universities, and they had come together as a political force out of fear that their institutions would soon be deprived of their lucrative tax advantages."[23] They wished to protect the tax breaks they enjoyed but would lose if their Jim Crow policies persisted. Falwell and others railed against abortion, homosexuality, pornography, "sex education, 'secular humanism,' and public education" as evidence that the US had become Sodom-and-Gomorrah-like. But "the threat that the Supreme Court might end tax exemptions for segregated Christian schools" mobilized them.[24] If they controlled the Republican Party, they might well take control of the Supreme Court and undermine *Brown*.

Rousas J. Rushdoony, the so-called "father" of Christian Reconstructionism, was a leading intellectual of the Christian nationalist cause and another admirer of Dabney. Maligning organizations like the Student Nonviolent Coordinating Committee, Rushdoony argues that Black "'civil rights' revolutionary groups" of necessity seek power rather than "equality." In his mind, African people are innately captive to magic, which seeks "control and power over God, man, nature, and society." According to Rushdoony, "Voodoo, or magic, was the religion and life of American Negroes. Voodoo songs underlie jazz, and old voodoo, with its power goal, has been merely replaced with revolutionary voodoo, a modernized power drive."[25] (So much for Wakanda.)

Rushdoony's whiteness runs deep:

> When New England began its existence as a law order, its adoption of biblical law was both a return to Scripture and a return to Europe's past. It was a new beginning in terms of old foundations. It was not an easy beginning, in that the many servants who came with the Puritans later were in full-scale revolt against any biblical faith and order. Nevertheless, it was a resolute return to the fundamentals of Christendom. Thus, the New Haven Colony records show that the law of God, without any sense of innovation, was made the law of the colony.[26]

Rushdoony thinks "the law of God" should govern twenty-first-century America: A Godfearing nation should imprison and even execute gays, and schools should be biblically based and private. His US "is a Redeemer Nation, chosen by God" and "tasked with becoming the orthodox Christian Republic in which" men will be over women, the Christian right will control education, and none will pay "taxes to support Black people."[27]

WHITE CHRISTIAN NATIONALISM AND TRUMPISM: BIRDS OF A FEATHER

Donald Trump, it bears repeating, is not a theologian, but like calls to like in the republic nonetheless: White Evangelicals know the America Trump would make great again is for whites like himself and Blacks like the would-be senator Herschel Walker. Do MAGA folk know Trump isn't a genius billionaire, his real estate projects have gone bust, and his debts are monumental?[28] His presidential maneuverings may be proved criminal,[29] but they don't appear to care. They think Trump's improprieties work to the glory of God, as he delivered the two justices critical to the rescinding of *Roe v. Wade*. They supported Trump because he extended their power. To quote Sarah Posner, "Trump is the first Republican to be treated with such leniency . . . because, unlike his predecessors, he has exhibited no compunction about flexing his executive power in unprecedented ways to implement long-sought Christian right policy and stacking the federal courts with conservative judges, in ways that will endure over generations."[30]

OVERCOMING TRUMP AND WHITE CHRISTIAN NATIONALISM

Dabney, Falwell, and Rushdoony appropriated the Hebrew Bible's patriarchal narratives as if white Americans had been exiled in sixth-century BCE Babylon. That's partly because the Bible was, as Rushdoony has pointed out, the sacred text of the Puritan elite for whom whiteness and Calvinism were identical. Their hegemony subliminally conveys that the Logos' iconic whiteness is their Godness, the Definition of Chalcedon notwithstanding. Although they seem to have the inside track on Christian soteriology, white Christian nationalists are blind to their idolatry.

Ludwig Feuerbach, the nineteenth-century left-wing Hegelian philosopher, argues that theologies are essentially anthropological.[31] It's credible to hold that the Bible reveals nothing but the values of human beings, especially if there's no transcendent Creator. It may be that the *creatio ex nihilo* is as mythic as the tale of Adam and Eve. History, sated with the bones of yesterday, belies, moreover, the resurrection of the dead. What appears likely eons from now is the black dwarf Sun and the ensuing lifeless abyss. The unborn may survive the Sun's death due to space travel (if we don't blow up Earth first). But bodily resurrection in a regenerated world seems unlikely. The claim, therefore, that the future, as pneumatologically, Christologically, and theologically construed, sublates the troubled present is suspect and useless unless believers embody humane ethics here and now. It's sobering to think that progressive theologies and the smarmily conservative ones have no object but their theologians' passions.

Whether Feuerbach is correct, one needn't capitulate to the Christian right. Theologies needn't be fascistically racist. Progressive Evangelicals, womanist theologians, and liberation theologians offer alternative hermeneutics. Although they can't erase the Bible's archaisms, they unveil the intrinsic relationship between "God" and the theologians' most heartfelt convictions. From this perspective, William Barber and Franklin Graham differ hermeneutically because they differ morally and politically. One might say they're a continuum of the difference between David Walker and Charles Colcock Jones. All those theologians—Jones, Walker, Graham, and Barber—evince that dogma alone doesn't challenge white supremacism. Only the theologian can do that and thus function therapeutically in our troubled times. Here, the symbols they deem sacrosanct empower transformative rather than reactionary activities. Christmas, Good Friday, and Easter—the Incarnation, the Crucifixion, and the Resurrection—can inspire resistance to hatred of the other. Light sometimes overcomes darkness, though the causalities of the night are astronomical.

Trumpism may retreat to the shadows if voters let their lights shine against anarchic predilections. But racist Christianity will persist if people solipsistically identify "God" with their heritage. White supremacy and the notion of biblical inerrancy are dangerous when paired. Hatefulness and ignorance are lethal. But we can take prophylactic measures against both through vigilant, democratically ethical actions. We can overcome white Christian nationalists and Donald Trump if humane citizens guard one another's liberty. But we can't approach that task somnolently. If we do, we'll likely wake up within a nightmarish republic. We can't go to sleep. The future depends on us.

NOTES

1. Anthea Butler, "Trump, Republicans, and White Evangelicals Are Forming a Powerful Trifecta," *MSNBC*, September 19, 2021, https://www.msnbc.com/opinion/trump-republicans-white-evangelicals-are-forming-powerful-trifecta-n1279504.

2. Jonathan Edwards, "An Unpublished Essay on the Trinity," *Monegrism.com*, https://www.monergism.com/thethreshold/sdg/Edwards,%20Jonathan%20-%20An%20Unpublished%20Essay%20on%20the%20Tr.pdf.

3. "Sermons by Jonathan Edwards," Biblesnet.com, https://www.biblesnet.com/Jonathan%20Edwards%20Sermons.pdf.

4. George Whitefield, *Selected Sermons of George Whitefield* (Grand Rapids, MI: Christian Classics Ethereal Library, n.d.), 519, https://ccel.org/ccel/w/whitefield/sermons/cache/sermons.pdf.

5. Whitefield, *Selected Sermons*, 519.

6. Whitefield, *Selected Sermons*, 519.

7. William A. Sloat II, "George Whitefield, African-Americans and Slavery," *Methodist History* 33, no. 1 (October 1994): 3–5.

8. Whitefield, *Selected Sermons*, 5.

9. Whitefield, *Selected Sermons*, 5.

10. Emphases are added to both pericopes.

11. Kenneth P. Minkema, "Jonathan Edwards's Defense of Slavery," *Massachusetts Historical Review* 4, Race and Slavery (2002): 23–59.

12. Frances FitzGerald, *The Evangelicals: The Struggle to Shape America* (New York: Simon & Schuster, 2017), 51.

13. FitzGerald, *The Evangelicals*, 51.

14. FitzGerald, *The Evangelicals*, 96.

15. FitzGerald, *The Evangelicals*, 110.

16. Robert Lewis Dabney, "Anti-Biblical Theories of Rights," 34, https://ia903105.us.archive.org/23/items/DiscussionsOfRobertLewisDabneyVol.3Philosophical/DiscussionsOfR.l.DabneyV.3.pdf.

17. Robert Lewis Dabney, *Defense of Virginia (and through Her of the South)* (New York: E. J. Hale & Son, 1867), 294–95.

18. Dabney, *Defense of Virginia*, 294–95.

19. Katherine Stewart, *The Power Worshippers: Inside the Dangerous Rise of Religious Nationalism* (New York: Bloomsbury Publishing, 2022), 105.

20. Max Blumenthal, "Agent of Intolerance," *The Nation*, May 16, 2007, https://www.thenation.com/article/archive/agent-intolerance/, accessed December 13, 2022.

21. Bruce Gerencser, "The Life and Times of Bruce Gerencser," Bruce Gerencser blog, August 17, 2017, https://brucegerencser.net/2017/08/is-segregation-scriptural-by-evangelist-bob-jones-the-founder-of-bob-jones-university/.

22. Sarah Posner, *Unholy: How White Christian Nationalists Powered the Trump Presidency, and the Devastating Legacy They Left Behind* (New York: Random House, 2021), 106–7.

23. Stewart, *The Power Worshippers*, 61.

24. Stewart, *The Power Worshippers*, 61.

25. Rousas J. Rushdoony, *The Institutes of Biblical Law* (Phillipsburg, NJ: Chalcedon, 2012), 75.

26. Rushdoony, *The Institutes of Biblical Law*, 10.

27. Stewart, *The Power Worshippers*, 113.

28. "Committee Uncovers Evidence That Trump Concealed Millions in Losses, Hid Debts, and Received Millions from Foreign Governments at Trump Hotel," Committee on Oversight and Accountability, October 8, 2021, https://oversight.house.gov/news/press-releases/committee-uncovers-evidence-that-trump-concealed-millions-in-losses-hid-debts.

29. Garth Evans, "Donald Trump: His Four Biggest Legal Problems," *BBC News*, October 21, 2022, https://www.bbc.com/news/world-us-canada-6108416.

30. Posner, *Unholy*, 25.

31. "Ludwig Feuerbach: Theology as Anthropology," Philosophy of Religion, https://www.philosophyofreligion.uk/arguments-for-atheism/the-psychogenesis-of-religion/ludwig-feuerbach-theology-as-anthropology/.

Chapter 19

Revolution and the Soul of White Christianity

Dean J. Johnson

The revolution for a more inclusive and equitable society is upon us. It has been building for decades and continues now. At the same time, we are at a moment ripe with the possibility of fascism because those who have been in power for the last five-hundred-plus years are not going to go quietly; this includes white Eurocentric Christians and churches. It is time to make a choice and answer the question, "Can white Christianity be redeemed?" Our choices, as white Christians, are to either go all in for revolution or give in to the ongoing pressure of maintaining the soul of a reinvigorated heteronormative, patriarchal, white supremacy. After decades of progressive movements for a more inclusive society, along with shifting demographics in the US, we are experiencing the death nail in the coffin of the way things have been and the white supremacist Eurocentric Christianity that holds it all together. If we are going to choose revolutionary change, then we must honestly discuss the rising fascism of the current moment, the problem of white supremacist Eurocentric Christianity, and what, if anything, can be done to redeem white Christians.

SOME DEFINITIONS

Before moving into a discussion about the moment in which we find ourselves, it is necessary to define some of the terms I will be using throughout this chapter. The first term is *revolution*. Revolution, as I am using it, comes from movement elder Grace Lee Boggs, who wrote:

> Revolution means reinventing culture. . . . With the end of empire, we are coming to an end of the epoch of rights. We have entered the epoch of responsibilities, which requires new, more socially-minded human beings and new, more participatory and place-based concepts of citizenship and democracy.[1]

For Boggs, *revolution* means beginning anew and tearing down the old structures. She argues that the progressive movements of the past have been organized around a human rights orientation working to secure those rights for everyone. Her call is for us to move the focus toward being responsible for the well-being of one another by engaging in community. To be in this revolutionary moment means to decide how we are responsible for one another, not "just what I need."

When I use the term *fascism*, I am not being hyperbolic. I mean there is an unapologetic movement toward authoritarian rule based on a white supremacist Christian nationalism. The movement is intended to bring together the state, paramilitary militias, and other organized groups to maintain the status quo. Some of the most overt ways this is happening is through the questioning and intentional dismantling of democratic and educational systems.

Finally, I define *white supremacist Eurocentric Christianity*. In this chapter, I am using an intersectional approach which takes into consideration the overlapping ways that power, privilege, and oppression function based on how people are identified as part of groups by the culture we live in. When using the term *white supremacist Eurocentric Christianity*, I mean the Christianity that created and continues to use the white, cisgender, heterosexual, able-bodied, male Christian as the supreme model against which all other human beings are compared and measured.[2] In other words, white supremacist Eurocentric Christianity depends on and perpetuates white supremacy, heteronormativity, patriarchy, and ableism for its survival.[3]

THE CURRENT MOMENT

Whenever there has been a movement toward a more inclusive society, it has been met with force and backlash. These movements toward cultural inclusiveness have existed whenever and wherever human dignity has been denied to a group of people. We see the backlash throughout the history of the US. The Southern Strategy was a response that appealed to white supremacy as backlash to Black-led freedom struggles in the South. The Southern Strategy appealed to the heteronormative, patriarchal values of white supremacist Eurocentric Christianity, giving rise to what eventually became recognized as the Religious Right. As the human rights movements of the 1950s–1970s made strides toward a more inclusive society, the backlash was embodied in the governorship and presidency of Ronald Reagan. Most recently, the presidency of Donald Trump and much of the Republican platform was the backlash to the first US biracial (Black) president, Barak Obama, the #MeToo movement, and the Movement for Black Lives.

Trump has found success in the demagoguery of heteronormative, patriarchal, white supremacist, Christian status quo. According to Patricia Roberts-Miller, "Demagoguery is discourse that promises stability, certainty, and escape from the responsibilities of rhetoric by framing public policy in terms of the degree to which and the means by which (not whether) the out-group should be scapegoated for the current problems of the in-group."[4] Trump has been able to whip up support by continuing to push narratives of hypermasculine, white, Christian nationalism. These narratives intentionally work to create and perpetuate the idea of victimhood among whites, Christians, and cis-hetero men.

Trump's success comes in part because some whites feel like they are victims. Evidence of the sense of victimhood can be found in a 2017 survey of "Young Americans" conducted by the Public Religion Research Institute and MTV. The survey report states, "Young white evangelical Protestants are significantly more likely to believe that evangelical Christians face more discrimination than most other racial, ethnic, and religious minority groups. Nearly six in ten (57%) young white evangelical Protestants say evangelical Christians face a lot of discrimination in the U.S. today."[5] The idea of victimhood is even more evident when respondents were asked about the idea of reverse discrimination. According to the report:

> White Americans overall are more likely to affirm this belief than white young people. A majority (55%) of white Americans—including roughly equal numbers of white men (55%) and white women (53%)—agree that "reverse" discrimination is as big an issue as other types of racial and ethnic discrimination. The politics of young people's parents also appears closely associated with views about "reverse" discrimination. A majority (55%) of young people whose parents voted for Trump agree that discrimination against whites is as serious a problem as discrimination against black people and other minorities, while only 19% of those whose parents voted for Clinton agree.[6]

Regardless of the accuracy, white perceptions of victimhood are useful to those willing to use such perceptions to maintain power.

The Trumpist narratives are effective because they appeal to the desires, imaginations, and/or experiences of the groups at which they are aimed. These Trumpist narratives provide comfort, simplicity, and clarity to those who are losing power due to the cultural changes created by progressive social movements and shifts in US demographics which have led to a more complex and intersectional way of being. People seek simplicity and resist complexity. Complexity tears at security in identity. As society has moved toward more fluidity in the definitions of identity (socially, politically, culturally), there has been pushback to maintain binary systems. Trump and his institutional followers have been effective in their narrative appeals. Evidence of this can be seen in the following facts: (1) white Evangelicals identified as followers of Trump during his presidency; (2) following his presidency there is an ongoing debate about support of Trump among white Evangelicals; and (3) although many Trump-endorsed candidates lost during the 2022 midterm elections, large numbers of Republicans, many of whom are white and men, still voted for them.[7] Being effective does not mean one wins over everyone, but that one wins over just enough people to still maintain some power and influence.

As was clear, Trump's announced candidacy for the 2016 election involved an increase in white hate groups, open hostility by groups of white men, and the (re)normalizing of racist, sexist, homophobic, transphobic, and xenophobic rhetoric and violence in the public sphere. Extreme examples of this open hostility can be seen in the bringing together of white and Christian nationalists in the so-called Unite the Right Rally in August of 2017 and the attack on the US Capitol on January 6, 2021, which included members from the Oath Keepers, Proud Boys, and Three Percenters. While it is important to name the extreme examples, we cannot allow ourselves to get distracted from the problem of everyday instances that allow white supremacist Eurocentric Christianity to persist. The extreme forms of hostility are what happens when the quiet part is said out loud and placed on public display. The extreme only exists with the assistance of active allies, passive allies, and those who think they are neutral.[8] Active allies are those who are committed to actively and overtly keeping in place the white supremacist Eurocentric Christian status quo. Passive allies are those who are not overtly active in the work to maintain the status quo and yet are supportive and believe the cause to have merit. There are, finally, those who believe themselves to be neutral. They are not engaging the work or the conversations that maintain the status quo. However, they benefit from the continuation of the status quo. In other words, in this case, there is no true neutrality. If one is not in active allyship, then one is reinforcing the system. The system is set up to take advantage of those who believe they are neutral. The system is not broken. It is working the way it was intended to work.

White supremacy, patriarchy, heteronormativity, and Christianity are built into the political, economic, and institutional structures and systems in the US and maintained by cultural narratives that legitimize their existence. White supremacist Eurocentric Christian rule in this country has always relied on the coalition of government forces, official police, extrajudicial vigilantism, churches, and public support working together to create/maintain ideological dominance. Our current moment is no exception, and yet there is something else at work that has disappeared for several decades. Many of the overt supremacists' narratives that resurfaced with Trump had been forced underground and were seen as taboo because they make the oppression overt. One of the ways dominant groups maintain power is by making themselves "invisible," by making the focus the political and cultural stories about the supposed abnormality of the oppressed and subordinated groups. In other words, the discourse functions to conceal the dominant group.[9] For example, when we hear the word *race*, we have been taught to think about Black and brown persons rather than whites. When we hear the word *religion*, we have been taught to think about Islam, Buddhism, and other religions rather than Christianity. The dominant groups are left invisible and function as the default norm. Demagoguery brings the invisible out into the open in overt ways to create clear sides of *us* and *them*. When such a distinction suites the power of the demagogue, the *us* is clearly named, made mainstream, to polarize the masses.[10]

Polarization and violence are being used to maintain power. The polarization is being perpetuated by demagoguery. Social media, the proliferation of ideological news media, and anti-intellectualism allow people to surround themselves with those with whom they agree, perpetuating an *us-versus-them* reality. Such a reality lends itself to violence by pitting one group against another. Hannah Arendt reminds us that violence and power have a relationship. According to Arendt, "Power and violence are opposites; where the one rules absolutely the other is absent. Violence appears where power is in jeopardy."[11] She argues that as those in power lose power, they use violence as a substitute for their lost power. If a group has power, there is no need to use violence. Part of the reason there has been an increase in white, Christian, male violence is because they believe they are losing power and control over society and their privileged place in it.[12]

THE PROBLEM OF WHITE SUPREMACIST EUROCENTRIC CHRISTIANITY

To answer the question about the redeemability of white Christians, it is necessary to discuss the problem of white supremacist Eurocentric Christianity. White supremacist Eurocentric Christianity has always been an undertaking of us versus them. The very roots of the undertaking are binary: One is either a follower of Jesus or one is not. From there, the narrative begins to have qualifiers, which provide a way of engaging in the world through binaries. This orientation sets the stage for colonial conquests and the creation of durable inequalities. Indeed, according to Charles Tilly, such "significant inequalities in advantages among human beings correspond mainly to categorical differences such as black/white, male/female, citizen/ foreigner, or Muslim/Jew rather than to individual differences in attributes, propensities, or performances."[13] For Tilly, durable inequalities are created by collective actors and reinforced through the adaptive behaviors of individuals. These inequalities (re)create the systems that objectify and separate human beings. Institutions, in this case white supremacist Eurocentric churches, have made these inequalities permanent through rituals and narratives. The binary construction of salvation, the rise of colonial conquests, and the perpetuation of monogenesis, the idea we are all from an original set of parents in Adam and Eve, inform the definitions and categories of good/evil, race, gender, sexuality, and able-bodiedness that persist today. It is these categories and definitions that perpetuate the superiority of white, cisgender, heterosexual men.

All white Christianity benefits from white supremacist Eurocentric Christianity. And yet, not all white Christianity is equal. The quality of white Christianity falls on a scale and can be measured by its beliefs, practices, and opposition to white supremacist Eurocentric Christianity. The reason for using a scale is that few, if any, white Christians can completely get outside the systems of oppression from which they benefit. All white Christians have work to do, and it is continuous until the systems of oppression are eliminated from society. The scale of white Christianity represents the wide-ranging beliefs and practices from those who work toward the greater good of humanity to those who want to maintain the power of the chosen few. On one end of the scale is a transformational white Christianity that has an orientation centered on and committed to community and works against a white supremacist Eurocentric way of being. On the other end of the scale is a transactional white Christianity that has an orientation focused on individualism and reinforces a white supremacist Eurocentric worldview. Let us explore the characteristics of each of these extremes.

A transformational white Christianity seeks to transform society into a place that recognizes the worth and dignity of every human being. Much like Martin Luther King Jr.'s theological beloved community, transformational white Christianity is community centered and operates out of the idea of the *imago Dei*, or the image of God in us all.[14] *Imago Dei* reminds us that we are all God's children, all loved, and all interconnected. The idea of *imago Dei* at its core is intersectional. It recognizes the complexity and the interconnectedness of human identities and the inherent worth of all human beings since we are all created in God's image. A transformational white Christianity orientation is about responsibility for one's neighbor and the earth as interpreted from Genesis 1.

The transformational type of white Christianity works to recognize its role in systems of oppression, confessing the sins of the past, and paying penance. Transformational white Christianity works to eradicate systems of oppression and white supremacist Eurocentric Christianity. White participants who ascribe to a transformational orientation are self-reflective, self-critical, and open to criticism from historically oppressed communities. Transformational white Christianity acknowledges the complexity of what it means to work against the white supremacist Eurocentric model. White participants realize that because they still benefit from the systems of white supremacist Eurocentric Christianity, there will always be some level of distrust. One will always be suspect and will always have to be self-reflective. One is caught in "damnable ambiguity," the idea that no matter how they choose to act, their motives and way of moving forward may be called into question due to their privileged place in society.[15]

Transformative white Christianity believes that education is about achieving knowledge and working to improve society. There is an understanding that the only way to revolutionary transformation is through relationships with and accountability to those who are and/or have been oppressed by white supremacist euro-Christianity.

On the opposite end of the scale, a transactional white Christianity has a worldview based in the idea that interactions are zero-sum, resulting in gains for oneself, or for one's own, at some cost. Sometimes this means gaining or giving up resources that are limited. Sometimes this means being competitive, always winning or losing because there are no ties. Transactional white Christianity focuses on individualism and centers on the individual's salvation and adherence to a set of biblical fundamentals. According to Dwight Hopkins, "Individualism [is] a smokescreen for a warped self-focus and unethical right to exploit people through maintaining hierarchy over others."[16] This way of engaging Christianity is me-centered—concerned with one's own salvation and right belief, as well as the salvation and right beliefs of a select few who are also "right with God" and who will also inherit the kingdom to come. This type of Christianity understands that it should have dominion over Earth and the animals, and that men should have power over women, as interpreted from Genesis 1.

Transactional white Christianity believes one has earned all they have, rather than having gained it because of systemic advantages. Self-criticism is missing from their understanding of the Bible. Transactional white Christianity interprets the world in individual terms to the degree that sin is about individual transgressions and not the function of systems of power, unless that system is questioning the group's doctrines and beliefs. Ultimately, this means that individuals and not systems are the reason for bigotry, prejudice, and oppression. Education is about indoctrination and proper beliefs and practices. When criticized by those outside the group, transactional white Christianity defends itself by claiming victimization. This type of white Christianity upholds white supremacist Eurocentric Christianity, believing it is the right order of things based on the will of God.

White supremacist Eurocentric Christianity has been shown to help create and still maintains the oppressive binary systems in place today. All white Christianity is tainted by it and benefits from it. However, not all white Christianity is equal. White Christianity can be measured on a scale with transformational white Christianity on one end and transactional white Christianity on the other end. The more transformational white Christianity is, the more it contributes to revolutionary change. Conversely, the more transactional white Christianity is, the more likely it will support the white supremacist Eurocentric Christian status quo which is leading the US toward fascism.

THE REDEEMABILITY OF WHITE CHRISTIANS

Several years ago, I was asked by movement elder Ruby Sales, "Do you believe white people are redeemable?"[17] I was asked because Sales wanted me to consider writing a white redemptive theology. It is a question that has haunted me ever since. The more I have thought about it, the question has changed to, "Can white Christians be redeemed?" I continue to be confounded as more and more people move away from identifying as Christian while at the same time there are white people who have doubled-down and seek shelter in the comfort of white supremacist Eurocentric Christianity. Ultimately, the answer to the question is messy. My answer is *no* and *yes* and needs to be unpacked.

Let me first clarify what is meant by *being redeemed*. Redemption is the process of recognizing harm, confessing about the harm, and making changes in one's life to stop the harm. All people have the capacity to change. Change comes through conflict and disruption to one's worldview and usually happens through the mechanisms of moral appeal, education, and/or personal experience. And yet, not all people are willing to change or want change. From their perspective, there is nothing wrong, and thus, redemption is unnecessary. We are living in a time when everyone knows what oppression is and evidence shows how it works. Not to believe something is wrong and that systems of oppression are not real is to be willfully ignorant. Redeemability comes down to one's willingness to change. In the context of the question about white Christianity, being redeemed means working for and supporting the revolution. Remember, *revolution* means creating society anew, where all human beings are valued, given equity, and cared for with dignity.

Therefore, to answer the question: "No, white Christians cannot be redeemed if they do not believe there is a need for redemption from white supremacist Eurocentric Christianity." How can someone be redeemed if they believe they are sinless and do not need to wrestle with the sins of their ancestors? Or if they do not see everyone as a worthy human being? Or if they believe themselves to be superior? When there is no recognition that harm has occurred and continues to occur, then there can be no confession, and as a result, redemption cannot take place. This would be true of those white Christians who find themselves on the scale leaning toward transactional white Christianity. The more characteristics from transactional white Christianity to which one subscribes, the less likely they are to see the need for change because they see no problem.

I can also answer the question as: "Yes. There is hope for those who seek redemption from white supremacist Eurocentric Christianity, who are willing to confess, and who make good on working for revolutionary change." White Christians who lean toward a transformational white Christianity can be redeemed.

USHERING IN THE REVOLUTION

The choice of becoming a part of the revolution or allowing fascism to further gain momentum continues to be upon those of us who identify as white Christians. There is still time for redemption, and there are concrete actions that can be taken to usher in the revolution.

First, strive to be transformational in your Christian beliefs and practices. Part of this process is reorienting yourself to thinking about your responsibilities to the wider community. To do this, you must do the work. Take anti-oppression workshops and read. You do not need to be "all together" or have professional credentials to start doing the work. There is always more to learn, and so you will not be perfect or get it right all the time. This process also includes maintaining humility and a willingness to be corrected. As someone who benefits from the systems of oppression, there will be times when you will mess up in your speech or actions. Bias, prejudice, and superiority are strong forces even when you are trying to be conscious of them. It is in those moments that one must be open to being corrected and to absorb such correction with humility.

Second, seek out others who are doing the work. You need to develop relationships locally with a variety of people getting out of white and heteronormative comfortable spaces. The first part of developing relationships is showing up and then to keep showing up over and over. Sometimes it may feel like you are not doing much, but showing up helps develop trust and ultimately relationships. In addition to showing up, your role in these spaces is to listen. You need to learn how to listen deeply and believe what people say. People who benefit from the systems of oppression often dismiss those who are experiencing the oppression. Things are what people say and as bad as they describe them. Your role is to believe them.[18] It means developing empathy for others, rather than just sympathy. Empathy is relational and develops community. It comes from understanding and compassion bringing people together. Sympathy, however, is a kind of pity that can have power implications and create isolation.

Third, find your place in the revolution. We all have different skills that can contribute. A few of the roles include organizer, reconciler, host, advocate, educator, helper, rebel, and theorist.[19] The role you take may not be clear in the beginning. You may also have to take on roles that do not suit you to be sure the work gets done. Gradually, you will find your way. Regardless of the specific kind of role(s) you take, it is important to follow the lead of those you are in solidarity with and to eventually move beyond allyship to becoming an accomplice in the work. Being an ally is an important step, but it is not enough. Allies may express solidarity but do little to engage in active change. According to Indigenous Action, "Accomplices are realized through mutual consent and build trust. They don't just have our backs, they are at our side, or in their own spaces confronting and unsettling colonialism. *As accomplices we are compelled to become accountable and responsible to each other, that is the nature of trust*" (emphasis in original).[20] We are all responsible for doing the work and being knowledgeable, and everyone must find their role in the work.

Fourth, look for ways to let people know you are safe. If you are easily identified as someone who benefits from the systems of oppression, how do people know you are safe? This is an easier task in places where you develop relationships and show up over time: churches, places of employment, schools, organizations, and neighborhoods. People can observe how you act. It is more complicated in public spaces where you are unknown. It becomes necessary in those public spaces to use signifiers that indicate you are safe. For example, if you carry a bag or backpack, you can place supportive buttons, patches, or stickers on it. Another example would be stopping, watching, and maybe asking to be sure everything is okay when you see a Black or brown person pulled over by white police officers. In some public spaces, the only way to signify your support is to be a witness.

Fifth, provide a counternarrative to white supremacist Eurocentric Christianity. If you are working for the revolution, you should take the opportunity to let people know that not all white Christians ascribe to a white supremacist Eurocentric way of being. Instead, you should share your vision of a world based on equity, inclusion, and the worth and dignity of all people.

You may find these opportunities at public meetings, in public forums, online, and at rallies.

Sixth, push back against the ideas of white cis-hetero male victimhood and xenophobia when you are a witness to it. This is especially true in your relationships and day-to-day encounters. One must be prepared to speak up in those moments. At the same time, it should be recognized that sometimes we are not the ones that will be best listened to. This can be true in family systems. Often a stranger will be heard in a way that we cannot.

Seventh, remember self-care. The revolution will not come overnight. It is a long haul. It is therefore necessary to find ways to care for oneself and for others in the fight. Too often people enter the revolutionary cause and feel guilty when they take time for themselves. There will always be work to be done, and if you are burned out you will not be of use to anyone. Learn to find an escape and time to rejuvenate.

CONCLUSION

It is possible for white Christians to be redeemed by assuming the characteristics of transformational white Christianity and doing the work. There are forces at work to keep the status quo and to roll back any revolutionary changes made in the last sixty-plus years. Throughout this chapter, I have demonstrated that white supremacist Eurocentric Christianity has been one of the sources for securing the systems of oppression which have been in place for centuries. Currently, transactional white Christianity provides support to the demagoguery and backlash to the progress made toward a more equitable society. The rise in social, cultural, and political polarization and violence has prepared the ground for fascism to take hold, *unless* there is revolutionary change. Are you ready to join the revolution?[21]

NOTES

1. Boggs and Kurashige, *The Next American Revolution*, xvii–xviii. Boggs's understanding of revolution is akin to how Martin Luther King Jr. discussed revolution in the years just before his assassination. See King Jr., "Conversations with Martin Luther King." See also King's articulation of a "revolution of values," first drafted by Vincent Harding, in his 1967 sermon, "Beyond Vietnam."

2. I have written about this elsewhere. See Johnson, "Weaving Narratives."

3. The use of the terms *heteronormative*, *patriarchal*, and *white supremacy* is informed by the works of hooks, *Feminist Theory*; Combahee River Collective, "The

Combahee River Collective"; and Andrea Smith, "Heteropatriarchy and the Three Pillars of White Supremacy."

4. Roberts-Miller, *Demagoguery and Democracy*, 33.

5. Vandermaas-Peeler, Cox, Fisch-Friedman, and Jones, "Diversity, Division, Discrimination."

6. Vandermaas-Peeler, Cox, Fisch-Friedman, and Jones, "Diversity, Division, Discrimination."

7. See Smith, "More White Americans Adopted Than Shed Evangelical Label"; Shellnutt, "'Political Evangelicals'?"; Rubin, "Just How Racist Is the MAGA Movement?"; Engler, "Political Polarization Is Pushing Evangelicals"; Garcia, "Herschel Walker Won Overwhelming Share of White Votes"; and Dale, "How 2020 Election Deniers Did."

8. The idea of active ally, passive ally, and neutral comes from "The Spectrum of Allies." The spectrum originates from the work of George Lakey and is an activist tool for analyzing your allies and opponents. See "Spectrum of Allies."

9. Katz, Young, Earp, and Jhally, *Tough Guise 2*.

10. *Visibility* and *invisibility* are much more complex than I am able to discuss here. For example, movement elder Ruby Sales argues that the racial categories of white and Black are intended to erase an individual's cultural heritage. This is true for all racial categories. For white people this means not understanding who your people are, making you dependent on the power and privileges of whiteness for your identity.

11. Arendt, *On Violence*, 56.

12. The so-called "Great Replacement" is an example of this phenomenon. See Wilson and Flanagan, "The Racist 'Great Replacement' Conspiracy Theory Explained."

13. Tilly, *Durable Inequality*, 7. See also Johnson, "Weaving Narratives."

14. I am building on Martin Luther King Jr.'s concept of *beloved community*. As I have written elsewhere, King's beloved community is rooted in the ideas of the *Imago Dei* and agape love in action. See Johnson, "Martin Luther King Jr. and the Search for Peace," 333–34.

15. Johnson, "The Problem of Whiteness in the Occupy Movement," 91–92.

16. Hopkins, *Being Human*, 109.

17. For more about the work and life of Ruby Sales, see the SpiritHouse Project, https://www.spirithouseproject.org/aboutruby.php; the Veterans of Hope Project, https://www.veteransofhope.org/veterans/ruby-sales/; and Sales, "Where Does It Hurt?"

18. Defining what it means to show up, listen, and believe came in conversation with Rev. Melissa Bennett.

19. Bill Moyer and Mary Lou Finley wrote about the different types of social activist in their work about the Movement Action Plan. For a summary of many of these roles, see Lakey, "What Role Were You Born to Play in Social Change?" See also Finley, "How Social Movements Work," 195–202.

20. "Accomplices Not Allies."

21. Acknowledgments: Thank you to Dr. David Fairchild and Rev. Jan Fairchild for your editing work on this chapter.

BIBLIOGRAPHY

"Accomplices Not Allies: Abolishing the Ally Industrial Complex." *Indigenous Action.* May 4, 2014. https://www.indigenousaction.org/accomplices-not-allies-abolishing-the-ally-industrial-complex/.

Arendt, Hannah. *On Violence.* London: Harcourt, 1970.

Boggs, Grace Lee, and Scott Kurashige. *The Next American Revolution: Sustainable Activism for the Twenty-First Century.* Berkeley: University of California Press, 2011.

Combahee River Collective. "The Combahee River Collective: A Black Feminist Statement." In *Resist, Organize, Transform: An Introduction to Nonviolence and Activism.* Edited by JoanMay Cordova, Matt Guynn, Dean Johnson, and Regina Shands Stoltzfus. San Diego, CA: Cognella Academic Publishing, 2020.

Dale, Daniel. "How 2020 Election Deniers Did in Their 2022 Midterm Races." *CNN Politics.* December 7, 2022. https://www.cnn.com/interactive/2022/11/politics/election-deniers-winners-losers-midterms-2022/.

Engler, Paul. "Political Polarization Is Pushing Evangelicals to a Historic Breaking Point." *Waging Nonviolence.* July 19, 2022. https://wagingnonviolence.org/2022/07/political-polarization-is-pushing-evangelicals-to-historic-breaking-point/.

Finley, Mary Lou. "How Social Movements Work." In *Resist, Organize, Transform: An Introduction to Nonviolence and Activism.* Edited by JoanMay Cordova, Matt Guynn, Dean Johnson, and Regina Shands Stoltzfus. San Diego, CA: Cognella Academic Publishing, 2020.

Garcia, Eric. "Herschel Walker Won Overwhelming Share of White Votes—The Only Group That Supported Him." *The Independent.* November 9, 2022. https://www.independent.co.uk/news/world/americas/us-politics/midterm-elections-2022/white-voters-georgia-herschel-walker-senate-b2221657.html.

hooks, bell. *Feminist Theory: From Margin to Center.* London: Pluto Press, 1984/2000.

Hopkins, Dwight N. *Being Human: Race, Culture, and Religion.* Minneapolis, MN: Orbis Books, 2005.

Johnson, Dean J. "Martin Luther King Jr. and the Search for Peace." In *The Wiley Blackwell Companion to Religion and Peace.* Edited by Jolyon Mitchell, Suzanna R. Millar, Francesca Po, and Martyn Percy. Hoboken, NJ: Wiley Blackwell, 2022.

———. "The Problem of Whiteness in the Occupy Movement." In *What Comes After Occupy? The Regional Politics of Resistance.* Edited by Todd Comer. Newcastle upon Tyne: Cambridge Scholars Publishing, 2015.

———. "Weaving Narratives: The Construction of Whiteness." In *We Have Not Been Moved: Resisting Racism and Militarism in 21st Century America.* Edited by Elizabeth "Betita" Martínez, Mandy Carter, and Matt Meyer. Oakland, CA: PM Press, 2012.

Katz, Jackson, Jason T. Young, Jeremy Earp, and Sut Jhally. *Tough Guise 2: Violence Manhood and American Culture.* Media Education Foundation and Kanopy Streaming, 2016. http://ucsb.kanopystreaming.com/node/216725.

King, Martin Luther Jr. "Beyond Vietnam: Time to Break the Silence." In *Resist, Organize, Transform: An Introduction to Nonviolence and Activism*. Edited by JoanMay Cordova, Matt Guynn, Dean Johnson, and Regina Shands Stoltzfus. San Diego, C: Cognella Academic Publishing, 2020.

———. "Conversations with Martin Luther King: 68th Annual Convention of the Rabbinical Assembly March 25, 1968." In *Martin Luther King, Jr.: The Last Interview and Other Conversations*. Brooklyn, NY: Melville House, 2017.

Lakey, George. "What Role Were You Born to Play in Social Change?" Waging Nonviolence. February 3, 2016. https://wagingnonviolence.org/2016/02/bill-moyer-four-roles-of-social-change/?pf=true.

Roberts-Miller, Patricia. *Demagoguery and Democracy*. New York: The Experiment, 2017.

Rubin, Jennifer. "Just How Racist Is the MAGA Movement? This Survey Measures It." *The Washington Post*. September 28, 2022.

Sales, Ruby. "Where Does It Hurt?" *On Being with Krista Tippett*. National Public Radio. September 15, 2016. https://onbeing.org/programs/ruby-sales-where-does-it-hurt/.

Shellnutt, Kate. "'Political Evangelicals'? More Trump Supporters Adopt the Label." *Christianity Today*. September 16, 2021. https://www.christianitytoday.com/news/2021/september/trump-evangelical-identity-pew-research-survey-presidency.html.

Smith, Andrea. "Heteropatriarchy and the Three Pillars of White Supremacy: Rethinking Women of Color Organizing." In *Color of Violence: The INCITE! Anthology*. Durham, NC: Duke University Press, 2016.

Smith, Gregory A. "More White Americans Adopted Than Shed Evangelical Label during Trump Presidency, Especially His Supporters." Pew Research Center. September 15, 2021. https://www.pewresearch.org/fact-tank/2021/09/15/more-white-americans-adopted-than-shed-evangelical-label-during-trump-presidency-especially-his-supporters/.

"Spectrum of Allies." Beautiful Trouble. https://beautifultrouble.org/toolbox/tool/spectrum-of-allies/.

Tilly, Charles. *Durable Inequality*. Berkeley: University of California Press, 1998.

Vandermaas-Peeler, Alex, Daniel Cox, Molly Fisch-Friedman, and Robert P. Jones. "Diversity, Division, Discrimination: The State of Young America." *MTV/PRRI Report*. Public Religion Research Institute. https://www.prri.org/research/mtv-culture-and-religion/.

Wilson, Jason, and Aaron Flanagan. "The Racist 'Great Replacement' Conspiracy Theory Explained." Southern Poverty Law Center. May 17, 2022. https://www.splcenter.org/hatewatch/2022/05/17/racist-great-replacement-conspiracy-theory-explained.

Chapter 20

The Hidden White Flesh of White Christian Nationalism

Anthropological Docetism and the *Forging* of *Idols*

José Francisco Morales Torres

For the wolflike white nationalism to cloak itself in "Christian" wool, it needs to use Christian sources malleable enough to deform so that they *appear* Christian but are, in actuality, used in a "heretical" manner that rejects the countercultural, last-shall-be-first praxis of the Gospel. In this way, it gives off the "feel" or "mood" of Christianity without needing to pay heed to the incarnate Word and brown carpenter-turned-preacher from Nazareth. The Gospel challenge is an incarnate word that calls for an embodied commitment to the revolutionary reign of God. Incarnational and embodied; hence, the words from the first Johannine epistle:

> By this you know the Spirit of God: every spirit that confesses that Jesus Christ has come in the flesh is from God, and every spirit that does not confess Jesus is not from God. And this is the spirit of the antichrist, of which you have heard that it is coming, and now it is already in the world.[1]

In this reflection, I argue that white Christian nationalism, to possess a "Christian" signature, *de*carnates the Word by rejecting the brown, fleshly messiah and by rejecting a fully theological anthropology that makes demands on the body and not just the "heart." The idolatry of white Christian nationalism is sourced by a docetism that rejects or evades embodiment to hide the oppressive machinations of white flesh, to deny the full humanity of the racialized Other, and to ignore the incarnational faith of that which orients us to "the weightier matters of the law: justice and mercy and faith."[2] (Docetism was an early heresy—still lingering in our midst—that rejected that "Jesus Christ has come in the flesh.") In other words, *Christian* nationalism forges idols to "seem" [*dokein*, from the Koine for "to seem"] Christian enough to "sanctify" the hidden ways white supremacy is enfleshed in the world.

This chapter is composed of five constructive moves. First, I speak to the nature of theology as having its origin in song (denoted as *hymno-theology*) and as being "orientational knowledge." In other words, it is a form of knowledge that orients and locates us to engage the world in a particular way. Second, I offer a phenomenological account of how racism works as a site of invisibilizing the white flesh so that it may likewise invisibilize the ways in which white privilege is enfleshed in the world. The intent of this white invisibility is political: to go undetected and continue in its insidious project of domination. Third, aided by this phenomenology of racialized invisibility, I offer a theological analysis that dissects the ways that white nationalism uses the disembodied theological anthropology (what I describe as an anthropological docetism) dominant in white hymno-theology to legitimize and make "sacred" its racist political ideology. I demonstrate that the decarnational, disembodied hymno-theology of white evangelical culture is malleable enough to serve white Christian nationalism because it evades embodiment and renders invisible the ways white flesh, systemic and political, is an agent of conquest and colonization. The invisible soul invisibilizes white flesh and its subjugating ploys. Fourth, I interpret the liberationist theopoetics of Father Ernesto Cardenal as a corrective theological anthropology that places enfleshment and its political entanglements at the center of its theological concern. Lastly, I end on a homiletical note, a kerygmatic summons to sing a new song rooted in a robust theological anthropology that embraces incarnational praxes and resists white supremafication and its ploys of invisibility.

I

Theology orients us to reality—to God, others, and the world. As "orientational knowledge," theology assists us "to *locate* ourselves in our world and to *order* the world with respect to us." In this sense, theology is "orientational knowledge."[3] What makes theology orientational knowledge is its "*localizing* and *organizing functions*."[4] To use phenomenological terms, theology attunes us to the world by interpreting the world into which we are "thrown" and in which we seek to act freely and authentically. Theology, at its best, moves us from merely existing to living authentically.[5]

If theology orients, then its magnetic force is song. Theology was creedalized later, but its origin, its "heart," is hymnic. Peter G. Heltzel rightly reminds us that the church *sang* the Trinity and performed it in ritual before it *understood* the Trinity.[6] The New Testament grew out of a communal experience of the risen Christ who even in his resurrected, eschatological embodiment, retained the scars of his political execution. Some of the earliest material in the New Testament are the hymns, songs, and liturgical confessions that preserved and nurtured the earliest Christians' mystical encounter with the Risen Christ. They would deepen their mystical contact with Christ as they sang "psalms and hymns and spiritual songs to one another."[7] Therefore, if theology is to have orientational power, it must retain the sonics of melody even as it strives for the exactness of logical explication. Theology is not just didactic. It is performative. It is drama.[8] As theologian Lakisha Lockhart notes, theology is "play."[9]

Unlike disputational prose, the lyrical and poetic word is porous and elastic, always opening space for the (nearly) inexpressible—that is, for the comical and the tragic, for the beautiful and the dreadful, for joyous exuberance and "groans too deep for words."[10] The metered lines of songs remain perennially open to the transcendence of faith that oozes through and beyond the written page. Therefore, to get at how theology impacts and operates in the shared *Lebenswelt*—a lifeworld disgraced by Christian supremacy and white nationalism—it behooves us to reflect upon how we *sing* our faith. It demands that our hymnody undergo hermeneutical criticism and that we scrutinize the cantillated language of faith and its political and economic manifestations.

II

As Paul C. Taylor posits, racism works by way of invisibilities.[11] The racist tactic of invisibility caricaturizes or monsterizes brownness and Blackness. It flattens Black and brown persons, limiting their fabricated profile to only a few possibilities: "thug,"[12] "illegal,"[13] or "welfare queen,"[14] among others. George Yancy dubs this "objecthood": Under the white gaze, the Black subject is "fungible and fixed essence," which distorts their particularity, "phantasmicizes" their embodiment, and "de-subjectivizes" them.[15] The white gaze depersonalizes persons of color. The multilayered histories, the rich personalities of actual persons, are never *truly* seen. What the white system of "colorblindness" sees is only the caricature or monster it has produced. Racial "mythologies" generate veils to invisibilize the other.[16] These "perverse forms of racialized typification"[17] are political strategies[18] that place persons of color in a *"present invisibility,"* a "being-there-not-there."[19]

Yet, Taylor continues, racism also fabricates a *white* invisibility as well, which makes white persons unaware of their whiteness and its affiliated privileges. (Supposedly) unaware of their whiteness, they cannot see, or refuse to see, their own whiteness. Also, white invisibility reinforces white dominance. Meaning, the privilege, centrality, and "normativity" of said dominance are also hidden,[20] eluding detection at first glance. Such fabricated normativity is easily "naturalized" when placed within the dominant white lifeworld, within its sociopolitical horizon of being carved by and for whiteness. Whereas Black and brown invisibility caricaturizes by casting monsters, white invisibility camouflages and mimics, permitting white supremacy to blend into a world it insidiously conquers and claims as its own.

Yancy theorizes this racialized invisibility with the language of "home" and estrangement. Within the racialized space of the white gaze, the racialized other becomes "'Black' anew," that is, it again becomes the "predator-stereotype" and "fantasized object" of the white imaginary.[21] Within this anti-Black horizon, the white gaze never truly sees the Black Other. In "seeing" the Black body anew, the white gaze attempts to render the Black body homeless, as that which doesn't have a home, as that which is always already estranged from its own embodiment. Conversely, white embodiment always has an exclusive "home" of its own making, protected by its own power and privilege and, thusly, "normalized."[22] Calvin Warren's analysis of Blackness as lacking an ontological "home" (what he calls black "onticide"[23]) comes to mind.

In sum, the sheep's clothes of racism are not invisible; rather, they are invisibilizing. Racism hides racialized flesh to insidiously oppress Black and brown flesh. And it deems invisible the oppressive entanglements of white flesh upon the bruised flesh of the world. Against a liberative, orthopraxic theology that orients toward the flourishing of flesh-and-bone humans, racism disorients toward the "ideal"—nay, toward the ideology—of disembodiment, so that it may try to conceal its privileging of white flesh and its supremacist policies emerging therefrom.

III

So far, my argument accounts for the insidious tactics of *white* nationalism. But what about the heretical tactics of white *Christian* nationalism? This move leads us to ask about the operative theology that sanctions and "blesses" Christian nationalism and how said theology (dis)orients the white gaze away from the embodied, racializing polity staffed by white flesh. And since (as stated previously) theology is song at its core, it calls for analysis of the hymnological themes and proclivities that source and manifest the heresy of Christian nationalism. To this, I now turn.

It might be an oversimplification to equate, in a one-to-one comparison, white Christian nationalism with white evangelical theological culture. (Although to be brutally honest, I am not so sure anymore, after four years of prominent white evangelicals supporting a racist, xenophobic, sexist, misogynistic, classist, and Islamophobic despot as [their] president.) Nevertheless, I contend that the white evangelical theological hymno-theology provides white nationalism with a theology—and more specifically, a theological *anthropology*—suitable for its Christian nationalistic idol making and idol worshipping.

I begin here by uttering, quite intentionally, the forthcoming (almost) tautology. Nonetheless, it is necessary to begin by *naming* the obvious: White Christian nationalism is sourced by white Christianity. Again, the claim is not that the former *is* the latter, but the latter provides the theological "raw material" for the former. What then is the *zeitgeist* of white *hymno*-theology? And how is this hymnic mood appropriated for the white nationalistic project? I seek not a full exegesis of the repertoire of the church's canticles. Rather I offer philosophical and theological reflections on how hymnic orientations reflect and influence political praxes.

Edmund Husserl contends that each "science" works from "a set of inferential relations" that are interconnected to and expressed in "a system of propositions." To grasp these systems, adds Husserl, it is necessary to analyze their "linguistic manifestations."[24] One need only skim through the discography of, say, some of the most popular and highest grossing praise and worship bands, singers, and "collectives,"[25] which come from largely white Evangelical circles. (There is not enough space here to go through the whole discography to demonstrate my basic assertion. I trust the curious reader to peruse for themselves if they are so inclined to investigate further.) Still, to deepen my point, I offer a phenomenological reading of "America's most beloved song,"[26] John Newton's "Amazing Grace."[27] Although this song is not a product of contemporary evangelicalism, it is an archetype for the hymnic mood set by Evangelical "worship culture."

In the spirit of full disclosure, I admit that there is much in Newton's "Amazing Grace" that moves me still. I am very much like the Apostle Paul: All too often, "I do not do what I want, but I do the very thing I hate."[28] So, I am counting on God to be amazingly gracious with me. Nevertheless, what stuns me most is how Newton does not name the body in this hymn, a hymn penned to recount his conversion after coming face to face with *bodily* death. Nor does this song contain a register that orients Newton toward the embodied other. It is purely an interior, isolating theological anthropology.

As a seaman, Newton[29] was involved in the transatlantic slave trade. He later had a change of *heart*. As the story is *erroneously* told, he had a near-death experience at sea, which led to his conversion *and to his turn to abolitionism*. However, this is not the story at all. In fact, even *after* his conversion, he continued his active participation in the slave trade, captaining three more voyages. He only quit the slave-trading enterprise after he retired from sailing altogether due to a stroke. Newton's personal story is richly embodied, both as a perpetrator and as the recipient of amazing grace. He sold African bodies and moved the "merchandise" of enslaved flesh "across the pond" for profit. He had a near-death experience—an intensely *bodily* event, I might add. Yet, the song, intended to mark his personal conversion, avoids strong incarnational language, except in the fifth stanza:

> Yes, when this flesh and heart shall fail,
> and mortal life shall cease . . .

William E. Phipps argues that the last line of the first stanza, "Was blind but now I see," refers to "his deliverance from the blindness that prevented his seeing the anti-Christian nature of slave trading."[30] Phipps's assertion intimates a bodily register in Newton's theological anthropology of conversion. Yet, this is not apparent within the larger mood set by the hymn, a mood oriented largely to the interior self.

Moreover, the chronology alone confirms that the song portrays spiritual conversion as only a reformation of one's interior states and not a bodily rehabilitation toward the just and good. Newton writes,

> How precious did that grace appear
> The hour I first believ'd!

Newton penned "first believed" and "grace appeared" in 1748. He did not claim an abolitionist position until 1754 or 1755. Hence, his lost-and-foundness, his blind-and-seeingness, is not an embodied conversion. It is not a reorientation toward the other. It does not display an honest embodied repentance, a turning away, with his body, from being an *active* extension of the enslaving apparatus of white political flesh. Nor does he decry the reducing of African bodies to an enslaved means of profitable production. His "conversion" does not call for an incarnational praxis that attends to those enslaved by empire and its army and markets. For Newton, this is a radical turn *inward* that completely occludes the very flesh he scarred and severed during his pre-graced lostness and blindness. "Grace has taught my eyes to see." Newton's theology of grace does not teach the "eyes" to see out into the wounded, whipped, shackled flesh of the world. The repentant gaze, the repentant *white* gaze, is interiorly oriented toward his invisible soul.

As hymo-theology, "Amazing Grace" orients us to neglect the flesh—even one's own—and to focus on the interior life. Its intended addressee is the invisible soul. Newton uses what Charles Taylor calls "reified and self-focused forms of modern subjectivism."[31] As this hymn demonstrates, white hymno-theology exaggerates "the inwardness of radical reflexivity."[32] This radical turn "imprisons"[33] the "self" in a reified interiority, so much so that one loses sight of one's own embodiment and how this embodiment has material and historical effects on the rest of the flesh of the world. It converts the (white) soul but makes no demands for sanctification on the (white) body.

The radical inwardness *at the expense of incarnation* defines the contemporary praise and worship phenomenon, a largely white evangelical manifestation. "Amazing Grace" has many children; its most boisterous child is the white Evangelical "worship culture," which continues to uphold this docetistic anthropology. When one surveys the hymno-theological culture and its "anthems," a particular lexicography emerges, which portrays a "man" (gender-exclusive term used with intention) of only interiority: "soul," "heart," and the ever amorphous "me." Moreover, that "me" is usually *un*placed—not *dis*placed, but unplaced. The "soul," which theologically anthropologizes white hymno-theology, is no-place. The tenor it sets is that of omnipresence. This disembodied, unplaced, omnipresent "man" is then oriented likewise toward a disembodied, unplaced, omnipresent *epistemology* and *praxis*. To draw from Yancy here, it "images" a whiteness "unconstrained" by the "norms" it sets to "generalize" whiteness and to "make strange" the other.[34] It blankets the particularities of oppression, always an enfleshed phenomena, in the cloak of vague generalities—in disembodied, unplaced, omnipresent "truth." Yet, these generalities are the luxury of those afforded and comforted by power. The theological anthropology of white normativity orients and locates itself to the world through a white epistemology of generality.

My point here is that the dominant theological anthropology, exemplified in "America's most beloved song" and exacerbated by the globalizing reach of white worship culture, centers the invisible soul and de-places the visible body beyond the radius of theological concern. Unlike the Black spiritual, which (as James Cone notes[35]) is a richly embodied hymno-theology, its white Evangelical counterpart never gets at what Miguel de Unamuno calls *el hombre de carne y hueso* ("the human of flesh and bone"). Rather, the resultant anthropology of this hymnic docetism is not human. It does not imagine "all of us who walk solidly on the earth." In Unamuno's words, it constructs a "no-man."[36] This hymno-theology is thoroughly docetistic. It overuses the invisible (white) soul to render invisible the white body.

To be clear, I do not object to "the inwardness of radical reflexivity." Such an inwardness is indispensable to authenticity. (After all, "the unexamined life is not worth living."[37]) Rather, my concern is how this call exclusively to the *interiorem hominem* generates *for white nationalism* a socioeconomic and political strategy of domination. White Christian nationalism sings its white invisibility by centering the invisible "soul," liturgically legitimizing its white supremacy by simply hiding the white flesh that animates said supremafication. The "gaze" of the white song turns *in interiore homine*, orienting the worshipper toward an approach to the world that does not see, or dismisses, its embodied, oppressive entanglements in the world. Phrased differently, the white hymno-theology, when interpreted "discographically" (i.e., as a whole), generates a theological anthropology that begins and ends with the *interiorem hominem*. It ignores the *homo in relationibus* and consequently orients toward a decarnational spirituality. Once unfleshed, it can evade the much-needed hamartiological deconstruction that calls to account all the ways white flesh operates oppressively in the world. White hymno-theology renders invisible white Christian hegemony by omitting from its litanies the white body. In doing so, it places the death-dealing ways of white supremacist flesh beyond theological admonition. A docetistic theological anthropology permits white Christian supremacist flesh to go unchecked (theologically speaking), so that gripping enfleshment of white Christian nationalism can continue suffocating Black and brown bodies. ("I can't breathe!")

By centralizing the invisible (white) soul, white hymno-theology invisibilizes the white flesh. In doing so, it constructs a theological anthropology ideal for the oppressive mechanics of white supremacy. White evangelical hymno-theology, on the one hand, equips white nationalism with the language and performance to showcase its "christianness." On the other hand, it capacitates nationalism to occlude its whiteness. Thus, the evasion of embodiment in white evangelical hymno-theology yields its intended sociopolitical end, namely, to intentionally orient the gaze *away* from white embodiment and its concomitant privilege. Theological docetism is a political docetism that hides (or attempts to obfuscate) the ways in which white bodies operate in colonizing the horizon of being (which should be shared by all of the living by virtue of our creatureliness) into their white space of comfort and conquest. It establishes for them what Yancy calls their "white innocence."[38]

IV

To resist the heretical docetistic lure of white Christian nationalism, theology needs to sing a new song. Where then shall we turn to find a liberating muse to inspire prophetic and incarnational hymno-theology that reorients us toward an antiracist, antinationalistic posture toward the flesh of the world? I suggest that we look south to Nicaragua and its poet-prophet, the late Father Ernesto Cardenal. The robust embodiment and political enfleshment of his liberationist theopoetics construct a theological anthropology that attends to the person of *carne y hueso* and attunes us to our enfleshed sociopolitical relations. Cardenal's hymno-theology *sees* the embodied Other. It names the body politic that materializes oppression and enfleshes injustice, refusing to theologize the former (human flesh) without the latter (political flesh). Working with her fellow Caribbean theorists Aimé Césaire and Édouard Glissant, Mayra Rivera notes how sociopolitical relations and their discourses are also enfleshments which entangle with our flesh. The individual is "flesh of the flesh of the world,"[39] and the world "a society of labyrinthine intracorporeal transformations" and "complex incarnations with no discernible end or beginning."[40] Within such a context that emphasizes the profound continuity and contiguity of enfleshment (not discreet edges), Yancy suggests "an ontology of no edges."[41]

Cardenal deploys his quill to do a liberationist paraphrase of the Psalms, *Salmos*.[42] Working from the already robust theological anthropology of the biblical Psalter, he extends embodiment into "the becoming flesh of social relations."[43] For example, he takes the opening address to God in Psalm 5:

> For you are not a God who delights in wickedness;
> evil will not sojourn with you.
> The boastful will not stand before your eyes;
> you hate all evildoers. (vv. 4–5)

—as chanted, directly and unequivocally, from his political circumstance:

> For you are not a God who befriends directors or supports of their politics
> nor are you influenced by propaganda
> nor do you partner with the "gangster"

Cardenal takes the already incarnationally rich corpus of the Psalms and, by way of paraphrase, extends their lyrical enfleshments to the sociopolitical. As Reginald Gibbons highlights, Cardenal incorporates "a recognizably Latin American material into his poetry." His brilliance, moreover, is found, among other things, in his deployment of "a diction that is concrete and detailed, textured with proper names and the names of things in preference to the accepted poetic language, which was more abstract, general, and vaguely symbolic."[44] Cardenal's narrator is never unplaced. They are always "on the ground" in the struggle against US-backed dictator-puppets used to extend the tentacles of the political dominance of white flesh. Nor is the poetic voice a disembodied one. The cantor of Cardenal's "Psalm 17" is the voice of "the defender of the exiled," "of the condemned by the War Trials," and "of prisoners in the concentration camps." In place and embodied, the narrative voice is not omnipresent; rather, it is always "here" or "there."

In *Epigramas*,[45] Cardenal denounces, by name, the sources of the inner fear, the Somoza regime, and summons forth an incarnational praxis to resist the diabolical political flesh:

> I've handed out clandestine pamphlets,
> yelling: VIVA LA LIBERTAD! In the middle of the street
> defying armed guards.
> I participated in the April rebellion:
> but I grow pale when I pass by your house
> and one look from you makes me tremble.

And as attended to the body politic, he attends to bodies. He depicts the fear as felt in the body. "I grow pale . . . makes me tremble": This is full anthropology theologized in poetry. As Rivera notes, the world's dealings "produce material effects that are woven in the textures of the flesh," "marking" and "scarring" the body.[46] The narrator of *Epigramas* has "hands" to distribute prophetic pamphlets. One *sees* him and his hands distributing printed prophecies ("clandestine pamphlets") that inculcate an embodied faith standing before the gangrened flesh of dictatorships backed by a "gangster" empire. The oppressive fear is felt in the body; the resistance, too, is bodily.

Cardenal's lyrical technique exemplified his "definition of his stance toward life."[47] He was a poet-theologian. As a hymno-theologian, his intone stanzas are saturated in an "orientational knowledge" that locates the reader and orients them to shift their gaze *outward* toward the other and the world. His "poetic stance" addresses sociopolitical forces "that shape—and often distort, damage, or destroy—life and feeling."[48] Cardenal's radius of theological anthropological concern is not imprisoned by inner angst or some inquietude of the interior in need of some psychological techniques for serenity.

Again, I am not arguing against introspection in our theological anthropology. Cardenal's theopoetic anthropology includes a robust interior life. Yet, he posits an interiority that (drawing from Helmuth Plessner) is "exocentric."[49] The inner self is always "out there" and not simply within. As Plessner notes, the human "core" is "not only with themselves but at the same time outside themselves."[50] Exocentricity means that inner selves "stand where they stand and at the same time do not stand where they stand."[51] One therefore cannot circumvent the body since the inner "I" is always embodied "out there" and not just "in here." And the swivel, the hinge, between "in here" and "out there" is *the body*. As a theopoet and psalmo-theologian, Cardenal constructs an exocentric anthropology that attunes the reader to a bodily register and locates them in a praxical posture committed to the embodied, placed, and present work of justice. The visible body, in praxis, is what will unveil (i.e., make visible), for direct hamartiological rebuke, the fleshy apparatuses of oppression. And the visible body, in relational and revolutionary praxes, is how justice is incarnated. To paraphrase "John's" first epistle, *every spirit that confesses that liberation comes in the flesh is from God.*

V

The esoteric (versus "exocentric") "inner man" in white hymno-theology comes with a political proclivity that, in white nationalist hands, is deadly. By evading embodiment, white Christian nationalism avoids the prophetic indictment against the ways that white flesh has dominated and conquered nonwhite flesh. As the Psalter, Prophets, and Cardenal's poetic corpus attest, prophetic rebuke always addresses by name the site of oppression, always rebukes the particular in its exorcisms. In calling out "evil," Isaiah names and rebukes not evil in some invisible, ephemeral way; rather, the prophet denounces the embodiments of evil:

> Look, you serve your own interest on your fast day
> and oppress all your workers.
> You fast only to quarrel and to fight
> and to strike with a wicked fist.
> Such fasting as you do today
> will not make your voice heard on high.[52]

In other words, true denunciation of evil (hamartiology) and true restoration (soteriology) require a concrete site of address (i.e., embodiment in place). By shifting the white gaze to the indeterminate and invisible "soul" at the core of white hymno-theology, white Christian nationalism can "sing its heart out" to God without ever addressing the site of white privilege, namely, white flesh. Its "soul" can enjoy the "sweet sounds" of grace without atoning for the embodied supremacism of whiteness that offers, as sacrifice to its idols, "the sinful transubstantiation of Black living bodies into dead flesh."[53] The anthropological docetism of white hymno-theology serves well the surreptitious tactics of white Christian nationalism that deceptively conceals its whiteness while explicitly posturing a semblance to the faith of the brown carpenter-turned-preacher from Nazareth.

White Christian nationalism finds usable material in this anthropological docetism for forging its nationalistic idols. The concealing of white embodiment serves the political telos of white Christian nationalism by invisibilizing white embodiment to hide, and foster an "innocence" toward, white supremafication. Moreover, this hymno-theological inattention to (white) bodies facilitates the evasion of the necessary and critical (and hopefully redemptive) self-reflection and dismantling of white systems of domination. White Christian nationalism goes unchecked because the white gaze is oriented hymnally away from its white enfleshments, not only its individuated and personal flesh, but also its concomitant systemic, institutional, political flesh. It is by way of anthropological docetism that white Christian nationalism forges its idols. It invisibilizes its oppressive flesh by orienting the gaze toward the invisible "soul."

The heart of theology is song. Therefore, hymnody reveals our ultimate "loves." And, our "god" is revealed in our *ultimate* love(s). Rabbi Abraham Joshua Heschel declares, "God is of no importance unless He is of supreme importance."[54] John Calvin asserts the same in negative form: "We may infer that the human mind is, so to speak, a perpetual forge of idols."[55] By way of song, theology "orients" and "locates" the body in the world.

To resist white Christian nationalism then, we need a new song. Might I suggest we go back to the very beginning, to a pregnant Mary, who through her own flesh enfleshes salvation. While the Word gestates in her womb, Mary intones a song of incarnational depth that iconoclastically praises God in a world of idols *and* denounces the injustice sanctioned by false gods. Mary's hymno-theology is not just a doxological hymn:

> My soul magnifies the Lord
> And my spirit rejoices in God my Savior.

It is also a protest chant, a song for activists:

> He has brought down the powerful from their thrones
> but he has lifted the lowly;
> he has filled the hungry with good things
> and has sent the rich away empty.[56]

The angels at the Nativity also join in Mary's new song. When announcing the Good News to "lowly" shepherds, the angelic choir sings a hymn-turned-protest. For their hymno-theology refused to separate doxology—"Glory to God in the highest heaven"—from the prophetic protest against injustice—"and on earth peace among those whom he favors."[57]

Only a hymno-theology that is hymn and protest—equal parts praise and praxis—can rebuke and resist white Christian nationalism. Only a doxology-turned-protest-chant can shake the pedestals upon which white idols perch. May we join Mary in singing doxologies that rip down idols "from their thrones." May we join the angelic choir in singing songs of resistance that orient us toward the antiracist, iconoclastic work of "peace on earth." Not a peace as elusive as souls. A true peace, a real peace, made of *carne y hueso*.

NOTES

1. 1 Jn 4:2–3. All biblical references are from the *NRSV*.
2. Mt 23:23.
3. Ingolf U. Dalferth, *Theology and Philosophy* (Oxford: Basil Blackwell, 1998), 197, 205.
4. Dalferth, *Theology and Philosophy*, 205.
5. Dalferth, *Theology and Philosophy*, 204. He writes, "We not only exist in the world but live in it, and we cannot live in it without interpreting it in order to orient ourselves and thus become capable of acting in it."
6. Peter Goodwin Heltzel, "Singing the Trinity," in *Chalice Introduction to Disciples Theology*, edited by Peter Goodwin Heltzel (St. Louis, MO: Chalice Press, 2008), 87ff.
7. Eph 5:18–19.
8. *Cf.* Hans Urs von Balthasar, *Theo-Drama: Theological Dramatic Theory*, translated by Graham Harrison (San Francisco: Ignatius Press, 1988), 26ff.
9. Here I am grateful to my colleague Lakisha R. Lockhart (Union Presbyterian Seminary), who is doing groundbreaking work on womanism, pedagogy, and theology as play. I await her forthcoming monograph with eager anticipation.
10. Rom 8:26.
11. Paul C. Taylor, *Race: A Philosophical Introduction*, 2nd ed. (New York: Polity Press, 2013). 147ff.
12. *Cf.* Rima L. Vesely-Flad, *Racial Purity and Dangerous Bodies: Moral Pollution, Black Lives, and the Struggle for Justice* (Minneapolis, MN: Fortress Press, 2017), 31ff.
13. *Cf.* Steven W. Bender, "Aliens, Illegals, Wetbacks, and Anchor Babies: The Dehumanization of Immigrant Workers and Their Families," in *Mea Culpa: Lessons on Law and Regret from U.S. History* (New York: New York University Press, 2015), 35–58.
14. Stephen G. Ray Jr. addresses the way that the caricature of "welfare queen" is leveraged in Christian sin-talk, even in liberal harmatiologies, which further propagate oppressive "discursive realities" even while attempting to construct liberate theological alternatives. See his *Do No Harm: Social Sin and Christian Responsibility* (Minneapolis, MN: Fortress Press, 2003), 7ff.

15. George Yancy, "The Danger of White Innocence: Being a Stranger in One's Own 'Home,'" *Schutzian Research* 13 (2021): 13.
16. Taylor, *Race*, 150.
17. Yancy, "The Danger of White Innocence," 13.
18. Sophia Rose Arjana, *Muslims in the Western Imagination* (New York: Oxford University Press, 2015), 12.
19. Eboni Marshall Turman, "Of Men and [Mountain]Tops: Black Women, Martin Luther King Jr., and the Ethics and Aesthetics of Invisibility in the Movement for Black Lives," *Journal of the Society of Christian Ethics* 39, no. 1 (2019): 58. I am temporarily repurposing Marshall Turman's usage of the phrase. Her intent for the phrase is "to explore the continuity between anti-Black racism and sexism that engenders un-freedom for Black women in church and society" (58).
20. Taylor, *Race*, 150.
21. Yancy, "The Danger of White Innocence," 21.
22. Yancy, "The Danger of White Innocence," 13, 14.
23. *Cf.* Calvin L. Warren, *Ontological Terror: Blackness, Nihilism, and Emancipation* (Durham, NC: Duke University Press, 2018).
24. Quoted in Christian Beyer, "Edmund Husserl," in *The Stanford Encyclopedia of Philosophy*, edited by Edward N. Zalta and Uri Nodelman, https://plato.stanford.edu/archives/win2022/entries/husserl/.
25. *Cf.* "CCLI Top 100," Worshipfuel, December 1, 2022, https://www.worshipfuel.com/ccli-top-100/; Kristina Kislyanka, "Most Popular Worship Songs of 2023," Worship Artistry, https://worshipartistry.com/greenroom/leadership/most-popular-worship-songs; "Top 10 Worship Songs of All Time," Tithely, September 16, 2022, https://get.tithe.ly/blog/top-worship-songs-of-all-time.
26. *Cf.* Steve Turner, *Amazing Grace: The Story of America's Most Beloved Song* (New York: Ecco, 2002); Kevin Lewis, "America's Heirloom Comfort Song: 'Amazing Grace,'" *Implicit Religion* 16, no. 3 (September 2013): 277–88.
27. John Newton, "Amazing Grace" (1779), public domain.
28. Rom 7:15.
29. For (auto)biographical sketches on Newton, see John Newton, *The Journal of a Slave Trader (John Newton), 1750–1754*, edited by Bernard Martin and Mark Spurrell (London: Epworth Press, 1962); Steve Turner, *Amazing Grace: The Story of America's Most Beloved Song* (New York: HarperCollins, 2002).
30. William E. Phipps, "'Amazing Grace' in the Hymnwriter's Life," *Anglican Theological Review* 72, no. 3 (Summer 1990): 306.
31. Charles Taylor, *Sources of the Self: The Making of the Modern Identity* (Cambridge, MA: Harvard University Press, 1989), 132.
32. Taylor, *Sources of the Self*, 131.
33. Taylor, *Sources of the Self*, 132.
34. Yancy, "The Danger of White Innocence," 13–14.
35. James H. Cone, *The Spirituals and the Blues: An Interpretation* (New York: Seabury Press, 1972).
36. Miguel de Unamuno, *Tragic Sense of Life*, translated by J. E. Crawford Flitch (New York: Dover Publications, 1954), 1.

37. Plato, *The Apology of Socrates*, 38a5–6.
38. Yancy, "The Danger of White Innocence," 14.
39. Aimé Césaire, *Notebook of a Return to the Native Land*, translated by A. James Arnold and Clayton Eshleman (Middletown, CT: Wesleyan University Press, 2013), 37; quoted in Mayra Rivera, *Poetics of the Flesh* (Durham, NC: Duke University Press, 2015), 123–24.
40. Rivera, *Poetics of the Flesh*, 130.
41. George Yancy, *Backlash: What Happens When We Talk Honestly about Racism in America* (Lanham, MD: Rowman & Littlefield, 2018), 110–11.
42. Ernesto Cardenal, *Salmos* (Madrid: Editorial Trotta, 1998). All references to his paraphrase of the Psalms are from this edition. All English translations of the same are mine.
43. Rivera, *Poetics of the Flesh*, 12.
44. Reginald Gibbons, "Political Poetry and the Example of Ernesto Cardenal," *Critical Inquiry* 13, no. 3 (1987): 649.
45. Ernesto Cardenal, *Epigramas* (Madrid: Editorial Trotta, 2001).
46. Rivera, *Poetics of the Flesh*, 133.
47. Gibbons, "Political Poetry and the Example of Ernesto Cardenal," 649.
48. Gibbons, "Political Poetry and the Example of Ernesto Cardenal," 649.
49. Maarten Coolen, "Bodily Experience and Experiencing One's Body," in *Plessner's Philosophical Anthropology: Perspectives and Prospects*, edited by Jos de Mul (Amsterdam: Amsterdam University Press, 2014), 111–27; Helmuth Plessner, *Political Anthropology*, translated by Nils F. Schott (Evanston, IL: Northwestern University Press, 2018), 54ff.
50. In Pannenberg, *Anthropology in Theological Perspective*, 37.
51. In Pannenberg, *Anthropology in Theological Perspective*, 67.
52. Is 58.3–4.
53. Elías Ortega Aponte, "The Haunting of Lynching Spectacles: An Ethics of Response," in *Anti-Blackness and Christian Ethics*, edited by Vincent W. Lloyd and Andrew L. Prevot (Maryknoll, NY: Orbis Books, 2017), 72.
54. Abraham Joshua Heschel, *Man Is Not Alone: A Philosophy of Religion* (New York: Farrar, Straus and Giroux, 1954), 92.
55. John Calvin, *Institutes of the Christian Religion*, edited by John T. McNeill and translated by Ford Lewis Battles (Philadelphia: The Westminster Press, 1960), I.11.8.
56. Lk 1:46–47, 52–53.
57. Mt 2:14.

Chapter 21

On White Christian Violence

Anthony Paul Smith

Sometime in summer 2017, bizarre ads began to show up on American television. They featured a teddy bear with a familiar shock of wispy blond hair, somehow both over-coiffed and messy looking. The name of this product was the "Trumpy Bear." The commercial begins with something that I can only describe as a pseudo-poem. In a mix of confused metaphors and images, it declares that a whisper spreads throughout the forest of an unstoppable storm coming, but another voice answers that it fears nothing and comes when the trumpet calls. In a moment of pseudo-poetic amphibology, it is unclear if there are one or two storms, but we are told that this storm is the "great American grizzly." The image of a real grizzly bear, seemingly in full-throated roar, dissolves into an image of the much less awe-inspiring, stuffed Trumpy Bear. The announcer proudly tells us that this bear's birthday is Flag Day (June 14), which somehow explains why secreted inside of the Trumpy Bear is an American flag blanket. This is revealed to us when an older woman cuddling the bear turns it around and unzips the back of its neck to pull the blanket out. The narrator entreats us to pull it out and "wrap yourself in the white, red, and blue for comfort and warmth." We are also introduced to a more masculine way of interacting with Trumpy Bear when we see him placed at the front of a motorcycle. In an apparent non sequitur, the rider of that motorcycle locks eyes with the camera and says that he is a former Marine. He goes on to say, "Once a Marine, always a Marine," with his face set in grim determination, expressing (against some unknown threat) a resolute hardness. A series of other characters parade across the screen, including an elderly woman who declares, "God bless America and God bless Trumpy Bear," an African American business owner who says that when business is great then he is great and America is great, and an elderly war veteran who solemnly tells us that he's proud to own a Trumpy Bear and will "always be proud to be an American." As you might expect, you too could own this bear for two payments of $19.95 (plus shipping and handling).

As this retelling of the commercial no doubt communicates, I was struck by this commercial, but not just due to its ridiculousness. What struck me was what it said about the nature of a rising American fascism. Because of the odd nature of this commercial, it would sometimes come up in conversation with friends and work colleagues. During a conversation with colleagues and administrators concerning challenges that our international students may face under planned immigration changes, the Trumpy Bear came up as we talked and wondered about the utter disdain that so many Trump-aligned conservatives have for academics. Anyone who has spent time at a small liberal arts university knows that these are not hotbeds of revolutionary radicalism, and yet academics, especially in the humanities, appear to be considered a major threat to the US and American ideals. One of us remarked, with mock horror, that it was offensive—personally insulting even—that this was the driving aesthetic of people who hate us so much, some who even seem willing to use violence to stop our work. And, of course, there is something comical and indeed offensive that the culture that produced Trumpy Bear is seen as a culture worth defending with violence. This is what is valued as beautiful by those who make jokes about killing academics and others deemed "threats" to a certain American way of life by throwing them out of helicopters.[1]

There is more than just comedy in this bizarre episode of American life, more than just a "what if." This is the same aesthetic of the white nationalists who marched in Charlottesville, Virginia, in August of 2017 and murdered Heather Heyer. Something is actually communicated through this aesthetic about the nature of white Christian nationalism. Consider again the scene in the commercial where the female viewer is invited to pull an American flag blanket from the neck of the Trumpy Bear and literally wrap herself in it for comfort. Or the former Marine-turned-motorcycle enthusiast telling us with the aggression of a "real man" that he's proud to ride with Trumpy and "once a Marine, always a Marine." In the US, but also throughout the white world, there's something about the need to shore up and viciously protect identity within white Christian nationalism. That need can never really be met, for identity is a matter of contestation and fabulation that has no eternal substance to it; no guarantee exists that we are what we think we are, what we want to be seen as being, or that what our identity was recognized as yesterday will have the same consistency tomorrow. More than that, nothing truly guarantees that we will even believe in our identity tomorrow. A fundamental claim behind this chapter is that the fear provoked by these realities is part of the latent phobic structures of the self and that white Christian violence arises in desperate response to that fear.

In the rest of this chapter, we will examine the problem of violence as it manifests within white Christian nationalism. We will examine the underlying political theology of white Christian nationalism before turning to a related philosophical account of violence developed in dialogue with the work of Frantz Fanon on violence. This will allow us to end by turning to a comparative analysis of the emergence of white nationalist violence within Weimar Germany and the underlying conditions for large-scale violence in the US.

WHITE CHRISTIAN NATIONALISM AS RELIGIOUSLY MOTIVATED VIOLENCE

The epistemology of violence can be thought of as divided between violence that is generally recognized as such and violence that is generally unseen or unremarkable. Under the category of recognized violence may be acts of criminal violence or terrorist violence, while unseen or unremarkable violence has generally tended to be carried out by the state or in some way generally sanctioned by the state. The issue of religiously motivated violence, which is often commonly referred to as "religious terrorism," rose in prominence after the 9/11 attacks and in popular consciousness focused mostly on Muslims who committed violence. This is remarkable, of course, since the majority of mass violence that could be said to be religiously motivated in the US is committed by those who self-identify as Christians or come from a Christian background.[2] Perhaps it is in part remarkable because the standard liberal conception of religiously motivated violence blocks our analysis from clearly seeing the nature of violence since it leaves unquestioned the unremarkable nature of violence aligned with the state.

The standard liberal conception of religiously motivated violence is best indexed by Mark Juergensmeyer in his book *Terror in the Mind of God: The Global Rise of Religious Violence*. The book, in its fourth edition, is a standard text for courses that deal with religiously motivated violence. In it Juergensmeyer presents several case studies that lead him to detail a theory of the common logic of religiously motivated violence. That theory begins by implicitly accepting the monopoly on violence held by the state.[3] The book's strength lies in its comparative nature with investigations of instances of violence emerging out of every major world religious tradition (Christianity, Judaism, Islam, Hinduism, Buddhism, and Sikhism). This alone justifies its continued use in the classroom, despite many of the historical references being in the 1990s. Additionally, the violence of white Christian nationalism is explored in depth by Juergensmeyer and has some usefulness for thinking about contemporary iterations of Christian nationalism. While he focuses on iterations of white Christian nationalism from the 1990s, he has connected those iterations to more recent examples, like the 2011 Norway attacks by Anders Breivik that saw him murder seventy-seven people, mostly children. Generally, however, Juergensmeyer is unable to account or even truly recognize if there is anything different about religiously motivated violence when it dovetails with the ideology of the state or otherwise shares interests with the state. This means that Juergensmeyer is unable to see how seemingly fringe recognized violence may easily become state-sanctioned violence, as we saw instances of during the Trump years.

Juergensmeyer's comparative study of religiously motivated violence produces a general theory of the logic of religious violence with four main aspects. First, religiously motivated violence is performative in the sense that it is intended to reach an audience.[4] Juergensmeyer does not make this connection, but we might connect this to the tactic of nonviolence advocated by Martin Luther King Jr. which sought to bring the violence of the state into view for others and so provoke them to action. Like nonviolent resistance as a tactic, the goal of religiously motivated violence is rarely to "win" some kinetic conflict. This symbolic aspect is extended in Juergensmeyer's second aspect, the guiding principle of "cosmic war."[5] Juergensmeyer claims that religiously motivated violence is structured by a "symbolic war" that pits good versus evil. Everything takes place within this war, the meaning inherent in *anything in this world is there because of this conflict*. This in turn leads to the third aspect, the creation of martyrs and demons.[6] Within the cosmic war of good versus evil, there is no "gray zone"; there are only friends and enemies. Finally, he ends with a psycho-sexual account of religiously motivated violence as predominately male violence undertaken by men who feel that they have been disempowered and cut off from less violent forms of accruing honor within their particular society.[7]

By all accounts, contemporary white Christian nationalism follows this logic. One cannot fail to see this in even a cursory read of the many journalistic profiles of the American far right. What is less clear, however, is the connection between this religious understanding of politics and just what politics actually is, especially American politics as it emerged during the presidency of George W. Bush. An analysis that suspends some liberal assumptions, especially around the nature of American claims to secularism, would reveal a politics that also appears to follow the logic laid out by Juergensmeyer. While this was a politics troubled with contradictions, like all religiously motivated violence, the Bush administration carried out violence intended to be seen (the doctrine of "shock and awe") and built around a worldview of good versus evil (America and its allies versus the axis of evil) and a strict friend/enemy distinction (the constant refrain of "you're either for us or against us" from Bush himself and the everyday advocates of US state violence).

We may find the field of political theology useful to understand the violence of white Christian nationalism and its connection with US state violence. Here I am making use of the understanding of political theology developed by Adam Kotsko. For Kotsko, political theology is a genealogical discipline that uncovers the ways in which Christian theological concepts are converted into secular political concepts *across time* and how Christian theological and secular political concepts share a similar structure *at the same time*.[8] In other words, political theology may allow us to see the deep but unacknowledged relationship between the political order and theological ideas. In this instance, there is the connection between the seemingly secular liberal order of the US and the theology of white Christian nationalism.

So, Kotsko's understanding guides us here because it takes seriously the intertwined nature of Christianity and secularism in the West.[9] This is a familiar claim in religious studies that is informed by critical theory, and we can see this intertwining present in the alliance between Christians (of Protestant, Catholic, and Orthodox traditions) and secular atheists within the white Christian nationalist movement. Richard Spencer is perhaps the most famous of the many intellectual heroes of contemporary white nationalism to describe himself as an atheist. Yet, even as an atheist, he ultimately supports Christianity because it helped to produce "the West."[10] The Proud Boys similarly call themselves "Western chauvinists" and welcome members from other faith traditions, like Hinduism, while claiming that Christianity (similar to contemporary Germany's notion of *Leitkultur*) is the best religion because it produces Western values, like a qualified secularism that allows for tolerance of other religions.[11] Christianity, in sum, should be supported over and above other religious traditions because Christianity produces Western values, while other religions, namely Islam and sometimes Judaism (though white nationalists tend to oscillate between antisemitism and philo-semitism, both ultimately rooted in a Christian-secular supersessionism), are aligned with values that undermine the West.[12]

What we find in the conception of Christian identity in white Christian nationalism is a political theology. What the various agents of white Christian nationalism really believe is not so much a matter of piety or even a concern for the global Christian Church; they believe in themselves. The shape of this belief is not that they have high self-worth—much of the evidence points to the opposite—but that they truly believe in the coherence of the identity of the white nation and in their identity. They believe that there is a self to protect. They fervently believe that they were born to be secure in their identity, to shape and rule the world, and it is being born into the Christian-cum-secular world that secures their birth right, denied them by the "evil forces" of feminism, Black empowerment, and LGBTQ+ culture. There may be differences of degree between this conception of the self and the American conception of the nation and its destiny, but there is no difference in kind.

Political theology is described by Carl Schmitt as "the sociology of concepts" that examines the ways in which "all significant concepts of the modern theory of the state [or politics] are secularized theological concepts." This must be read alongside Schmitt's definition that politics is the identification of the distinction between friend and enemy, between who one lives with and who one does not live with, even unto death.[13] This distinction, of course, is also a theological concept. It may be traced back to the earliest foundational writings of Christianity, as Daniel Colucciello Barber has done in his reading of Paul's distinctions, which continues into modernity with the founding colonial distinctions found in the Papal Bulls *Dum Diversas* (1452) and *Romanus Pontifex* (1454). These documents determined that Muslims were killable and hereditarily enslavable while Africans and the Indigenous Peoples of the Americas were deemed enslavable because Muslims were not-quite-human and the Africans and America's indigenous were not human at all (though through the efforts of some, most famously the Jesuit Bartolomé de las Casas, the Indigenous were raised to the level of "not-quite-human").[14] These distinctions among the human, the killable, and the socially dead are secularized today through the positioning of the global Muslim as subject to international extrajudicial killing of "enemy combatants" and the ways in which, as Frank Wilderson says, "black bodies magnetize bullets."[15] Political theology is concerned, at the beginning of the colonial period and in our age, with these distinctions of identity and the securing of the borders between them.

FRANTZ FANON'S POLITICAL THEOLOGY OF VIOLENCE

In what follows, I will trace the elements of Fanon's thinking that appear isomorphic to works in political theology but show that Fanon's work marks a critical analysis of political theology from the exterior to the assumed desires of political theologians.[16] In his 1961 text, *The Wretched of the Earth*, Fanon anticipates the kind of political theology identified by Kotsko earlier. There readers will find an analysis of the generic structure of the shift from Christiandom to the secular political order as part of a single colonizing series. Fanon, regardless of his own atheism, was able to see through the lie of secularism's separation from Christianity, while being able to recognize that the various traditions deemed "religions" were more complexly related to the struggle against colonialism. Secular authority will make use of Christianity in the process of marking as depraved or diabolical the myths, practices, and beliefs of the colonized. Fanon thus links Christianity with DDT, which is an insecticide, saying that both are used to root out evil.[17] The church in the colonies is a device of welcome, a conversion of bad religion into good religion, of bad people into good people: "The Church in the colonies is a white man's Church, a foreigners' Church. It does not call the colonized to the ways of God, but to the ways of the white man, to the ways of the master, the ways of the oppressor. And as we know, in this story many are called but few are chosen."[18]

Yet, Fanon's engagement with political theology is not merely critical; it is also poetic or aesthetic in a constructive sense. Fanon can be said to be promulgating, among other things, a positive political theology in "On Violence." In describing decolonization, he calls upon the Christ's proclamation that the last shall be first; the definition of decolonization "can, if we want to describe it accurately, be summed up in the well-known words: 'The last shall be first.'"[19] In this theologico-political proclamation is elaborated the distinction between colonial order and its necessary disordering through decolonization. "Decolonization," Fanon says, "which sets out to change the order of the world, is clearly *an agenda for total disorder*."[20]

Fanon's description of the colonial world as a Manichean world is well known and the most easily recognizable gnostic thematic in his work. "Challenging the colonial world," he writes, "is not a rational confrontation of viewpoints. It is not a discourse on the universal, but the impassioned claim by the colonized that their world is fundamentally different. The colonial world is a Manichaean world."[21] Fanon's reference to the Manicheanism of the world appears to be largely dependent upon the idiomatic rendering of Manichean to refer to any stark dualism between good and evil. But there is a deeper truth of Manicheanism, not explicitly referenced by Fanon, but that nonetheless still permeates his thinking. Namely, Manicheanism is a philosopheme of the world that presents the world we live in as an utter failure, as a lie, and says that there is something true beyond all the worldly stories—beyond even the story of Mani! A truth we cannot yet speak of, for we lack even the basic grammar. We can see this in Fanon by reading his discussion of the creation of the world as something akin to the politico-poetic metaphysics of the Gnostic narration of the creation of the world. One, though, that finds its grammar and its characters within the scope of a relatively secularized historical and material world. Let's now sketch that politico-poetic metaphysics.

The colonized world is a Manichean world because it is a world of distinctions and divisions, of separations linked to moral categories. As Fanon summarizes this:

> The colonized world is a world divided in two. The dividing line, the border, is represented by the barracks and the police stations. This compartmentalized

world, this world divided in two, is inhabited by different species. . . . The colonial world is a Manichaean world.²²

When decolonial violence breaks out, there are often various forms of discomfort and horror that take place within the psyches of those in the dominant culture. This results in some expressing sympathy for the plight of the colonized, for the most wretched among them, but at the same time demanding that the oppressed recognize the common humanity shared by the colonist and the colonized. Yet, this shared humanity is simply not true for the colonized. Fanon tells us, "Decolonization is quite simply the substitution of one 'species' of mankind by another."²³

How is it that these two "species" came to be? The bio-political resonance of this word is impossible to escape. Fanon uses *espèces* rather than *genre* (kind or sort), which has a more performative sense to it than a biological or natural one as *espèces* does. There is the weight of a natural reality that settles over the distinction between the species of the colonist and the species of the colonized, with an even starker distinction between these two general species and the wretched, which is marked not even as a species but as a disease, "the gangrene ever present at the heart of colonial domination."²⁴ I note here that casual readers of Fanon, those who wish to decolonize dialectics, for example, tend to ignore the very real questions he has regarding the success of revolution. For throughout "On Violence" and the other essays of *The Wretched of the Earth*, there is a question of distinctions within the colonized such that the wretched, the *lumpenproletariat* and the peasantry, are not likely to carry on with the revolution past its early explosive and spontaneous violence. The people, we might say, do not exist, just as no nations truly exist.

But returning to our main analysis, how do these two species and the disease of being emerge? We might say, with fidelity to Fanon's text, that they are the creation of the demiurge, here given the name colonization, and the colonists are the incarnation of that god or share in the filiation of the colonial nation, to the point of a divine or sovereign immanence: "The cause is effect: You are rich because you are white, you are white because you are rich."²⁵

The identity of the colonized is one "gifted" by the colonizers and the system of colonization generally. The decolonial violence that the dominant culture wrings their hands over is a violence of response or reaction to the original violence of the creation of the colonial system that bestows the identity of colonist and colonized. The violence of decolonization, the violence of making the last first, is a violence that responds to the violence of division, cession, and dividing up first found in the differential creation of the world.

The distinction between the two species and subsequently the disease of being begins to emerge in the encounter with the Indigenous populations that the colonist comes into contact with. The colonist comes into a land and sees the land as held in reserve, like Martin Heidegger says the industrialist sees the forest as wood or the river as water power (an instance of the European colonists turning inward to "their own land," just as they turned inward to their own internal colonized using of technologies perfected in the outer colonies).[26] They see the land in this way simultaneously as they see the people who inhabit this land as potentially standing reserve (enslaveable) or as diabolically inhabiting the land with different practices and customs than their own.[27] These practices are not at all diabolical in themselves, but to create the hierarchal structure and to control that population, in part by undermining their Indigenous practices, the colonists create a division or a *heresis* (a separation). The division and the diabolic at first only exist in the mind of the colonizer and the various persona of the colonial system (the missionary, the cop, the overseer, etc.), but in so marking this distinction it becomes real as the world. The colonized, in their various forms, are then *interpellated* as a distinct species of humanity or subhumanity or even as an animal or evil supernatural being. The practices or culture of the colonized then must become diabolical when used to satisfy the need for ridding the land of the colonist. Fanon himself analyzed an example of one such "diabolical practice" in his discussion of the veil in "Algeria Unveiled" (collected in *A Dying Colonialism*): "Removed and reassumed again and again, the veil has been manipulated, transformed into a technique of camouflage, into a means of struggle."[28] Fanon's insight here is that all tools, all weapons, in the agenda for total disorder are changed through their prior colonial casting. We have no real access to the meaning or use of the veil prior to colonialism, just as we have no access to the world other than as it has been created by colonialism.

THE PHOBIC STRUCTURE OF THE WHITE CHRISTIAN SELF AND THE GRACE OF ITS ABOLITION

What does Fanon's analysis of violence in the colonial world allow us to understand about white Christian nationalism in the US?[29] Though Fanon's title "On Violence" might lead us to think it undertakes a direct analysis of violence, it never actually looks directly at it in an ontological sense. Fanon never says, "This is what violence is." Rather, what we find is a phenomenological, contemplative understanding of violence. In another part of *The Wretched of the Earth*, Fanon argues that violence is the means by which knowledge of social reality is gained by the masses.[30] Violence is then not primarily a means of politics so much as a means of mass or generic contemplation. To attend to violence, where such attention is now understood as "thinking about thinking," is to attend to the world formed and forming of our grammars of coherence. His analysis of violence allows us to see that violence in part emerges from the desire for coherence.

Indeed, this desire is the cause of the very deadlock that Fanon presents regarding decolonization. He writes, "Decolonization, we know, is an historical process: In other words, it can only be understood, it can only find its significance and become self-coherent in so far as we can discern the history-making movement which gives it form and substance."[31] Later he writes of history, "The colonist makes history and he knows it."[32] It might seem, considering that Fanon goes on to mark a distinction between the history of the country the colonist is despoiling and the history of the colonist's own nation's looting, raping, and starving to death and says, "The immobility to which the colonized subject is condemned can only be challenged if he decides to put an end to the history of colonization and the history of despoliation in order to bring to life the history of the nation, the history of decolonization."[33] What can emerge from the conflict between the history of the colonist and the history of decolonization but more history, more coherence?

This is the pessimistic lament we saw with Fanon's analysis of the Manichean world and why his is not a simple description of conflict that leads to resolution. It is also an analysis of the ways in which the postcolonial situation can result in the afterlife of colonialism. This happens given the repetition of the historical structures in the new contemporary moment, with new figures or new configurations within the general architecture. While usually taken as Fanon's handbook for decolonization, *The Wretched of the Earth*, and especially "On Violence," spells out the path of failure for decolonization as it becomes the postcolonial nation. The violence of decolonization gives way to a new colonial relationship where the bourgeoisie and intelligentsia of the colonized *separate* themselves from the wretched rather than seeing that they are the same. This calls forth ever more violence, whether it be the decolonial kind or the unseen violence of international debt.

Decolonization is an agenda for total disorder. At its most beautiful, we might name the political theology of "the first shall be last and the last shall be first" the undoing of coherence. Whether that exists in the postcolonial world is a matter for those who live there to figure out. As a white man living the US, my concern is with the white Christians who do not see such disorder as the blessing it is but as a threat to their very sense of self. While the decolonial struggle may petrify into a postcolonial nation, the leap that is taken in decolonization is one that would stop telling stories, that can only appeal to the concept of the tabula rasa or what ultimately cannot be said. The tabula rasa names the truth that there is only abyss before us. David Marriott characterizes it this way: "To read is to take a step, to be inventive, but this outcome cannot be prepared for nor prescribed. For Fanon, in brief, the leap remains a question; it has no thematic content (materialist, humanist, political), and yet without it no decision is possible, or is recognizable as such. This is why its locus (to name only one) is the tabula rasa: an inscription that is always the abyss of itself, for it is written on nothing."[34] The abyss, the unknown God.

But the God that is worshipped in white Christian nationalism is a familiar God. It is the God of inner self, the God as the regulatory superego, the God within. *Male Fantasies*, Klaus Theweleit's brilliant but underused two-volume study of the proto-fascist consciousness of German men, which paved the way for the rise of the Nazi Party in post-Weimar Germany, provides us with a major insight into the subjective constitution of men drawn toward and as participants in fascist violence. Namely, that the obsession with violence seen in *Freikorps* narratives (memoirs and other writings by far-right-wing paramilitary men in post–World War I Germany) emerges as an ego defense against their fears regarding the integrity of their own bodies and their unconscious linking of the integrity of their own male bodies to other male bodies gathered under the national body. Their fears regarding their bodies bursting are cathected onto the bodies of women and their symbolic connection to floods (of water, blood, and immigrants). The *Freikorps* man was a product of a theology that turned ever inward after Luther's Reformation. A punitive God was synonymous with fear of one's body, with fear of coming apart in pleasure. Summarizing this point, Theweleit writes, "The 'all-seeing' god lives inside your own skin, in your peripheral areas, in your body's orifices and musculature. He is a part of the perception of pleasure itself; he is the one who converts pleasure into anxiety. The punitive god-figure owes his effectiveness (in the culture of 'mopping up') to the fear that phenomena of dissolution may occur along the borders of the body."[35] This God within, however, also comes to die and is replaced in turn by a "god without," who "dwelt on the skin and whose name was Cleanliness."[36] The bio-political desire for a clean body, purified of pollution from the bodies of others.

There is an extreme phobia of the body and pleasure that can be seen in white Christian nationalism. This is most obvious in its relationship to the incel movement and in bizarre rants from the likes of Nick Fuentes, an antisemite, alt-right intellectual, and congressional intern for Marjorie Taylor Greene who entreats his followers not to have sex and claims that pursuing romantic relationships with women is ultimately a homosexual act. His direct words are: "If we're really being honest, never having a girlfriend, never having sex with a woman, really makes you more heterosexual, because honestly, dating women is gay. And if you want to know the truth, the only really straight, heterosexual position is to be an asexual incel."[37] The fear of losing oneself is inherent in the fear of sex, the fear of being seen in the frail body of a human being, even or especially as one erotically charged; fear that one is nothing is inherent in the fear of a sexual encounter with another. The subjective constitution of the white Christian nationalist is fully on display here: desiring a self that it can never be (and that none of us can ever be) and willing to destroy everyone around him because of his fear of incoherence, of being the same nothing he believes that those below him are.

The violence of the white Christian is, from their perspective, a defensive violence. Theirs is a violence ultimately taken up in the service of protecting a world created by colonial violence. And, of course, they are not wrong in thinking that the world is ending, at least a particular world, and thank God for that. What is coming next is not so clear, and one can understand why people may be worried or pessimistic when you consider how demands for justice have been turned into diversity, equity, and inclusion statements on websites while the basic structures of our institutions remain the same (seen most perversely in these statements often being written by Black colleagues or colleagues of color who did not receive extra compensation for their extra work). But regardless of what comes next, good or ill, what exists now should still be abolished. It was and remains indefensible, and its destruction is a kind of grace, a liberation from the deathly self. What should give us pause and demand our attention and thought is how this phobic structure exists and manifests in mainstream white Americans as well and for all those whose "destiny may be white."[38] While the intensity of reaction to the fear of incoherence may be more extreme among self-identifying white Christian nationalists, that structure exists as part of the makeup of the US and Americans themselves. A fear of losing Christian-secular identity, of losing the power consolidated under this political theology, can produce much greater violence because it may be unremarkable violence.

NOTES

1. The historical reference that contemporary American fascists are making is to actions of the Argentine military during the Dirty War (1976–1983) and the Augusto Pinochet regime where left-wing opponents to the regime and others were extrajudicially executed by being thrown from helicopters. This often took place after the individual was horrifically tortured. Online activists and provocateurs in the so-called "alt-right" have made memes out of this barbarism, and one can even purchase T-shirts referencing the murders.

2. This can be gleaned from reading recent FBI and Department of Homeland Security reports on domestic terrorism. See the latest: Federal Bureau of Investigation and Department of Homeland Security, *Strategic Intelligence Assessment and Data on Domestic Terrorism*, 2022, https://www.fbi.gov/file-repository/fbi-dhs-domestic-terrorism-strategic-report-2022.pdf/view.

3. See his "Introduction," where Juergensmeyer admits that the "disenfranchised groups" who are more commonly associated than any nation state with "terrorism" are unable to "kill on the scale that governments with all their military power can,"

yet he still goes on to consider religiously motivated violence to be the most concerning form of violence. Mark Juergensmeyer, *Terror in the Mind of God: The Global Rise of Religious Violence*, 4th ed. (Oakland: University of California Press, 2017), 4.

4. Juergensmeyer, *Terror in the Mind of God*, ch. 7.

5. Juergensmeyer, *Terror in the Mind of God*, ch. 8.

6. Juergensmeyer, *Terror in the Mind of God*, ch. 9.

7. Juergensmeyer, *Terror in the Mind of God*, ch. 10.

8. Adam Kotsko, *The Prince of this World* (Stanford: Stanford University Press, 2016), 12.

9. For a summary of this argument, see Anthony Paul Smith, "Postsecularism," in *Reading the Abrahamic Faiths: Rethinking Religion and Literature*, edited by Emma Mason (London: Bloomsbury Academic, 2014), 221–35.

10. Richard Spencer, Interview by David McAfee, "Listening to the Other Side: A Conversation with White Nationalist Richard Spencer," https://archive.fo/vwgyw.

11. See Damon T. Berry, *Christianity and the Alt-Right: Exploring the Relationship* (London: Routledge, 2022), chs. 1–2.

12. On the Proud Boys in particular, see Margo Kitts, "Proud Boys, Nationalism, and Religion," *Journal of Religion and Violence* 8, no. 3 (2021): 22–27.

13. Carl Schmitt, *Political Theology: Four Chapters on the Concept of Sovereignty*, translated by George Schwab (Chicago: University of Chicago Press, 2005), 45, 36.

14. Daniel Colucciello Barber, "The Immanent Refusal of Conversion," *The Journal of Cultural and Religious Theory* 13, no. 1 (2014): 145–46. The distinction I am making regarding human, not-quite-human, and not human at all is borrowed but modified from Alexander G. Weheliye, *Habeas Viscus: Racializing Assemblages, Biopolitics, and Black Feminist Theory of the Human* (Durham, NC: Duke University Press, 2014).

15. Frank B. Wilderson III, "The Prison Slave as Hegemony's (Silent) Scandal," *Social Justice* 30, no. 2 (2003): 20.

16. The reader of Fanon and secondary literature on Fanon may be surprised to read here my implicit claim that Fanon's concern with decolonial politics is marked by mystical and Gnostic thematics. This reading is only possible because it follows in the wake of the intensive work of David Marriott in *Whither Fanon? Studies in the Blackness of Being* (Stanford: Stanford University Press, 2018). This study shows and examines the deep ambiguity of Fanon's proclamations. In Marriott's reading, Fanon's ambitious proclamations constitute a leap where the reader is suspended over an abyss rather than rising out of the ground of a masculinist, revolutionary faith. Fanon's work is not the confident, unrelenting gaze of a Lenin (as Peter Hallward describes him), but it presents a demand to take a leap into the abyss, the work of the tabula rasa. Concerning the reading that presents Fanon in a purely Marxist way, Marriott writes, "It strikes me as odd that Fanon should be consistently read as committed to a teleological 'narrative of freedom' rather than to maintaining freedom as a difficult question that cannot be resolved." He continues, "Finally, I would like to say that it is precisely this question that will always *come after* the question of how we ought to read Fanon, a reading that cannot be entirely predicted or known in advance, and in whose future inheritance we necessarily remain bewildered and perplexed"

(Marriott, *Whither Fanon?* 36). The mystical and Gnostic reading presented here is one that follows from how reading the bewilderment in Fanon's text allows for a shift in perspective on political theology. Not one that moves beyond intertwined Christian and secular political theology, but one that maps out the hostile terrain of Christianity and the secular and how to speak of freedom within such a constrained grammar.

17. Franz Fanon, *The Wretched of the Earth*, translated by Richard Philcox (New York: Grove Press, 2004), 7.
18. Fanon, *The Wretched of the Earth*, 7.
19. Fanon, *The Wretched of the Earth*, 2.
20. Fanon, *The Wretched of the Earth*, 2 (my emphasis).
21. Fanon, *The Wretched of the Earth*, 6.
22. Fanon, *The Wretched of the Earth*, 3, 5, 6.
23. Fanon, *The Wretched of the Earth*, 1.
24. Marriott, *Whither Fanon?* 154.
25. Fanon, *The Wretched of the Earth*, 5.
26. Martin Heidegger, "The Question Concerning Technology," in *Basic Writings*, edited and translated by David Farrell Krell (San Francisco: HarperSanFrancisco, 1993), 317–18, 320.
27. For more on this colonial relation to land and the people who inhabit it, see Malcom Ferdinand, *A Decolonial Ecology: Thinking from the Caribbean World*, translated by Anthony Paul Smith (Cambridge, MA: Polity Press, 2022).
28. Frantz Fanon, *A Dying Colonialism*, translated by Haakon Chevalier (New York: Grove Press, 1965), 61.
29. It moves us too far from our argument, but readers should understand that I follow the analysis of Bobby Seale, Huey P. Newton, and others in the Black Panther Party who used Fanon to argue that the colonial situation is the same situation one finds in the US. Joshua Bloom and Waldo E. Martin Jr., *Black against Empire: The History and Politics of the Black Panther Party* (Berkeley: University of California Press, 2016), 66–73.
30. Fanon, *A Dying Colonialism*, 96.
31. Fanon, *A Dying Colonialism*, 2.
32. Fanon *A Dying Colonialism*, 15.
33. Fanon, *A Dying Colonialism*, 15.
34. Marriott, *Whither Fanon?* 276.
35. Klaus Theweleit, *Male Fantasies, Volume 1: Women, Floods, Bodies, History*, translated by Stephen Conway (Minneapolis: University of Minnesota Press, 1987), 413.
36. Theweleit, *Male Fantasies*, 419.
37. Quoted in Matt Prigge, "An 'America First' Leader Railed Against Losing His Virginity, Saying That 'Dating Women Is Gay,'" *Uproxx*, May 14, 2022, https://uproxx.com/viral/america-first-nick-fuentes-dating-women-is-gay/.
38. Frantz Fanon, *Black Skin, White Masks*, translated by Richard Philcox (New York: Grove Press, 2008), xiv.

Closing Poem: Original Sin

Michael Simms

America

    Beside the highway outside McKeesport PA
    a state trooper has pulled over a Black man
    who leans against his rusty Ford
    palms flat, feet apart
    assuming the position
    as we say in America
    The smokey wears his broad brimmed hat
    with its menacing chin strap
    which is leather, like the leather of his boots
    and belt and holster,
    low, his face in shadow
    Beside us, the Monongahela River
    quickens, making its way
    through abandoned pastures
    and ruined river towns
    on its way to the Ohio
    As the smokey rummages through
    the car, the man shrinks in his clothes,
    catches my eye, then looks down
    as if ashamed. *What's he done? I wonder*
    Then *What's the trooper done?*
    What have I done,
    what have I ever done
    but look away / up the road
    toward the beautiful Laurel Highlands
    hidden in the white mist of America?

Night School

I used to teach policemen
at the community college—diligent, respectful, curious,
the only students who craved grammar lessons
because they knew their dialect marked them
as *Yinzers* from the Mon Valley
One evening I showed up early.
Three students wearing chinos and cologne,
smelling for all the world like stockbrokers
on their day off, didn't notice me
They were laughing
about an *ass whoopin* they'd delivered
to a Black kid the night before
As the cops took turns beating him,
the *boot*, as they called the rookie,
broke a bone in his hand
Bill, the gray one they called *Sarge*, said
Son, never hit a guy with your fist.
Carry a sap. Use the tools of the trade
Most cops like truncheons
for the intimidation factor Sarge said
But I like a tool I can carry in my pocket
He pulled out
a leather sack of lead pellets
and slapped it on his palm
Hitting the skull, spine, groin or sternum
is considered deadly force—illegal
Sarge warned
but we do it all the time
*

I remember walking home at 2am from a bar
in Iowa City, joining an angry crowd surrounding
a policeman beating a dark man crouched in the street
begging for mercy, hands protecting his face
The cop, intent on his work,
hadn't noticed the crowd until he looked up startled
put his hand on his holster and ordered us to disperse.
Then he bundled the man into the squad car and drove off
The next day at the police station
a captain politely nodded, took a few notes,
thanked me for my citizen's report,
then shook my hand and assured me
he *would* investigate and be in touch
I believed him. I was very young.

Since then, I've often wondered
how it feels to think of oneself
as the hammer of justice.
How does it feel to inflict pain
as a joyful act
of public service, an obligation,
a jubilation, almost
a prayer?
*

Last week I ran into Sarge on a street corner.
He'd retired from the force, lost weight
and stopped drinking. He said he was happy
teaching his grandkids how to fish
I still didn't want to like him
but I did. We were just
two old white guys standing on the sidewalk
talking about stuff
Later I thought about Sarge
all those years ago in my classroom
explaining how to beat a suspect in handcuffs
When I remembered the ecstasy
on his ruddy face
I hated him all over again

How My Brother Tried to Save Us

Forty-four years ago, when my brother Ken confronted
our sister's boyfriend Gary, and the lowlife
took a wild swing at him, Ken ducked
The blow hit him on the forehead
knocking him down and breaking Gary's hand.
The pimp, who'd been selling our sister
to his friends, ran away crying
My father joked
when I told you to use your head, Ken,
I didn't mean like that.
My brother said, *Well I didn't lose the fight*
But he did lose. We all lost.
As revenge for betraying him
Gary kidnapped Elizabeth
and kept her in a cage for weeks
farming her out until he broke her
*
Reader, this is not a metaphor.
This is the world I come from.

My sister was literally kept in a cage
like an animal and raped repeatedly
Elizabeth didn't tell us for twenty-five years.
By then, she was ready to die
*
Elizabeth's suicide broke my mother,
and it nearly broke me
but my father never spoke of it.
Nor did Ken.
The two men seemed unsurprised
as if they were so beaten down
there was nothing more life could do to them.
I'm not sure what broke my father.
A crazy mother maybe.
Or maybe just being an average American guy
overworked and frightened.
As for Ken, he hasn't spoken to me
since his last suicide attempt
six years ago
*
As we sat in the visitors room
of the psych hospital
Ken, his wrists bandaged, told me
a few months before Dad died
Ken had confronted the old man
about the way he treated me
when I was small
He said Dad had chuckled
well maybe at times I went a little too far
My brother responded *you didn't go a little too far*
You abused him because you enjoyed it
and you knew you could get away with it
because he couldn't speak
A few days later, Dad called me to apologize.
Sobbing, he tried to explain his life to me
but there's no explaining what's in a man's heart
when he hurts someone just because he can

The Sentence

After sentencing four young women
for placing water jugs in the desert,
the judge returns to his chambers,
removes his black robes
and puts his face in his hands.

Behind him, law books stare down—
sentries on the walls of a crumbling city

Brotherly Love

AWP conference, Philadelphia, March 2022
I broke from the colloquy of ten thousand poets,
walked down Arch Street with the March wind
in my face and a few flakes falling. I was headed
for dinner but, as things turned out, I became a witness
to love. Evening filled the air with light and shadow.
Two young men walked toward me holding hands—
the air was cold but the men were warmed by laughter.
A stylish older couple passed by arm in arm,
their faces pink and happy in their woolen scarves.
I walked past the Kabuki Sushi and the TexMex Grill,
past the elegant Notary Hotel with its marble floors
and mirrored halls where we'd discussed Dickinson,
past the magnificent City Hall in the Second Empire style
of 88 million red bricks and thousands of tons of white marble,
over 700 rooms and 250 sculptures, capturing artists,
educators, and engineers who embodied American ideals
and contributed to this country's genius as the bronze says
and the tall clock tower, witness to the slow decay
of this glorious city of brotherly love and anguish.
I came to the *Fogo de Chão* Brazilian Steakhouse
on Chestnut Street where a great haunch of roasted calf
is carved beside each table and I tried not to think
of the terrified yearling who'd given his life for this spectacle
of consumption. Not having tasted flesh for 15 years,
I filled up on fresh greens, beans, fruit and light fluffy
Pão de Queijo at the lavish salad bar
and my young friends and I laughed and gossiped
and ranted about the current war and the past president
and who'd won the big-ass poetry prize
and whether someone else, meaning one of us,
should've. Next, the U-Bahn with live loud music
by SlamJam but I couldn't hear anyone talking,
hadn't had a drink in 37 years, too old for sloppy,
and my friends were heading to the Good Dog Bar
The Black Sheep Pub or the Harp and Crown—
they couldn't decide—so I said goodbye and walked away
calling it a night after 68 years of mostly good luck
and walked up Filbert toward Thirteenth where it passes
beneath the Convention Center, the wind becoming fiercer

and the snow faster and harder, white in the darkness.
People hunched over as they walked,
holding their collars close around their throats
and I remembered going to the Flower Show
at the Convention Center the day before
where the air was heavy with jasmine and gardenia
and I thought heaven if it's anything at all
must surely and entirely be warmth, scent and color.
I turned onto thirteenth street, a block-long tunnel
where people sleep on the sidewalk huddled in blankets
and plastic sheets, hoodies hiding their faces,
their hands neither black nor white but gray
with the dust of the city, a few zombie drug addicts
but mostly just people with nowhere to sleep
except this dark cold cave their lives had become.
A man with a puppy snuggling inside his coat
glanced up, puzzled. People like me usually walk
the long way around to avoid people like him
because we're afraid to look deprivation
in the eye, resent admitting our own dumb luck,
but in my superior compassion, my arrogant morality
I decided to risk walking among the indigent
as if I were Mother Teresa and not just a tourist
of misfortune. A car stopped. A white woman
in jeans handed a Styrofoam box
to a man hunkered and trembling on the sidewalk.
He nodded thanks and the car moved to the next man
and the next, each one receiving supper,
perhaps a Last Supper I thought wryly, immediately
ashamed of finding irony in compassion.
The car came to a woman with two small girls,
the mother dressed in rags but her children in pink parkas,
the woman giving everything to her children,
keeping nothing for herself, and the small family
received the dole of fried chicken, mashed potatoes,
brown gravy, a dinner roll, a small heap of chopped greens
and a delicate plastic fork, tines breaking off
in their food. The car pulled up
to the last man standing on the sidewalk,
gray hoodie pulled back revealing a scarred face,
dreadlocks like a black halo.
The social worker handed him his dinner
and the man leaned over to kiss her cheek,
a chaste thank you, an affectionate reward
for her kindness, but the woman yanked

her head back, avoiding his kiss
and the two stood surprised,
their faces a hand's breadth apart,
two travelers caught in a web,
uncertain how to break loose
from the other's gaze

AUTHOR'S NOTE

In the five cantos of "Original Sin," I describe incidents which I've witnessed of police brutality, child abuse, rape, slavery, forced prostitution, denial of refugee status, and criminalization of acts of conscience, as well as my own blithe assumption of privilege, which are presented as examples of the Original Sin of dehumanization, out of which all other sins arise. The argument of the poem is that racism, sexism, and classism—and the resultant poverty, humiliation, and violence—arise from *rejection of one's Inner Light* in the Quaker sense and *suffering resulting from separation*, in the Buddhist sense, also known as *dehumanization of the other* in contemporary social theory. (See, for example, the work of Nour Kteily, a psychologist at Northwestern University whose research is about dehumanization, our acquired ability to see fellow men and women as species inferior to ourselves.) I might add that everyone in Western society has developed this ability to objectify others. Even the good-hearted social worker in *Brotherly Love*, the last canto, is disgusted by a homeless man trying to give her a chaste thank-you kiss, rejecting the intimacy of his gesture because it would break down the caste wall between them.

Index

AAVE. *See* African American Vernacular English
abortion, 65n58, 112, 292, 295
Abraham (Biblical), 149–50
"activist indoctrination," 95–96
Advanced Placement African American Studies, 117–18
affirmative action, 281
Africa: British empire and, 235, 239–40, 244, 246–48; Cullinan Diamonds from, 244; fetish religion and, 21; Mau Mau uprising in, 246–47; Nigerian-Biafran War and, 247–48
African American Vernacular English (AAVE), 58–59
African Command, US (AFRICOM), 30
Ahmed, Sara, 172–73
Alexander VI (Pope), 53–54, 131
Alliance Defending Freedom, 213–14
allies, 302, 308, 310n8
Allison, Richard, 22–23
"Amazing Grace" (Newton), 317–19
America, as "Promised Land," 53–56
American exceptionalism, 120–22
American identity, 145
Anderson, Elizabeth, 201n30
anthropological docetism, 319–20, 323–24
anti-Catholicism, 127

antidemocratic violence, 46
Antioch church, 228
anti-racist training, 29–30
antisemitism, 25, 226; colonialism and, 74; conquest and, 56–59; "The Order" and, 257; supersessionism and, 58–59
anti-white discrimination, 94–95, 301
Anya, Uju, 247
apocalypse, 7
apocalypticism, 52–53, 269–76
apologies, 159–60, 163–64, 165n10
Appiah, K. Anthony, 264
Applebaum, Barbara, 282–84
apprenticeship, 13
Arendt, Hannah, 303
Aristotle, 180, 182–83, 187–89, 201n15
Armaly, Miles T., 270
Aryan race, 24, 64n45, 257–58
atonement, 273–74
Attiah, Karen, 242
Augustine of Hippo, 290
Auld, Thomas, 212–13
authoritarianism, 6–8, 111–12, 117

Backlash (Yancy), 26
"bad theology," 151–52
Baldwin, James, 6, 130, 179–81
Baptists, 291

Barber, Daniel Coluccicllo, 334
Barber, William, 81, 230, 295
Beamer, Todd, 53
Beecher, Henry Ward, 222
being, 182–83
Bell, Derrick, 180, 190, 197–99
beloved community, 304, 310n14
Berg, Alan, 257
Bible: "Biblical citizenship" and, 110; hymns, 314–15; liberation in, 323; Psalms and, 321–22; race in, 226–29; slavery in, 291; transformational white Christianity and, 305; Trump and photo shoot with, 157–58, 163. *See also* God; Jesus Christ
Biden, Joe, 36n47, 58, 94, 195, 270
Bird, Michael F., 243
The Birth of a Nation (Griffith), 107
Black bodies, 1, 4–5, 159, 181, 189–90, 246–48
Black Christianity, 13, 96–97
Black citizenship, 104
Black freedom, 103–4, 107, 132, 272–73
Black History Month, 118
Black identity, 12, 256–66
Black leadership, 153–54
Black liberation theology, 76, 79–80, 190–92
Black Lives Matter, 118–19, 162
Black ontology, 5
Black Panther Party, 117–18, 342n29
Black people: blackness as "evil" or enemy, 5, 169–70; colonialism and, 56–58; demonization of, 184; listening to, 285–86; medical experimentation on, 210–12, 217n15; "Negro rule" against, 103–4; origins and "necessity" of, 179–80, 186–88; political theory, racism, and, 187–89, 201n30; redemption for, 170–71; "scientific" taxonomy of race and, 56–58; as "soul-less," 184; theodicy and anti-Blackness, 169–72; voodoo and, 293; wokeness and, 58–59. *See also specific topics*
Black Power Movement, 117–18
"Black rapist" figure, 43, 216n6
Black wisdom, 285–86
Blum, Edward, 132, 136
boarding schools, 208–9
body politic, 321–23
Boebert, Lauren, 52, 62n11, 66n69, 110, 112
Boggs, Grace Lee, 299–300, 309n1
books: banning of, 1, 7–8, 106; textbooks, 105–6, 113–14
Booth, John Wilkes, 104
Bowers, Claude, 103–4, 107, 119–20
Bradford, William, 59–60
Breivik, Anders, 331–32
British empire, 235–40, 243–49, 291–92. *See also* Elizabeth
Bromley, Roger, 61n1
Brown v. Board of Education (1954), 109, 292
Buchanan, Patrick, 85, 89
Buddhism, 21, 22, 349
Buhari, Muhammadu, 247
Bunche, Ralph, 190–91
Burke, Edmund, 119
Bush, George W., 110–11, 332
Butler, Anthea, 171, 214–15
Butler, Judith, 22, 283–84
Butler, Richard, 257
Byrne, Martin, 142n65

Cabot, John, 53–54
Calvin, John, 290, 324
Calvinism, 23, 54, 60, 290, 294
Camp Constitution, 269–70, 271
Canaanite conquest, 53–56
Canada, 159–60
capitalism, 92–93, 236
Capitol insurrection, January 6, 2021, 16; Congress and, 173–74; gender and, 224; as "legitimate political discourse," 167–68, 173; philosophy and, 194–95; race and, 224; Trump

Index   353

and, 173–74, 194–95, 270, 275–76;
white Christian nationalism and,
3–4, 20, 80, 92–94, 167–75, 221–22,
225–26, 302; white evil and, 173–74;
white mob and, 39–49, 195–97;
whiteness, theodicy and, 169–75;
white violence and, 167–68
Cardenal, Ernesto, 314, 320–23
Carter, Jimmy, 90–91
Carter, J. Kameron, 24–26, 35n30
Carter, Louisia, 207
Casas, de las (Bishop), 158–59
Catholic Church, 11; in Canada,
159–60; colonialism and, 130–32;
conquest and, 53–54, 65n52; papal
decrees and, 130–32, 334
Catholicism: anti-Catholicism and,
127; *Christ in Majesty* mosaic and,
132–35; Irish Catholics and, 128–29;
white Christian nationalism and,
127–37; whiteness and, 127–37;
white supremacy and, 127–32
Catholic Worker Movement, 80
Caucasians, 64n48
causality, 183
censorship, 94–95, 117
Cham, 56–57
Chansley, Jacob Anthony, 225–26
Charlottesville, Virginia, protest,
285, 330
Chauvin, Derek, 279
Cheney, Dick, 18
Child, Brenda, 208
children: boarding schools and, 208–9;
family values and, 208–9; imagery
and, 136; racism and, 255–57, 260,
264–65; slavery and, 209–10; white
violence and, 206–10, 332
Chordiya, Rashmi, 161
Christian flag, 269
Christianity: American identity and,
145; damaging religion of, 96–98;
fetish religion and, 21; love and,
6, 48, 227, 239–40; politics and, 7;
progressivism and, 45–47; systemic

racism and, 284–86; as "true
religion," 21–22; white supremacy,
misogyny, and, 205–16. *See also*
white Christianity; *specific topics*
Christian mission, 210–13, 271, 274–75
Christian nationalism: apocalypticism
and, 269–76; church and, 157–58;
citizenship and, 12–13, 19; conquest
and, 51–61; convergence of
racism, antisemitism, and, 56–59;
Evangelicalism and, 81n3, 91–93,
97; history of, 103–22; identity of,
81n3; Jericho story and, 55–56;
politics and, 52–53, 55–56, 58–59,
64n39; politics of exclusion and,
221–30; "Promised Land" in rhetoric
of, 51; Republicans denouncing,
111–12; white supremacy and,
257–66. *See also* white Christian
nationalism
Christian symbolism, 22
Christian theology, 2; faith and, 182;
law and, 181–82, 189–93, 198–99;
nihilism and, 182–84; "onto-
theology" and, 180–85; philosophy
and, 179–200; political theory and,
189–93; racism in, 180–93, 197–200;
theological irony and, 145–54;
transcendental idealism and, 180–85,
201n30
Christian "utopia," 61
Christ in Majesty mosaic, 129, 132–35
Christmas messages, 236, 238–40
church: Antioch, 228; as "barrier-
breaker," 227–30; Catholic, 11,
53–54, 65n52, 130–32, 159–60;
Christian nationalism and,
157–58; complacency of, 158–62;
Eastminster, 227–29; of England,
243–46; moral imperatives for
restitution and reparation dialogue
by, 162–64; racial justice initiatives
from, 227–29; racism and, 160–64;
reparations and, 228–29; restorative

justice and, 161–64; slavery and, 158–61; and state, 110, 114
citizenship: "Biblical citizenship," 110; Black, 104; Christian nationalism and, 12–13, 19; Native Americans and, 272; Naturalization Act and, 272; white Christianity and, 44; white Christian nationalism and, 12–13, 19, 76
civic life, 71–72
Civil Liberties Act, 165n10
Civil Rights Act (1964), 292–93
Civil Rights Movement, 80–81, 86; voting and, 120; white Christian nationalism and, 89–91; white violence and, 109
Civil War, 12, 80, 103–7, 119–22
Clark, Kenneth, 186
classroom conflict, 280–83
Cleage, Albert, 139n22
cleanliness, 339
Clinton, Bill, 165n10, 275
Clinton, Hilary, 275, 281
CNP. *See* Council for National Policy
Coates, Ta-Nehisi, 279, 283
collective forgetting, 133
colonial countergaze, 237
colonialism, 6; antisemitism and, 74; Black people and, 56–58; British empire, monarchy, and, 235–38, 243–49, 291–92; Catholic Church and, 130–32; Christianity as "true religion" and, 21–22; conquest and, 73; crucifixion and, 31–32; decolonization and, 335–39, 341n16; dehumanization and, 72–78; discipleship and, 73; Doctrine of Discovery and, 1, 53–56, 63n19, 63n21, 131–34, 236; exceptionalism and, 86–88; Fanon on, 334–39, 341n16, 342n29; imperialism, race-making, and, 23–30; Jews and, 25; Manifest Destiny and, 75, 89; neocolonialism and, 19; slavery and, 72, 130–32, 158–59, 291–92;

white Christianity and, 11–12, 27–28; white colonial gaze and, 237, 243–44, 319–20, 324; white mob and, 39–40, 44; white violence and, 7, 11–12
Columbus, Christopher, 52, 53–54, 62n10, 130–31
Commonwealth nations, 240, 245
Cone, James, 6, 76, 79, 162, 273, 319
Confederacy, 104–5
Congress, 173–74
Connell, Raewyn, 225
conquest: America as site of Canaanite, 53–56; Catholic Church and, 53–54, 65n52; Christian nationalism and, 51–61; colonialism and, 73; Columbus and, 52; divine appointment, prophecy and, 52–53; imperialism and, 52, 53–54; of Indigenous people, 53–57, 60; racism, antisemitism, and, 56–59; violence in name of God and, 59–61; war and, 75; white violence and, 56–57, 59–61
conspiracies: Civil War and, 107; in politics, 56; white violence and, 270, 275
Constantine, 7
Constitution, US, 23, 55, 89, 110, 188, 223
Cooper, Amy, 279
Cooper, Anderson, 160
Cooper, James Fenimore, 272
Copeland, M. Shawn, 72, 78–79, 129, 131–32
Coppage v. Kansas (1915), 191–92
Cornet v. Winton (1826), 54
corporate power, 8
corporate-warrior state: crucifixion and, 31–33; military power and, 18; politics and, 29–30; race-making in, 23–30; religion-making in, 21–23; white Christianity and, 17–33
Cotton, John, 54
Cotton, Tom, 171

Council for National Policy (CNP), 92–93
counternarratives, 308–9
coups, 41
covenant justice, 161–62
The Crescent Observed (Allison), 22–23
Crist, Charlie, 116
critical race theory (CRT), 1, 114–18, 121, 190–91
Critique of Pure Reason (Kant), 181–82
cross, 273. *See also* crucifixion
CRT. *See* critical race theory
crucifixion: colonialism and, 31–32; corporate-warrior state and, 31–33; crucified Jesus in wake of empire, 30–33; imagery of, 273–74; politics and, 31–32; religion-making and, 32–33; sin and, 31; white Christianity and, 30–33; white Christian nationalism and, 78–79
Crusades, 271, 274–75
Cruz, Ted, 195–96
Cullinan Diamonds, 244
cults, 16
culture: cultural heritage and, 310n10; multiculturalism and, 29–30, 119–20, 142n65, 167; white mob and, 42–43; worship, 317–20
Curry, Tommy J., 201n30

Dabney, Robert Lewis, 291–94
Dalferth, Ingolf U., 325n5
damnable ambiguity, 305
Danforth, Samuel, 63n29
Daniel, Carey, 76–78
Day, Dorothy, 80
Day, William Howard, 119
Declaration of Independence, 89
decolonization, 335–39, 341n16
dehumanization: colonialism and, 72–78; of dehumanized "other," 1, 315–16, 349; exploitation and, 157–64, 334; of Jews, 74; racism and, 73–74, 315–16; slavery and, 130–32, 209–10, 223

deicide, 131
Delffs, Dudley, 242
demagoguery, 301
democracy, 13–14; exceptionalism and, 86–88; white Christian nationalism and, 14, 85–98; white mob and, 41–42
Democrats, 52, 58, 90, 98, 224–25. *See also* politics
DeSantis, Ron, 52–53, 55, 56, 58–59, 115–16
Dewey, John, 13–14
diamonds, 244
DiAngelo, Robin, 280
Ding-an-Sich, 180
Dirty War, 340n1
discipleship, 72–73, 78–81
discrimination: anti-white, 94–95, 301; in British empire, 245–46; religious, 269–70; white Christian nationalism and, 89–91. *See also* racism
disjunctive syllogism, 184–85
diversity, equity, and inclusion statements, 340
divine appointment, 52–53
docetism, 319–20, 323–24
Doctrine of Discovery, 1, 53–56, 63n19, 63n21, 131–34, 236
"doing work" and learning, 307–8
"Don't Say Gay" law, 115–16
Douglas, Kelly Brown, 75
Douglass, Frederick, 4–5, 187, 212–13, 222
Du Bois, W. E. B., 36n46, 95, 120, 127–28, 130, 260
Dukakis, Michael, 259–60
Dum Diversas, 131
Du Mez, Kristin Kobes, 224, 230, 231n15
Dunning, William Archibald, 104, 107
Dunning School, 104–7
duplicity, 72

Easter message, 240–42
Eastminster Church, 227–29

Ebony and Ivy (Wilder), 27
economics, 92–93, 217n4, 236
education, 95; Advanced Placement African American Studies in, 117–18; authoritarianism in, 117; boarding schools and, 208–9; censorship and, 117; classroom conflict and, 280–83; CRT and, 1, 114–18, 121; DeSantis and, 115–16; at Dunning School, 104–7; KKK and, 108–9; law and, 12, 115–18; LGBTQIA community and, 109–13, 118, 120–21; Moms for Liberty and, 116–17; multiculturalism and, 119–20; politics and, 104–22; "The Professor Watchlist" and, 2, 9n2; racism and, 255–57; Republicans and, 109–22; Rutherford and, 105–6; school boards and, 109; teaching about race in, 280–86; textbooks and, 105–6, 113–14; Trump and, 114–15; voting and, 121; white Christian nationalism and, 104–22; white solidarity on campus and in, 280–86; white supremacy in, 26–27; wokeness in, 115–19
Edwards, Jonathan, 76, 78, 290–93
ego, 270–71
eliminationism, 12, 261–66
Eliot, John, 65n55
elite white men, 86–89
Elizabeth (Queen), 11; bishops and, 245–46; Black bodies and white queen, 246–48; Christmas messages by, 236, 238–40; Church of England and, 243–46; Commonwealth nations and, 240; coronation speech by, 236; death of, 243–44, 247–48; Easter message by, 240–42; Evangelicalism and, 242–43; funeral of, 243–44; introduction to, 235–38; Jesus Christ and, 238–41; Mau Mau uprising and, 246–47; monarchy, British empire, and, 235–40, 243–49; Nigerian-Biafran War and, 247–48; racism and, 240–42, 245–49; white supremacy and, 236–38
Elkins, Caroline, 18, 23
Emerson, Michael O., 226–27
empathy, 308
empire: British, 235–40, 243–49, 291–92; crucified Jesus in wake of, 30–33; liberal imperialism and, 23; race-making and, 23–30; religion-making and, 21–23; Roman, 5; white Christianity and wake of, 5, 30–33
Enlightenment, 24–25, 104, 183–84
Epigramas (Cardenal), 322–23
Espionage Act, 18
ethnic cleansing, 66n61
ethno-nationalism, 151–52
Evangelicalism: Black Christianity and, 97; Christian nationalism and, 81n3, 91–93, 97; othering and, 226–27; politics and, 91–93; Queen Elizabeth and, 242–43; Trump and, 91–92, 294–95, 302; white Christian nationalism and, 226–27, 231n15, 289–95
Evangelical Moral Majority, 91
evil, 323; blackness as, 169–70; good versus, 332, 333–35; structural, 158–64; white, 173–74
exceptionalism, 47, 86–88, 120–22
The Executed God (Taylor, Mark Lewis), 32
exploitation, 157–64, 334. *See also* colonialism; slavery

faith, 78–80, 182
false idols, 135, 147–51
Falwell, Jerry, 91, 113–14, 292–94
family values, 206–10, 292–93
Fanon, Frantz, 25–26, 117, 260–61; political theology of violence and, 334–39, 341n16, 342n29
fascism, 17; liberalism and, 18–19; neocolonialism and, 19; war and, 18–19; white Christian nationalism and, 19–20, 330–31, 340n1; white

supremacist Eurocentric Christianity and, 300, 306, 307; white supremacy and, 19–20
Fea, John, 63n25
Feagin, Joe, 128, 130, 132–33, 137n3
fear, 199, 230; of God, 290, 339; racism and, 93–94, 196–97; white violence and, 339
federalism, 104
Feimster, Crystal Nicole, 216n6
fetish religion, 21
Feuerbach, Ludwig, 294–95
FitzGerald, Francis, 291
Fletcher, Jeanine Hill, 24, 26–28
Floyd, George, 157, 171
Founding Fathers, 27, 60, 88–89, 105
Francis (Pope), 159–60
freedom, 6–7; Black, 103–4, 107, 132, 272–73; religious, 168–69; slavery and, 132, 272–73
free-market capitalism, 92–93
Freikorps narratives, 339
Freire, Paulo, 6
Freud, Sigmund, 273–74, 275
Fuentes, Nick, 339

gender: Capitol insurrection and, 224; identity, 12, 14, 65n58, 114
genocide: eliminationism and, 12, 261–66; ethnic cleansing and, 66n61; of Native Americans, 60, 61, 228, 271–72
geopolitics, 29
Gestell, 181
Gibbons, Reginald, 321
Giglio, Louie, 171
God, 15; deicide and, 131; fear of, 290, 339; idolatry and, 147–51; imagery and conceptualization of, 135; *imago Dei* and, 11–12, 180, 304; Jesus Christ and, 313; justice and, 284–85; nihilism and, 182–84; revisiting local gods, 148–51; violence and, 59–61, 290; white Christian nationalism and, 289–93; whiteness of, 179–80

God of the Oppressed (Cone), 162
God's Fierce Whimsy (Mud Flower Collective), 16
Goldhagen, Jonah, 262
Goodman, Eugene, 196–97, 225
goodness, 46–47, 169–75
good versus evil, 332, 333–35
Gordon, Lewis, 169–70
Gorski, Philip S., 51, 63n25, 92
Goshen-Gottstein, Alon, 150–51
Gospel movement, 80
Graham, Billy, 242
Graham, Franklin, 295
Gray, Robert, 54
Great Awakening, 61, 76, 290–94
Great Depression, 191–92
Greene, Marjorie Taylor, 339
Griffith, D. W., 107
Grovey v. Townsend (1935), 190–91
gynecology, 210–12, 217n15

Haidt, Johnathan, 283
Ham, 56–57, 65n49, 222
Hampton, Fred, 19
Harper, Lisa Sharon, 242, 244
Harper, Stephen, 159
Harvey, Paul, 132, 136
Hawley, Josh, 224–25
Hayes-Tilden compromise, 196
health care, 210–12, 217n15, 218n26
Hedges, Chris, 110–11
Hegel, G. W. F., 182, 260–61, 295
hegemonic masculinity, 225
hegemony, pedagogy of, 103–22
Heidegger, Martin, 180–85
Heltzel, Peter G., 314–15
Heschel, Abraham Joshua, 3, 5, 324
Heyer, Heather, 330
hiding, sin of, 283–86
Hill, Jemele, 247
Hillbilly Elegy (Vance), 272
Hinduism, 22
history: Black History Month and, 118; of Christian nationalism, 103–22;

Jesus Christ in, 138n8; memory and, 61n1, 213; philosophy of, 193–97
Hitler, Adolf, 257
Hodges, Daniel, 225
Holocaust, 262
homelessness, 271–72
homeostasis, 275
homosexuality, 339–40
hooks, bell, 225, 227
Hoover, Herbert, 103
hope, 2–3
Hopkins, Dwight, 305
Horne, Gerald, 188–89
housing segregation, 217n14
Husserl, Edmund, 317
hybridized identity, 152–54
Hying, Donald, 134
hymno-theology, 316–24
hymns, 314–15

ICWA. *See* Indian Child Welfare Act
ideal theory, 192–93, 201n30
identity: American, 145; Black, 12, 256–66; of Christian nationalists, 81n3; ethno-nationalism and, 151–52; fluidity and complexity of, 301–2; gender, 12, 14, 65n58, 114; hybridized, 152–54; narratives and, 302; phobic structures of white Christian self and, 337–40; racial, 260, 263–65, 310n10; racism and, 256–66, 280–81; religious, 152–54; sexual, 12, 339–40; social, 280–81; white, 270–71
idolatry: race and, 147–51, 313–14; of white Christian nationalism, 187–89, 199–200, 313–14, 323–24; worship culture and, 317–20
idol-making, 183–84
idols: definition of, 5; false, 135, 147–51
ignorance, 94–96
imagery: in *Christ in Majesty* mosaic, 129, 132–35; of crucifixion, 273–74;

of God, 135; multicultural, 142n65; white supremacy and, 134–37
imago Dei, 11–12, 180, 304
imago hominis, 12, 179–80; Black bodies and, 181; white supremacy, racism, and, 189, 193–200
imperialism: colonialism, race-making, and, 23–30; conquest and, 52, 53–54; geopolitics and, 29; liberal, 23; military power and, 29; politics and, 29–30. *See also* colonialism; empire
incarnation, 318–19
Incidents in the Life of a Slave Girl (Jacobs), 221–22
inclusivity, backlash to, 300–303
Indian Child Welfare Act (ICWA), 66n61
Indian Removal Act, 61
Indigenous Action, 308
Indigenous people, 248–49; conquest of, 53–57, 60; Doctrine of Discovery and conquest of, 53–56; founding of US and, 27; Mau Mau uprising and, 246–47. *See also* Native Americans
individualism, 305
inner self, 318–20, 322–23
"insubordinate space," 227–30
Inter Caetera (1493), 53–54
interracial marriage, 77–78
interruption, 281
"In the Penal Colony" (Kafka), 31–32
The Invention of World *Religions* (Masuzawa), 147–48
invisibility. *See* racialized invisibility
inwardness, 318–20
Iraq, 18
Irish Catholics, 128–29
irony, theological, 145–54
Is God a White Racist? A Preamble to Black Theology (Jones, W. R.), 170
Islam, 21–23

Jackson, Andrew, 61
Jackson, Jesse, 259–60
Jackson, Mahala, 207

Jacobs, Harriet, 221–22
James, Joy, 3
"Japheth's inheritance," 27
Jefferson, Thomas, 89
Jeffersonian era, 88–89
Jennings, James, 73, 74
Jennings, Willie, 130
Jericho March, 275
Jericho story, 55–56
Jesus Christ, 19; atonement and, 273–74; Black liberation theology and, 79–80; in *Christ in Majesty* mosaic, 129, 132–35; God and, 313; in history, 138n8; Queen Elizabeth and, 238–41; re-membering, 32–33; in wake of empire, 5, 30–33; as white, 11, 24–25, 127–37, 185. *See also* crucifixion
Jewish Theology and World Religions (Goshen-Gottstein), 150
Jews: colonialism and, 25; dehumanization of, 74; idolatry, Christianity and, 147–51; othering of, 24–26, 52, 66n59; in South, 146. *See also* antisemitism
Jim Crow, 41, 75, 86, 181, 228–29, 293
Johnson, Alderman Richard, 56–57
Johnson, Andrew, 66n61, 103–4
Johnson, Philena, 208
Johnson, Robert, 57
Johnson v. McIntosh (1823), 54, 63n19
Jones, Alex, 274
Jones, Bob, Sr., 292
Jones, Charles Colcock, 295
Jones, Robert P., 91
Jones, William R., 170
Joseph, Peniel, 120
Judaism, 25, 50n15, 58, 65n58
Juergensmeyer, Mark, 331–32, 340n3

Kafka, Franz, 31–32
Kant, Immanuel, 24–25, 180–85, 193–95, 201n30
Kelly, Megyn, 7, 127–28
Kendi, Ibram X., 222

Kesey, Ken, 272
Kierkegaard, Søren, 182
King, Martin Luther, Jr., 80, 186, 227, 309n1, 332; on beloved community, 304, 310n14
King, Richard, 22
KKK. *See* Ku Klux Klan
knighthood, 242
Kotsko, Adam, 333
Ku Klux Klan (KKK), 12, 42, 107–9, 182, 273
Kurashige, Scott, 309n1

labor laws, 191–92
Lacan, Jacques, 270–71, 272, 274–75
Last of the Mohicans (Cooper, J. F.), 272
Latinx community, 159, 160, 163
law: Black liberation theology and, 190–92; Christian theology and, 181–82, 189–93, 198–99; education and, 12, 115–18; labor and, 191–92; political theory and, 189–93, 198–99; racism in, 12, 115–18, 189–93, 198–99; voting and, 190–91
learning, 307–8
Lebenswelt, 315
Lee, Robert E., 120, 285
Legacy of Violence (Elkins), 18
legal realism, 191–92
Lepore, Jill, 93
LGBTQIA community, 59, 333; education and, 109–13, 118, 120–21; Pride flag and, 269; rights of, 112; transgender youth and, 213–14, 218n26, 218n28
liberal imperialism, 23
liberalism, 18–19, 243
liberation: in Bible, 323; redemption and, 170–71; theopoetics, 314, 320–23. *See also* Black liberation theology
"Liberty State" movement, 257–58
lies, 4, 6–7, 45, 119–20
Lincoln, Abraham, 103–6

Lipsitz, George, 227
Lockhart, Lakisha, 315
logos, 180, 190–93
Lost Cause movement, 12, 104–7, 119–22
Lost Narratives (Bromley), 61n1
love, 230, 324, 347–49; Christianity and, 6, 48, 227, 239–40; racism and, 6; violence and, 48
Lovejoy, Elijah, 41
Lowry, Rich, 118
Luckerson, Victor, 42
lynching, 216n3; cross and, 273; lynch mobs and, 43, 206–8; public displays of, 206–7; torture and, 216n4; white Christian nationalism and, 4, 20, 272–73
Lyons, Betty, 133–34

Madison, James, 122
Maimonides (Moses ben Maimon), 148–50, 154n11
Male Fantasies (Theweleit), 339
Manifest Destiny, 61, 75, 89
marriage, 77–78
Marriott, David, 341n16
Marshall, John, 53, 131–32
Martinot, Steve, 45
Marx, Karl, 240
Mary, 324
"Mary Magdalene Sings" (Thompson), 15–16
masculinity, 224–25
mask, 5–6, 273–75
Massingale, Bryan, 127, 135
master-slave narrative, 260–61
Mastriano, Doug, 52, 53, 55, 58
Mastriano, Rebbie, 56
Masuzawa, Tomoko, 147–48
Mather, Cotton, 23, 55–58, 60, 63n25, 65nn53–55; white Christian nationalism and, 75–76, 78–79
Matthews, Robert Jay, 258
Mau Mau uprising, 246–47

A Measuring Rod to Test Text Books and Reference Books in Schools, Colleges and Libraries (Rutherford), 105–6, 115
medical experimentation, 210–12, 217n15
Mehl, Caroline, 283
memory: collective forgetting and, 133; history and, 61n1, 213; laws, 12, 117–18
Metaline, Washington, 255–58, 261–63, 265–66
metaphysical violence, 131–32
Metaphysics (Aristotle), 182–83, 187–89
Methodists, 291
Mid-Atlantic Reformation Society, 113
migrants, 73
militant masculinity, 224–25
military power: corporate-warrior state and, 18; geopolitics and, 29; imperialism and, 29; war and, 18; white Christianity and, 29, 300
Mills, Charles, 42, 192–93
misinformation, 94–96, 106
misogynoir, 212
misogyny: "Black rapist" and, 216n6; family values and, 206–10; resistance to, 215–16; sexual violence and, 205–6, 209; white supremacy and, 205–16; white violence and, 205–16
Mohler, Al, 243
Momaday, N. Scott, 131
Moms for Liberty, 116–17
monarchy, 235–40, 243–44, 246–49, 291–92. *See also* Elizabeth
Moorish people, 23, 26
"Moral Majority," 113–14, 120, 292–93
Moral Mondays Movement, 81
moral philosophy, 193–95
Mormon church, 16
Moses ben Maimon (Maimonides), 148–50, 154n11
Mud Flower Collective, 16

multiculturalism, 29–30, 119–20, 142n65, 167
Muslims, 22–23, 52, 271, 334
Mystic Ford, 60

Narrative of the Life of Frederick Douglass (Douglass), 212–13
narratives, 120–22, 260–61; counternarratives and, 308–9; *Freikorps,* 339; identity and, 302; polarization and, 301–4; Trumpist, 301–3; white violence and, 339
National Conservatism Conference, 224–25
nationalism. *See* white Christian nationalism
Native Americans: children, 208; citizenship and, 272; conquest of, 56–57, 60; Doctrine of Discovery and, 132–34; genocide of, 60, 61, 228, 271–72; ICWA and, 66n61; Indian Removal Act and, 61; metaphysical violence against, 131; restitution for, 159–60; "scientific" taxonomy of race and, 56–58, 63n18; "Trail of Tears" and, 61
Naturalization Act (1790), 272
Nazis, 257, 339
"Negro rule," 103–4
Neiwert, David, 262
neocolonialism, 19
neoliberalism, 18
neutrality, 279, 283–86, 302
New Apostolic Reformation, 52
Newton, John, 317–19
The Next American Revolution (Boggs and Kurashige), 309n1
Ngugi, Mukoma Wa, 246–47
Nicaragua, 320–23
Nicholas V (Pope), 130
Nietzsche, Friedrich, 265
Nigerian-Biafran War, 247–48
nihilism, 182–84
Noakes-Duncan, Thomas, 161
"non-ideal" theory, 201n30

Norway, 331–32

Oath Keepers, 173–74, 302
Obama, Barack, 275, 301
ObeySumner, ChrisTiana, 161
objecthood, 315
objectification, 349
One Flew Over the Cuckoo's Nest (Kesey), 272
"onto-theology," 180–85
Onyebuchi, Kelachi, 248
Operation Resist (film), 112
"The Order," 257–60
Orientalism and Religion (King, R.), 22
"orientational knowledge," 314–15
"Original Sin" (Simms), 343–49
origins, 187–89, 201n15
O'Sullivan, John, 89
othering: dehumanized "other" and, 1, 315–16, 349; Evangelicalism and, 226–27; of Jews, 24–26, 52, 66n59; of Muslims, 22–23, 52; objecthood and, 315; race-making and, 23–30; racialized invisibility and, 314; "saved," "unsaved," and, 28; white Christianity and, 22–23

pandemics, 108
papal decrees, 130–32, 334
Parental Rights in Education, 115–16
Parousia, 291
patriotism, 93–94, 108
Payne, Buchner, 184–85
Peckham, George, 54
pedagogy of hegemony, 103–22
Pence, Mike, 3–4, 20, 225
Pepinster, Catherine, 238–39
Perry, Samuel L., 51, 63n25, 71–72, 92
Pew Research Center, 96–97, 113, 279
Phillips, Kevin, 85–86
philosophy: Aristotle on, 180, 182–83, 187–89, 201n15; Black bodies in, 181; Capitol insurrection and, 194–95; Christian theology and, 179–200; Heidegger on, 180–85; of

history, 193–97; Kant on, 180–85, 201n30; moral, 193–94; nihilism and, 182–84; political theory and, 189–93; pseudo-knowledge and, 182, 188; reason and, 180–85; skepticism and, 186–87
Phipps, William E., 318
phobic structures, of white Christian self, 337–40
Pinochet, Augusto, 340n1
place, as "insubordinate space," 227–30
Plantinga, Alvin, 184
pleasure principle, 275
Plessner, Helmuth, 322
poetry, 8, 15–16, 314, 320–23, 343–49
polarization, 301–6
police brutality and abuse, 30, 43, 157, 163–64, 344–45
political theory: Black people, racism, and, 187–89, 201n30; Constitution and, 188; CRT and, 190–91; economics and, 217n14; law, racism, and, 12, 115–18, 189–93, 198–99; white violence and, 334–37
politics: Black people and, 58–59; Christianity and, 7; Christian nationalism and, 52–53, 55–56, 58–59, 64n39; *Christ in Majesty* mosaic and, 132–33; conspiracies, 56; corporate-warrior state and, 29–30; coups and, 41; crucifixion and, 31–32; education and, 104–22; Evangelicalism and, 91–93; of exclusion, 221–30; Fanon and, 334–39, 341n16, 342n29; geopolitics and, 29; imperialism and, 29–30; of interruption, 281; Jericho story and, 55–56; liberalism and, 18–19; misinformation and, 94–96; political theory, law, and, 189–93; racism and, 90–93; Reconstruction and, 104–9, 121; religious terrorism and, 332–33; Republican Thought Police and, 4–5; of resentment, 7–8, 10n28; secularism and, 333–34; supersessionism and, 58–59; Supreme Court and, 292–93, 295; voting and, 36n47; white Christian nationalism and, 3–5, 7–8, 20, 81, 104–22, 259–60, 262–63; white solidarity and, 279–80; white violence and, 60–61; white violence and political theology, 334–37; wokeness and, 58–59. *See also* Capitol insurrection
Pollard, Virginian Edward, 104
populism, 113, 116–17
Posner, Sarah, 111, 292–93, 295
poverty, 3, 191, 292
The Power Worshippers (Stewart), 111, 291–92
predominantly white institution (PWI), 280–86
Pride flag, 269
"primitive" religions, 148
"The Professor Watchlist," 2, 9n2
progressivism, 47–48
Project Blitz, 93
"Promised Land," 51–56, 75–78
prophecy, 52–53
Protestants, 11
Protonentis, Adana, 161
Proud Boys, 20, 224, 302, 333
Psalms, 321–22
pseudo-knowledge, 182, 188
psychoanalytic theory, 270–75
public safety, 308
public theology, 71–72, 74–78
Puritans, 54–55, 63n29, 73; slavery and, 75–76; white Christian nationalism and, 75–76, 78–79, 87–88. *See also* Mather, Cotton
PWI. *See* predominantly white institution

Quakers, 349
"The Question Concerning Technology" (Heidegger), 183

race: in Bible, 226–29; capitalism and, 92–93; Capitol insurrection and, 224; cultural heritage and, 310n10; idolatry and, 147–51, 313–14; invisibility and, 310n10, 314; redemption and, 170–71, 174; religion and, 15–16, 147–54; "scientific" taxonomy of, 56–58, 63n18; as social construct, 226–27; teaching about, 280–86; white Christianity as race-making, 23–30, 179–80, 186–88; white mob and race riots, 42–43; white racial frame and, 127–37. *See also* critical race theory; white Christianity
racial contract, 42–43
racial entitlement, 196–97
racial identity, 260, 263–65, 310n10
racialized invisibility, 310n10, 314–24
racial justice initiatives, 227–29
racial profiling, 281
racial "purity," 6–7, 14
racial realism, 191–92
racial segregation, 109; housing segregation and, 217n14; Jim Crow and, 41, 75, 86, 181, 228–29, 293; "justifications" for, 76–78, 88; supersessionism and, 77; white Christian nationalism and, 76–78, 292
racism: children and, 255–57, 260, 264–65; in Christian theology, 180–93, 197–200; church and, 160–64; conquest and, 56–59; dehumanization and, 73–74, 315–16; economics and, 217n14; education and, 255–57; eliminationism and, 12, 261–66; fear and, 93–94, 196–97; health care and, 210–12, 217n15; identity and, 256–66, 280–81; *imago hominis* and, 189, 193–200; in law and political theory, 12, 115–18, 189–93, 198–99; love and, 6; medical experimentation and, 210–12, 217n15; "The Order" and, 257–60; patriotism and, 93–94; in philosophy of history, 193–97; political theory, Black people, and, 187–89, 201n30; politics and, 90–93; "Promised Land," slavery, and, 75–78; in PWI, 280–86; Queen Elizabeth and, 240–42, 245–49; racist thinking and white mob logic, 39, 45–49; religious identity and, 285; reverse, 59, 66n61, 94–95, 301; settlers and, 56–57; social hierarchy and, 88; spirituality and, 197–99; structural evil and, 158–64; systemic, 280–86; theodicy and anti-Blackness, 169–72; transgender youth and, 213–14; white Christianity and, 16, 233n60; white privilege and, 280–81; "woke agenda" and, 58–59. *See also specific topics*
radical reflexivity, 319–20
Rauschenbusch, Walter, 80
Rawls, John, 192–93
Ray, Stephen G., Jr., 325n14
Reagan, Ronald, 90–91, 165n10, 292, 300–301
reason, 180–85
rebellion, 2–3
Reconstruction, 66n61, 181; Hayes-Tilden compromise and end of, 196; "Negro rule" during, 103–4; politics and, 104–9, 121; Rushdoony and, 293
redemption, 170–71, 174, 306–7, 309
religion: fetish, 21; Marx on, 240; origins of, 147–48; Pew Research Center on, 96–97; "primitive," 148; race and, 15–16, 147–54; religion-making, 21–23, 32–33; religiosity and, 96–97. *See also specific religions; specific topics*
Religion, Politics and the Christian Right (Taylor, M. L.), 32
"religio-racial project," 27
religious discrimination, 269–70
religious freedom, 168–69

religious identity, 152–54, 206, 285
religious terrorism, 331–34
reparations, 161–64, 228–29
replacement theory, 12, 74, 106–7, 109
Republicans: denouncing Christian nationalism, 111–12; education and, 109–22; misinformation and, 94–96; Moms for Liberty and, 116–17; National Conservatism Conference and, 224–25; Pew Research Center surveys on, 113; Republican Thought Police and, 4–5; in South, 90–93; Supreme Court and, 292–93; Tea Party and, 64n39; white Christian nationalism and, 52–59, 85–86, 90–93. *See also* Capitol insurrection; politics; Trump, Donald
resentment, politics of, 7–8, 10n28
restitution, 159–64, 165n10
restorative justice, 161–64
reverse mimesis, 180
reverse racism, 59, 66n61, 94–95, 301
revolution, 2–3; actions for ushering in, 307–9; allies and, 302, 308, 310n8; backlashes to inclusivity and, 300–303; definition and term usage, 299–300; different roles in, 308; finding your place in, 308; narrative and, 301–3; redemption and, 306–7; white Christianity and, 299–309
Revolutionary War, 188–89
Rhodes, Stewart, 173–74
riots, 42–43, 157
Roberts, Paul, 227–30
Roberts, Steven O., 135
Roberts-Miller, Patricia, 301
Robertson, Pat, 114
Rocha, Guido, 31
Roche, Michael, 225
Roe v. Wade (1973), 292, 294
Roman empire, 5–6, 61
Roof, Dylann, 136, 279
Rosen, Jan Henryk de, 134
Rothstein, Richard, 217n14
Royal Collection Trust, 244

Rushdoony, Rousas J., 293, 294
Rutherford, Mildred Lewis, 105–7, 115

safety, in public spaces, 308
Sales, Ruby, 306, 310n10
salvation, 305, 306–7, 309
"saved," 28
Schmitt, Carl, 334
school boards, 109
secularism, 333–34
Seitz, Mark J., 162
self-care, 309
self-criticism, 304–6
settlers: Doctrine of Discovery and, 53–56, 131–34; racism and, 56–57; white violence and, 60–61. *See also* colonialism
Seven Mountain Mandates, 114
sexual identity, 12, 339–40
sexual violence, 205–6, 209–13
Shelby v. Holder (2013), 120
Shem, 56–57, 64n45
Simmons, William, 107–8
Simms, Michael, 343–49
Sims, James Marion, 210–12, 217n15
sin: crucifixion and, 31; of hiding and neutrality, 283–86; interracial marriage depicted as, 77–78; in "Original Sin," 343–49; redemption and, 306–7
"The 1619 Project," 121
skepticism, 186–87
slavery: in Bible, 291; children and, 209–10; Christian "utopia" and, 61; church and, 158–61; Civil War and, 80, 104–5; colonialism and, 72, 130–32, 158–59, 291–92; Constitution and, 223; dehumanization and, 130–32, 209–10, 223; Doctrine of Discovery and, 54, 131–34; faith and, 78–80; freedom and, 132, 272–73; Great Awakening and, 290–93; Jim Crow and, 228–29; "justification" for, 75–77, 88; master-slave narrative and, 260–61; medical

experimentation and, 210–12, 217n15; as "necessary evil," 171; Newton's "Amazing Grace" and, 317–19; "Promised Land," racism, and, 75–78; Puritans and, 75–76; Revolutionary War and, 188–89; "scientific" taxonomy of race and, 56–58; white Christian nationalism and, 56–58, 291–93; women and, 209–10
Smith, Al, 103–4, 119–20
Smith, Harold, 77–78
Smith, Henry, 207
SNCC. *See* Student Nonviolent Coordinating Committee
Snyder, Timothy, 117
social contract theory, 192–93
social hierarchy, 88
social identity, 280–81
social justice, 29–30, 58–59, 161–64, 282–83
social media, 94–95
Socratic questioning, 6–7
soteriological motive, 74
South: Confederacy and, 104–5; Great Awakening in, 61, 76, 290–93; Jews in, 146; Jim Crow and, 41, 75, 86, 181, 228–29, 293; Republicans in, 90–93; theological irony in, 145–54; white Christian nationalism in, 90–93
Spain, 52, 53–54, 65n52, 73, 130–31, 158–59
Spanish influenza pandemic, 108
spirituality, 197–99
sports, 218n28
Stacy, Rubin, 216n3
Stannard, David, 26
state oppression, 6–8
Sterling, Jeffrey, 18
Stewart, Katherine, 94–95, 111, 121, 291–93
Stiles, Ezra, 27
Stone Mountain Park, 246–47
Stop W.O.K.E. Act, 117, 119
Strachey, William, 57

structural evil, 158–64
Student Nonviolent Coordinating Committee (SNCC), 293
suffering, 3
Sullivan, Shannon, 133, 201n30
Sun Ceremony, 131
supersessionism, 50n15, 58–59, 74–78
Supreme Court: Camp Constitution and, 269–70, 271; Doctrine of Discovery and, 54, 63n19, 63n21; politics and, 292–93, 294
surveillance, 18
Swainsboro, Georgia, 145–48, 152–54
Swinfen, Anne, 16
symbolism: Christian, 22; symbolic capital and, 27–28; of white Christian nationalism, 80
sympathy, 308
systemic poverty, 3
systemic racism, 280–86

Taíno people, 52–53
Taking America Back for God (Whitehead and Perry), 71–72
tautology, 317
taxes, 293
Taylor, Charles, 319
Taylor, Kandiss, 60–61
Taylor, Mark Lewis, 32, 237–41
Taylor, Paul C., 264, 315–16
teaching about race, 280–86
Tea Party, 64n39
Terror in the Mind of God (Juergensmeyer), 331–32, 340n3
terrorism, religious, 331–34
Texas voting rights, 190–91
textbooks, 105–6, 113–14
theodicy: anti-Blackness and, 169–72; whiteness and, 169–75; white violence and, 170–74
theological irony, 145–54
A Theory of Justice (Rawls), 192
Theweleit, Klaus, 339
Thomas, Kendall, 61n1
Thompson, Becky, 15–16

Thornwell, James Henry, 223
Thurman, Howard, 180, 197–99
Tilly, Charles, 303–4
Tisby, Jemar, 153, 227, 228
Torre, Miguel de la, 280–81
torture, 31–32, 210–13, 216n4
toxic masculinity, 224–25
The Tragic Era (Bowers), 103–4, 119–20
"Trail of Tears," 61
transactional white Christianity, 304–6
transcendental idealism, 180–85, 201n30
transformational white Christianity, 304–6, 307
transgender youth, 213–14, 218n26, 218n28
Tricontinental Institute, 30
Tricontinental Institute for Social Research, 30
Trinity, 314–15
Trump, Donald, 281; Bible photoshoot with, 157–58, 163; Biden and, 36n47; Capitol insurrection and, 173–74, 194–95, 270, 275–76; education and, 114–15; Evangelicalism and, 91–92, 294–95, 302; on Jews, 66n59; narratives and, 301–3; overcoming white Christian nationalism and, 289, 294–95; success of, 301–2; "Trumpy Bear" and, 329–30; "vigilante justice" and, 111; white Christian nationalism and, 3–4, 7, 18–19, 58, 94, 97–98, 274–75, 301–3; white solidarity and, 279; white supremacy and, 285, 302. *See also* Capitol insurrection
Trumpsters, 20, 80, 225–26, 259, 294–95
truth, 106
Truths of History (Rutherford), 106, 115
Turkish Muslims, 271
Turman, Eboni Marshall, 325n19
Turning Point USA, 2
Turtle Island, 54

Underhill, John, 60
unemployment, 93–94
Unholy (Posner), 111, 292–93
United States (US): Constitution, 23, 55, 89, 110, 188, 223; Founding Fathers of, 27, 60, 105; founding of, 26–30, 53–57, 60–61, 131–34, 168–69; as site of Canaanite conquest, 53–56
"unsaved," 28
Urban II (Pope), 271
US. *See* United States

Vance, J. D., 272
Viganò, Carlo Maria, 275
"vigilante justice," 111
violence: decolonization and, 335–39, 341n16; love and, 48; metaphysical, 131–32; in name of God, 59–61, 290; police abuse and, 30, 43, 157, 163–64, 344–45; power and, 303; sexual, 205–6, 209–13. *See also* genocide; lynching; white violence
Virginia Company, 56–57
visibility, 310n10. *See also* racialized invisibility
voodoo, 293
voting: Civil Rights Movement and, 120; education and, 121; KKK and, 108–9; law and, 190–91; politics and, 36n47; rights, 190–91, 292–93; voter fraud and, 194–95; voter suppression and, 81, 108–9; white Christian nationalism and, 90–91; white solidarity and, 279
Voting Rights Act (1965), 292–93

Walker, David, 295
Wallace, George, 109
war: conquest and, 75; fascism and, 18–19; in Iraq, 18; military power and, 18; white mob and, 42. *See also specific wars*
Washington, George, 27
Washington, Harriet A., 217n15
Weaver, Randy, 258

Welch, Edgar Maddison, 275
"welfare queens," 90, 315, 325n24
Wells, Ida B., 206–8
West, Cornel, 5, 7–8
White, Paula, 114, 270
white bodies, 174–75
white brainwashing, 94–96
white Caucasian origins, 64n48
white Christianity: affective provocations and theoretical postures of, 17–20; anti-racist training and, 29–30; atonement and, 273–74; citizenship and, 44; colonialism and, 11–12, 27–28; corporate-warrior state and, 17–33; crucifixion and, 30–33; goodness and, 46–47; *imago Dei* and, 304; Jesus Christ and wake of empire, 5, 30–33; Jesus Christ as white and, 11, 24–25, 127–37, 185; legitimacy and, 22; liberation theopoetics and, 314, 320–23; mask of, 5–6, 273–75; military power and, 29, 300; othering and, 22–23; phobic structures of white Christian self and, 337–40; as race-making, 23–30, 179–80, 186–88; racism and, 16, 233n60; redeemability of, 306–7, 309; as religion-making, 21–23; "religio-racial project" of, 27; revolution and soul of, 299–309; scale of, 304; term usage and expression of, 20–21; transactional, 304–6; transformational, 304–6, 307; white mob and, 39–49; white supremacist Eurocentric Christianity, 299–300, 303–7. *See also specific topics*
white Christian nationalism: antecedents of, 289–93; authoritarianism and, 6–8, 111–12; as "bad theology," 151–52; Capitol insurrection and, 3–4, 20, 80, 92–94, 167–75, 221–22, 225–26, 302; Catholicism and, 127–37; Caucasus mountains, Caucasians, and, 64n48; Christianity damaged by, 96–98; Christianity today and, 75–81; Christian "no" to, 71–81; citizenship and, 12–13, 19, 76; civic life and, 71–72; Civil Rights Movement and, 89–91; crucifixion and, 78–79; dangers of, 1–8; democracy and, 14, 85–98; discipleship and, 72, 78–81; discrimination and, 89–91; education and, 104–22; Evangelicalism and, 226–27, 231n15, 289–95; fascism and, 19–20, 330–31, 340n1; Founding Fathers and, 88–89; God and, 289–93; heretical tactics of, 316–20; hymno-theology and, 316–24; idolatry of, 187–89, 199–200, 313–14, 323–24; ignorance and, 94–96; "insubordinate space" and, 227–30; in Jeffersonian era, 88–89; KKK and, 12, 42, 107–9, 182, 273; lynching and, 4, 20, 272–73; Mather and, 75–76, 78–79; "The Order" and, 257–60; overcoming Trump and, 289, 294–95; philosophy of history and, 193–97; politics and, 3–5, 7–8, 20, 81, 104–22, 259–60, 262–63; public theology and, 71–72; Puritans and, 75–76, 78–79, 87–88; racialized invisibility and, 314–24; racial segregation and, 76–78, 292; as religiously motivated violence, 331–34; Republicans and, 52–59, 85–86, 90–93; slavery and, 56–58, 291–93; in South, 90–93; symbolism of, 80; as threat to Christianity, 14; Trump and, 3–4, 7, 18–19, 58, 94, 97–98, 274–75, 301–3; Trumpsters, Trumpism and, 294–95; untangling elements of, 223–26; voting and, 90–91; white American exceptionalism and, 86–88; white brainwashing and, 94–96; white violence and, 1–7, 26, 270, 274–76, 329–40; worship culture and, 317–20

white colonial gaze, 237, 243–44, 319–20, 324
white denial, 245–46
white discourse, 271
white elites, 86–89, 245–46
white evil, 173–74
Whitefield, George, 61, 290–91
white fragility, 270, 274–75, 280–84, 301, 309
Whitehead, Andrew, 71–72
white homogeneity, 168–69
white identity, 270–71
white invisibility, 315–16
white mob: Capitol insurrection and, 39–49, 195–97; colonialism and, 39–40, 44; culture and, 42–43; democracy and, 41–42; examples of, 42–44; exceptionalism and, 47; goodness and, 46–47; logic, 39, 45–49; lynch mob and, 43, 206–8; race riots and, 42–43; racial contract and, 42–43; war and, 42; white Christianity and, 39–49; white dominance and, 43–44; white privilege and, 43; white solidarity and, 47–48; white violence and, 39–49, 206–8, 216n4
whiteness: Catholicism and, 127–37; challenging, 2–3; in *Christ in Majesty* mosaic, 129, 132–35; of God, 179–80; as goodness, 169–75; of Jesus Christ, 11, 24–25, 127–37, 185; as performative, or an enactment of power, 283–86; racial "purity" and, 6–7, 14; redemption and, 170–71; refusal to accept white racism and, 6; sin of hiding and, 283–86; theodicy and, 169–75; white racial frame and, 127–37
white persecution complex, 94–95
white privilege, 49n9, 80–81, 95, 171; damnable ambiguity and, 305; racism and, 280–81; white elites and, 86–89, 245–46; white mob and, 43
white savior, 6–7

white solidarity: on campus, 280–86; neutrality and, 279; politics and, 279–80; resisting, 286; Trump and, 279; voting and, 279; white mob and, 47–48; women and, 279
white supremacy, 5; Aryan race and, 24, 64n45, 257–58; backlash to inclusivity and, 300–303; Catholicism and, 127–32; Charlottesville, Virginia, protest and, 285, 330; Christian mission as cover to, 210–13; Christian nationalism and, 257–66; cross and, 273; in education, 26–27; eliminationism and, 12, 261–66; family values and, 206–10, 292–93; fascism and, 19–20; founding of US and, 26–30; hymno-theology and, 316–24; imagery and, 134–37; *imago hominis* and, 189, 193–200; KKK and, 12, 42, 107–9, 182, 273; misogyny and, 205–16; Oath Keepers and, 173–74, 302; "The Order" and, 257–60; Proud Boys and, 20, 224, 302, 333; Queen Elizabeth and, 236–38; race-making and, 23–30, 179–80, 186–88; racial entitlement and, 196–97; racialized invisibility and, 310n10, 314; resistance to, 215–16; Rutherford and, 106–7; Trump and, 285, 302; white solidarity and, 47–48, 279–86; white supremacist Eurocentric Christianity, 299–300, 303–7
white "victimhood," 270, 274–75, 280, 283–84, 301, 309
white violence: analyzing white Christian violence, 329–40; antidemocratic violence and, 46; apocalypticism and, 269–76; Capitol insurrection and, 167–68; children and, 206–10, 332; Civil Rights Movement and, 109; colonialism and, 7, 11–12; conquest and, 56–57, 59–61; conspiracies and, 270, 275; eliminationism and, 12, 261–66; fear

and, 339; medical experimentation and, 210–12, 217n15; metaphysical violence and, 131–32; misogyny and, 205–16; narratives and, 339; in "Original Sin," 343–49; patriotism and, 93–94; phobic structures of white Christian self and, 337–40; polarization and, 301–3; police abuse and, 30, 157; political theology, political theory, and, 334–37; politics and, 60–61; redemption and, 173–75; religiously motivated violence and, 331–34; settlers and, 60–61; sexual violence and, 205–6, 209–13; theodicy and, 170–74; torture and, 31–32, 210–13, 216n4; white bodies and, 174–75; white Christian nationalism and, 1–7, 26, 270, 274–76, 329–40; white evil and, 173–74; white mob and, 39–49, 206–8, 216n4. *See also* genocide; lynching; slavery

Whither Fanon? (Marriott), 341n16
Wilder, Craig Steven, 27
Wilderson, Frank, 334
Wilensky-Lanford, Brook, 138
Wilkerson, Isabel, 279
Windrush Generation, 245
Winthrop, John, 54–55, 87–88
wokeness, 58–59, 115–19
Wolfe, Patrick, 25

women, 8; abortion and, 65n58, 112, 292, 295; "Black rapist" and, 43, 216n6; children and, 208–9; family values and, 206–10; gynecology and, 210–12, 217n15; medical experimentation on, 210–12, 217n15; misogyny, white supremacy, and, 205–16; sexual violence and, 205–6, 209–13; slavery and, 209–10; sports, transgender youth, and, 218n28; white solidarity and, 279
World War I, 273, 339
World War II, 262
Worse Than War (Goldhagen), 262
worship culture, 317–20
The Wretched of the Earth (Fanon), 334–39, 341n16, 342n29
Wynter, Sylvia, 131

Yancy, George, 26, 288n26, 316, 319–21
"yellow dog" contracts, 191–92
Young, Graydon, 173–74
Youngkin, Glenn, 116
youth: transgender and, 213–14, 218n26, 218n28; young Americans and, 301

Zack, Naomi, 263
Zeitz, Joshua, 41

About the Contributors

Brock Bahler is a teaching professor and director of undergraduate studies in the Department of Religious Studies at the University of Pittsburgh, where he specializes in the intersection of philosophy of religion, Jewish philosophy, and philosophy of race. He is the author of three books, including the edited collection *The Logic of Racial Practice: Explorations in the Habituation of Racism* (2021).

Bill Bywater is professor emeritus philosophy at Allegheny College. He received his PhD from the University of Michigan. In his early years, he published on aesthetics and media studies, including a book on the English art critic Clive Bell. His most recent work on social justice, education, and democracy can be found in edited volumes by Solymosi and Schook, Hanes and Weisman, George Yancy and Kimberley Ducey, Clevis Headley, and Joe Feagin, as well as in an interview with Noelle McAfee in the *Kettering Review*. He is a pragmatist in the tradition of John Dewey.

J. Kameron Carter was professor of religious studies and English at Indiana University and co-director of Indiana University's Center for Religion and the Human. He is currently professor of comparative literature and African American studies at the University of California, Irvine. Professor Carter engages questions of race and ecology with religion and literature. He is the author of *Race: A Theological Account* (Oxford University Press, 2008), editor of *Religion and the Futures of Blackness* (South Atlantic Quarterly, 2013), and editor of *The Matter of Black Religion* (American Religion, 2021). Most recently, Professor Carter is the author of *The Anarchy of Black Religion: A Mystic Song* (Duke University Press, 2023). His next book, *The Religion of Whiteness: An Apocalyptic Lyric* is forthcoming with Yale University Press.

Laurie Cassidy currently teaches in the Christian Spirituality Program at Creighton University and was an associate professor in the religious studies department at Marywood University in Scranton, Pennsylvania. An award-winning author and editor, her latest book is *Desire, Darkness, and Hope: Theology in a Time of Impasse*, edited with M. Shawn Copeland. Her forthcoming book is *Praying for Freedom: Racism and Ignatian Spirituality in America*. Cassidy's teaching and research explore the intersection of personal and social transformation. Raised in Massachusetts, she now makes her home in the foothills of the Rocky Mountains, traditional homeland of the Ute, in Colorado.

Kimberley Ducey (white settler) was born and raised on the ancestral homelands of the Mi'kmaq, Beothuk, Innu of Nitassinan, Inuit of Nunatsiavut, and Inuit of NunatuKavut in what is now called Newfoundland and Labrador. She currently lives and works in the territories of the Anishinaabeg, Cree, Dakota, Dene, Métis, and Oji-Cree Nations on Treaty 1 territory, the ancestral and traditional homeland of Anishinaabe Peoples. She is a professor in the Department of Sociology at the University of Winnipeg and an adjunct professor of peace and conflict studies at the University of Manitoba.

Joe Feagin is distinguished professor in sociology at Texas A&M University. He has done much internationally recognized research on racism, sexism, and political economy, which has been published in eighty scholarly books and more than two hundred articles. His books include *Systemic Racism* (2006), *How Blacks Built America* (2015), *Elite White Men Ruling* (2017, with K. Ducey), *Racist America* (2019, with K. Ducey), *The White Racial Frame* (2020), and *White Minority Nation* (Routledge, 2023). He is a recipient of the American Association for Affirmative Action's Lifetime Achievement Award and the American Sociological Association's W. E. B. Du Bois Career of Distinguished Scholarship Award.

James Garrison is an assistant professor of philosophy at Baldwin Wallace University in Berea, Ohio. His work focuses on ethics, aesthetics, intercultural philosophy, and social/political philosophy, all of which he explores in his upcoming Lexington Books project *Black Bodies That Matter: Mourning, Rage, and Beauty*. Additionally, he is the co-editor of the collected volume *Political Philosophy from an Intercultural Perspective: Power Relations in a Global World* (Routledge, 2021) and also the author of his own book *Reconsidering the Life of Power: Ritual, Body, and Art in Critical Theory and Chinese Philosophy* (State University of New York Press, 2021).

Sheldon George is chair of the Department of Literature and Writing at Simmons University in Boston, Massachusetts. His scholarship centers on the application of cultural and literary theory to analyses of American and African American literature and culture. George's book *Trauma and Race: A Lacanian Study of African American Identity* was published in 2016. He is coeditor, with Jean Wyatt, of *Reading Contemporary Black British and African American Women Writers* (2020). His most recent publications include a collection, coedited with Derek Hook, titled *Lacan and Race: Racism, Identity and Psychoanalytic Theory* (2021) and a collection, coedited with Jean Wyatt, titled *Experimental Subjectivities in Global Black Women's Writing: Race and Narrative Innovation* (2024).

Kathy Glass is a professor of English at Duquesne University, where she teaches African American literature. She is the author of *Politics and Affect in Black Women's Fiction* (2018) and *Courting Communities: Black Female Nationalism and Syncre-Nationalism in the Nineteenth-Century North* (2006). Her work on gender, race, spirituality, and pedagogy also appears in numerous journal articles and book chapters.

Timothy J. Golden is visiting professor of philosophy at Whitman College in Walla Walla, Washington. He specializes in philosophical theology in nineteenth-century philosophy (Kant, Hegel, and Kierkegaard) and twentieth-century philosophy (Heidegger, Husserl, and Levinas). He also specializes in African American philosophy, jurisprudence, and critical race theory (Derrick Bell). His books include the monograph, *Frederick Douglass and the Philosophy of Religion: An Interpretation of Narrative, Art, and the Political* (Lexington Books, 2022), and an edited volume titled *Racism and Resistance: Essays on Derrick Bell's Racial Realism* (SUNY Press, 2022). His second monograph, *Reason's Dilemma: Subjectivity, Transcendence, and the Problem of Ontotheology*, is forthcoming from Palgrave Macmillan.

Biko Mandela Gray is an associate professor of religion at Syracuse University. He has published three books, including the edited volume *The Religion of White Rage* (2020) and, coauthored with Ryan Johnson, *The Phenomenology of Black Spirit* (2022). His first monograph, *Black Life Matter: Blackness, Religion, and the Subject* (2022), speaks to his ongoing concern with the real-world effects of anti-Black philosophical and religious logics masquerading as unspoken and given norms. His pressing question remains the same: *How do Black people live in a world marked by profound anti-Blackness?*

Marinus Chijioke Iwuchukwu was an associate professor in theology at Duquesne University, in Pittsburgh, Pennsylvania. His areas of research included interreligious dialogue, inclusive religious pluralism, world religions, and media and religious studies. He was the author of two books and a coeditor of another, as well as the author of dozens of peer-reviewed journal articles, book reviews, and book chapters. He served as a guest editor for a special issue of the *Journal of Religions* titled "Religious Pluralism in the Contemporary Transformation Society." He was a chair of the Consortium for Christian-Muslim Dialogue and the immediate past chair of the theology department at Duquesne University.

Dean J. Johnson is a professor of philosophy and an affiliated faculty of women's and gender studies at West Chester University of Pennsylvania. An interdisciplinary activist scholar, Johnson teaches courses on peace studies, religious studies, and women's and gender studies. As an activist and scholar, Johnson is a consultant for nonviolent campaigns and initiatives. He provides workshops and trainings in the areas of nonviolent direct action, community organizing, and (with his partner, Melissa Bennett) anti-oppression, queer solidarity, and antiracism. He is membership chair (as well as a founding board member) of the Peace and Justice Studies Association and a member of the Association of Pennsylvania State College and University Faculties.

Leah Kalmanson is an associate professor and the Bhagwan Adinath Professor of Jain Studies in the Department of Philosophy and Religion at the University of North Texas. She received her PhD in philosophy from the University of Hawai'i at Mānoa in 2010. She is author of *Cross-Cultural Existentialism* (2020) and coauthor, with Monika Kirloskar-Steinbach, of *A Practical Guide to World Philosophies* (2021). Her articles appear in the journals *The Arrow*, *Comparative and Continental Philosophy*, *Continental Philosophy Review*, *Frontiers of Philosophy in China*, *Hypatia*, *Journal of the Pacific Association for the Continental Tradition*, *Journal of World Philosophies*, *Philosophy East and West*, *Pragmatism Today*, *Shofar*, and *Studies in Chinese Religions*, as well as the online magazines *Aeon*.

Todd M. Mealy is an adjunct professor of history at Dickinson College in Carlisle, Pennsylvania, and a public school educator working in urban and rural districts for more than two decades. He often writes about the antislavery and civil rights movements' short- and long-term implications on the education system. *Shades of Brown*, a forthcoming publication, offers new insights about educator Jane Elliott and the blue eyes, brown eyes exercise. Mealy serves as CEO of the National Institute for Customizing Education, where he manages a team that helps school districts customize programs and initiatives, and supports particular student and staffing needs.

José Francisco Morales Torres is an assistant professor of Latinx studies and religion at Chicago Theological Seminary. As a historical and comparative theologian, his approach is thoroughly interdisciplinary, weaving together comparative theology, history of religious thought, and philosophy (especially philosophies of race, ethnicity, and culture). His most recent book is *Wonder as a New Starting Point for Theological Anthropology: Opened by the World* (2023), which proposes a new theological anthropology informed by the experience of wonder.

Anna Floerke Scheid is an associate professor at Duquesne University. Her teaching and research areas are theological and religious ethics, with attention to religion and US political life; religion, war, and peacebuilding; forgiveness and reconciliation in the aftermath of conflict; and faith-based activism. She is the author of *Just Revolution: A Christian Ethic of Political Resistance and Social Transformation* (2015) and numerous essays and articles. Through her work and community engagement she is committed to helping people understand and exercise their own power over the forces that shape our social, economic, and political lives together.

Michael Simms, who identifies as a person with autism, is the founder of *Vox Populi*, an online forum for poetry, politics, and nature, as well as Autumn House Press, a publisher of books. He's the author of four full-length collections of poetry, including *Strange Meadowlark* (2023), and two novels, including *Bicycles of the Gods* (2023); the coauthor of a college textbook about poetry; and the lead editor of more than one hundred published books, including the best-selling *Autumn House Anthology of Contemporary Poetry*, now in its third edition. In 2011, the Pennsylvania Legislature awarded Simms a Certificate of Recognition for his contribution to the arts.

Anthony Paul Smith is an associate professor in the Department of Religion and Theology at La Salle University in Philadelphia, Pennsylvania. In addition to a number of translations of François Laruelle and Malcom Ferdinand, he is the author of *A Non-Philosophical Theory of Nature: Ecologies of Thought* and *Laruelle—A Stranger Thought*. His current project explores theodicy as philosophical form and examines the conceptions of suffering and violence that emerge from that form.

Mark Lewis Taylor is the Maxwell M. Upson Professor of Theology and Culture at Princeton Theological Seminary. Among his most recent books are *Religion, Politics, and the Christian Right: Post 9-11 Powers and American Empire* (2005) and *The Theological and the Political: On the Weight of the World* (2011). He received the Best General Interest Book Award for his 2001 book, *The Executed God: The Way of the Cross in Lockdown America* (2nd edition, 2015). Over the years, he has been committed to ending antideath penalty, solidarity work in Mexico and Central America, and working to support political prisoners (he is founder of Educators for Mumia Abu-Jamal). Further publications and resources are available at www.marklewistaylor.com

Karen Teel is a professor in the Department of Theology and Religious Studies and affiliated faculty in the Department of Ethnic Studies at the University of San Diego, located in the traditional, unceded homeland of the Kumeyaay Nation. Her scholarly endeavors center on the Christian dimensions of the problems of racism and white supremacy, especially considering how whiteness has evolved as a racial, cultural, and Christian identity in what is now the United States. Her ancestors actively participated in creating and enforcing the racial inequity that endures today. Considering herself accountable, she consciously theorizes and theologizes her own positionality as a cisgendered, female, Roman Catholic, white US American. She is the author of *Racism and the Image of God*.

Becky Thompson is the author of *To Speak in Salt*, winner of the Ex Ophidia Poetry Book Prize. Her scholarly books include *Teaching with Tenderness*, *Survivors on the Yoga Mat*, and several other books centering on social justice activism. She has coedited two poetry anthologies, including *Making Mirrors: Righting/Writing by and for Refugees* (with Jehan Bseiso) and *Fingernails Across the Chalkboard: Poetry and Prose on HIV/AIDS across the Black Diaspora*. She has held appointments at China Women's University, Princeton, Duke, and the University of Colorado, and is currently at Simmons University.

Elisabeth Vasko is an associate professor of theology at Duquesne University. She teaches and researches in the areas of theological anthropology, Christian ethics, and liberation theologies. She prioritizes collaborative, interdisciplinary, and community-based methods in her work because she believes they are building blocks for expanding the moral imagination and creating a more just society. She is the author of multiple publications, including *Beyond Apathy: A Theology for Bystanders* (2015) and *True Crime and the Justice of God: Ethics, Media, and Forensic Science* (2022).

Traci C. West is a scholar-activist who serves as the James W. Pearsall Professor of Christian Social Ethics and African American Studies at Drew University Theological School in New Jersey. Her teaching, research, and activism have focused on gender, racial, and sexuality justice, particularly in relation to gender-based violence. In addition to many published articles, book chapters, and books, she is the author of *Solidarity and Defiant*

Spirituality: Africana Lessons on Religion, Racism, and Ending Gender Violence (2019).

George Yancy is the Samuel Candler Dobbs Professor of Philosophy at Emory University and a Montgomery Fellow at Dartmouth College, and he was the University of Pennsylvania's inaugural fellow in the Provost's Distinguished Faculty Fellowship Program (2019–2020). At Academic Influence, Yancy is cited as one of the top-ten influential philosophers in the last ten years, 2010–2020, based on number of citations and web presence. He has authored, edited, and coedited more than twenty books. He has published over two hundred combined scholarly articles, chapters, and interviews appearing in professional journals, books, and at various news sites. He is well-known for his influential essays and interviews at the *New York Times* philosophy column "The Stone," and at the prominent political nonprofit news organization *Truthout*. Lastly, Yancy is the Philosophy of Race book series editor for Lexington Books.

Josiah Ulysses Young III is a professor of systematic theology at Wesley Theological Seminary in Washington, DC. His scholarship focuses on the theological implications of African American experience and spirituality. His monograph *Black Lives Matter and the Image of God: A Theo-Anthropological Study* is soon to be released.